Hispanic Lands and Peoples

Dellplain Latin American Studies

DELLPLAIN LATIN AMERICAN STUDIES

PUBLISHED IN COOPERATION
WITH THE DEPARTMENT OF GEOGRAPHY
SYRACUSE UNIVERSITY

EDITOR

David J. Robinson
Syracuse University

EDITORIAL ADVISORY COMMITTEE

John K. Chance
Arizona State University

William M. Denevan
University of Wisconsin

W. George Lovell
Queen's University

Robert McCaa
University of Minnesota

Linda Newson
University of London

EDITORIAL ASSISTANT
Judith A. Routson

JAMES J. PARSONS

In Río Negro, Antioquia, Colombia, November 8, 1987. Photo by
Pedro J. Restrepo. Reproduced by permission.

Hispanic Lands and Peoples

Selected Writings of
James J. Parsons

edited by William M. Denevan

Dellplain Latin American Studies, No. 23

Westview Press

Boulder, London, & San Francisco

Dellplain Latin American Studies

Photos on pages 222 and 223 reproduced by permission of their owner, Mrs. Betty Parsons.

This Westview softcover edition is printed on acid-free paper and bound in softcovers that carry the highest rating of the National Association of State Textbook Administrators, in consultation with the Association of American Publishers and the Book Manufacturers' Institute.

Copyright © 1989 by the Department of Geography, Syracuse University

Published in 1989 in the United States of America by Westview Press, Inc., 5500 Central Avenue, Boulder, Colorado 80301, and in the United Kingdom by Westview Press, Inc., 13 Brunswick Centre, London WC1N 1AF, England

Library of Congress Cataloging-in-Publication Data
Parsons, James Jerome, 1915–
  [Selections. 1989]
  Hispanic lands and peoples : selected writings of James J. Parsons
/ edited by William M. Denevan.
    p. cm.—(Dellplain Latin American studies; no. 23)
  ISBN 0-8133-7638-6
  1. Latin America—Historical geography. 2. Spain—Historical
geography. 3. Canary Islands—Historical geography. 4. Human
ecology—Latin America. 5. Human ecology—Spain. 6. Human ecology—
Canary Islands. I. Denevan, William M. II. Title. III. Series.
F1408.P332 1982
909'.097468—dc19
                                                                                        89-5420
                                                                                        CIP

Printed and bound in the United States of America

The paper used in this publication meets the requirements of the American National Standard for Permanence of Paper for Printed Library Materials Z39.48-1984.

10   9   8   7   6   5   4   3   2   1

CONTENTS

ILLUSTRATIONS

TABLES

FIGURES

PHOTOS

Preface

Mentors are forever, they say. This has certainly been true of Jim Parsons for me, as it was with Carl Sauer for him, and Rollin Salisbury for Sauer. But although I was an undergraduate in geography at Berkeley in 1951-53 and later periodically a graduate student there for a decade, I didn't take a course from Parsons or scarcely speak with him for several years. I did run into him out of the blue at a sidewalk cafe in Belém at the mouth of the Amazon in September of 1956. Clearly something in common had brought us to that tropical place. It took awhile, but once the connection had been made it became a firm and lasting one, as it has been for most of Jim's many students. The association has been one of edification, inspiration, and support for me, and with this anthology of selected papers I wish to both honor and thank Jim for all of us.

James Parsons is a geographer. He is a cultural geographer, an historical geographer, a biogeographer, a conservation geographer, an economic geographer, a tropical geographer, and a Latin Americanist geographer. But just plain geographer will do--the kind who looks at questions about people, economy, and environment in a regional context. And he is one of the very best at this sort of thing, venturing out into near and far corners of the world to try to make some sense out of what is going on there by means of field observation, talking to people, reading the newspapers, and delving into libraries and archives, records and maps.

To be in the field with Jim is a humbling experience, as he describes, explains, and clarifies what is not at all so clear. He scribbles things on backs of envelopes and scraps of paper, probably in field notebooks but I have never seen one. And if he is driving he may get lost temporarily, not because he doesn't know where he is but because his eyes are not on the road but on the land, while his mind is somewhere else putting it all together. A lot of what he sees must be stashed away deep inside permanently, not for a few days or weeks as with most of us. Then he comes home to Berkeley, does some more library research, and after awhile it all comes out in an article or monograph, well reasoned, well documented, and in some of the finest prose we can find in geography. We have brought together pieces of Jim's best research and best writing in the collection of papers presented here.

The idea for this anthology arose in discussions with Kent Mathewson, with encouragement from David Robinson, editor of the Dellplain Latin American Studies series. The selections included are largely my choices but with suggestions from Kent, and they also reflect some of Jim's own preferences. The emphasis is on Parsons' work in Latin America and in Spain, with the resulting neglect of his publications on other regions, particularly California.

The organization of the 30 papers included here is somewhat arbitrary but does reflect Parsons' major research themes and regions; a number of items could be placed in more than one category. Part I contains statements about geographical research in general and in Latin America. Part II focuses on Colombia, the scene of Parsons' most persistent field work. Part III consists of historical geographical studies elsewhere. Part IV is on ancient agricultural fields in South America. Part V is a sampling of Parsons' many publications on the human impact on the natural environment of Latin America. Part VI covers a variety of topics on Spain and the Canary Islands. The Postscript is a plea for the humanistic approach to geography, as well as to learning in general.

To meet space limitations and still retain diversity, an emphasis has been given to including mostly shorter publications. Only portions of some articles appear (Chapters 1, 2, 3, 17). From Parsons' monographs chapters were selected which would make sense independently (Chapters 5, 7, 8, 9, 23). Chapter 4 on "Geographical Research in Latin America" has been reworked by Parsons for this volume. Otherwise, the texts of the articles are as originally published except for a few minor corrections. Most of the original photos have been deleted, as well as a few of the maps.

A capsule biography is in order. James J. Parsons was born in Cortland, New York, on November 15, 1915, but moved with his family to Pasadena, California, in the early 1920s. He received an A.B. in Economics from Berkeley in 1937 and an M.A. in Geography from Berkeley in 1939, with a year in between as news editor for the Ukiah *Redwood Journal*. He served in the U.S. Army from 1941 to 1945 (private to major), applying his geographic skills to Air Force intelligence in the Pacific Theater. He and Betty were married in 1942. He returned to graduate school at Berkeley in 1945 to pursue a Ph.D. under Carl Sauer, with a dissertation on "Antio-queño Colonization in Western Colombia" in 1948.

Parsons has spent his entire academic career at Berkeley. He entered the faculty as an Instructor in 1946, rising to Professor in 1960, and retiring in 1986. He was Chairman of Geography in 1960-66 and 1975-79. He was Chairman of the Center for Latin American Studies at Berkeley in 1965-66, 1970-73, and 1979-80. His services to professional geography are also considerable, including President of the Association of Pacific Coast Geographers (1954-55) and Councilor (1960-62), Vice President (1973-74), and President (1974-75) of the Association of American Geographers.

Honors awarded include Guggenheim Fellow (1959-60), Doctor Honoris Causa from the Universidad de Antioquia (Colombia, 1965), Estrella de Oro Medal (Colombia, 1977), Honors from the Conference of Latin Americanist Geographers (1978), Honors from the Association of American Geographers (1983), the David Livingston Memorial Medal from the American Geographical Society (1985), The Berkeley Citation (University of California, 1986), Honorary Professor, Universities of Caldas (Colombia, 1987), and El Orden de Pedro Justo Berrio (Colombia, 1987).

Parsons has made so many trips for research and meetings to Latin America, Europe, and elsewhere that even he would be hard pressed to list them all. Colombia has seen the most of him, as he has returned again and again. However, he has also undertaken substantial field work in the Caribbean, Mexico, Nicaragua, Ecuador, Costa Rica, Spain, and the Canary Islands. He has been a prolific writer, with some five books and monographs and over 100 articles and notes in a wide variety of journals in and out of geography. A significant contribution has been his willingness to prepare book reviews, far more than his share, with nearly 70 in all.

Since 1950, Parsons with Sauer, plus Hilgard Sternberg and Bernard Nietschmann, have maintained at Berkeley probably the premier center in the world of graduate training in Latin American geography (37 Ph.D. dissertations). Jim has supervised 34 Ph.D. dissertations, of which 17 are on Latin America. The latter are by Charles Alexander (Venezuela, 1955), John Street (Haiti, 1959), Campbell Pennington (Mexico, 1959), David Harris (West Indies, 1963), William Denevan (Bolivia, 1963), Lee Pederson (Chile, 1965), Gene Wilken (Mexico, 1967), Jim Krogzemis (Colombia, 1968), David Radell (Nicaragua, 1969), Elinore Barrett (Mexico, 1970), Peter Rees (Mexico, 1971), Thomas Veblen (Guatemala, 1975), Janet Crane Schuh (Peru, 1977), Gerald Fish (Mexico, 1980), Michael Murphy (Mexico, 1983), Luis Calero (Latin American Studies, Colombia, 1987), and Karl Zimmerer (Peru, 1989).

Non-Latin American Ph.D. dissertations supervised by Parsons include: Ward Barrett (1959), Alvin Urquhart (1962), Robert Frenkel (1967), Bret Wallach (1968), Tom Pagenhart (1969), Christopher Salter (1970), Bryce Decker (1970), Robin Doughty (1971), William Bowen (1972), Rowan Rowntree (1973), Marshall McLennan (1973), Marijean Eichel Hawthorne (1975), Franco Ferrario (1977), Randall Rossi (1979), Krimhilde Henderson (1980), Noritaka Yagasaki (1982), and Barbara Brower (1987).

These are the facts about Jim Parsons. The "Introduction" by Robert West, a fellow grad at Berkeley in the 1940s, and the "Appreciation" by Kent Mathewson, a third generation Parsonite, give insight into the man, the scholar, and the teacher. Then comes our sampling of his thoughts and scholarship regarding geography and Hispanic lands and people. A full listing of Parsons' publications to date follows the text. "We shall be known by our works and saved by them alone," Jim once said. He provides us here with some pretty fine works.

William M. Denevan
Madison

Introduction

James Parsons stands as one of the most influential, best known, and in terms of publications one of the most prolific geographers in the United States today. His fields of inquiry have been concentrated mainly in Latin America, especially northern South America, in Spain, and lately in the Canary Islands. But he has also published on various parts of the United States, principally California, his adopted state, where he has lived most of his life. And several of his works deal with the world distribution of a particular phenomenon, the destructive exploitation of the green sea turtle.

In both teaching and research Parsons' philosophy of geography appears to have evolved from several sources. Paramount was the teaching of Carl Sauer, who helped to instill in him the historical approach for the understanding of landscape and the ecological concept of man's relation to his environment. Equally important was Sauer's insistence on fieldwork in geographical research, a tenet that Parsons adopted enthusiastically as evidenced by his lengthy travel experience abroad and at home. A keen observer of man and nature and an indefatigable worker in library and archive, Parsons has been able to amass quantities of data for his numerous publications and classroom lectures. More than once he has stated publicly his belief that geographical research is fundamentally an exercise in "exploration and discovery," not necessarily in the sense of a James Cook or a Robert Parry, but in a desire to satisfy personal curiosity about areas and peoples and to impart one's findings to student and public. Like Sauer, Parsons is basically a humanist.

By no means, however, has Parsons been a clone of his mentor in ideas and writings. Whereas Sauer's contributions, particularly those on Latin America, dealt largely with the past, those of Parsons usually include explanatory description of the contemporary scene and emphasize the economic bases of livelihood, historically derived. That emphasis may in part stem from his early training in economics at Berkeley. It also may have been encouraged by his early experience in journalism, having worked as a reporter on a local California newspaper. And that same experience may well have enhanced his ability to produce the precise, facile prose that characterizes his professional writings. His simple, direct English, unencumbered by jargon, makes all of his works a delight to read.

Parsons' renown among both peers and students derives not only from his publications but also from his long association with various geographical organizations in the United States and abroad. Since the mid-1950s he has rarely missed an annual meeting of the Association of American Geographers, having served on various of its committees and as its president. Active participation in other organizations, such as the Association of Pacific Coast Geographers, the California Geographical Society, and the Conference of Latin Americanist Geographers, further enhanced his exposure to colleagues and students alike. From all these societies he has received awards for excellence for his studies in the Latin American tropics and in Spain. Moreover, Jim's affable personality has helped gain him lasting respect among all who meet him, especially among students.

Parsons' first and one of his most lengthy research papers was his doctoral thesis on Colombia, done under Carl Sauer. Published in the *Ibero-Americana* series in 1949, "Antioqueño Colonization in Western Colombia" (see Chapter 5) immediately caught the eyes of Colombian scholars, and a year later a Spanish translation appeared; two subsequent Spanish editions have been published. Here was the first organized presentation of Antioqueño settlement history--the story of a unique segment of the Colombian people who have developed an agricultural economy based on coffee and stock raising and eventually a thriving industrial complex within the rugged northern Andes. This study has served as a model for other historical and geographical investigations in Colombia and a challenge to others, including historians and sociologists, to expand on and in some cases to correct a few of Parsons' original ideas on Antioquian expansion.

Although Parsons' interests have turned to many other themes, the call of Colombia has remained with him until the present, having returned to his adopted "patria chica" many times for work in field and archive. His monographs *Antioquia's Corridor to the Sea* (1967) (see Chapters 7 and 8) and *San Andrés and Providencia* (1956) (see Chapter 9) and their Spanish translations, as well as several journal articles attest to this attraction. For his work in Colombia he has received at least three prestigious awards from his

Antioqueño friends and colleagues. Parsons' frequent revisits to Colombia illustrate his firm belief that a geographer, to understand well a foreign land and people, must return repeatedly over a long period of time to the locale of study. Whenever he returns to Medellín or some other city in Antioquia he is still hailed in the local press as "Parsons, el antioqueñólogo."

An important contribution to the historical geography of aboriginal agriculture in the Americas stems in part from Parsons' work in Colombia. On one of his field excursions to Antioquia (*ca.* 1963) quite by accident Parsons observed from the air a large area of geometrically arranged swales and ridges, theretofore unreported, in the seasonally inundated San Jorge River floodplain in northern Colombia. These he termed "ridged fields," and subsequent investigation on the ground with air photos suggested their construction by pre-Columbian Indians for planting surfaces raised above flood level. Somewhat similar features had been briefly reported as early as 1901 in the Lake Titicaca Basin, but it was not until the early 1960s that William Denevan, one of Parsons' graduate students, thoroughly investigated ridges in lowland Bolivia and described them in his doctoral thesis. Parsons also found ridged fields in the lowlands of eastern Ecuador (see Chapter 15) and others reported them in Surinam and in the Venezuelan Llanos. After publication of Parsons' (and coauthor Bowen's) initial report on the Colombian ridged fields (see Chapter 14), their finds were written up in *Time* magazine (August 5, 1966), giving the authors national recognition among the general public. Subsequently anthropologists and geographers began to search for evidence of long abandoned raised fields in other parts of the lowland tropics, especially in southeastern Mexico, where they have been found in wet areas of southern Veracruz, the Yucatan peninsula, and also in neighboring Belize. Thus, new evidence of a sophisticated aboriginal agriculture in the tropical lowlands of America long before European contact may help to give credence to suggestions for high lowland densities among pre-Columbian populations.

Colombia was not the first Latin American country that Parsons visited during his graduate days at Berkeley. During the intersemester break, December 1940-January 1941, when I was still working on my dissertation under Professor Sauer, Jim and I made a trip into northern Mexico and, being adventuresome souls, crossed the Sierra Madre Occidental over the colonial "Topia Road," a trail that led from Tepehuanes, Durango state, to Culiacán on the Pacific lowlands. We drove from Berkeley to Chihuahua City in Jim's car, then by rail to Tepehuanes where we obtained mules and a guide to take us to Valle de Topia in the sierra. From there we followed a mailman and a loaded burro on foot down a treacherous dry-season trail, crossing a stream some 300 times, and finally arrived at Culiacán. The trip across the sierra took ten exhausting days of travel by mule and foot. From Culiacán we returned to Durango City in an old three-engine passenger plane, recrossing the sierra in one hour, and thence home by rail and car. This may have been Jim Parsons' first "fieldwork" in Latin America, and perhaps it whetted his desire to continue geographical investigations in that part of the world. After returning to Berkeley we composed a joint paper on the historical geography of the Topia Road and brazenly sent it to the *Geographical Review*. We soon received work from editor Gladys Wrigley that our paper had been accepted for publication in the July 1941 issue of the *Review* (see Chapter 11), in which Carl Sauer's famous paper "The Personality of Mexico" would appear. This was Jim's second publication (his first, on hops in California in 1940). Through the years Parsons on occasion attended conferences in Mexico City, but he did not return to the country for investigations of any import until recently. In 1985 he began a study of native Mexican ornamental plants, delving into their origin, distribution, and role in pre-Columbian Indian and present-day cultures.

Although his first substantial work in Latin America resulted from his research in Antioquia, no less important are Parsons' concerns and resulting publications relative to present-day ecological problems that he has encountered in the tropical lowlands of northern South America and Central America. Foremost among such problems, in his view, has been the impact of man on natural vegetation, much of which has resulted in environmental deterioration. Likely, it was Carl Sauer who introduced him to this phenomenon, and once in the field he was quick to recognize the change in the extent and composition of tropical forest and savanna effected through human action. Parsons' work on vegetation began in 1953 with his study of the anomalous pine savanna along the rainy Caribbean coast of Nicaragua and easternmost Honduras (see Chapter 17). Later studies involved the grasslands of northern Colombia, the Llanos of Colombia and Venezuela (see Chapter 18), and the pastures of Central America (see Chapter 19). All of these studies carry the theme of rapid clearing of the rain forest and its replacement by grasses to further the livestock industry. Once established the grasses are maintained largely through the use of fire, a process long known to cattlemen and Indian hunters. However, this activity has not been overly detrimental to the environment in some cases, as Parsons indicates in his revealing study on the introduction of African grasses into tropical America, where they have replaced the less nutritious native species, making pastures in both highland and lowland more productive for the livestock industry (see Chapter 20). Nonetheless, the progressive disappearance of the lowland rain forest, especially in Central America, may well result in the loss of an enormous floral and faunal diversity, a decrease in soil fertility, and serious soil erosion in hilly terrain (see Chapter 21).

In his studies of man's impact on the environment Parsons has dealt with only one animal, the green sea turtle. His interest in this reptile and its exploitation probably began while he was engaged in work on the Colombian Caribbean islands of San Andrés and Providencia, where a number of turtle fishermen are based. In the Caribbean the depletion of the sea turtle through overhunting and egg robbing is representative of a world-wide pattern of the exploitation of a living resource to the brink of extinction. Thus, ever curious, Parsons extended his study to include all of the world's tropical seas, resulting in a book-length treatise, one of its kind, but probably appreciated more by biologists than by most geographers (see Chapter 23; also 22).

Parsons' concern with ecological problems coincides with the growing public interest in the environmental movement within the United States, Canada, and a few Latin American countries. The Geography Department at Berkeley is one of the few in the U.S. where students are made keenly aware of such problems. Among geographers, Parsons, with his departmental colleagues Sternberg, Nietschmann, Luten, and others, has been in the forefront of the environmental movement on the Berkeley campus, including supervision since the 1960s of numerous doctoral dissertations related to that subject.

In 1959 Parsons received a Guggenheim Fellowship for a year's travel and study in Spain and Portugal. Visits to the Iberian Peninsula are logical and necessary steps taken by many Latin Americanists seeking information on European origins of culture traits found in the New World, or searching for documents in archives to reconstruct aspects of Hispanic-American colonial history and geography. Parsons, however, was concerned not so much with those goals as with the exploration of the countryside in a land new to him. The title of his grant proposal to the Guggenheim Foundation is: "The Forest Gathering and Herding Economy of the South of Spain and Portugal." Thus, in his writings on Iberia he concentrated on explanatory description and historical development of various present-day economic activities that dealt with the exploitation of natural resources, mainly vegetation and its deterioration through human misuse (see Chapter 25). Innovative farming techniques that he encountered also intrigued him (see Chapter 27), as did aspects of architecture.

To date, Parsons, with wife Betty, has made four study trips to Spain and surrounding areas (1959-60, 1972, 1979, 1984). Having devoted his attention to southern Spain and Portugal during the first two field seasons, he spent the last two mainly in the Canary Islands, where various landscape features aroused his curiosity (see Chapter 30). And some of his latest writings are concerned with the role of the Canaries in the transfer of artifacts and lifeways to the New World, including the extraordinary migrations of Canary Islanders into the Americas during the last 400 years (see Chapter 28).

Probably most of Parsons' colleagues would consider his accomplishments through his many contributions to geographical literature. But others, especially his students, will rarely forget his warm, relaxed demeanor, his unfailing positive attitude, and his strong encouragement to achieve. Even in the field those personal characteristics reveal themselves in his down-to-earth rapport with both rural informants and urban intellectuals, who, responding to his open, friendly nature, have often looked upon him as one of their own.

Robert C. West
Baton Rouge

An Appreciation

When thinking of James Parsons, many qualities come to mind. Openness and accessibility are two of the obvious ones. My own introduction came through correspondence as a prospective graduate student. My inquiry was addressed to Professor J.J. Parsons, Graduate Advisor. I indicated interests in Latin America, biogeography, cultural historical studies, and noted that I had been editor of my college newspaper. I knew Parsons to be a student of Sauer's and also of Latin America and biogeographical topics, but I had no idea of the extent of his wide-ranging expertise beyond these rather standard Berkeley School pursuits. Neither did I realize that citing experience in journalism would strike such a sympathetic chord, nor did I know that Parsons' term as Graduate Advisor had lapsed, and that he was on sabbatical in Spain. But instead of receiving a routine response (given the circumstances) from the department, I soon had a long hand-written letter from Parsons in the field. He strongly encouraged me to pursue the directions I had mentioned. Remarkably, there was little emphasis on recruitment *per se*; rather there was this enthusiastic invitation to join in the adventure and challenge of doing geography along lines that I only sketchily understood at the time.

As it turned out, I never made it formally to California and studied instead at Wisconsin. This seems to have made little difference. I soon discovered, as others have, that being one of Parsons' students is not something limited to Berkeley enrollment or even to being a geographer. I hope to speak for all of his many students, both formal and informal, especially those who have become part of this collectivity in recent years, in thanking him for his advice, encouragement, and example. There is the temptation to elaborate on the full range of his many contributions, but that can and will be done in other contexts. Now is the time to enjoy what is available here and elsewhere and to anticipate what still awaits us. I would like to make a few general observations on the ways his writings can inform future generations of geographers.

The work presented in this volume is by no means the complete Parsons. While it covers much of the core, important pieces from what some might assume to be the periphery are necessarily omitted. These include his work on California and on the economic geography of the United States. A larger picture emerges than just the cultural geography of Latin America and Spain. Involved in part is the integration of economy and ecology. At the same time, Parsons' eclecticism, with no apologies, is startling, and is not fully apparent in this volume (e.g., letters in the landscape, residential choices of airline pilots, domestication of the canary, fog drip, subdivisions without homes).

Appreciation has various meanings. Of course, the main sense implied here is that of saluting one of geography's most esteemed scholars. But another of its meanings, "to increase in value," might also be invoked. Parsons, through his own highly personal style and efforts has not only added significantly to many subfields of the discipline, but he has "appreciated" the whole enterprise of geography with his example, his leadership, and above all his infectious curiosity and enthusiasm. In an age when nominations for the title of "total geographer" are apt to be proffered to those who have striven to reduce the logos of place to the most parsimonious theorems and operations possible, Parsons' approach is indeed far afield. But in the long view he is clearly in the mainstream, marking for those who will follow currents that are strong and durable.

Agreeably, the collection in hand confirms the image most hold of James Parsons as a devoted student of cultural, historical, and regional geographic topics. He is one of this century's most accomplished Latin Americanist and Iberianist geographers. In the various places he knows well and is well known, such as Colombia, the western Caribbean, and the Canaries, local scholars have no difficulty locating him in the tradition (and often in the company) of those who have gone before: Humboldt, Hettner, and Sapper. However, in focusing on his accomplishments as an authority on particular places, we are in danger of losing sight of his range of interests and expertise. Even after close inspection of his publications list, synopsis does not come easily. In a sense, the contents of this bibliography are a resounding affirmation of his own stated belief in the importance of studying questions of geographical diversity and uniqueness. And befitting his own training under Sauer at Berkeley, one can readily see the importance given to asking genetic questions and pursuing historical themes.

The directions of Parsons' scholarly productions and persona were already apparent in his early publications. His article with Robert West on the Topia Road in Mexico (*Geographical Review*, 1941) anticipated a Latin American and culture history bent well before field work in Colombia. His first published effort, however, dealt with "Hops in Early California Agriculture" (*Agricultural History*, 1940). The article is based on his 1939 Master's thesis in geography at Berkeley on "The California Hop Industry: Its Eighty Years of Development and Expansion." Seeds of subsequent interests and projects are quite evident in this study. The predictable historical themes of agricultural diffusions and colonization are well developed, but one can also see that Parsons was well aware that California agriculture was taking on an "industrial" character, or in Cary McWilliams' now famous phrase, becoming "factories in the fields." This willingness to follow the facts wherever they lead, including into the industrial present, was no doubt reinforced by his stint as a journalist after college before he turned to geography full time. Somewhat in contradistinction, one can imagine his mentor Carl Sauer taking the hop theme and tracing it back along its diffusion paths to the plant's earliest uses and domestication.

Parsons' work on hops in California represents the beginning of a sustained commitment to writing on topics investigating different aspects of California's regional geography--some 16 publications, culminating in his masterful study of the San Joaquin Valley (*Geographical Review*, 1986). This aspect of his scholarly production has been somewhat overshadowed by his better-known writings on other Hispanic lands. Included are economic studies of agriculture, home-building and residential location, manufacturing, and energy use. These are hardly topics that one associates with Berkeley School geography. Yet each is written with the verve and inquisitiveness that distinguishes Parsons' best work on tropical landscapes, or historical studies of ecological disruptions.

Parsons' undergraduate training was in economics. Apparently, allegiance to this earlier training, if not calling, has prevented him from abandoning the discipline he studied for his first degree. Even at present he lists among his geographic specializations "descriptive economic geography." Surely he is among the only, if not the only economic geographer today who is willing to qualify his epistemological orientation in such honest if unfashionable terms. Yet an earlier generation of economic geographers also saw their task to be essentially one of doing "an honest job of reporting" as Parsons (here echoing Sauer) is fond of saying. Perhaps the worst causalities of the recent but now waning Great Enforced Modernization of Geography Campaign have been within some of the very precincts from which it was launched. Parsons' continuing contributions to the literature of economic geography are poignant reminders of these losses.

One might even look back to economic geography's halcyon days when direct observation of phenomena in the field played a large part. In important ways Parsons' work and outlook is an implicit realization that the sciences of economy and ecology not only share the same etymological origins or grounds, but, as Kenneth Boulding and others have also pointed out, the two disciplines are necessarily interdependent whether or not the practitioners of either field care to acknowledge it. Parsons in his unassuming way has given us some first rate examples of how the mediations might proceed.

In perhaps more obvious ways, Parsons' prospectings have added many facets to his and our knowledge of specific regions. From California-as-home to New Caledonia to Colombia and beyond and back again, he has crisscrossed both the Caribbean Mainland and Rimland, seeing California each time anew, and finally back tracking all the way to Iberia--the Hispanic source lands along with their Atlantic isles. Mediterraneanist of both the New and the Old Worlds, Parsons is exemplary as chorologist on these terrains. This distinction is a reflection of not only his extensive direct knowledge of these places, but also his willingness or even insistence that one must see and study economies and ecologies as indivisible. All of this is in tune with current "rediscovery" of regions and the regional approach throughout geography. It is of course to his credit that Parsons never abandoned these interests.

If this persistence strikes some geographers as mildly prophetic, his labors before a larger audience have a similar resonance. Parsons has been well received by various publics, especially in places in which he has come to feel at home. Return visits to favorite places elicit newspaper headlines of his arrival. His work appears in local newspapers in Colombia and elsewhere. Scholars in various countries have written on his style of geography and his contributions. For example, in the Catalan journal *Documents d'Anàlisi Geogràfica* (7:177-191, Barcelona 1985), Xavier Sanclimens i Solervicens discusses "L'obra de James J. Parsons sobre Espanya." There is also the interview of Parsons by Antioqueño sociologist Alejandro Reyes Posada (*Estudios Sociales*, 1:195-211, Medellín, 1986). Parsons is known to Californians outside the academy as well as to the readership of popular publications such as *Co-Evolutionary Quarterly* and *Whole Earth Review*. At a time when "public intellectuals" are said to be largely a vanished tribe, and academics, even those who profess a duty to make a public difference, are caught up in ever more centripetal forms of discourse, it is indeed a pleasure to hear of the range of audiences Parsons reaches.

Unfortunately, little of this informal record of the public Parsons is immediately retrievable. However, the written record we do have is certainly a generous one. In describing the man himself, this remarkable spirit of generosity may be the single attribute that will come to mind most quickly. Those who have been fortunate in knowing James Parsons in the field, in the classroom, at conferences, as a colleague, or simply as admirers of his work, will attest that his contagious sense of affinity for all sorts of people and a multiplicity of remarkable places is something that is impossible not to share. As his written work here and elsewhere attests, Parsons' circle of admirers should only grow wider and wider with time.

Kent Mathewson
Chapel Hill

PART ONE

The Geographer in Latin America

1

An Independent Field of Inquiry*

   Geography stands as an independent field of inquiry by virtue
of its concern with the place-to-place variation of the earth's surface
and its human societies and the causes and consequences of this
variation. It is unique as to point of view, of which the map is an
effective mirror. Man's evaluation of the relative habitability of the
earth, in good part a cultural judgment, is expressed through the
uneven distribution of population and such material marks of his
occupancy as houses, cities, factories, roads, farmsteads, and fields--
and these features and their distributions are the raw material of
most geographical investigation. The understanding of why and how
people live where they do and the nature and durability of man's
relationship with and dependence upon the physical environment are
major themes within geography.
   Although geography's organizing principle is spatial, as that
of history is chronological, the manner in which a contemporary
landscape has evolved cannot be understood without the perspective
of time. The historical orientation of geography has been especially
pronounced in the Latin American field, where the lines of history
are deeply etched on the land and its people. Indeed, the interests of
cultural anthropologists, historians, and geographers have often fused
in Latin American studies, as in investigations of the origins, spread,
limits, and modifications of culture traits or cultural complexes, until
the distinction between them often becomes blurred. Much of geography's strength stems from its flexibility--its ability to work with

---

materials from both the physical and social sciences from its own distinctive and integrating point of view.

For its relative lack of concern for theory, its neglect of methodological innovation, its wariness of broad generalizations, and its past tendencies to be satisfied with "mere description," geography of late has been chided by some of its own and passed by unrecognized by others. There are many misconceptions of what geography is, even its confusion with "geology" or the not infrequent assumption that it is little more than the study of place names, the proving of "influences" of the environment on human activity, or gazetteer-like description.

Most geographical work transcends the boundaries of the social sciences, drawing on the ideas, field techniques, and observations of natural science. It considers the whole wherever possible in terms of mapped distributions and the interrelationship of physical phenomena, cultural attitudes, and economic activities. As a bridge between the natural and the social sciences, but with its own distinctive set of problems, the field of geography has a unique opportunity to contribute to the fuller understanding of man's place in nature, especially through its emphasis on empirical relationships and on the application of spatial and ecologic thinking to the human use of the earth. Potentially it has important contributions to make to scientific programs concerned with land utilization, food production, water supply, industrial development, urban and regional planning, and natural resources conservation. It may equally be concerned with man's attitudes about the earth and his attachments to the local character of places. The appreciation and enjoyment of landscapes for their own sake, and a naive curiosity about the arrangement of things in space, has attracted many workers to geography. So too has the "conservation ethic," a concern for the husbanding and protection of the earth against man's destructive exploitation and despoliation. The engineering of economic and social development in itself, the provision of resources for an expanding world population at rising levels of living, if not a geographical goal, may nevertheless have profound geographical consequences.

Traditionally geography has been committed strongly to direct field observation. This could well be its unique challenge and its opportunity. Nowadays, with new techniques and the proliferation of the printed work, more and more scholars are doing their work in the office or laboratory, well removed from contact with the countryside and the enormously difficult task of analyzing complex reality. Indeed, the provision of trained field workers, sensitive to both culture and environment and willing to get their boots muddy, may be one of geography's more important contributions to scholarship generally and to area studies in particular.

Scholarly geography is placing more emphasis on problems, concepts, ideas, and techniques today than ever before. Yet the world of scholarship still properly looks to geography for information about places and will doubtless continue to do so. The term "geography" means "writing about the earth," by which the Greeks understood "describing the earth." Good regional description, as much art as science, is likely to be useful to scholars of the future long after the theories and models toward which so much of contemporary social science is geared have been forgotten or have been enshrined as quaint relics of another era. Although the facts the geographer perceives must be examined, labeled, and perhaps measured with care and accuracy, the presentation of these facts involves personal choice, taste, and judgment. The reading of the landscape, the interpretation of scenery, whether for its own sake or for some specific end, involving as it does the intricate interplay of its physical and cultural elements, is in a manner comparable to art or music appreciation, a legitimate subject of humanistic inquiry. A sympathetic review in *Landscape* magazine (P.G.A., 1951:34) put it this way:

> For the manner in which the environment is exploited, the attitude toward nature as she manifests herself in that environment, is a cultural trait second to none in importance. The human landscape is the visible sign of that attitude. It is in the interpretation of that landscape that ecology falters, and where human geography comes into its own. Skeptical of "scientific" laws, aware of the enormous diversity among human groups, disdaining no discipline in its effort to understand the manmade environment, it does much to bring together and moderate the various professions which have undertaken to study man and his habitat. More than anything else, perhaps, human geography is a way of looking at man and the world; it is a new word for humanism. If so, we must see to it that...its qualities become generally diffused [among other disciplines], ecology taking over its human concern, its earthier aspects being absorbed by the social sciences.

Such interpretive insight depends on long and intimate familiarity with place, language, and culture. This is the first requisite of the "area specialist," whether in Latin America or elsewhere, but especially so of the geographer.

In recent years quite another direction has come to geography, an abstract and mathematical concern for space and space-distance relations, centering on the search for verification of observation and the search for generalizations and laws through systems analysis, spatial and stimulation models, and the methods, concepts, and approaches of the physical sciences applied to economic and cultural data. William Warntz (1959), perhaps representative of those striving to bring the subject more in line with the more theoretically oriented social sciences, has called for "a macroscopic geography aimed at developing concepts at a more meaningful level of abstraction so as to make possible the understanding of the whole economic system and to provide a conceptual framework into which to put the micro-descriptions." In this macroscopic analysis and especially through the application of gravity and potential models in which earth variables are purposefully disregarded, he has envisioned a step towards "the forging of a theory of human society [that] can be greatly aided by finding regularities in the aggregate." Others complain that this is hardly geography's responsibility. Labeling this doctrine "the new teleology of the equilibrium and functional concepts," Lukermann and Porter (1960:504) conclude that, "if this is the high level of abstraction that geography is searching for--the seventeenth century lies dead ahead."

The lively ferment in contemporary geography cannot but have its effect on Latin American studies. As elsewhere the winds of change blow strongly within geography, yet what Sauer called the subject's "lingering sickness," a consequence in part of its work being too much ruled "not by inquisitiveness but by definitions of its boundaries," cannot be said to have been entirely eradicated. While extricating itself from the quagmire of pedagogy, it runs the risk of splintering today into quantitative economic geography, historical-cultural geography, and physical geography, with limited communication between the segments. It seems likely, however, that geographers working in Latin America may be less affected by this threatening schism than those working in the more developed parts of the world.

References

Lukermann, F., and P.W. Porter. 1960. "Gravity and Potential Models in Economic Geography" (review article), *Annals of the Association of American Geographers*, Vol. 50, pp. 493-504.

P.G.A. 1951. Review of *Culture in Crisis*, by Laura Thompson, *Landscape*, Vol. 1, No. 2, pp. 32-35.

Warntz, William. 1959. "Progress in Economic Geography," in *New Viewpoints in Geography*, Preston E. James, editor. Twenty-Ninth Yearbook of the National Council for the Social Studies, Washington, D.C., pp. 54-75.

2

By Way of Preface*

From Herodotus to Heyerdahl the far-off and seldom visited lands that have been but little known or understood have been a particular concern of geographers. The public is still apt to think of geography primarily in terms of geographical discovery and exploration, and it is often a bit disillusioned upon learning how seldom geographers actually are concerned with far-away and romantic places and peoples. This, I think, is rather unfortunate. Certainly it was the prospect of satisfying deep-seated curiosities about distant and dimly-known corners of the earth that lured many of us initially into this thing we call Geography, stimulated perhaps by a childhood collection of stamps or rocks or by those wonderful pictures in the National Geographic. When we saw there was a chance to make a living at this sort of thing we became professionals. In the beginning we have had a good bit of the unabashed hedonist in us. The trouble seems to be that somewhere along the line we "get religion"; we spend less and less time on the problems and areas that really excite us, the things we really would like to do, and more and more time doing the things that we are asked to do or feel that we should do, usually because they seem to bear on local and contemporary problems for which answers are being demanded. We start taking ourselves too seriously, we seem to tense up, and we begin to merit the charge of the former editor of that excellent magazine of human geography called *Landscape* that professional geographers as a group

*Excerpted (pp. 3-5, 16) from "English Speaking Settlement of the Western Caribbean," *Yearbook of the Association of Pacific Coast Geographers*, Vol. 16, pp. 3-16, Oregon State University Press (1954). Only the introduction and conclusion are included here. Presidential Address delivered at the 17th Annual Meeting of the Association of Pacific Coast Geographers, Pullman, Washington, June 24, 1954.

ment are not being properly exercised. As we concern ourselves increasingly with enumeration and description, we stop asking "why" and how." What is worse, our descriptions too often lack life and imagination. The dearth of widely-read semi-popular books on geography in America is in embarrassing contrast to the situation in Europe. Nor can all the blame be laid to high publishing cost. Good writing, of course, requires practice as well as imagination and persistence. This may be why newspaper experience has been in the background of so many of our most respected geographers--Ratzel and Reclus, to name two.

In the days when German geography was great, one or more field seasons or *wanderjahre* in an unfamiliar physical and cultural environment in one of the further reaches of the earth was almost a requisite of graduate training. To be thrown into the midst of a totally unfamiliar setting, preferably one that has not been picked over too much by the experts and faced with the task of pulling together observations into a meaningful pattern and interpretation is certainly one of the best tests of geographical competence. I should like to put in a good word for the thesis that to know ourselves and our own culture such a point of reference in other lands, in other cultures and even other times puts us on much firmer grounds. And further, that the time to stake them out is in graduate student days, when enthusiasms and physical endurance are at full strength, before children, house payments, and heavy teaching loads make arm-chair geographers of us by force of circumstances or habit.

At Berkeley, in a certain measure through the influence of Carl Sauer, we have found in Latin America a convenient and relatively inexpensive proving ground for graduate students which has been curiously little exploited by American geographers. It offers not only areas of rich geographical content but enticing problems in systematic geography as well. Moreover, a thesis based on extensive field study in Middle America or the Caribbean frequently has opened the door to a teaching job with course work in Latin American geography, in tropical geography, or in culture history which would have been closed to the candidate whose field experience has been confined to the familiar urbanized industrial North American culture region of the mid-twentieth century with which we are all more or less inevitably identified. And there is yet another reward from foreign field work; it is an almost sure-fire way to gain a competence of sorts in at least one other tongue than English. I well recall that my own decision to initiate theses research in Colombia was based in part on the reassuring realization that, if worst came to worst, I would at least come home with some competence in the Spanish language to show for the considerable expenditure of time and money involved. In Sweden, in Borneo, in Madagascar, or in Brazil the reward would have been comparable.

Our Canadian colleagues seem to be discovering that the Arctic regions offer another accessible yet new and challenging environment which sharpens and intensifies their focus. I do not think that it is mere chance that some of the best regional writing on North America has been done by foreigners such as Bauling, Bartz, DeGeer, and Schmieder, nor that some of our own members have done such effective interpretations in Europe, in Mexico, in New Zealand, or the Orient. The stimulus of the new landscape, and the unfamiliar culture, cannot but sharpen the perception of the acute observer; it may go a long way toward explaining why so much of our really enduring geographic literature has been by "scientific travelers," from Peter Kalm, Arthur Young, Humboldt, Wallace, and Darwin to the reconnaissances of Sven Hedin, von Richthofen, Pendleton, Sauer, or Robert Cushman Murphy.

Geography, no more than any other academic discipline, can expect to long endure or command respect as a teaching field alone. In America, at least, this does not always seem to have been properly recognized. Do we really lack the curiosity, the ability to pose problems and to write effective prose that the scantiness of our published researches suggests? Professor Trewartha's stinging critique should be required reading for all who are complacent about the contents of the volume entitled *American Geography: Inventory and Prospect*. He writes:

> "A discipline involves a special and particular segment of the whole field of knowledge and those who operate under the banner of any discipline have a dual responsibility which involves the creation as well as the imparting of knowledge. Teaching is not enough. It is required of us, also, that we discover new truths and offer new interpretations. This is research, and no discipline can be considered in a healthy state unless its members are both creators and teachers."[1]

As Professor Trewartha disconsolately observes, we are in general operating with great success at teaching and administration, at text-book writing, at committee work, and at University "politicking," and in general leading energetic lives eagerly devoted to good works. Yet, as we beat the drums for the undeniably high educa-

---

[1]Glenn Trewartha, "Some Thoughts on the Functions of the Regional Divisions," *The Professional Geographer*, Vol. 5, pp. 35-44 (1953).

12

tional values of geography to build up budgets and enrollments, our scholarly activities and thus our academic reputations suffer accordingly. If we are to defend our place of honor within the tradition of liberal learning we must pay more attention to the cultivation of the critical and exploratory spirit, concern ourselves more with additions to knowledge and become once more creative thinkers and intellectual pioneers. Such an association as this has a definite responsibility to further the attainment of such goals, to encourage expertness and depth in a field that has become increasingly characterized by shallowness. Only by charting such a course can we hope to attract the superior young students in whose hands we would like to see the fate of geography eventually rest.

But we shall be known by our works and saved by them alone. With this in mind I turn now to a summary of my current field and library research into the Geography of the English-speaking, Protestant Settlements of the Western Caribbean. It is not a problem, nor an area of any particular practical significance at the moment, nor did a desire to demonstrate any particular "field method" motivate my visit to the area. I went there for the old-fashioned reason that it interested and intrigued me and because it was one of those blank spots on the map and in the literature that seems never to have received much attention. What I found whetted my curiosity and has sent me scurrying back to the library for the answers to many questions which can only be found by the collation of field and documentary evidence....

It is in such out-of-the-way corners of the earth that some of the richest nuggets await the cultural geographer. We geographers may have a tendency towards preoccupations with our own familiar culture, landscape, and the urgent problems of the moment. There is an antidote for this, I think, in the tropics, in the arctic, in every foreign land and unfamiliar landscape for those who, to borrow a phrase from John Leighly, would look at the land, the sea and the sky with questioning eyes seeking understanding. It is, I submit, worthwhile and revealing to get off the beaten track, seek out the forgotten, inaccessible peoples and cultures. If one is concerned with perspective in the understanding of cultural processes, and with historical geography, the value of such experience can hardly be exaggerated. And, perhaps most important of all, it is often an exciting adventure, both physically and intellectually, of the very sort that originally endeared geography to so many of us, but which somehow in the course of years, we have failed to take advantage of as we had originally intended.

3

Geography as Exploration and Discovery[*]

   We geographers are an unlikely lot. At times the one common denominator among us seems to be that we call ourselves "geographers," with little consideration as to what that grand word really means. Yet we do have shared values and a common, almost mystic, bond--our curiosity about this planet and the human experience on it--ways of looking at the world that seem to us both unique and worthwhile. Best of all, we are busy doing things that we like to do.

   I am among the privileged ones in this fragmented company who find fascination above all in places and people and the interplay between them. In my undergraduate days "geography" never occurred to us, either as a major or a career. As with so many of us, my conversion was due to a chance encounter with a professor who had charisma, wisdom, and a profound "geographical sense." The geography that has most appealed to me has been a kind of historically based "landscape appreciation," and I confess a certain uneasiness with the current compulsion for precision of analysis, the often sterile straining for statistical content and significance.

   Geography, so magnificently interdisciplinary, seems an ideal vehicle for the joining of hands of science and humanism, including the taking of moral positions on environmental and spatial issues. This world, after all, is seriously out of balance with regards to production and consumption of food and raw materials, environments are deteriorating, resources and opportunities are unevenly available.

---

[*]Excerpted (pp. 1-3, 14-16) from *Annals of the Association of American Geographers*, Vol. 67, pp. 1-25 (1977). Only the introduction and conclusion are included here. Presidential Address delivered at the 72nd Annual Meeting of the Association of American Geographers, New York, April 13, 1976.

As students of the relations between nature and culture we are asking surprisingly few of the really critical questions. How have things gotten this way? Can we possibly use the planet's resources at this rate without using them up, without fouling our nest beyond reclaim? What kind of a jaycock world is it where annual expenditures for armaments is equal to the entire income of the poorer half of mankind? How long can this and the idiot idea of unending growth, this unquenchable thirst for material goods, be sustained? World population has increased from three to four billion since the A.A.G. met in Dallas just 15 years ago. More people need more food, more energy, more of everything.

Busied elsewhere, we geographers have too largely left to others, and perhaps especially the biologists, the task of exploring the man-nature relationship and facing up to the consequences of the materialistic philosophy with which we have infected so much of the world. Among the more relevant, the most rewarding, of the approaches to our subject, if it is to be a living force, would seem to be the ecological perspective, which is really the long view, from the distant past, into the twentieth century and beyond. It focuses on the earth as the home of man and our responsibilities for the maintenance of its diversity and productivity. We are still an earth science as surely as *geo* is Greek for "earth," yet much of what is being passed off as geography today is simply the study of man, of society, without serious regard for place or time.

The Attractions of Geography

Many of us are in geography because it involves using our eyes, and for the latitude it allows for wonderment at the world around us, for travel and exploration, for knowing in some depth at least one people and environment other than our own. The excitement of distant places, a colorful map, or the sound of certain place names may first have excited our geographical instincts. In my own case I suspect it was those memorable transcontinental auto trips in high school and college days when considerable stretches of even the Lincoln Highway and Route 66 were still gravel and when gasoline was ten cents a gallon, and even less in East Texas. Or it may have been that stamp collection. I still recall those brightly colored Tanganyikas, with their graceful giraffes browsing on the savanna trees, the caribou on that set from Newfoundland, and our own Columbian Exposition commemoratives of 1892. Whatever the original stimuli, it took. One hopes that at least some of our present recruits are still coming into geography through this door.

Having started out as a newspaperman, I still find myself looking at the world in much the same way that I did as a young reporter on the Mendicino County *Redwood Journal*. The linkage between journalism and geography--at least the geography that interests me, based on observation, conservation and digging through the records leading to a story hopefully expressed with clarity and simplicity--is something that is not properly appreciated. Indeed, geography in one sense may be seen as basically a higher form of journalism. Like Bernal Díaz we could well ask if our best hope for immortality might not be that "we wrote the truth and were never dull." We have an unmatched entrée to our supporting public in the naturally given interest of students of all ages in the wonders of the world about us. It would be sad if geography should permit itself to become identified principally as a discipline that can provide techniques and mechanics of control and manipulation for urban, regional, and environmental management. Ours is a major opportunity that transcends mere method. The faculties of description and evaluation are those most in need of cultivation if we are to interpret the relationships of land and life and better illuminate the esthetic qualities of landscapes so that men may live more wisely and happily.

My own focus within geography has come to be the tropical world, especially the American tropics, and, because I live where I do, areas of summer-dry Mediterranean climates. I have come to be impressed, in both life zones, with the significance of vegetation and, in the face of increasing human disturbance, the dynamics of vegetation succession. It is the plant cover, more than anything else, that gives character to the land, to what we see and sense. Vegetation, with its associated wild fauna, is not only a rewarding field for study for its own sake but it also provides an incomparable and sensitive ecologic indicator of the state of the environment, its equilibrium, its productivity, and its potential for supplying human needs, whether for food, industrial raw materials, or simply as wildland to be appreciated and perhaps preserved.

In considering a topic for this occasion, accordingly, I have been strongly drawn to a long held interest, that of the process and consequences of tropical forest destruction, especially the conversion of forest to artificial pasture in Latin America. From here it would have been a short step to the world protein problem, the question of the food producing potential of the earth and especially of the warmer lower latitudes where most of the remaining land reserve lies.

Alternatively, the bicentennial year of the nation seemed to suggest something relating to the American experience, perhaps our westward expansion and its terminal expression out on what Wallace Stegner likes to call "the handsome side of the content," in the warm folds of California's hills and valleys where America runs out of land. But I was reminded that if 1776 marks the departure of imperialism from the East Coast, it was in the same year that it arrived, under the flag of Spain, on the shores of San Francisco Bay. And that is hardly a theme in the spirit of the Bicentennial!

Instead I have settled on an almost autobiographical review of what I have learned about a particular part of the world with which I have become more or less familiar during recurrent visits and study during the past 30 years. I shall resist cataloguing the intriguing complexity of geographical facts and ecological relationships of the area. Rather, through selected examples, I shall seek to demonstrate what I perceive as the extraordinary advantages of viewing a particular area or set of phenomena over a continuing period of time. It provides the opportunity to observe processes, not at a given moment, but to see them over a substantial period and thus from a variety of perspectives. Even more important to me has been the demonstration of how familiarity and continued exposure may lead to recognition of unexpected themes, problems and relationships within an area--especially an unfamiliar landscape and culture to which one comes with the fresh perspective of an outsider. The significance of what one is seeing may not fully register until it has been repeatedly observed, from different angles and at different points in time. A further and obvious advantage is the growing mastery of sources. Friendships and the confidence of acquaintances mature and yield fruit. With good luck one may come to be considered a part of a community as sympathy and understanding deepen, to be taken into confidence, perhaps encouraged to think that one is doing something that may bring satisfaction and succor to others, not simply exploiting a foreign area as a lucrative research pasture for whatever professional kudos it may promise.

I chose northwestern Colombia as my area almost by accident. I had thought, after nearly 5 years in the military during World War II, that I had earned the right to a year of field study in a region of optimal attractiveness--in my personal ordering of priorities a tropical highland with shirtsleeve weather, where the mountains were tall and green, the people kindly, and with the colonial Spanish imprint still clearly visible. My original objective had been to study the coffee economy of the mountain province of Antioquia and its impact on the rapidly growing commercial center of Medellín, its orchid-decked mile-high capital. Vaguely it had occurred to me, too, that its geographical position at the stem end of the southern continent potentially gave it a special significance, for the flood tide of human migrations that swept down from the north to people South America quite clearly funneled through it. But most of all it was an area curiously little known to the outside world, a blank spot on the map of the short I had always imagined it was up to geographers to explore and to elucidate....

On Going Back

In my corner of South America, and I suspect elsewhere, everything in the end has seemed to be hitched to everything else. I have found that it pays to keep going back to an area, a people. I have found that significant phenomena or relationships continue to present themselves, things that were at first completely missed or whose significance was not originally apparent. In my experience these linkages are quite accidentally discovered. They are seldom of the sort that can be conjured up in one's study. Repeated visits and growing familiarity with an area continually enlarge one's range of vision and concern. You see, you hear, or read something new, something out of place, something irregular, and you are moved to investigate further. There may be many false leads, many a dead end, but if one is lucky and persists there may be undreamed of rewards awaiting. The experiences, the acquaintances made along the way, can make geography enormously good fun. You learn the ropes, how to get around in the libraries and archives, how to use the local newspapers as the rich sources of information they often are, who the people are who know their area, who are at heart the "geographers" with a reservoir of local knowledge and insight above and beyond the norm. In such company time moves fast. Life becomes worth living. As Carlos Casteñeda's "Don Juan" says "We are going to be here in this stupendous, awesome, unfathomable world only a short while, too short for witnessing all the marvels of it." We have got to learn to make every act count, even though it may on occasion mean taking risks, living dangerously.

Area as Integrating Concept

For me, at least, it all comes back to place, to area as the integrating concept, to the supremacy of observed geographic data over any pyramid of deductions or formal theories, however powerful the apparatus brought to bear. Geography by its nature offers the promise of carrying us beyond generalizations to more exact knowledge of the interaction of man and environment. Diversity, we are learning, seems to be a major stabilizing force in the natural order, and probably in the social order, too. It is something to analyze and understand, not something to be gotten rid of. Interest in the unique, moreover, may be the single most powerful recruiting agent we have for bringing students into geography. We must be aware of those who would brainwash us into thinking it is something shameful or secondary, that only generalizations or theory are wholly respectable.

It does of course take time, access to a minimum of travel, money (and here a personal bow to my own university and to the Office of Naval Research for support), and perhaps a certain perverse propensity for roughing it. Having one's share of good fortune can help, too, perhaps beginning with choosing the right area in which to work. Rosalie Wax, in an autobiographical review of her own ethnographic field career, observes that the "most valuable thing any fieldworker can take with him into the field is good luck."[1] Luck, she suggests, is a gift of the Powers and cannot be acquired by determination or study. Being at the right place at the right time is part of it, but it also helps to know that you are there. The next most useful thing to take into the field, she continues, is intelligence manifested as common sense, shrewdness, and flexibility--the property called "having one's wits about one." "I cannot tell a student how to acquire or develop wits," she writes, "but I can tell him this: that if he does not have his wits about him while in the field the chances are that he will not be given the opportunity to exercise any of his other attributes or virtues."

As we seek out paths to expanded awareness through teaching or writing we would do well not to forget that our subject was originally rooted in the comparative observation and analysis of places. The field experience that such geography almost inevitably entails has the special virtue of lifting us quite decisively from the quagmire of definitions of our subject and from methodology and it gets us back into the open air. It reaffirms the spirit of geographical adventure and the validity of personal observation and of intuitive knowledge. It may encourage the integration of large general themes, the weaving together of disparate strands into a tapestry of land and

---

[1]R. H. Wax, *Doing Fieldwork: Warnings and Advice* (Chicago: University of Chicago Press, 1971), reference p. 268 (cited in J. C. Friberg, "Field Techniques and the Training of the American Geographer," Discussion Paper Series No. 5, Department of Geography, Syracuse University, 1975, p. 15).

life in a regional context that is both satisfying and useful.[2] It makes us, I suppose, as much humanists and historians as scientists. But it may just be that such knowledge and the understanding deriving from it is what the future will most want and expect from us. At least I detect a current flowing that way. I hope that I am right, that geographers to come may continue to experience the joys of exploration and discovery that have been one of the wellsprings of our subject's strength since antiquity.

[2]The points of view here expressed have found repeated affirmation in the works of C. O. Sauer. See also, D. W. Meinig, "Environmental Appreciation: Localities as a Humane Art," *Western Humanities Review*, Vol. 25 (1971), pp. 1-11; and D. Hooson, "Rejuvenating Regional Geography: Ends and Means," *Proceedings*, 21st International Geographical Congress, New Delhi. Vol. 4 (Calcutta, 1972), pp. 91-94.

4

Geographical Research in Latin America:
The Ecological Dimension*

Among the great world culture areas Latin America stands unique, in many ways still a New World, largely unknown and un-studied. The extraordinary fact of its discovery, and the infinitely complex process of its absorption into the larger world, begun on the shores of Hispaniola in 1492 and still in process, represents one of the great epics of human experience. The origin and character of the indigenous societies of America, previously unknown and un-dreamt of, as well as the proper relationship of European society to them, have provided the basis for intense philosophical speculation and scholarly investigation for generations of Western scholars. Latin America stands alone, too, as the one major world area in which effective racial and cultural mixing has been achieved. Its 420 mil-lion people [in 1987] represent in large part a quite recognizable new race and culture, however diverse their political and social com-ponents. But Latin America is also the home of major Indian sur-vivals, even integrated cultural entities, and these stubbornly con-servative groups themselves have importantly influenced the nature of the dominant society. Here exists a unique blend of the European and native cultures, the indigenousness of which remains largely un-studied. The Catholic church, the Spanish and Portuguese languages,

*James Parsons has written several bibliographic surveys of geographical research in Latin America (1964, 1971, 1973, 1981). His essay on "Latin America" for the 1972 University of Chicago conference on *Geographers Abroad*, ed. Marvin Mikesell, is reprinted here (University of Chicago, Department of Geography Research Paper No. 152, pp. 16-46, 1973). Excerpts are added (indented) from his more recent presentation on "The Ecological Dimension: Ten Years Later," *Proceedings of the Conference of Latin Americanist Geographers*, Vol. 8, pp. 22-33 (1981). Minor changes, corrections, and deletions have been made in consultation with Professor Parsons. The citations have been considerably reduced in number; although the text has been updated in a few places, the baseline remains 1980.

and Iberian institutions, even the flattening steamroller called modernization, in many areas only thinly veneer the persistent and deep roots in the aboriginal and colonial American past.

Interest in these contrasting cultures and economies of Latin America, in complex spatial and temporal juxtaposition, is further heightened for geographers by the extreme diversity of the physical environment they inhabit, from the rainless Atacama to the Amazonian rain forest and to some of the highest inhabited mountains on earth. Climatically, only the extreme continentality of the northern hemisphere mid-latitudes is missing. This richness of cultural and environmental dimensions is heightened by the availability of an extraordinary documentation in European languages, much of which has been published and the rest of which is preserved in well-organized and preserved archives. Further, and increasingly, Latin America is in a sense a part of us--in the Hispanic-American Southwest, in California, in the Cuban colonies of Florida and the Puerto Rican barrios of Manhattan--with increasing relevance for the understanding of the contemporary society of the United States. Finally, for North Americans, these foreign lands directly to the south are uniquely accessible, and often at minimal cost. No cultural boundary on earth offers more striking contrasts than those on either side of the United States-Mexican frontier between the mouths of the Rio Grande and the Tijuana rivers, and few are easier to cross. Only the peculiar Anglo-Saxon block against foreign languages, coupled at times with a curious and possibly growing inhibition among geographers against trying to know things first hand, of getting away from the difficulties of time and place, has kept more of our kind from pursuing their studies in these extraordinary lands.

If one were designing on a *tabla rasa* an ideal but imaginary New World it would be difficult to conceive, even in one's wildest dreams, of a set of human and environmental circumstances more extraordinary, more original than that offered by the Americas. The English and French speaking lands north of the Rio Grande, much later occupied, were to become firmly attached to the Old World as economic and cultural extensions of Europe. To the south, in Ibero-America, a very different society or societies emerged--at the same time monolithic and plural--strongly influenced by aboriginal cultures, by the dominant tropicality of the climate, by the existence of extraordinary metallic riches, and by the historical accident of the political dominance of two strongly Catholic and centralist European powers.

Latin America is almost an island in the world ocean, standing in contrast and isolation from the other great world island, the Old World. Distance and isolation have played a very real role, often not fully appreciated, in its evolution. Even today it stands at one side from the great avenues of world commerce. The links and strands connecting these two worlds, the interchange of plants and animals, ideas, and institutions provide us with one of the grand and continuing themes of scholarly investigation. Such isolation, combined with unique cultural and ecologic circumstances, offers unparalleled opportunities for comparative studies, as yet but little exploited.

Pre-Historical and Historical Geography

Work in Latin America by English-speaking geographers[1] has been strongly dominated by the historical approach, often with a strong environmental emphasis. The lines of history are here deeply etched on the land and people, and an understanding of the present is heavily dependent on the past. More than one geographer, with an original intent to do a conventional--or unconventional--contemporary field study, has been lured irrevocably to the pre-Columbian or colonial past once he has confronted the Latin America reality, with its strong and diverse cultural survivals, and the impressive archaeologic remains and archival documentation that makes historical study and elucidation both feasible and compelling. The extent of the historical bias is documented in William Denevan's (1971a) bibliography of Latin American historical geography. It shows, too, the very strong predominance of work on Spanish-speaking areas as compared to that on Portuguese-speaking Brazil. This in part reflects the extraordinary attraction to scholars of the problems associated with the origins of Meso-American and Andean high cultures and the persistence of aboriginal influences--language, customs, ways of life--particularly in Mexico, Guatemala, Ecuador, Peru, and Bolivia. This bias is also explained in part by the low position and prestige of Portuguese language study in our schools, and, in the case of Mexico and Central America, the obvious ease of access to the North American scholar. Finally Brazilians themselves, much more than Spanish Americans, have been oriented to the present, to problems of modernization and development, despite the lateness of their independence from European control. The bibliography just mentioned, which seems representative of English language research, contains some 446 items. Of these 214 are localizable in Mexico and Central America, and 165 in South America, of which only 20 are in Brazil proper.

---

[1]Editor's note. The emphasis in this essay is on English-speaking geographers. For a discussion of European and Latin American geographers, see Parsons, 1964:37-44.

Geographical work on Latin America often tends to fuse with that of cultural anthropologists and historians as in community studies and in studies of the origins, spread, limits, and modifications of culture complexes or traits. The links with anthropology and with anthropological method are in part a result of that subject's greater dependence on field work and direct observation than characterizes the other social sciences. The data of physical geography, soils, land forms, climate, and climatic change, are increasingly relied upon to resolve the knotty problems of past habitats and societies as the so-called ecological approach has given new vigor and direction to that profession and its handmaiden, archaeology. The door is increasingly open to geographers for collaboration. The first volume of the *Handbook of Middle American Indians*, edited by Robert West (1964), and the contributions in Volume 6 of the *Handbook of South American Indians* (Steward, 1950) on physical geography and biogeography are examples of the recognition by anthropologists of the role of the physical environment in human affairs, something some geographers paradoxically seem willing to ignore or even deny.

A significant contributing factor to this emphasis on cultural and historical geography has been the strong and persistent influence of the maestro of Latin American historical geography, Carl Sauer of Berkeley, whose work, with that of his students, comprises a very significant part of this literature, virtually all of it on Spanish-language areas. The *Ibero-Americana* monograph series at the University of California, founded by Sauer and the anthropologist Alfred Kroeber in 1932, has been the vehicle for much of this work. Of its 54 volumes to date (1987), some 19 have been by professional geographers, the rest by colleagues working on the fringes of the field with an active concern for human ecology and demographic or cultural history. A comparable number of monographs in the *University of California Publications in Geography* have been on Latin American or Caribbean topics, while several other Berkeley studies have had more limited distribution as Office of Naval Research reports.

Considering the remarkable consistency with which Sauer's ideas or "hunches" have been verified in time by archival research, archaeology and ethnobotany, it is perhaps curious that more geographers have not been attracted into the lines of prehistoric inquiry that he pioneered. His wide-ranging contributions have included studies on the antiquity of man in the Americas, pre-Columbian population densities, the origins and dispersal of domesticated plants and animals, pre-Columbian contacts between the Old World and the New World, native agricultural systems, and the nature and extent of environmental deterioration through time.

It is a striking and singular fact that it has been the archaeologists and anthropologists who have most seriously engaged themselves in developing hypotheses and evidence on man-land or culture-environment relationships in Latin America. They have, in fact, often tended to see in cultural ecology a new kind of magic, perhaps in partial reaction against a too rigid cultural determinism (e.g., Meggers 1954, 1971; Palerm and Wolf, 1957). Past climates and climatic change, in particular, become increasingly relevant as we push back in time with our evidence, but work here has not as yet resulted in any overall synthesis.

The anthropological literature on pre-historic land and livelihood in Latin America is probably more extensive than the totality of all geography writing on the area. It has been conspicuously reported in journals like *Science, Scientific American, Natural History*, and in the popular press, and the work has been generously supported by funding agencies. It is not a fad and it is not a minor theme of only peripheral significance to the understanding of man's place in nature. It is in the mainstream of contemporary scientific inquiry. It involves the laws governing climate and landscape evolution, and it involves perception of human habitats, production systems, and settlement patterns and a host of other concerns close to the heart of any reasonably defined geography. Yet here, in our own back-yard, we continue to be outflanked and out-numbered.

Pre-historic and primitive agricultural production systems and techniques--milpa farming, irrigation, terracing, raised fields--have perhaps most attracted our attention within this context (see Denevan, 1980, for references). Again, Sauer's (1935) early classic work in northwest Mexico set the example for numerous later studies of pre-Columbian population densities and the thorny issue of carrying capacity and its relationship to cultural levels and dietary patterns (e.g., Gordon, 1957; Aschmann, 1959; Denevan, 1966, also 1976). The convergence of human geography with classical historical ethnogeography is exemplified by the work of several of Sauer's students (e.g., Meigs, 1939; Aschmann, 1959, 1960; Pennington, 1963, 1969). Others have made regional studies among modern Indian populations which may be conceptually indistinguishable from those of ecologically oriented anthropologists (e.g., Schmeider, 1930; McBryde, 1947; West, 1948; Brand, 1951; Denevan, 1971b). Aschmann (1971) has considered some of the problems associated with such work, not the least of which is the physical durability of the investigator. Among themes heavily dependent on Indian cultures, that of plant and animal domestication is perhaps outstanding. Sauer's (1952) earlier work has been continued by others (e.g., J. Sauer, 1950; Johannessen, 1966, 1970a, 1970b; Harris, 1972). The studies of

Edwards (1965) on aboriginal sailing craft on South America's west coast are of the same genre, as are land tenure investigations involving Indian systems (Borde and Góngora, 1956). Aschmann's (1959) perceptive analysis of the human ecology and demography of Baja California provides an example of the importance of understanding not only the activities of individuals and communities but also the motivations and goals that induce them.

More recently, contemporary subsistence farming practices have been the object of critical attention by an increasing number of geographers. A seminal paper by the Colombian anthropologist Reichel-Dolmatoff (1976) describes the highly adaptive behavioral rules and beliefs that control population growth and the exploitation of the natural environment in the rain forest, a blueprint for ecological adaptation that has been compared to modern systems analysis. Yet another anthropological contribution of special interest to geographers relates to vertical ecological zonation as exploited by native Andean populations (Murra, 1972). Agricultural origins have been of lesser concern, a recent discovery of an unexpectedly early maize in Ecuador having brought into question some widely held earlier views. The research field of ethnobotany, with roots reaching back to Sauer, seems to have been largely usurped by anthropologists and botanists, although some geographers (e.g., Johannessen, Gade, Harris) continue to make significant contributions to it. Hunting and fishing societies, however, have received considerable attention (Nietschmann, 1972, 1973; Smith, 1978, 1979).

The reconstruction of aboriginal populations and population densities at the time of the conquest, stimulated by the earlier work of Sauer, Cook, Borah, and Simpson, have continued (Denevan, 1976; Turner, 1976; Veblen, 1977). Crosby (1972) has elegantly summarized the impact of the European conquest on aboriginal populations and vice versa. Remaining native populations both in the tropical forest and in the highlands continue to be shamelessly pressured for living space. Protectionist legislation and public interest groups dedicated to the interests of Indian people have been increasingly evident and, in a growing number of cases, effective.

The Physical Environment

From the time of Humboldt to the present the problems associated with the land forms, climate, and vegetation of Latin America have attracted the attention of numerous and often prominent European geographers--e.g., Hettner, Sapper, Sievers, Kühn among an earlier generation, Troll, Kinzl, Maull, Wilhelmy, Czaja, Termer, and Gierloff-Emden more recently--without straying beyond the German-speaking scholars. Then there are Borde, De Martonne, Dresch, Dollfus, Ruellan, and others among the French, and King of South Africa, as well as a number of significant Latin American contributors. It is curious indeed that the pioneering work of Bowman (1916) in the Central Andes seems to have had no later parallel among U.S. geographers.

The sparseness of the contributions of North Americans to the study of the physical geography of Latin America reflects, of course, the relatively low status of the physical side of our subject, a condition which the recent ecological awakening may be at long last changing. The environment is increasingly being recognized as humanized nature rather than merely as a physical category, a part of the philosophy of man as inhabitant and transformer of the earth. Brunnschweiler (1971), in pointing to the paucity of work on land forms, and climate, most of which has been done by geologists and meteorologists, has urged the importance of a more coherent and practically oriented physical geography that may be relevant to our increasing ecologic and environmental concerns. Only in coastal studies, thanks in good measure to the program developed by the late R.J. Russell and his colleagues at Louisiana State University, and perhaps in studies of the natural and man-altered vegetation, can we hold our heads at all high. As things now stand, it has been noted, the average student is likely to get a more meaningful elaboration of the natural factors in the environment of a region from a Madariaga or a Ted Szulc than from geographers.

As man increasingly intervenes in nature, the maintenance of the man-land system in some sort of ecological equilibrium is more and more recognized as our principal challenge and responsibility. In this the involvement of our Latin American colleagues must have the highest priority. One obvious task is identification and analysis in human terms of the extreme and fragile environments that seem more characteristic of Latin America than most other world regions. The problems associated with tropicality and aridity--especially as related to soil fertility, human disease, and water surpluses or shortages--are fundamental concerns over wide areas. Such "short-term phenomena" as earthquakes, volcanic eruptions, landslides, avalanches, hurricanes, floods, drought, and wild fires have also had serious long-term consequences here for man. But there have been few geographic analyses or even case studies of such phenomena and none of the type of hazard research that has come to be so strongly identified with geography at Clark, Chicago, and Toronto.

28

In Latin America natural cataclysmic events have been significant modifiers of the physical landscape (e.g., Horst et al., 1976; Veblen and Ashton, 1978; Schlemon, 1979). When man is in the way, of course, they become "disasters." Such events have been unusually numerous in recent years, with the geographer's attention usually being directed towards their perception and human responses to them. The decade of the seventies was a particularly active one in this regard. Two Central American capitals suffered devastating earthquakes during the period. Managua was leveled in December 1972 for the third time in 90 years (8-12,000 dead, 700 city blocks destroyed). Little more than 3 years later came the 7.5 Richter scale Guatemala quake which took at least 17,000 lives and left some 55,000 injured, the worst natural tragedy to hit Central America since the conquest. Even more deadly had been the May 1970 temblor on the Pacific coast of South America that destroyed the coastal port of Chimbote, Peru, triggering massive avalanches and mud slides in the interior that left some 64,000 dead with another quarter million injured, one of the greatest disasters in recorded history. There were at least four other earthquakes in the 1970s with major loss of life: in the Mexican states of Michoacan and Puebla in 1973, in San Juan province, Argentina in 1977, and at Tumaco on the southwest coast of Colombia in 1979. The renewal of activity at Soufriere, which affected much of St. Vincent in 1902-1903, failed to bring with it the destruction predicted although extensive evacuations were carried out.[2]

Caribbean hurricanes tended to concentrate their force northwards towards United States coasts during the decade. But not "Fifi," which devastated the San Pedro Sula area of Honduras in September 1974, with 5,000 lives lost, mainly through flooding and mud slides. Five years later "David" leveled Santo Domingo, taking 1,500 lives. Damage from these tropical storms was massive, estimated in excess of 1 billion dollars for each.

There were other major natural catastrophes in the 1970s: "El Niño" with its destructive rains on the desert coast of Peru [the most severe coming later, in 1983-84]; droughts in Chile, Mexico, and the Nordeste of Brazil; frosts damaging to coffee in southern Brazil; recurrent floods in the Magdalena valley

[2]Editor's note. In November 1985 the eruption of Volcan Ruíz in Colombia and consequent mudflows left more than 20,000 dead or missing. Two months earlier an 8.1 magnitude quake left 10,000 dead in Mexico City.

and elsewhere following on progressive deforestation; and land-slides on the steep slopes of the rainier Andes, some of which wiped out whole villages.

Other environmental disruptions have been more directly the result of human action. Continuing soil erosion, urban air pollution, contamination of water supplies by mining and in-dustrial wastes and sewage, pesticide and herbicide poisonings, a major supertanker spill in the Straits of Magellan, the oil well blowout (Ixtoc I) off the Mexican gulf coast, and the near destruction of the once great Peruvian anchovy fishery, are but examples of how modern technology may "backfire" with major deleterious environmental consequences.

The Revitalization of Biogeography

One of the more encouraging recent developments within geography has been the revitalization of the sub-field of bio-geography. Much of this work, and more especially the history of vegetation modification through human activity, has centered in tropical America, where one tends to become especially sensitized to the importance of vegetation as the essential geographic factor that more than anything else defines and gives character to the visible landscape. The relationship of plant cover to human activity seems much closer here than in temperate lands so that for the field geographer the ability to make proper identifications of growing things and to recognize indications of disturbance becomes of considerable importance.

Vegetation and vegetation change provide some of the most sensitive indicators of ecological potential and environmental deterio-ration and it is here that some of the most important contributions by geographers have been made (e.g., Waibel, 1948; Tosi, 1960; Wagner, 1962; Gordon, 1969). In numerous explicitly regional studies, too, special attention has been given to vegetation and its modification and use by man (e.g., Gordon, 1957; West, 1957). Maps of ecological potential, drawn on the basis of a predictive climatic model created by Leslie R. Holdridge, have been published for almost all of the Spanish-speaking countries from Guatemala to Peru using a terminology relating to plant formations. Perhaps the most sustained efforts have been focused on the vexing question of tropical savannas, including a series of some 16 volumes published by the McGill Savanna Research Project. Geographers have been giving attention to the pampas question (e.g., Walter, 1967), to strand vegetation (e.g., J. Sauer, 1968; Vann, 1959; Wet, 1956), and to problems of high mountain geoecology (e.g., Troll, 1959, 1968).

The deserts and tropical forests have been more largely left to the botanists and ecologists. All of these major associations have been modified importantly by human activity, but it is the relentless attack on the tropical rain forest that recently has been the object of special concern.

Vegetation Alteration

Denevan's (1973) dramatic warning of the "imminent demise of the Amazon rain forest" at the 1971 Conference of Latin Americanist Geographers meeting has been followed by much speculation as to the ecologic consequences of the rush of new highway construction and the new land clearing technology it has brought with it. In recent years the attention of researchers has tended to switch from the *vías de penetración* reaching down from the Andes to the crash program of road building in Brazilian Amazonia that followed the creation of the Superintendencia do Desenvolvimiento da Amazonia (SUDAM) in 1966 This push to open the empty selva, pressed with unparalleled speed and intensity, has been widely documented (e.g., Smith, 1980). Its brutal ecological consequences seem likely for the most part to be irreversible.

Whether the eight-nation Treaty of Amazonian Cooperation signed in Brasilia in 1978 will hasten or slow the progress of forest clearing is uncertain. There are recent indications that both Brazil and the Andean nations may be becoming increasingly sensitized to the dangers of this uncontrolled destruction of the world's greatest lowland forest. One hope may be a new agroforestry based on plantations of fast-growing trees. In tropical environments this is still in the experimental phase, although in more temperate Brazil and Chile vast, man-made tracts of eucalyptus and *Pinus radiata* have been producing lumber, wood pulp, and charcoal for many years. The conversion of large-scale, biologically diversified forests to monocultural systems, however, opens the way to disease, insect infestations, and soil deterioration, and may extract other ecological and social costs. In the equatorial zone nothing has matched the audacious and much publicized venture of Daniel K. Ludwig, the secretive United States shipowner and industrialist, who converted much of a 6,000 square mile tract of rain forest on the remo Rio Jarí, a left bank Amazon tributary, into a vast plantation of fast-growing *Gmelina arborea* from India and Burma, together with *Pinus caribaea* on thinner soils. We should learn much from this "experiment," more recently under the control of Brazilian interests.

Most of the land cleared of tropical forest in the Americas is converted to pasture, either directly or after a short period in subsistence crops. This process of "grassification" which threatens to convert much of the tropical lowland of Latin America into cattle ranching has been well documented by geographers and ecologists. Encouraged by the availability of cheap land, easy credit, and favorable tax laws, multinational as well as local interests have moved aggressively into the production of beef cattle, often for export (e.g., West, 1978; Nations and Nigh, 1978; Feder, 1979). Everywhere the forest is yielding to the axe and the bulldozer. Within 10 years of being cleared and planted to introduced pasture grasses, most properties along the new highways of Amazonia have reverted to worthless secondary scrub. The Panama Canal is threatened by deforestation that is causing a severe shortage of water needed to operate the canal. In Mexico reservoirs are rapidly silting. Some areas, like Haiti, are at an almost irreversible stage of environmental degradation. A recent President of Costa Rica made deforestation a major issue in his inaugural address, stating that his country was "approaching the point of no return in regard to management of its renewable resources." During the decade 1965-1975 the area in pasture increased by some 64 million acres, almost entirely at the expense of forest, in tropical America.

The functioning of tropical forests as systems and especially the rate and the potential consequences of their destruction has recently become a major research concern of numerous private, governmental, and international agencies, as documented in the "Tropical Moist Forest Conservation Bulletin," which began publication in 1978 under the auspices of the Natural Resources Defense Council, Washington, D.C. (see also Norman Myers' National Research Council report, 1980). An unpublished report to the President by a United States Interagency Task Force on the world's tropical forests (1979) decries the lack of internationally qualified professionals available for tropical forestry programs. In this general area there would appear to be growing opportunities for properly trained professional geographers.

There has been a revolution in thinking about the history of the rain forest. Some evidence indicates that the Amazonian selva, instead of being an ageless and static entity, may be of relatively recent origin and that during the last glaciation it was semi-arid, a quiltwork of savanna landscapes and forest refugia. Its bird fauna, for example, is said to be explicable only if the Amazonian rain forest were divided into several discrete blocks in the Pleistocene. Pollen studies and the distribution of fossil sand dunes, too, have been cited as contradicting the long prevailing view of the stability of climate and vegetation at low latitudes. Attempts to relate this view to the culture history of Amazonia is generating considerable controversy (e.g., Whitten, 1979; Meggers, 1979) and has dramatically emphasized how the tropical moist forest is tied to the preservation of species diversity. In most of these new interpretations there has been an attempt to draw on the theory of island biogeography. Both the diversity and the successful regeneration of the forest has been held to be a function of the size of the forest block preserved. Recent reviews of the history of tropical forests continue to emphasize the meager data base available and the speculative nature of many currently held ideas. The pre-eminent role of soils and soil weathering processes within it is increasingly recognized.

Plant succession in disturbed situations such as abandoned agricultural plots provides important clues to the process of vegetational change (Budowski, 1963), and this often involves changes in the soil and micro-climate. Weedy immigrant species, usually introduced through human agency, have contributed largely to the reconstitution of secondary formations throughout the American tropics as well as frequently being the cause of abandonment of agricultural plots. Selective protection of useful items in the second-growth (*rastrojo*) has favored certain palms, leguminous trees, chicle, *Brosimum*, pitahaya, calabash, and a host of other species in many parts of tropical America. Elsewhere exotic invaders, such as cashews, oranges, limes, and mangoes have established themselves so successfully they may be mistaken for natural elements of the vegetation.

One of the best examples of this replacement of native by exotic elements is the gradual invasion of African grasses in tropical America, often with the aid of fire or grazing (Parsons, 1972). This establishment is in part on old savanna surfaces but more largely on recently cleared tracts of tropical forest where, after 2 or 3 years of cropping, the land has been converted to pasture. In terms of area covered we may be dealing here with one of the greatest ecological invasions in history. Its consequences are uncertain. In the short run, at least, it would seem to offer not only superior protein content but resistance to fire and overgrazing. But the durability of such a tropical "grass economy" is questionable. A similar replacement of native grasses by introduced species, from the Mediterranean region, is occurring in middle Chile. In Argentina species from the more humid mid-latitudes of Europe are involved.

It has been shown that grazing animals replaced man in the tropical lowlands of Mexico with the decline of Indian populations in the sixteenth century, thus promoting the invasion of adventive woody species (Simpson, 1952). Overgrazing may also have so reduced fuel supplies in some areas that fires were eliminated as an ecologic factor (Johannessen, 1963), with a resultant advantage to unpalatable woody species, especially those adapted to drought. Pines, widely distributed in Middle America, have attracted special attention as successional species adapted to fire, although fire may kill seedlings during the early stages of growth (Parsons, 1955; Denevan, 1961). Ecological assemblages, although not climax or in equilibrium, are thus being established and maintained.

The appropriation of wild plants for use by man has been a recurrent theme in the literature of cultural biogeography. However, animal geography has remained, like ecological plant geography, largely the domain of the professional biologists, although man's use of wild game and fish has tended increasingly to come within the scope of the geographers' concern (e.g., Bennett, 1962, 1968; Nietschmann, 1972; Parsons, 1962; Henderson, 1972).

The Significance of Tropicality

One of the more important geographical aspects of Latin America is its predominant tropicality. Most of its land mass lies within 30° of the Equator. From Mazatlan to the Norte Chico and from Tampico to Sao Paulo seasonal contrasts in temperature are minimal; a full two-thirds of the area is wet enough to support tropical or sub-tropical forest associations. In such environments, as Gourou (1966), Pendleton (1955), and others have pointed out, problems of soil fertility, soil exhaustion, human disease, and dietary deficiency take on a special character quite unfamiliar to mid-latitude observers. The familiar struggle between man and nature often seems weighted in favor of the latter, and the delicately balanced ecosystems may be subject to serious, even irreversible alteration, unless handled with the utmost care. Land abandonment among milpa farmers has not been due solely to soil exhaustion. Grass and weed invasion, insect infestations, and cultural tradition may prove to be at least equally important factors. Yet shortened fallow periods caused by population pressures and the local unavailability of land may lead to impoverishment of second growth and eventually to savanna conditions and ecological disaster (Budowski, 1956, 1968). A real controversy rages over the extent to which the tropical lowlands of the New World, and more especially the leached upland surfaces of Amazonia, may be amenable to permanent occupancy by sedentary farmers, even if a system of mixed farming with wet rice and tree crops, or a livestock economy, is adopted.

As food production has fallen behind population growth in much of Latin America, concern for the functioning of peasant agricultural systems has heightened. Critics have argued that the Green Revolution, with its new high yielding varieties, may have widened the gap between rich and poor, increasing dependency on energy inputs and foreign technology and threatening the genetic diversity of crop plants accumulated during thousands of years. The distinctive problems, character- istics, and limitations of tropical agro-ecosystems have been brilliantly delineated in a widely quoted essay by biologist Dan Janzen (1973) which cites extensively from geographers. Like others he criticizes the temperate zone bias of most work being done in the American tropics. Watters' (1971) well-known FAO report on shifting cultivation has been supplemented by numer- ous papers on traditional farming systems and technology[3] and on the incorporation of subsistence societies into commercial systems (Nietschmann, 1977, 1979).

The impact of man's activities on the physical environment of South America has been catalogued by Sternberg (1968). It is an impressive listing, and it has many roots deep in human history. Man has been in Latin America for a long time, longer than any but a Sauer dared to imagine only a few years ago. The evidence for Pleistocene occupation of the New World seems irrefutable. Man must have been well established in South America at a time when the Pleistocene ice sheet still covered much of the New World. Between 7000 and 1500 B.C. most of the major plant foods had been domesticated and a form of settled life achieved. Population estimates for pre-Columbian America have been going up, as ar- chaeological and archival data are increasingly brought to bear on the problem. It is now believed by best authority to have exceeded 100 million, a figure that has been attained again only in the past decades. The drastic decline in native populations following the Conquest did not significantly reduce the pressures on the environ- ment. The introduction of European livestock, European crops, and

---

[3]Editor's note. Gene Wilken has been particularly productive. His articles on traditional agriculture in Mexico and Guatemala have been incorporated into a recent book (1987). For a bibliographic essay that includes South America, see Denevan (1980).

European plows brought an acceleration of an already serious soil erosion in many areas, a process that is still going on. Geographical analyses of such erosion, together with the effectiveness of terracing and other devices designed to alleviate it, largely remain to be done. They should be vastly facilitated by use of aerial photography.

Vogt (1946, 1948, 1963) went further than anyone in placing the erosion problem in clear perspective, coupling it with continuing and largely uncontrolled population growth. He specifically urged geographical case studies of the history of land use and productivity of specific areas, especially in Mexico and Central America. More recently conferences sponsored by IUCN, UNESCO, and the IGU regional conference in Mexico City have further focused attention on related environmental issues. Sauer (1958) repeatedly pointed to the role of destructive exploitation in the non-western world, arguing that man has long been the ecologic dominant and that true "natural vegetation" probably no longer exists anywhere in tropical America.

Given the latent energy of the continuing population explosion, it is clear that Latin America, with a still vigorous 2.4 percent annual increase, is faced with providing for a vastly increased number of mouths, and at higher dietary standards, in the next decades. The continent is crying out for regional land resource and land use evaluations such as Preston James long urged. Now, with the availability of radar and satellite imagery, this is at last within our grasp. It seems likely that intensification of production in already settled areas holds more promise than the continued forest destruction associated with the opening of new lands which, after a few crops of maize or manioc, most commonly are converted to low intensity pasture use....

Land Tenure and the New Colonization Schemes

One of the more pressing problems in Latin America is the uneven distribution of land and the inefficiencies in production that this has often engendered. Latifundia and minifundia have deep historical and cultural roots, but despite the early classic studies of McBride (1923, 1936), few geographers have pursued the subject in any depth. It has been economists, political scientists, and sociologists, as at the Wisconsin Land Tenure Center, who have done most of the work in this field, although often oblivious to the ecological factors involved. Government colonization schemes, on the other hand, have attracted considerable attention from geographers. So has export-based tropical plantation agriculture and other types of large-scale corporate agricultural enterprises, especially when associated with irrigation developments.

The opening of "new lands" in the *tierra caliente* and the impact of the *vías de penetración* that have been reaching down from the Central American and Andean highlands into the adjacent lowlands and from the Brazilian coast into the heart of Amazonia has probably been the single most intensively pursued theme within Latin American geography (e.g., Eidt, 1962, 1971; Stewart, 1965, 1967, 1968; Parsons, 1967; Dozier, 1969). A recurrent theme in this has been the contrasts between spontaneous and planned colonization in such areas and the cultural adaptations of highlanders (often Indians) to a drastically different lowland environment. The literature on agricultural colonization in Latin America has been reviewed by the sociologist, T. Lynn Smith (1969). The process of forest clearing and its replacement, chiefly by pasture, is visibly conspicuous and peculiarly adaptable to geographical analysis, as the classic studies by Sandner (1961, 1962, 1964) in Costa Rica and Central America have shown. There has been a spate of excellent German-language research on forest clearing and agricultural settlement along the Andean front. The ecologic effects of this massive alteration of the face of the tropical lowlands by man is but dimly perceived. In some areas archaeologic evidence of formerly large native populations suggests that production systems other than the popular Western monoculture model may offer more efficient use of the land (e.g., Gordon, 1969; also see Dickinson, 1972, on high-diversity systems). The frontier philosophy views the conquest of the forest with pride and enthusiasm, much as North American pioneers saw the replacement of woodland by cropland as inevitable and desirable. For Brazil, for example, the Belém-Brasilia and Trans-Amazon highway projects epitomize the national aspirations to open the empty interior to settlement and civilization, although a kind of genocide of the Indian inhabitants of the Amazonian forest may be a by-product of this process. As long as land is viewed as a cheap resource, intensification of effort on existing settled lands will be delayed and the destruction of the rain forest ecosystem will continue.

Agricultural colonization often has been by cohesive cultural groups in temperate as well as tropical Latin America and has been the object of our frequent attention (e.g., Stewart, 1967; Winsberg, 1968; Williams, 1968; Sawatzky, 1971; Hiraoka, 1980). Although rich in historical detail, such studies seldom have been characterized by the innovative research designs associated with work in some other parts of the tropical world.

Conclusion

In 1986 there were about 450 professional geographers in North America with an active area concern in Latin America. Probably fewer than 40 of these have accounted for half or more of the published English-language literature. Some 11 percent (171 out of 1,582) of all geography Ph.D. dissertations between 1901 and 1969 were on Latin American topics (Browning, 1970:95), but the proportion has probably dropped since the 1970s. Two-thirds (114) of the dissertations were on Middle America and only one third (57) were on South America. The degree of interest in Middle America is worth special note, perhaps a reflection of both easier access and the existence of several organized research and instructional programs there (e.g., the Organization for Tropical Studies in Costa Rica).[4]

Our publication record is less impressive. There have probably been as many monographs on Latin American topics published by French and German geographers in the recent decades as the combined English language output. This is indicative less of the relative input of research effort than our lack of publication outlets and policy. For virtually all German and French dissertations publication is mandatory. Of the English language Ph.D.s it seems likely that fewer than one in ten appears in print although the majority are probably abstracted in part in journal articles. The charitable view would be that this is no reflection on their quality. There has been a recent and significant revival of Latin American interest among British geographers, in part a consequence of the Parry Committee report which gave a strong push to Latin American Studies in the United Kingdom. The cadre of active workers in 1980 included Browning, Crossley, Donkin, Fifer, Fox, Harris, Preston, C.T. Smith, and Robinson, the last relocated since 1973 in the United States. Even remote Australasia has at least two major contributors (Butland, Watters). The work of this active group, like that of North Americans, has been to date strongly cultural and historical in its orientation, and based on extended periods of field study.

The recent profusion of international and interdisciplinary symposia has underscored the new environmental and ecological awareness. Participation of geographers in these has been modest. Much of the best material on the issues and their policy implications is being provided by journalists and essayists and it is worth the effort to keep abreast of it through the local Latin American press. The malfunctioning of ecologic

---

[4]The statistics in this paragraph have been revised by the editor.

systems and the misuses of resources, too, have begun to attract the attention of "radical" social scientists, who see the redistribution of power and wealth rather than unbridled population growth and inappropriate technologies as at the root of the Third World's problems.

Our coterie of ecologically minded geographers has tended to be more proficient at documenting environmental degradation and decrying ecologically unsound development than in showing the way to alternatives. Yet looking back through the sessions of The Conference of Latin Americanist Geographers (CLAG), perhaps we have progressed. No longer is it necessary to argue that man is ecosystem dependent, or that tropical environments are fragile and finite systems that present special problems. Cultural diversity is being seen more and more not as a part of the problem but as part of the solution (Bennett, 1976). No longer are we quite so stereotypically divided, either "for" or "against" development. For those of us who profess to make the study of this congenial and magnificently diverse culture area our concern, Latin America continues to offer endless unmet challenges and opportunities. The ecologic dimension of our concern becomes larger and more critical with each passing year.

The kind of understanding we seek is not, of course, exclusively subject to examination either by analytic method or by humanistic discourse. Our task here, as in the other world areas, is to bridge the gap between our culture and another. In the context of area studies it is to seek understanding of the interaction of mankind and his environment in a particular regional context, some part of Latin America with which we are more than commonly familiar, taking account of similarities and uniqueness alike. For this there is no substitute for field work. The essential interests of geography are clear enough--the diversity of the earth, the patterns of diversity and repetition, and often of how things came to be and the process of their alteration (Sauer, 1970). The danger is that we may spend ourselves in exhortation, telling each other what we ought to be doing and how to do it. Better by far that we get on with the task, each in his own, idiosyncratic way.

Bibliography

Aschmann, Homer. 1959. *The Central Desert of Baja California: Demography and Ecology, Ibero-Americana*, No. 42, Berkeley.

_____. 1960. "Indian Pastoralists of the Guajira Peninsula," *Annals of the Association of American Geographers*, Vol. 50, pp. 408-418.

_____. 1971. "Indian Societies and Communities in Latin America: An Historical Perspective," *Proceedings of the Conference of Latin Americanist Geographers*, Vol. 1, pp. 124-137.

Bennett, Charles F. 1962. "The Bayano Cuna Indians, Panama: An Ecological Study of Livelihood and Diet," *Annals of the Association of American Geographers*, Vol. 52, pp. 32-50.

_____. 1968. *Human Influences on the Zoogeography of Panama*, Ibero-Americana, No. 51, Berkeley.

_____. 1976. "Cultural Diversity in Central America and Panama: Its Relationship to Conservation and Planning," *Revista Biología Tropical*, Vol. 24, Suppl. 1, pp. 5-12.

Borde, Jean and Mario Góngora. 1956. *Evolución de la propriedad rural en el Valle de Puangue*, 2 vols., Instituto de Sociología, Universidad de Chile, Santiago.

Bowman, Isaiah. 1916. *The Andes of Southern Peru*, American Geographical Society, New York.

Brand, Donald. 1951. *Quiroga: A Mexican Municipio*, Institute of Social Anthropology, Publication 11, Smithsonian Institution, Washington, D.C.

Browning, Clyde E. 1970. *A Bibliography of Dissertations in Geography: 1901 to 1969*, Department of Geography, Studies in Geography, No. 1, University of North Carolina, Chapel Hill.

Brunnschweiler, Dieter. 1971. "The Study of the Physical Environment in Latin America," *Proceedings of the Conference of Latin Americanist Geographers*, Vol. 1, pp. 220-231.

Budowski, Gerardo. 1956. "Tropical Savannas: A Sequence of Forest Felling and Repeated Burnings," *Turrialba*, Vol. 6, pp. 23-33.

_____. 1963. "Forest Succession in Tropical Lowlands," *Turrialba*, Vol. 13, pp. 42-44.

_____. 1968. "La influencia humana en la vegetación natural de montañas tropicales americanas," *Colloquium Geographicum (Bonn)*, Vol. 9, pp. 157-162.

Crosby, Alfred W. 1972. *The Columbian Exchange: Biological and Cultural Consequences of 1492*, Greenwood Press, Westport, Connecticut.

Denevan, William M. 1961. *The Upland Pine Forests of Nicaragua: A Study in Cultural Plant Geography*, University of California Publications in Geography, Vol. 12, No. 4, pp. 251-320.

_____. 1966. *The Aboriginal Cultural Geography of the Llanos de Mojos of Bolivia*, Ibero-Americana, No. 48, Berkeley.

_____. 1971a. *A Bibliography of Latin American Historical Geography*, Pan American Institute of Geography and History, Special Publication No. 6, Washington, D.C.

_____. 1971b. "Campa Subsistence in the Gran Pajonal, Eastern Peru," *Geographical Review*, Vol. 61, pp. 496-518.

_____. 1973. "Development and the Imminent Demise of the Amazon Rain Forest," *The Professional Geographer*, Vol. 25, pp. 130-135.

_____ (editor). 1976. *The Native Population of the Americas in 1492*, University of Wisconsin Press, Madison.

_____. 1980. "Latin America," in *World Systems of Traditional Resource Management*, G.A. Klee, editor, pp. 217-244, Edward Arnold, London.

Dickinson, Joshua C. 1972. "Alternatives to Monoculture in the Humid Tropics," *The Professional Geographer*, Vol. 24, pp. 217-222.

Dozier, Craig L. 1969. *Land Development and Colonization in Latin America: Case Studies of Peru, Bolivia, and Mexico*, Praeger, New York.

Edwards, Clinton R. 1965. *Aboriginal Watercraft of the Pacific Coast of South America*, Ibero-Americana, No. 42, Berkeley.

Eidt, Robert. 1962. "Pioneer Settlement in Eastern Peru," *Annals of the Association of American Geographers*, Vol. 52, pp. 255-278.

_____. 1971. *Pioneer Settlement in Northeast Argentina*, University of Wisconsin Press, Madison.

Feder, E. 1979. *Lean Cows - Fat Ranchers: The International Ramifications of Mexico's Beef Cattle Industry*, Research Institute of the Berghof Stiftung für Konfliktforschung, Berlin.

Gordon, Burton LeRoy. 1957. *Human Geography and Ecology in the Sinú Country of Colombia*, Ibero-Americana, No. 39, Berkeley.

_____. 1969. *Anthropogeography and Rain Forest Ecology in Bocas del Toro Province, Panama*, Office of Naval Research Report, Department of Geography, University of California, Berkeley. A much amplified version was published as *A Panama Forest and Shore: Natural History and Amerindian Culture in Bocas del Toro*, Boxwood Press, Pacific Grove, 1982.

Gourou, Pierre. 1966. *The Tropical World: Its Social and Economic Condition and Its Future Status*, 4th edition, Wiley, New York.

Harris, David R. 1972 "The Origins of Agriculture in the Tropics," *American Scientist*, Vol. 60, pp. 180-193.

Henderson, David. 1972. *Men and Whales at Scammon's Lagoon*, Dawson's Book Shop, Los Angeles.

Hiraoka, Mario. 1980. *Japanese Settlement in the Upper Amazon: A Study in Regional Geography*, Latin American Studies, Vol. 1, University of Tsukuba.

Horst, O., D.W. Kuenzi, and R.V. McGehee. 1976. "Sedimentación reciente en la planicie costera del suroeste de Guatemala y su relación con la actividad volcánica," *Publicaciones Geológicas del ICAITI, Guatemala*, Vol. 5, pp. 113-131.

Janzen, Daniel. 1973. "Tropical Agroecosystems," *Science*, Vol. 182, pp. 1212-1219.

Johannessen, Carl L. 1963. *Savannas of Interior Honduras*, Ibero-Americana, No. 46, Berkeley.

_____. 1966. "The Domestication Process in Trees Reproduced by Seed: The Pejibaye Palm in Costa Rica," *Geographical Review*, Vol. 56, pp. 363-376.

_____. 1970a. "The Domestication of Maize: Process or Event?," *Geographical Review*, Vol. 60, pp. 393-413.

_____. 1970b. "The Dispersal of *Musa* in Central America: The Domestication Process in Action," *Annals of the Association of American Geographers*, Vol. 60, pp. 689-699.

McBride, George M. 1923. *The Land Systems of Mexico*, American Geographical Society, New York.

_____. 1936. *Chile: Land and Society*, American Geographical Society, New York.

McBryde, Felix W. 1947. *Cultural and Historical Geography of Southwest Guatemala*, Institute of Social Anthropology, Publication No. 4, Smithsonian Institution, Washington, D.C.

Meggers, Betty J. 1954. "Environmental Limitation on the Development of Culture," *American Anthropologist*, Vol. 56, pp. 801-824.

_____. 1971. *Amazonia: Man and Culture in a Counterfeit Paradise*, Aldine, Chicago.

_____. 1979. "Climatic Oscillation as a Factor in the Prehistory of Amazonia," *American Antiquity*, Vol. 44, pp. 252-266.

Meigs, Peveril. 1939. *The Kiliwa Indians of Lower California*, Ibero-Americana, No. 15, Berkeley.

Murra, John V. 1972. "El 'control vertical' de un máximo de pisos ecológicos en la economía de las sociedades andinas," in *Visita de la provincia de León de Huánuco en 1562, Iñigo Ortiz de Zúñiga, Visitator*, Vol. 2, pp. 427-476, Universidad Hermilio Valdizán, Huánuco.

Myers, Norman. 1980. *Conversion of Tropical Moist Forests*, National Research Council, Washington, D.C.

43

Nations, James D. and Ronald B. Nigh. 1978. "Cattle, Cash, Food, and Forest: The Destruction of the American Tropics and the Lacandon Maya Alternative," *Culture and Agriculture*, No. 6, pp. 1-4.

Nietschmann, Bernard Q. 1972. "Hunting and Fishing Focus Among the Miskito Indians, Eastern Nicaragua," *Human Ecology*, Vol. 1, pp. 41-67.

_____. 1973. *Between Land and Water: The Subsistence Ecology of the Miskito Indians, Eastern Nicaragua*, Seminar Press, New York.

_____ (editor). 1977. *Memorias de Arrecife Tortuga*, Banco de América, Managua.

_____. 1979. "Ecologic Change, Migration, and Inflation in the Far Western Caribbean," *Geographical Review*, Vol. 69, pp. 1-24.

Palerm, Angel and Eric R. Wolf. 1957. "Ecological Potential and Cultural Development in Mesoamerica," *Social Science Monographs III: Studies in Human Ecology*, pp. 1-37, Pan American Union, Washington, D.C.

Parsons, James J. 1955. "The Miskito Pine Savanna of Nicaragua and Honduras," *Annals of the Association of American Geographers*, Vol. 45, pp. 36-63.

_____. 1962. *The Green Turtle and Man*, University of Florida Press, Gainesville.

_____. 1964. "The Contribution of Geography to Latin American Studies," in *Social Science Research on Latin America*, Charles Wagley, editor, pp. 33-85, Columbia University Press, New York.

_____. 1967. *Antioquia's Corridor to the Sea: An Historical Geography of the Settlement of Urabá*, Ibero-Americana, No. 49, Berkeley.

_____. 1971. "Ecological Problems and Approaches in Latin American Geography," *Proceedings of the Conference of Latin Americanist Geographers*, Vol. 1, pp. 13-32.

_____. 1972. "Spread of African Pasture Grasses to the American Tropics," *Journal of Range Management*, Vol. 25, pp. 12-17.

_____. 1973. "Latin America," in *Geographers Abroad: Essays on the Problems and Prospects of Research in Foreign Areas*, Marvin Mikesell, editor, pp. 16-46. University of Chicago, Department of Geography Research Series No. 152.

_____. 1981. "The Ecological Dimension: Ten Years Later," *Proceedings of the Conference of Latin Americanist Geographers*, Vol. 8, pp. 22-33.

Pendleton, Robert L. 1955. "The Place of Tropical Soils in Feeding the World," *Smithsonian Institution Annual Report*, pp. 441-458.

Pennington, Campbell W. 1963. *The Tarahumar of Mexico: Their Environment and Material Culture*, University of Utah Press, Salt Lake City.

_____. 1969. *The Tepehuán of Chihuahua: Their Material Culture*, University of Utah Press, Salt Lake City.

Reichel-Dolmatoff, Gerardo. 1976. "Cosmology as Ecological Analysis: A View from the Rain Forest," *Man*, Vol. 2, pp. 307-318.

Sandner, Gerhard. 1961. "Agrarkolonisation in Costa Rica," *Schriften des Geographischen Instituts der Univ. Kiel*, Vol. 20, No. 3. Spanish translation, *La Colonización Agrícola de Costa Rica*, 2 Vols., Instituto Geográfica de Costa Rica, San José, 1964.

_____. 1962. "El concepto espacial y los sistemas funcionales en la colonización espontánea costarricense," *Informe Semestral*, Julio a Diciembre, Instituto Geográfico de Costa Rica.

_____. 1964. "Die Erschliessung de karibischen Waldregion im südlichen Zentralamerika," *Die Erde*, Vol. 95, pp. 111-131.

Sauer, Carl O. 1935. *The Aboriginal Population of Northwest Mexico*, Ibero-Americana, No. 10, Berkeley.

_____. 1952. *Agricultural Origins and Dispersals*, American Geographical Society, New York.

_____. 1958. "Man in the Ecology of Tropical America," *Proceedings of the Ninth Pacific Science Congress*, Bangkok, 1957, Vol. 20, pp. 104-110.

_____. 1970. "The Quality of Geography," *California Geographer*, Vol. 9, pp. 5-9.

Sauer, Jonathan. 1950. "The Grain Amaranths: A Survey of Their History and Classification," *Annals of the Missouri Botanical Garden*, Vol. 37, pp. 561-632.

_____. 1968. *Reconnaissance of Seashore Vegetation along the Mexican Gulf Coast*, Coastal Studies Institute, Louisiana State University, Baton Rouge.

Sawatzky, Harry L. 1971. *They Sought a Country: Mennonite Colonization in Mexico*, University of California Press, Berkeley.

Schmeider, Oscar. 1930. *The Settlements of the Tzapotec and Mije Indians, State of Oaxaca, Mexico*, University of California Publications in Geography, Vol. 4, Berkeley.

Shlemon, Roy. 1979. "Zonas de deslizamientos en los alrededores de Medellín, Antioquia, Colombia," *Publicaciones Geológicas Especiales de Ingeominas* (Bogotá), No. 5, pp. 1-45.

Simpson, Lesley B. 1952. *Exploitation of Land in Central Mexico in the Sixteenth Century*, Ibero-Americana, No. 36, Berkeley.

Smith, Nigel. 1978. "Human Exploitation of Terra Firme Fauna in Amazonia," *Ciencia e Cultura*, Vol. 30, pp. 17-23.

_____. 1979. *A Pesca no Rio Amazonas*, INPA, Manaus.

_____. 1980. *Transamazonica: Colonizacao nos tropicos humidos*, Universidade Federal do Pará, Belém. English revision, *Rainforest Corridors: The Transamazon Colonization Scheme*, University of California Press, Berkeley, 1982.

Smith, T. Lynn. 1969. "Studies of Colonization and Settlement," *Latin American Research Review*, Vol. 4, pp. 93-124.

Sternberg, Hilbard O'R. 1968. "Man and Environmental Change in South America," in *Biogeography and Ecology in South America*, E.J. Fittkau et al., editors, Vol. 1, pp. 413-445, W. Junk, The Hague.

Steward, Julian H. (editor). 1950. *Physical Anthropology, Linguistics, and Cultural Geography of South American Indians*, Handbook of

46

South American Indians, Vol. 6, Bureau of American Ethnology Bulletin No. 143, Smithsonian Institution, Washington, D.C.

Stewart, Norman R. 1965. "Micgration and Settlement in the Peruvian Montaña: The Apurimac Valley," *Geographical Review*, Vol. 55, pp. 143-157.

_____. 1967. *Japanese Colonization in Eastern Paraguay*, NAS-NRC Publication 1490, Washington, D.C.

_____. 1968. "Some Problems in the Development of Agricultural Colonization in the Andean Oriente," *Professional Geographer*, Vol. 20, pp. 33-38.

Tosi Jr., Joseph A. 1960. *Zonas de vida natural en el Perú: Memoria explicativa sobre el mapa ecológico del Perú*, Instituto Interamericano de Ciencias Agrícolas de la OEA, Zona Andina, Lima.

Troll, Carl. 1959. "Die tropischen Gebirge," *Bonner Geographische Abhandlungen*, Vol. 25, pp. 1-93.

_____ (editor). 1968. *Geo-Ecology of the Mountainous Regions of the Tropical Americas*, Colloquium Geographicum, Geographischen Institut der Universität Bonn, Vol. 9.

Turner II, B.L. 1976. "Population Density in the Classic Maya Lowlands: New Evidence for Old Approaches," *Geographical Review*, Vol. 66, pp. 73-82.

Vann, John. 1959. "Landform-Vegetation Relationships in the Atrato Delta," *Annals of the Association of American Geographers*, Vol. 49, pp. 345-360.

Veblen, Thomas T. 1977. "Native Population Decline in Totonicapán, Guatemala," *Annals of the Association of American Geographers*, Vol. 67, pp. 484-499.

_____ and D. Ashton. 1978. "Catastrophic Influences on the Vegetation of the Valdivian Andes, Chile," *Vegetatio*, Vol. 36, pp. 149-167.

Vogt, William. 1946. *The Population of Venezuela and Its Natural Resources*, Pan American Union, Washington, D.C.

_____. 1948. *Road to Survival*, Sloane, New York.

_____. 1963. *Comments on a Brief Reconnaissance of Resource Use, Progress, and Conservation Needs in Some Latin American Countries*, Conservation Foundation, Washington, D.C.

Wagner, Philip. 1962. "Natural and Artificial Zonation in a Vegetation Cover: Chiapas, Mexico," *Geographical Review*, Vol. 52, pp. 253-274.

Waibel, Leo. 1948. "Vegetation and Land Use in the Planalto Central of Brazil," *Geographical Review*, Vol. 38, pp. 529-554.

Walter, Helmut. 1967. "Das Pampaproblems in vergleichend ökologischen Betrachtung und seine Lösung," *Erdkunde* Vol. 21, pp. 181-202. Rejoinder by C. Troll and W. Lauer, *Erdkunde*, Vol. 22, pp. 152-158, 1968.

Watters, Ray F. 1971. *Shifting Cultivation in Latin America*, FAO Forestry Development Paper 17, UNESCO, Rome.

West, Robert C. 1948. *Cultural Geography of the Modern Tarascan Area*, Institute of Social Anthropology, Publication No. 7, Smithsonian Institution, Washington, D.C.

_____. 1956. "Mangrove Swamps of the Pacific Coast of Colombia," *Annals of the Association of American Geographers*, Vol. 46, pp. 98-121.

_____. 1957. *The Pacific Lowlands of Colombia: A Negroid Area of the American Tropics*, Social Science Series No. 8, Louisiana State University Press, Baton Rouge.

_____ (editor). 1964. *Natural Environment and Early Cultures*, Handbook of Middle American Indians, Vol. 1, University of Texas Press, Austin.

_____. 1978. "Recent Developments in Cattle Raising and the Beef Export Trade in the Middle American Region," *Actes du XLII Congrés International des Americanistes*, Vol. 1, pp. 391-402, Paris.

Whitten, Richard G. 1979. "Comments on the Theory of Holocene Refugia in the Culture History of Amazonia," *American Antiquity*, Vol. 44, pp. 238-251.

48

Wilken, Gene C. 1987. *Good Farmers: Traditional Agricultural Resource Management in Mexico and Central America*, University of California Press, Berkeley.

Williams, Glyn B. 1968. "The Welsh in Patagonia: A Geographic Perspective," *Revista Geográfica (Rio de Janeiro)*, No. 69, pp. 121-144.

Winsberg, Morton. 1968. "Jewish Agricultural Colonization in Entre Rios, Argentina," *American Journal of Economics and Sociology*, Vol. 27, pp. 285-296, Vol. 28 (1969), pp. 179-181, 423-428.

PART TWO

Colombian Roots

5

The People of Antioquia*

The temperate uplands of the northernmost Andes of western
Colombia are the home of the energetic and thrifty Antioqueños, the
self-styled "Yankees of South America." They are shrewd, aggressive individualists whose extraordinary colonizing genius and vigor
have made them the dominant and most clearly defined population
element of the republic. Their long and effective geographical
isolation in the interior highlands of Colombia is reflected in a
determined conservatism and a marked cultural particularism. Being
Antioqueño means more to them than being Colombian.

In a surge of colonizing fervor which began a century and a
half ago, before the Viceroyalty of New Granada became Colombia,
they have pushed their frontier southward along the rugged Andean
slopes until today they occupy a zone some 400 kilometers long by
160 kilometers wide between the Magdalena Valley and the rain
forest of the Chocó. The heart of the settlement area is bisected by
a belt of darker-skinned peoples living in the hot lowlands along the
Río Cauca, which cuts a furrow through the western Colombian
highlands (Fig. 5.1).

The "Antioqueño country" includes much more than the old
Province of Antioquia, within which lives only half of the four
million Colombians who call themselves Antioqueños. Besides the
coffee-rich department of Caldas, "proudest achievement of the
Antioqueños," and its recent offshoots, Risaralda and Quindío, the

*Reprinted from *Antioqueño Colonization in Western Colombia*, Revised Edition,
pp. 1-9, University of California Press, Berkeley (1968). Originally published as
Ibero-Americana: 32 (1949).

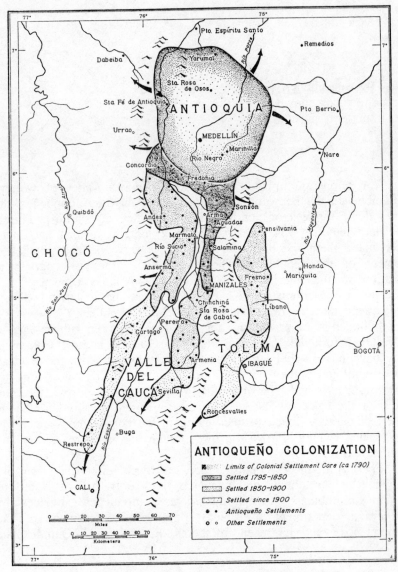

Figure 5.1 Antioqueño Colonization (Circa 1950).

area of settlement includes the coffee lands of northern Tolima and Valle de Cauca, extending southward along the slopes of the Central Cordillera and Western Cordillera to the new Antioqueño *municipios* of Roncesvalles and Restrepo, and beyond. Despite this geographical expansion all the cultural ties and allegiances of these people lead back to the old heartland of highland Antioquia and to the beautiful, mile-high valley of Medellín. The rural society of Antioquia is composed of small landholders and homesteaders and is in sharp contrast to most of latifundian Latin America. Notwithstanding dependence on coffee as the single cash crop, Antioqueño agriculture has shown a reasonably healthy diversity; cattle raising is an important subsidiary undertaking. The economy has remained aloof from the speculative rushes into tobacco, quinine, indigo, and cotton which characterized much of nineteenth-century Colombian economic history.[1]

The quest for gold was the immediate cause of the sixteenth-century Spanish settlement of the Province of Antioquia. Drawn by legends of fabulous hidden riches and by news of actual strikes, the first conquistadores were soon followed by the more numerous Basque and Austrian immigrants. The hill of Buriticá, in the Western Cordillera behind the old capital of Santa Fé de Antioquia, was the place of greatest interest to the early gold seekers, the source of much of the Indian gold from the Quindío and Sinú graves. However, most of the lodes and placers, worked by primitive, hand-washing methods, left little surplus beyond that needed to pay for foodstuffs brought in on the backs of Indian carriers over trails often made difficult by tropical rains. Moreover, the Indian labor supply was rapidly reduced by virulent diseases introduced by the Spaniards, and capital necessary for the importation of Negroes from the Cartagena slave market was seldom available. While the richer settlers exploited the gravels and quartz ore bodies with their slave gangs, others went with pan and pickax as independent prospectors (*mazamorreros*). Many of the Spaniards, as well as their mestizo offspring, were thus forced into productive labor for their own account. This situation gave an early impetus to Antioquia's democratic tradition of work, which has contrasted sharply with the class structure to the south and west where the Indian element has remained more numerous.

There is a curious quality to the Antioqueño picture, reminiscent of French Canada. The notably small number of surnames suggests

[1]Luís Eduardo Nieto Arteta, *Economía y Cultura en la Historia de Colombia* (Bogotá, 1942).

the selection imposed by geography on the very few hundreds of Spanish immigrants from which the present-day families have sprung. Such names as Restrepo, Uribe, Mejía, Londoño, Jaramillo, and Arango are recognized as typically Antioqueño throughout Colombia. The credentials which the great majority of these settlers brought with them from their home parishes on the Peninsula indicate that they were "Old Christians" (cristianos viejos, limpios de toda mala raza).[2] Yet the fable still persists that early Antioquia was settled by Sephardic Jews. It has been nurtured by the Antioqueños' reputation as ambitious, hard-headed businessmen with a superior aptitude for trade and commerce. In 1720, when the Crown ordered all foreigners expelled from the colonies, only two were found in the Province of Antioquia, both Italians. The descendants of one, Juan Botero, are so numerous today that the surname is as characteristically Antioqueño as Restrepo or Uribe.

The arduous river journey up the Río Magdalena and Río Cauca to the head of navigation at Zaragoza or Puerto Espíritu Santo, and then ten or more hard days over mountain mule trails, could hardly have enhanced the attractions of Antioquia to new arrivals in Cartagena. The alluvial valley lands around Medellín and Santa Fé de Antioquia had been granted to conquistadores and their mestizo descendants, and the deeply weathered crystalline uplands were of value only for their mining rights, so that the opportunities for a landed gentry were restricted. Among the immigrants there were no courtiers and probably fewer Spanish women than the patrilineal genealogists of Antioquia would admit. But women did come, especially in the surge of settlement in the seventeenth century which brought a shift from the old, hot-country capital at Santa Fé to the new villa of Medellín. The conquistador Jorge Robledo had earlier set the precedent by returning from a visit to Spain with a new wife and a party of 16 ladies-in-waiting. One of these, Doña Mencia de Carvajal, is said to have lived in the province to the ripe old age of 110 years, personally directing the operations of her mine and ranch interests. Although several of the more aristocratic branches of the early families have kept their blood lines "pure," the basic tri-ethnic quality of the Antioqueño stock is clearly evident in the rural areas, as well as in the working-class suburbs of Medellín and Manizales.

From the early mixture of the Spanish, and Indian and Negro slave elements there evolved the people who today, in ethnological heresy, call themselves la raza antioqueña. Although this misap-

---

[2]Gabriel Arango Mejía, Genealogías de Antioquia y Caldas, 2 vols. (Medellín, 1942), contains the results of a lifetime of genealogical research by the director of the Biblioteca y Archivo de Antioquia in Medellín.

plication of the term "race" to cover a cultural concept has been criticized by local scholars, it is firmly entrenched in popular usage. Indeed, a regional magazine recently established in Medellín carried the title *La Raza*. The characteristic Antioqueño physical type has been described as tall, dark, with large and piercing eyes, an aquiline nose, high forehead, and hair and beard abundant, but it is their cultural cohesion rather than any physical similarities which distinguishes them. The social and economic distinction between whites (*blancos*) and half-castes (*gentes de color*), precisely marked in an earlier day, has become increasingly obscured. Until 1918 the national census regularly included a breakdown according to "color" which, of course, merely reflected the social attitudes of the interrogator and interrogated. Yet the preponderance of mixed blood, indicated in Table 5.1, is in striking contradiction to the frequent assertion that Antioquia is a white province. In the new Antioqueño department of Caldas both the 1912 and 1918 censuses showed a similar preponderance of mestizos and mulattos. In the populous Quindío region, for instance, the mixed bloods (*mezclados*) outnumbered the whites by nearly four to one.

TABLE 5.1

RACIAL COMPOSITION OF ANTIOQUIA

Race	Census of 1808[a]	Census of 1912	Census of 1918
Mestizo and mulatto	57.7[b]	45.0	52.4
White	25.6	34.6	31.1
Negro	12.2[c]	18.2	15.3
Indian	4.5	2.2	1.2
Total Population	106,856	735,470	823,226

[a]Computed from statistics in Filipe Pérez, *Jeografía Física i Política del Estado de Antioquia* (Bogotá, 1863), p. 3.
[b]Includes free Negroes.
[c]Slaves only.

56

During colonial times the whites constituted an honored if un-
polished aristocracy whose position was unquestioningly accepted by
the lower classes.

The governor reported to the Crown in 1776:

> They have a great enthusiasm for nobility and are so inordinate-
> ly proud that all are immersed in the study of their titles and
> their relationships with the first conquistadores and settlers.
> They ordinarily contract marriage with very immediate relatives
> within their own family (in my judgment with no little gain in
> privilege) because each is reputed among themselves as better
> than the others.

> They dearly love tedious and ceremonious formalities in public
> functions, perpetuating tenaciously the customs of the times of
> the conquistadores. . . . Their luxury and fashion have a very
> limited sphere, for all vanity is reduced to wishing to be people
> of quality and position. Their dress styles are the most out-
> moded and strange. Some newly arrived Spaniards and other
> patricians who have had business with the outside or go abroad
> to study occasionally introduce new dress, but within a few
> days they all return to the old.[3]

Until the end of the colonial period most observers were struck
by the general backwardness, illiteracy, and poverty of the province.
Agriculture was almost completely neglected for the mines, and
commerce was undeveloped. For want of iron the land continued to
be cleared by flint-headed Indian axes (*macanas*). Most of the till-
able valleys, as well as the granitic uplands, were held by a few
wealthy grantees like Antonio de Quintana, whose immense domain
included the present municipios of Carolina, Angostura, and parts of
Yarumal and Santa Rosa de Osos.

The cultural and economic renaissance which transformed this
tranquil but impoverished backwoods province into a virile, literate,
and relatively wealthy state was initiated under the energetic leadership of the royal inspector (*oidor*) appointed by the Crown in 1784
at the request of Governor Francisco Silvestre, whose detailed and
thoughtful reports on the province had been one of the first products

---

[3]Francisco Silvestre, "Relación del Estado de la Provincia de Antioquia cuando la
entrego a Don Cayetano Buelta" [December 1, 1776], *Archivo Historical* (Manizales), July, 1919, pp. 569-605. Editor's note: for an extended treatment of Silvestre's role in Antioquia see David J. Robinson, *Relación de la Provincia de
Antioquia por Franciso Silvestre* (Medellín, 1988).

of the new period of French enlightenment in New Granada. The Oidor Juan Antonio Mon y Velarde, although in the province only 3 years, has been called "The Regenerator of Antioquia."[4] His far-reaching social, economic, and juridical reforms stirred the lethargic community to activity. New towns, the first truly agricultural settlements in the province, were established in the cooler, malaria-free uplands, and bounties were offered for the introduction of new crops. Vagrancy laws were enforced and the idle sent to help people the new towns and till the new fields. His was the discipline of work under which the Antioqueño economy and culture was to flower in the following century, and he wrote:

> We are all born to work and it is necessary to consider as delinquents of human society those who are not useful to their country and who do not employ their energies and talents in providing at least their own subsistence.[5]

In his last report to the King he predicted that "this Province of Antioquia, today the most backward in all the New Kingdom of Granada, will one day be the most opulent."

By the late eighteenth century both gold production and immigration had fallen off sharply. The scattered nature of the mineral deposits had encouraged a gradual expansion of settlement into the cooler uplands, so that for a time Ríonegro (elev., 2,120 m.) challenged Medellín (elev., 1,540 m.) as the first city of the province. Early marriage and large families favored a rapid increase in the population which, in turn, brought increasing pressure on available food supplies. The new emphasis on agriculture which followed Mon y Velarde's *visita* and the termination of the prolonged litigation between Ríonegro and the old villa of Santa Fé de Antioquia for ownership of the Río Negro meadowlands brought the first significant spilling over of Antioqueño settlers into the empty, forested slopes to the south and southwest at the beginning of the nineteenth century. Here the unproductive, red surfaces of the Antioquia

---

[4]Tulio Ospina, "El Oidor Mon y Velarde, Regenerador de Antioquia" [1901], *Repertorio Histórico* (Medellín), September, 1918, p. 412. After leaving his Antioquia assignment Mon y Velarde served briefly as president of the Real Audiencia of Quito until named, in 1790, to the Royal Council of the Indies at Seville, but he died of poisoning en route to his new post. See also, Emilio Robledo, *Bosquejo Biográfico del Señor Oidor Juan Antonio Mon y Velarde* Bogotá, 1954).

[5]Quoted in Ramón Franco, *Antropogeografía Colombiana* (Manizales, 1941), p. 177.

58

highlands gave way to the deep, fertile volcanic soils of the Mellizos and Ruiz-Tolima areas. Here, too, was the principal break in the girdle of tropical rain forest which hemmed in Antioquia to the north, east, and west.

Sonsón and Abejorral in the south, and, later, Fredonia to the west, became general headquarters for pioneers advancing into the present Caldas and Tolima and westward across the Río Cauca into the *Occidente* of Antioquia. For nearly a century and a half this homesteading frontier has pressed steadily southward along the middle slopes of the cordillera in three separate lobes (Fig. 5.1) until today there are outliers of Antioqueño colonies even beyond Popayán, in the volcanic lands of Moscapán in Huila, on the slopes of the Bogotá Cordillera, in the Florencia area of Caquetá, and even in northernmost Ecuador. More recent colonization has taken place on the northern fringes of the Antioqueño country and toward the Magdalena valley, but the traditional Antioqueño frontier has remained in the mountains to the south.

The frequent litigation over land titles is reminiscent of early California. Most of these unoccupied mountainsides were claimed *in absentia* under Spanish land grants, but the squatters won out in the end. In Colombia, too, possession has always been nine-tenths of the law. Between 1847 and 1914 the Congress of the Republic attempted to regularize and encourage settlement. Land grants, usually of 12,000 hectares (29,640 acres), were made to more than twenty new towns in Caldas and Tolima, either voiding or disregarding colonial claims. The consequent insecure position of landholders, together with almost constant political unrest, seems to have operated as an impetus to push the frontier ahead.

As the empty lands to the south have filled in and the "growing edge" of Antioqueño settlement has moved farther from Medellín and Manizales, the pace of colonization has slackened. Agrarianism is today being challenged by an explosive new industrial urbanism which, in considerable measure, is an outgrowth of a revolution in transportation. Almost overnight greater Medellín, with a population of one million persons, has become one of the most important manufacturing centers of Latin America. Within the memory of many adults the city was dependent on pack trains or human carriers for its links with the outside world. Today it is a road hub, and its airport handles some fifty scheduled passenger flights a day. The other major Antioqueño cities, Manizales (pop 190,000 in 1964), Pereira (150,000), and Armenia (125,000), have experienced an almost equally explosive growth.

Once the objects of pity and concern, the frugal, hard-working Antioqueños today boast the highest standard of living in Colombia.

Amongst them tradesmen and small proprietors have achieved a dignity and economic opportunity not common in other parts of Latin America. Even before coffee and textiles had begun to pour new wealth into the department a German traveler had observed:

> There are probably few places of similar size in South America where as many important fortunes are concentrated as in Medellín. The number of families considered as rich is considerable, but with few exceptions they appear so unassuming that their wealth, won mostly by trade and mining, and less commonly through farming and stock-raising, is not apparent. Even the middle classes or artisans are well situated.[6]

There has been a certain reorientation of Antioqueño colonizing energies in the past 15 years toward the rainier tropical lowlands of Urabá, the Sinú country, the lower Cauca (Bajo Cauca), and the middle Magdalena valleys. Facilitated by revolutionary improvements in highway and air transport, it has been of a character quite different from the traditional Antioqueño settlement on the southern frontier. Here capitalists and merchants tend to replace the colonist. Antioqueño economic and cultural penetration involves no moving frontier but rather a leapfrogging to favored nuclei of settlement, often far removed from the mountainous heartland. The community cohesiveness of an earlier period is replaced by a looser set of ties, for now the hard labor of felling the forest and establishing maize plantings and pasture is largely in the hands of day laborers from the coast or Magdalena lowlands. The Antioqueño is the entrepreneur, not the settler. In place of individual initiative in establishing the frontier infrastructure, dependence is increasingly on such government agencies as the Land Reform Institute (INCORA), which provides supervised credit, confirmed land titles, access roads, and technical assistance.

From a colonial mining-camp society there developed in Antioquia a kind of Latin puritanism which still prevails throughout the rural areas and which survives in only slightly modified form in the strict social and moral codes of modern Medellín and Manizales. In piety and devoutness the Antioqueños are far ahead of other Colombian ethnic groups, for they embrace Catholicism with the conscientious passion of their forefathers. The frequent occurrence of Bibli-

---

[6]Ferdinand von Schenck, "Reisen in Antioquia," *Petermanns Mitteilungen* (1883), Vol. 29, p. 39. Another German observer of the Antioqueño character in this period was Ernst Röthlisberger, *El Dorado...* [1897] (Bogotá, 1963), pp. 346-348.

cal place names, such as Belén, Betulia, Betania, Jericó, Líbano, Palestina, and even Antioquia itself, further attests to this.

The strong regional character of Antioqueño diet, dress, and speech is being stubbornly and proudly preserved. The extensive local poetry and literature continues to extol the simple virtues of the traditional subsistence agricultural economy (*la vida maicera*) of these mountains. In dress it is still the inevitable *carriel*, a fur-covered side back of countless hidden pockets, that is the surest mark of the true Antioqueño (*de pura cepa*), whether it is worn under a white cotton *poncho* or its dark woolen counterpart, the *ruana*. Outside of his native habitat the Antioqueño can usually be identified by his accent and his loquacity--of both he is extra-ordinarily proud. Although it is often held that the Spanish spoken around Medellín is the purest to be found in the Americas, a large number of provincialisms of Carib and Quechua origin have crept into the direct and graphic speech. An acute consciousness of this penetration is reflected by the poet Gregorio Gutiérrez González when he says, in the prologue to his beloved *Memoria Sobre el Cultivo del Maíz*, "I write not Spanish but Antioqueño."

Although elsewhere in the republic the down-slope migration of agriculture and settlement has been a persistent theme for more than a century, the Antioqueño countryman (*campesino*) has retained his mountaineer's attitude. The introduction of coffee as a major cash crop after 1880 simply reinforced the pattern of small mountainside holdings which characterized the earlier homestead frontier. Wherever the settler has gone he has transplanted his unique cultural heritage. Thus Caldas has become a second Antioqueño department "more Antioqueño than Antioquia." This cultural cohesiveness has its roots deep in the past, in the time before the limited opportunities of an impoverished homeland sent the Antioqueño searching for new lands to the south and west.

6

The Settlement of the Sinú Valley of Colombia[*]

In aboriginal times the Río Sinú Valley of Colombia was densely peopled. A brief orgy of grave looting by the Spaniards followed the Conquest, after which they almost forgot the area, for its gold had come from elsewhere and few Indians remained to be exploited as a labor force. Its effective resettlement has been accomplished only in the past 75 years.

First came the American and French lumber interests, which cleared the forest; they were followed by the big cattlemen and, more recently, the cotton kings. Montería, in 1950, was as heady with anticipation as a Texas oil-boom town, as Medellín capitalists, some with farming experience and others with only their check-books, poured in to make their fortunes from cotton planting in the Sinú. A relatively few families still hold the better alluvial valley lands in large blocks, acquired either by crown grant or, more commonly, by purchase from a financially distressed government. As the population has pyramided, the landless Sinuano peasant, who as tenant or wage laborer cleared the large haciendas, has gone to the hills to claim his own maize-hog farm from the foreste *baldíos* (government lands). He has extended the frontier of settlement westward well into the Department of Antioquia, but into lands that

[*]Reprinted from *The Geographical Review*, Vol. 42, pp. 67-86 (1952). Field work for this study was carried out during the summer of 1950 under the auspices of the Office of Naval Research. Acknowledgement of assistance is also made to the members of the staffs of the Socony-Vacuum Oil Company and R.J. Tipton and Associates, Bogotá, and to Mr. Roy Gordon, field companion and graduate student in geography at the University of California.

have had little appeal for the highland Antioqueño, himself a vigorous colonizer who has shown a marked preference for the cooler
uplands of the *tierra templada* and *tierra fría*.[1] While the Sinuano
has been occupying the empty, steamy hills along the Caribbean
coast, the headwater area of the Río Sinú (the Alto Sinú) has been
somewhat more slowly colonized from interior Antioquia, and
increasingly heavy pressure has been exerted on the remaining
Chocó-type Indians.

Climate and River Silting

The Sinú Valley is the principal structural depression within the
zone of parallel, north-northeast-trending Tertiary hills that lies
between the Magdalena trough and the Gulf of Urabá in northwestern Colombia. It has a tropical climate, sufficiently · humid to
support a luxuriant, semi-deciduous high forest in most undisturbed
situations despite a marked dry season during the first months of the
year. The rains normally begin in April and continue intermittently
until early December, but in some years the last 2 weeks of June
and the first days of July constitute a recognizable secondary dry
season. At Cereté, in the middle valley, the average annual precipitation over a 34-year period has been 43.41 inches, and deviations
from the mean have been relatively small. January, February, and
March are commonly rainless. Then the cattle on the parched hill
pastures move into the overflow lands (*ciéngas*) along the river, and
the air becomes murky with smoke from the fires of *colonos* burning
pastures or opening new clearings in the forest. Destructively heavy
rains and unseasonal drought are rare, and high winds are virtually
unknown. A greater hazard to agriculture is the floods that may
follow prolonged heavy rains in the Alto Sinú and turn the lower
valley into a series of great shallow lakes. However, in contrast
with the poorly drained San Jorge and Magdalena Valleys, such
damaging floods seem not to occur in the Sinú oftener than once in
a decade.

The fertile, irregularly shaped flood plain of the Sinú extends
inland from the coast for 100 miles to the point where the river
emerges from a forested gorge cut in sandstone and shale. The
plain is bounded on the east by the low, maturely dissected Sabanas
hills, which have a much longer settlement history, and on the west
toward Antioquia and the Gulf of Urabá by a series of higher,
roughly concordant anticlinal ridges that near the mouth of the river

---

[1]J.J. Parsons: Antioqueño Colonization in Western Colombia, *Ibero-Americana No.
32*, Berkeley and Los Angeles, 1949.

are aligned in echelon parallel to the coast line. At Lorica the river is sharply deflected to the left by the 700-foot Cispata Hills, which partly block off the lower valley from the sea. Other outlier Tertiary hills extend to the river on the east side of the valley between Montería and Ciénaga Betancí. The antecedent character of the Sinú is indicated in both areas, for it cuts across spurs of resistant, cherty hills rather than following the more obvious course across the alluvium to the west[2] (Fig. 6.1).

The hazards of flood in the Sinú are greatly reduced both by Ciénaga Betancí and by the complicated grouping of old river channels and swamps associated with the bifurcation of the river between Cereté and Lorica, which serve as natural catchment or overflow basins during high water. The maintenance of navigation in the Aguas Prietas, once the principal channel of the river, and its tributary sloughs was troubling the provincial legislature as early as 1867, but its choking with silt and debris was especially accelerated by later lumbering above Montería. Efforts to save the commerce of the towns of the Aguas Prietas and such now landlocked settlements as Ciénaga de Oro, San Carlos, and San Pelayo brought negligible results. Today ships plying between Lorica and Montería use the shorter Aguas Blancas channel exclusively. Other communities have been stranded on abandoned oxbow lakes and silted-up sloughs by the vagaries of the meandering channel of the main river. Cereté, to cite the principal example, is now isolated for all but a few months of the year by the new (1936) Lara cutoff, despite the best efforts of the government engineers.

Within the past century the once ample and secure anchorage of Cispata Bay has been almost completely choked by river silt. Old maps indicate that during the colonial period there were depths of 5 to 6 fathoms at points now as much as 6 miles inland from the present beach.[3] The river seems then to have debouched through Caño Salado at Punta Mestizos, but by the beginning of the nineteenth century a break-through on the right bank had diverted the main flow into Cispata Bay. The silting of the bay, which seems to

---

[2]T.A. Link: Post-Tertiary Strand-Line Oscillations in the Caribbean Coastal Area of Colombia, South America, *Journal of Geology*, Vol. 35, 1927, pp. 58-72. There is clear evidence that the Sinú Valley was once a shallow arm of the sea.

[3]The oldest map of Cispata Bay I have found is one credited to Don Juan de Herrera, chief engineer of Cartagena. It is reproduced in Thomas Jefferys: *A Description of the Spanish Islands and Settlements on the Coast of the West Indies, Compiled from Authentic Memoirs* (London, 1762), Pl. 7.

64

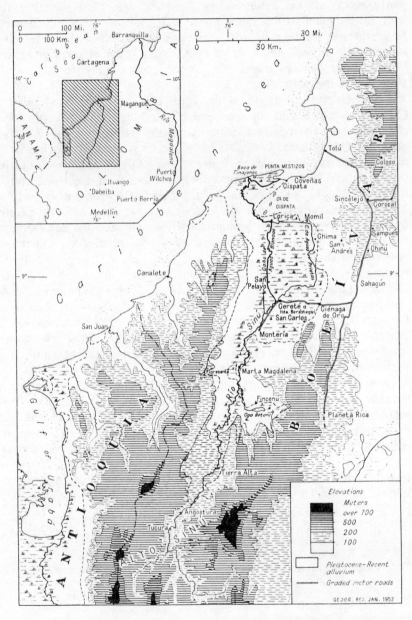

Figure 6.1 Location Map of the Sinú Valley.

stream, has been much reduced since August 1943, when the river broke through the 200 yards between the Tinajones meander and the sea to open a new mouth, which shortened its length by some 10 miles crews soon diverted the river into a newly excavated cutoff channel two miles above the break, but, incredibly, no diversion barrier was provided at the downstream re-entrant; as a result, an increasing amount of water continued to reach the new mouth by a reversal of the direction of flow in the lower half of the meander. The reduced flow through the old channel, accompanied by increased silt deposition within it, threatens the future of navigation on the river, for an exposed position and shifting sand bars have prohibited shipping from using the new entrance. The closing of the well-established Tinajones break, were it feasible, would wipe out a considerable squatter population that has reclaimed parts of the old channel bottom for rice cultivation, but it would relieve the increasingly serious problem of salt-water encroachment that faces the rice growers in other parts of these recently settled delta lands.

Indian Cemeteries and the Gold Seekers

The founding of Cartagena by Pedro de Heredia in 1533 marks the beginning of active Spanish interest in this part of *Tierra Firme*. Guided by a young Indian, the first, 250-man Heredia *entrada* reached the interior pueblo of Fincenú early in 1534. Fincenú was almost certainly located on the north side of Ciénaga Betancí in the midst of what was apparently an extensive, culturally induced grass-land. The land had once been populous, the surviving Indians stated, but with the first bearded conquerors had come an epidemic that killed most of the inhabitants. Indeed, Spanish arms and equipment found in the houses indicated that others had been there, possibly the Becerra expedition out of Urabá, whose fate had never been known. The density of the population in pre-Columbian times is evidenced by the traces of an almost unbelievable profusion of burial mounds, which stretched for at least 15 miles along the margin of the Ciénaga and its meandering overflow channel to the Río Sinú.

Most of the graves were low mounds, many of them pyramidal in shape. From some grew giant ceiba and jobo (*Spondias*) trees, an indication of their great antiquity. The largest grave, called by the Spaniards *la Tumba del Diablo*, was visible for more than a league away. Others were level with the ground and could be distinguished only after the coarse grass that covered them had been burned. Descriptions of the wealth of gold taken from the graves of Fincenú stagger the imagination. Individual graves yielded more than 30,000 pesos in gold; the deepest were the most lucrative. El Diablo itself was only partly excavated because of cave-ins, but 150,000 pesos was taken from 12 graves surrounding it, each of which was reported to be more than 30 feet high. In all, Heredia and his companions were said to have taken close to two million pesos from Fincenú over a period of 18 months.[4]

This and later expeditions to Cenú, as the site came to be known, made several fruitless forays into the upper San Jorge seeking the source of the gold, which had been traded down from Zenúfana (Antioquia) for salt, fish, and hammocks and other textile products. At Ayapel they found other large cemeteries, but less rich than those of Cenú. As the flush of excitement over the first discoveries abated, the interest of the Spaniards waned. Moreover, food supply had become an increasingly critical problem. When the *Oidor* Badillo visited Cenú in 1537, he found the Spaniards there living in slovenly fashion in two of the Indian communal houses.[5] His order that a town be laid out and a church built seems never to have been carried out. Already reports from the César expedition which had penetrated into Antioquia and the great mines of Buriticá were causing restlessness among those who remained.

The great necropolis of Fincenú, lost to the world for more than 300 years, was rediscovered at the beginning of the twentieth century by colonos clearing the forested wilderness of this part of the Sinú. The forest, undisturbed by the annual burnings that must have characterized the Indian occupancy, had re-established itself on all save the most poorly drained areas surrounding the Ciénaga, but the enormous revetments, pyramids, and other earthworks, including what must have been El Diablo, remained as tantalizing evidence of a lost culture. Although the area has been well probed by professional ghouls, it still awaits study by archaeologists. Here is the possible key to much of the confused culture history and ethnology of this important but little-known part of Caribbean Colombia. It is not even certain who the Cenúes were. Their goldwork and decoration are strongly suggestive of the Quimbaya of the middle Cauca

---

[4]Joaquín Acosta: Compendio histórico del descubrimiento y colonización de la Nueva Granada en el siglo décimo sexto (Paris, 1848), pp. 121-128. The principal original sources are Castellanos, Herrera, and Oviedo. See also "Las naciones indígenas que poblaban al Occidente de Colombia, el tiempo de la Conquista, según los Cronistas Castellanos," an appendix to J. Jijón y Caamaño's "Sebastián de Benalcázar" (2 vols., Quito, 1936 and 1938), Vol. 2.

[5]"Colección de documentos inéditos relativos al descubrimiento, conquista y colonización de las posesiones españolas en América y Oceanía" (42 vols., Madrid, 1864-1884), Vol. 41, 1884, pp. 356-400.

Valley, who have been described as recent arrivals from the north. They can also be shown to have had close affinities with the Chibcha and the Cuna of Urabá. Their poison arrows and hammocks, among other things, clearly indicate that they were not akin to the modern Chocó folk of the Alto Sinú. The few "Indians" reportedly still living in the remote rural parts of the Sabanas *municipio* of San Andrés may be the last representatives of this group, but they seem never to have been scientifically investigated.

The Colonial Economy

The *villa* of Tolú, founded in 1535 amidst friendly coastal Indians to supply Cenú and Cartagena with foodstuffs, remained the administrative and commercial center for the Sinú and the Sabanas throughout the colonial period. Moreover, as the only defended place between Cartagena and Nombre de Díos, it had also a certain military significance. Most of the 40 *repartimientos* of tribute-paying Indians were located on the Sabanas de Tolú (now Sabanas de Bolívar), the limestone-sandstone upland to the south, which had been largely cleared of its forest cover, perhaps before the Spaniards' arrival. These Sabanas settlements communicated with the coast by the Aguas Prietas arm of the Río Sinú. The Sinú lowlands were largely unoccupied, and even on the Sabanas the population was small; according to one 1610 account,[6] only San Andrés, Sampués, and Chenú (Chinú) counted as many as 40 tribute-paying males.

Maize, the principal tribute commodity, went chiefly to the Cartagena market. Each repartimiento, under a resident *mayordomo*, maintained one community field for tribute maize, in which it was permitted to plant yuca (*Manihot*) between the rows; yuca, together with maize *bollos* and *chicha*, formed the basis of the native diet. Two crops of maize a year were customarily harvested, but the same field was never planted a second year. Much of the maize was fed to hogs, which were early being shipped in quantity from Tolú to Cartagena.

During the dry season, when there was no work in the maize fields, the *monte* yielded wild fibers, aromatic resins, dyewoods, lumber, beeswax, and honey. The small river and coastal pueblos also took fish, fresh-water turtles, and manatee, the last for oil as well as for meat. Other important sources of protein in the native diet were tapirs and peccaries, such large aquatic rodents as the

---

[6]Oidor Juan de Villabona Zubiaurre, in "Visitas de Bolívar," Vol. I, Folio 279, Archivo Nacional, Bogotá (manuscript).

capybara, the paca, and the agouti, and the flesh and eggs of alligators and iguanas.

Gathering the long, narrow leaves of the pineapple-like pita (*Aechmea magdalenae*), a common understory element of the forest, seems to have been a main activity of several of the Tolú pueblos. Some of the cleaned, bleached pita fiber was shipped to Cartagena, but much of it was woven into hammocks, saddle blankets, and cordage by the women and girls. Although some cotton textiles were made, more were imported from Santa Marta.

It was especially for the aromatic balsams of its forests that this coast was known in Europe during the colonial period. The famous Tolú balsam came from the large, leguminous *Myroxylon* tree, as does the balsam of El Salvador, which supplies the world market today. The viscous exudations of vanilla-scented resin were collected in a gourd or calabash attached to the trunk below a V-shaped incision in the bark. Balsam was known and collected throughout the jurisdiction of Tolú, but the finest and clearest was said to come from Colosó. Toluene, a common coal-tar derivative known to the modern world as a constituent of trinotrotoluene (TNT), was named for the Tolú balsam, from which it was distilled by a French chemist in 1841. Once credited with great medicinal value, Tolú balsam is now used chiefly as a fixative in soap and perfumery and as a pleasant ingredient in ointments and cough medicines. The *Myroxylon* is relatively rate in the region today, having been extensively cut for its compact, reddish-brown, and fragrant wood and to make way for maize fields and pasture. An occasional tin of the resin still finds its way to Cartagena from the Colosó district, but most of the balsam exported from Colombia is *canime* (copaiba balsam), inferior oleoresin still taken in some quantity by tapping the heartwood of a forest tree (*Copaifera*) of the Alto Sinú.

Before the end of the seventeenth century free mestizo and mulatto elements of the Sinú area had become numerically dominant over the Indians. "The inhabitants of this province [of Cartagena]," wrote one observer, "are descendants of Army and Navy deserters, stowaways, escaped slaves, murderers, and other criminals fleeing punishment or imprisonment...who are scattered through the forests and swamps in small *rancherías*."[7] In 1772 a census listed an adult population of 26,237 for the three *partidos* that made up the jurisdiction of Tolú, of whom 28 percent were Indians and 4 per cent Negro slaves. Lorica, Corozal, Sincelejo, and Tolú were the prin-

---

[7]Quoted in Ernesto Restrepo Tirado: *De Gonzalo Ximénez de Quesada a Don Pablo Morillo* (Paris, 1928), p. 24.

cipal towns.[8]   The land west of the Río Sinú and inland above the new town of San Jerónimo de Buenavista (Montería) was considered under the control of the hostile Urabá Indians, who frequently raided the Sinú settlements during the eighteenth century.[9]

Throughout the colonial period the Tolú towns functioned chiefly as the breadbasket of Cartagena and, occasionally, Portobelo. To foreign corsairs looking for fresh meat, fruits, and vegetables the loaded Sinú *canoas de víveres* were tempting targets. As the rusted cannons along its water front attest, the villa of Tolú, too, was subjected to frequent piratic raids, beginning as early at 1569, when it was twice taken by the French. Between 1655 and 1671 alone it was sacked eight times by the English.[10]

The Lumbering Era

The exploitation of the cedar and mahogany forests of the Sinú by foreign lumber interests, which began about 1880, marked a turning point in its settlement history. For 300 years small amounts of wood had been floated down the river for local and Cartagena consumption, but exports had been limited to an occasional cargo picked up by sailing vessels stopping at Cispata or Tolú. In 1879 the United States consular agent at Cartagena had begun calling attention in his reports to Washington to the "inexhaustible" stands of tropical hardwoods above Montería. Dealers were urged to come and see for themselves the quality of the Spanish cedar and ma-hogany that could be laid down for delivery at Cispata for $30 or less a thousand board feet. The cedar was described as of cigar-box quality, comparable with that of Mexico or Cuba; the mahogany, which may have included some "Colombian mahogany" (*Cariniana pyriformis*) as well as true mahogany, was only fair and inferior to that of Santo Domingo.

The most important single factor in the developing lumber trade was the Boston firm of George D. Emery Company (Casa Emery),

---

[8]Diego de Peredo: Noticia historial de la Provincia de Cartagena [1772], in Documentos para la historia de Cartagena, edited by Jose P. Urueta (Cartagena, 1890), Vol. 3, pp. 311-345.

[9]Antonio de la Torre Miranda: Noticia individual de las poblaciones nuevamente fundadas en la Provincia de Cartagena [1788], in Documentos...(see footnote 8, above), Vol. 4, pp. 33-78.

[10]C.H. Haring: The Buccaneers in the West Indies in the XVII Century (New York, 1910), p. 267.

which between 1883 and 1915 carried on extensive operations, first in the Sinú Valley above Montería and later in the Canalete, San Juan, and Urabá districts to the west. The Emerys closed their Montería office and their Colombia operations in early 1915; their concessions had expired, and the merchantable timber near enough to the river to be logged with oxen had been exhausted. Further, the bulk of the output had been cedar, not mahogany, and the market demand had weakened. The Americans, though they never returned, had literally cleared the way for the modern colonization of the Sinú. In some 30 years the company had revivified the economy of the area and, according to the local press, had been largely responsible for the growth of Montería to a prosperous city of 10,000 population (1950 population, about 30,000).

Ahead of the lumbermen had gone the hard-bitten, self-reliant men who gathered the lesser products of the forest, grubstaked by Montería buyers of rubber, balsams, ipecac, sarsaparilla, and gum copal (algarroba resin). At times Castilla rubber had been the principal source of outside cash income in the Sinú, but the *caucheros* felled the trees for greater recovery of the latex, so that a sharp decrease in production was inevitable. During the rainy season they also collected ipecac, the elongated, warty rhizome of a trailing plant of the forest floor (*Cephaelis*), of which there is still a considerable production from the virgin forests of the Alto Sinú and Urabá. It is known to the drug trade as "Cartagena ipecac," to distinguish it from the commoner Brazilian variety.

Stock Raising

As is so often the case in the seasonally dry lowlands of tropical America, the modern economy of the Sinú and the adjacent Sabanas is dominated by the stockman. The cradle of the cattle industry in colonial new Granada was the periodically inundated natural grasslands of the lower San Jorge and Magdalena, from which it early spread westward toward the Sabanas. By 1892 the Sinú was beginning to send substantial numbers of steers to Antioquia markets, today the most important outlet for the red Bolívar cattle. The commerce was stimulating colonization along the route, which led from Montería past Ciénaga Betancí to the lower Río Cauca and Medellín.

It has been the overseas markets, however, that have given cattle raising in the Department of Bolívar its bonanza quality. As early as 1876 at least, soon after the introduction of the invaluable *admirable*, or Pará grass (*Panicum barbinode*), and guinea grass (*P. maximum*) into the Sinú from Brazil and Venezuela, exports from

Cispata to Cuba had begun. Strife-torn Cuba remained a major market for 25 years, but the War of the Thousand Days, which ravaged Colombia between 1899 and 1902, saw the wholesale liquidation of the Sinú-Sabanas herds to foreign buyers at panic prices, sometimes as low as $1 a head. The exportation of heifers and cows in large numbers made the subsequent rebuilding of the decimated herds a slow process.

World War I brought a resumption of exports from the Cispata chutes, but now the market was the Panama Canal Zone. During the war years more than 100,000 head of cattle and 20,000 pigs were shipped to Panama, and in the immediate postwar period Mexico, Peru, and Cuba entered the market to take an additional 40,000 cattle. Again in 1941 the Canal Zone began to take cattle from Cispata in large numbers, and for the next 5 years shipments from that port numbered more than 20,000 head annually. In 1949 oil-rich Venezuela, traditionally a cattle exporter, began to bid for Colombian cattle in quantity. The Colombian government, concerned with rising domestic meat prices, has placed exports to Venezuela on a quota basis. For the last 6 months of 1950 the export quota was set at 26,500 head, of which one-half were to come from Bolívar, shipping through Cispata. The department's quota was allocated among ten large haciendas in the Sinú and 10 more in the Sabanas-San Jorge area.

As early as 1908, British and American meat packers, already established in Argentina, had begun to make inquiries concerning the possible construction of a packing house on the Colombian coast. The Cispata export trade had withered with the imposition of new Cuban tariffs, and the big stockmen of the Lorica area, especially, were becoming increasingly anxious to locate new overseas markets. The concession for such a plant, which carried with it substantial subsidies, was thrown open to bidders by the government in Bogotá and, in 1918, was finally awarded to the International Products Company of Chicago and Paraguay.[11] This company held a 51

---

[11] In reporting that the Englishman Robert Cunninghame Graham was to be one of the bidders, a Montería newspaper editorial remarked that it would be a thousand times better for English rather than American capital to be involved, a sentiment that apparently traced back to the Panama affair. Graham wrote a popular account of his stay in Colombia, "Cartagena and the Banks of the Sinú" (London, 1920). Much more satisfactory, and a classic in its way, is Luis Striffler's "El Alto Sinú: Historia del primer establecimiento para la extracción del oro en el Alto Sinú" (Cartagena, 1875), a vivid geographic description by a sensitive young Alsatian engineer who was in charge of a well-organized but unsuccessful mining venture on the Río Sinú below Tucará in 1844, when much of the area was still a green

percent interest in a new corporation especially constituted to exploit the concession, the remaining stock of which was held by Cartagena and Lorica capitalists.

Construction at the site selected on the coast a few miles east of Cispata at Coveñas was delayed somewhat by the war, but in early 1924 the plant was completed. It included a handsome 5-foot slaughtering building and a six-story brick refrigeration plant with a 6000-carcass capacity. It had its own modern wharf, reservoir, hydroelectric plant, and hospital, together with a town of trim brick houses and barracks to house the workers. But it turned out to be a 3-million-dollar white elephant that was never to operate on a commercial basis.

Although there had been skepticism regarding the availability of enough cattle in northern Colombia to support a large-scale packing house, in the end it was the lack of markets that spelled failure for the Coveñas *frigorífico*. Samples sent to London had been graded fifth class and not to British taste. Negotiations with other European governments were similarly fruitless, apparently because of the substandard quality of the product, though in the Sinú there were dark hints of intrigue and boycott among the big United States packers. The long-idle plant was sold in 1939 to an American oil company, which uses a part of the facilities for its Barco pipeline terminus.

Of the 100,000 cattle shipped annually from the Sinú Valley for sale in Colombian markets, only a relatively few go to Cartagena. The largest numbers are trailed overland as 4-year-olds to a point near Magangué, on the Río Magdalena. From here they are shipped on special cattle boats to Barranquilla or upriver to such interior markets as Bucaramanga, Medellín, and Bogotá, which are reached by railroad lines that climb into the Andean highlands from the river towns of Puerto Wilches, Puerto Berrío, and La Dorada-Puerto Salgar (Fig. 6.1) By this route the trip to Medellín, the principal market, requires some 20 days. On the alternative, 40-day overland route to Medellín driving costs are lower, but the cattle lose as much as 30 percent weight, so that the 3-year-olds, which are normally dispatched by this route, must be fattened in the Antioqueño Cauca for 4 to 12 months before they are ready for sale. Recently a considerable number of fat Sinú and San Jorge cattle have been sent to a modern slaughterhouse at Planeta Rica, which is shipping warm, freshly dressed carcasses in chartered cargo planes to Medellín, 1 hour's flight away.

---

wilderness.

Although the rangy, red *criollo* cattle, descendants of Spanish colonial stock, constitute the base of the modern Bolívar herds, the introduction of new blood, especially by some of the larger haciendas, has greatly altered the genetic composition of the livestock population in recent years. From crossings of criollo with Aberdeen Angus and Red Polled has come the handsome Romo-sinuano, a semi-fixed type of red, hornless stock of good growth characteristics. Of greater economic significance has been the widespread introduction of zebu (Brahman) blood, especially during the past 10 years. Compared with European breeds, these humped Indian cattle have much better developed sweat glands, which, with the large superficial area of loose skin, permit continuous grazing for long hours under the hot tropical sun, when other cattle would be forced to retire to the shade to rest. A zebu-criollo cross at 3 years may weigh as much as a 4-year-old criollo in the same pasture--sufficient explanation for its recent and rapid rise to popularity. Notwithstanding early prejudices against it, today probably half of the livestock in the Sinú carry some zebu blood, and the proportion is rising rapidly.

Four out of five of the fenced *potreros* of the Sinú are in planted pasture. Pará grass is grown on the low, wet lands subject to occasional flooding; guinea grass and *puntero* (*Andropogon rufus*) are confined to the thinner, well-drained soils of the uplands. Most of the larger haciendas have extensive areas in both types of grass, so that year-round grazing is provided for the stock. Sabanas stockmen may have to rent range in the Sinú or San Jorge bottoms during the dry season, both for better feed and to obtain access to water for the stock. Most of the stock are fattened and sold to the export markets by such large proprietors, who purchase the young stock from smaller operators specializing in breeding. Much pasture is still burned during the dry season, especially on the Sabanas, but more satisfactory results are obtained by cleaning off the weeds and new woody growth with machetes where labor is available.

Cacao and Sugar

Commercial plantings of cacao seem to date from 1882, with the initiation of the first of several French agricultural ventures on the forested baldíos of Marta Magdalena. Here, as on the several French and Belgian plantations established above Montería shortly afterward, selected forest trees were left to provide the necessary shade for the cacao. Although the beans found favor on the Paris market, the yields were low, and the *cacaotales* were gradually transformed into Pará-grass pastures. Some of the properties have

74

remained in French hands,[12] but the first and largest, Marta Magdalena, was sold in 1912 to a syndicate of Antioqueño stockmen.

Despite the failure of plantation cacao on the alluvial Sinú
lowlands, it is a major cash crop for the Indians and the Antioqueño
smallholders on the better-drained, newly cleared lands of the Alto
Sinú above Tierra Alta. The peak of production here was reached
some 25 years ago; parasite and fungus infestations subsequently
brought on a decline that forced the replacement of the high-quality
native (criollo) types with the disease-resistant, high-yielding foreign
(forastero) varieties. Although much good cacao soil still remains,
labor shortages and inadequate transport facilities, the two great
problems of the Sinú, will probably continue to limit further planting.

Sugar cane, too, has had a role in the economic history of the
area. During the nineteenth century, production centered on the
Sabanas. The population of Sincelejo, for instance, was reported to
be "dedicated exclusively to the cultivation of cane and the distillation of aguardiente"[13] until new taxes and restrictions on rum
brought disaster to the industry in 1904. As the price of cane juice
dropped precipitously, most of the sugar lands were converted into
the planted pastures in which they remain today.

During recent years commercial sugar production in Caribbean
Colombia has been confined to two large properties near Cartagena
and to the Hacienda Berástegui, between Cereté and Ciénaga de Oro.
The 50,000-acre Berástegui grant, probably originally the largest
single holding in the Sinú, has been much subdivided, though the
parent company still controls perhaps one-sixth of the area within
the colonial grant. It was primarily a livestock operation until 1928,
when a modern steam sugar mill was installed. Yields have been
low, apparently because of the poor drainage and the fact that
production has been almost entirely from old ratoons, but cheap
labor and recurrent sugar shortages in Colombia seem to have made
the venture profitable. Harvesting is done by hand during the dry
season; the cane is hauled to the refinery on narrow-gauge tracks
that crisscross the 5,000 acres of cane fields. Between 700 and

---

[12]Among the French surnames common in the Montería area today are Dereix,
Kerguelen, Lacharme, and Leclerc. Most of these families were in one way or
another connected with the cacao ventures of the late nineteenth century. Some
had previously been associated with French canal-building activities at Panama
(Jaime Exbrayat: Reminiscéncias Monterianas [Montería, 1930], pp. 81 ff.).

[13]J.J. Nieto: Geografía historica, estadística y local de la Provincia de Cartagena
(Cartagena, 1839), p. 132.

1200 men are normally employed during the operating season, but in 1950, as a result of interfamily management quarrels, the 5-million-dollar property was temporarily abandoned, and for the first time no cane was cut.

The New Cotton Boom

The bonanza crop of the modern Sinú is cotton. The first large-scale planting was made in 1940 across the river from Montería, but the big "cotton rush" has occurred only within the past 3 years. The area in cotton rose from 700 acres in 1948 to 25,000 acres in 1950, and substantial further expansion seems inevitable. A guaranteed market at a liberal, government-fixed price coupled with extraordinarily high yields, averaging 300 to 450 pounds of lint per acre on plots that have been in cotton for 10 consecutive years, has meant fortunes in cotton. The Colombian government, shy of dollars and anxious to reduce imports of raw cotton, has subsidized the purchase of American-made farm machinery, distributed free certified seed, and, in partnership with the textile mill owners, constructed the necessary new gins.

The pitch of the cotton fever can perhaps best be gauged in the lobbies of Montería's hotels, where equipment salesmen discuss delivery quotas with suitcase farmers from Medellín who have come to bargain with the landowners for short-term leases. Cotton is for capitalists in the Sinú; it has burst forth full-blown as a wholly mechanized crop. In mid-1950 it was estimated that 250 cotton *equipos*[14] had been delivered in the area, and further sales were contingent on factory allocations and the condition of the road from Cartagena.

Physical conditions in the Sinú seem to be extremely favorable for cotton growing. The seed is planted in September or early October, the dependable late rains bring the plant to its full growth, and, as the *verano* sets in, the bolls mature under ideally high temperatures and low humidity. By the end of January the harvest is at its height. Cotton cannot be double-cropped here as it is in the parts of Colombia (for example, Tolima) where there are two well-marked dry seasons, but maize and sesame have been experimentally planted as second crops after the cotton harvest. Fertilization has not yet been practiced, and cotton pests, troublesome in other producing districts, have not yet appeared in force.

---

[14]In the Sinú an *equipo*, which will handle about 150 acres, usually consists of a tractor, plow, harrow, planter, cultivator, and duster.

Plantings have been made chiefly on the better-drained alluvial soils around Montería and Cereté, with smaller outlying areas near Tierra Alta and Lorica. Damaging floods, which apparently may be expected at intervals of perhaps 10 years, are reported to have caused substantial damage to the crop harvested in January-February, 1951, and this may have cooled the ardor of some of the marginal growers. Colombia still imports more than half of the raw cotton consumed in its booming textile industry. In the Sinú alone there seems to be enough good land not only to make the country self-sufficient in cotton but to provide a small export surplus for Venezuelan and European markets; this land is going under the plow at a rapid rate. One possible limiting factor on the future of cotton in the Sinú is the shortage of labor during the picking season. Another is transportation. To reach the large mills in Medellín, the bales must be moved by truck over the treacherous and often impassable highway from Montería to Magangué, then by river boat to Puerto Berrío, where they are transferred to the Antioquia railroad. Costs are high and the service both slow and uncertain, so that growers and mill owners are pressing vigorously for the completion of an all-weather highway from Montería to Medellín via Planeta Rica and the lower Cauca. A part of the 1951 crop of some 10,000 bales is reported to have been moved to Medellín by cargo aircraft.

Petroleum

Before cotton, petroleum had stirred men's hopes for finding quick riches in the Sinú, but the millions of dollars invested by foreign oil companies have to date produced negligible results. The abundance of oil and gas seeps associated with the folded and faulted marine Tertiary formations on each side of the Sinú Valley alluvium have long attracted attention. Although shallow wells had been drilled earlier by both English and German interests, the first well-organized attempt to find petroleum in the Sinú was made by the Standard Oil Company of New York between 1914 and 1916. Its substantial investment breathed new life into the economy of the Sinú much as the American lumber interests had done earlier. Several camps were set up, many miles of motor roads constructed, and three shallow wells drilled, two near Lorica and a third a few miles west of Montería, before World War I, possibly coupled with lingering anti-United States sentiment from the Panama affair, terminated operations.

Before 1944 and 1947 drilling was resumed in the Sinú Valley by the Socony-Vacuum Oil Company, which sank two deep tests and ten shallow wells on the Floresanto Concession, 25 miles southwest of Montería near Marta Magdalena. In 1947 the concession was abandoned as noncommercial, though it had produced small amounts of oil from shallow horizons. The deepest test hole had been bottomed in Oligocene at 10,876 feet.[15] Other American oil companies have been active on the Sabanas, where at least eight wells have been drilled in the San Andrés area and southeast of Sahagún.

Repeated dry holes, together with the lack of satisfactory petroleum and tax laws, are discouraging further exploratory work in Bolívar, though a few geophysical and mapping crews are still active in the area. North American travelers, even in the remotest areas, are inevitably considered to be in the employ of one or another of the petroleum companies, however forceful their protests to the contrary.

Transportation

Today the jeep, the truck, and the airplane are bringing an economic revolution to the long-isolated Sinú, and the river has lost much of its importance as a transportation life line. Montería, a city of jeeps, is connected with Cartagena and Magangué by daily bus and truck service and should soon be linked to Medellín, 330 miles to the south, if politics do not interfere with the completion of the unbuilt section of the road between Planeta Rica and the Antioquia boundary. Commercial air transport has increasingly tended to concentrate the economic activity of the area on Montería. There is excellent daily DC-3 passenger service to both Medellín and Cartagena, and surprisingly numerous feeder fights to and from cow-pasture landing fields at such points as Tierra Alta, San Juan Urabá, Planeta Rica, Sincelejo, and Tolú. Lorica is served by twice-weekly service from Cartagena, and at Coveñas there is a private airport. More impressive, however, than the passenger service is the large amount of cargo carried by air, especially between Montería and Medellín. In 1950 the three companies operating on this run were averaging more than 50 round trips monthly and transporting just about all the cargo, except cotton and cattle, that moved between the two cities. "Going up," these planes may carry live hogs, lard, lumber, cacao, cheese, furniture, and even occasional shipments of ginned cotton. From Medellín come the manufactures of Antioquia's factories, everything from structural steel and hardware to textiles,

---

[15]Geoffrey Barrow: Colombia, in World Geography of Petroleum, edited by Wallace E. Pratt and Dorothy Good, *American Geographical Society Special Publication No. 31*, 1950, pp. 100-119; reference on p. 110.

crockery, clothing, coffee, and the inevitable daily newspapers. During the first 6 months of 1950, more than 3,500 live hogs were shipped from Montería to Medellín, and tinned lard sometimes filled as many as 10 planes a week. In the rainy season shipments drop off sharply, not because of poor flying conditions but because of the difficulties of moving produce from rural districts to the airport. In 1949 and 1950, as a result of the operations of rebel bands of political "bandits" in the Alto Sinú, some hogs may have been shipped by air that might otherwise have moved on the hoof over the tough mountain trails from Tucurá to Ituango or Dabeiba in Antioquia.

Launch service to Cartagena, perpetually plagued with the problem of crossing the wide 4-foot bar at the mouth of the Sinú, has deteriorated greatly, for now it is largely a cargo trade. Most passengers go to Cartagena by the much faster and more comfortable plane or bus. During the verano the upper limit of navigation is Lorica, but for most of the year Montería's water front is the terminus for the Cartagena boats. When the water is high, there is also service from Lorica to Chimá and Momil and from Montería to Tierra Alta and the small settlements on the Caño Betancí. Giant dugout canoes, as much as 75 feet long, still carry considerable amounts of cargo between intermediate river points, and the much larger Cartagena-built sailing vessels occasionally are poled up the river as far as Lorica by black-skinned boatmen from the offshore islands.

Cultural and Commercial Relations

Everywhere in Colombia regional consciousness is sharp. In the geographically isolated Sinú it is embodied in the proposals recurrent since 1916 for the establishment of a new department, with its capital at Montería, which would separate all of the Sinú and parts of the Sabanas and the San Jorge Valley from the jurisdiction of Cartagena. Actually, Lorica and the lower Sinú have so far been but little affected by the new vitality that has swept the Montería area and the Alto Sinú, where Antioqueño and foreign influences have been most strongly felt. In Lorica the leading merchants are Syrians; in Montería they are Antioqueños or second-generation French or, occasionally, persons from Cartagena. The business and cultural ties of Lorica are with Cartagena and the coast, of Montería with Medellín and Bogotá. Like Antioquia, Montería is politically Conservative; Lorica and the Sabanas are Liberal. Montería reads Medellín newspapers, sends its children to Medellín schools, and sells its cattle, hogs, lard, rice, and cotton in Medellín markets, a most remarkable situation in view of the difficulties of land transportation between the two cities.

Because of its off-side location in relation to the main routes of commerce, the Sinú has long been one of the least-appreciated and least-known parts of Colombia. Today, as Colombian agriculture and settlement move irresistibly downslope from the crowded Andean highlands, the need is for more good land capable of supporting rural colonization in the *tierras calientes*. In these terms the Sinú Valley would appear to be one of the better-endowed lowlands of tropical America. *Desgraciado para el Perú si se descubre el Sinú* went an old refrain of the sixteenth century that indicated the Spaniards' obsession with finding the source of the gold of the Fincenú graves. Today the Sinú has become another El Dorado--a symbol of the unexplored agricultural potentialities of the long-neglected Caribbean coast.

7

Urabá in the Sixteenth Century*

To Rodrigo de Bastidas and Juan de la Cosa, coasting westward along the northern shore of South America in the late months
of 1501, this "tierra firme" must have seemed a green and abundant
land. The native people who were encountered by the first Spanish
expedition to the coast of Colombia had gold in abundance, and it
was for gold alone that the Spaniards had come.[1] The expedition
had coasted westward as far as the Gulf of Urabá, which it had
entered and explored. Its hilly eastern shore offered the principal
attraction to settlement and the best protection against the north-
easterlies, and the expedition spent some time there before turning
back to Española loaded down with gold trinkets traded from the
friendly Indians. The combination of precious metals in abundance
and a docile native population could scarcely have been more to the
Spaniards' liking.

San Sebastian de Urabá

The mounting of a follow-up expedition to Urabá was natural
and expected. To achieve this, Juan de la Cosa secured the post of
alguacil mayor or high constable of Urabá, with permission to
enslave any rebellious Caribs, i.e., cannibals encountered. There
seems to have been no reason to so label the natives of this area,
with whom the first expedition had had amicable relations, and in
Carl Sauer's considered view persuading the queen to do so was a

---

*Reprinted from *Antioquia's Corridor to the Sea*, Ibero-Americana: 49, pp. 3-14,
University of California Press, Berkeley (1967).

[1]Carl O. Sauer, *The Early Spanish Main* (1966).

82

low trick perpetrated by Cosa, the principal solicitant.[2] The *capitans* could now proceed as they wished by affirming that the natives were cannibals or simply that they resisted the Christians. Cosa's 1504 expedition raided the town of *cacique* Urabá on the east coast of the gulf and later that of Darién on the other side, then was stranded for some eighteen months on returning to Urabá's village where new ships were built to replace the worm-ridden ones in which they had arrived. Less than 50 men were in the party of survivors that reached Española.

In Spanish minds the land of Urabá, roughly interpreted as the east coast of that gulf (Fig. 7.1), had already come to be associated with gold, although it was known that the metal was traded in from the interior rather than being locally mined. The native population of this coast as well as that of the Sinú country to the east was probably of Chibchan stock, whose culture traits included the prizing of gold, but because they were so harried by the early Spaniards ethnological data on them is extremely rudimentary. The breakdown in relations between invader and native was early and complete. Beyond Cartagena, in Sauer's words, "the natives were classed as hostile, were thus treated, and so reacted."[3] This was a land, he observes, where the Spaniards expected to be met with warfare.

In concessions granted by the Junta de Burgos in 1508, rights to exploit the west coast of the gulf (Darién) were given to Diego de Nicuesa, while the east coast, from the domain of Urabá as far as Cartagena, was allocated to Alonso de Hojeda and Cosa, the latter as pilot and financial angel. Cosa was killed by Indian arrows near Cartagena, but Hojeda, after pillaging along the coast, debarked early in 1510 at the Indian town of Urabá, where a fort and a settlement called San Sebastián were built. Some have presumed this to be at or near the present town of Necoclí, the site of Cosa's shipyard 6 years earlier. Here a ridge of high ground reaches into the gulf, providing a defensible site, quiet water, and easy access to the Atrato and Sinú valleys. Frey Severino de Santa Teresa places it 4 kilometers to the north of Necoclí, at a place presently known as Cañaflechal.[4]

---

[2]Ibid., p. 162.

[3]Ibid., p. 171.

[4]Frey Severino de Santa Teresa, *Historia documentada de la iglesia en Urabá y el Darién* (1956-1957), 4:460.

83

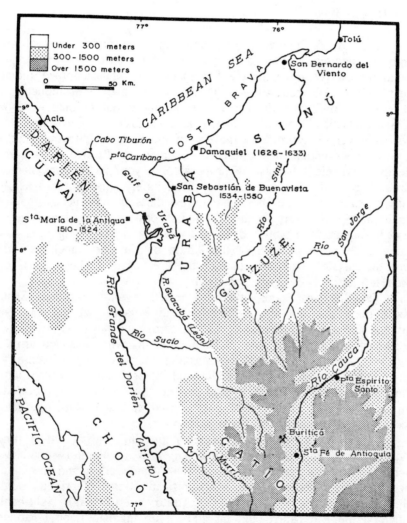

Figure 7.1 Northwest Colombia and the Urabá Region in the Sixteenth Century.

84

Although it was to be short-lived, San Sebastián de Urabá, as the the first Spanish settlement on the mainland of the New World,has earned a unique place in the annals of history. It lay within what was later to become the Gobernación of Antioquia.

The Darien Base

The Urabá Spaniards were short on men and rations almost from the beginning. Forced to raid into the interior for food, they found themselves up against a formidable and unaccustomed Indian weapon, the poisoned arrow. Their number had been reduced to some 60 "hungry and dispirited men...sitting it out in the sweatbox of San Sebastián,"[5] when Hojeda took leave, ostensibly to search for aid but never to return. By the end of the year the situation of the outpost, now under the command of Francisco Pizarro, was completely untenable. It was the proposal of a young stowaway named Vasco Nuñez de Balboa that they seek safety among the friendly natives of the opposite shore that turned disaster into success. As a result the Spanish fort on the Antioquia coast was abandoned and a new headquarters established at Santa María de la Antigua, a few miles north of the mouth of the Atrato on the Río Tanela, at that time the last left bank tributary of the great river. The trespass on Nicuesa's territory was not contested.

The Spaniards, soon much augmented in numbers, made Santa María their base for the exploration and pillaging of the adjacent isthmus and the Atrato valley. Urabá, across the bay, seems to have been looked upon as a land of hostile Indians with poisoned arrows that was best avoided. Balboa, asking the Crown for license to carry them as slaves to Española and other islands peopled with Christians, described them as bad Indians (no quedase memoria de tan mala gente.)[6] They could not be used at Santa María, he said, because there it would be too easy for them to escape.

Despite nearly a decade of reconnoitering, during which time Balboa discovered the Pacific and *entradas* (exploratory marches) were mounted for Central America, the Atrato valley, and the Sinú, the Spaniards failed to locate any significant source of primary gold. They had been far enough up the Atrato and its major right-bank tributary, the Río Murrí, and far enough up the Río León ("Río de

---

[5]Sauer, *Early Spanish Main*, p. 173.

[6]"Fragmento de carta de Vasco Nuñez de Balboa al Rey. Santa María de la Antigua del Darién 20 enero, 1513," in Martin Fernández de Navarette, *Colección de los viages y descubrimientos que hicieron por los Españoles* (1925-1929), 2:222.

los Redes" or "river of nets") to confirm the existence of the great lord Dabeiba who ruled over an extensive "savanna" country rich in gold in the mountains to the south.[7]   With the decimation of the local indian population and the probable exhaustion of the modest gold placers of the short Darién streams, the Santa María area was abandoned.   It was to be repeopled by Cueva (Cuna) people from the southwest, who were later to spread out to the San Blas Islands and even to Urabá, the so-called Darién Indians who were to trouble the Spaniards so for the next three centuries.

The evacuation of Santa María de la Antigua, completed in 1524, was in part a political move by the governor, Pedro Arias de Avila (Pedrarias), but it also reflected the shift of Spanish interest westward across the isthmus towards the more open Coiba country on the Pacific versant.[8]   Santa María had been a good march site, but its function could now be better served by Panamá.   The only Spaniards on the Caribbean coast of Darién were thenceforth to be found at the coastal settlement of Acla (Fig. 7.1).   It lay some 90 kilometers to the north, where there was good anchorage behind two small islands, adequate fresh water, alluvial soil, and lumber for shipbuilding and ship repair.   It had been from Acla that Balboa had opened the route across the isthmus to the Pacific Ocean in 1513, and it was here that he had been sent by Pedrarias 3 years later to found the second town in Castilla del Oro, only to be beheaded on its plaza on orders from the headstrong governor, who was also his father-in-law.   Gil González Dávila had mounted his successful expedition to Central America from here in 1520, crossing over to the Pacific side to appropriate Balboa's abandoned ships for the voyage.   As late as 1527 the chronicler Oviedo could still describe Acla as the principal town on the isthmus, not excluding Panamá.[9]

A Second San Sebastian

Under Julián Gutiérrez, lieutenant of the Governor of Panamá, Acla was gradually converted into a base for the pacification of the Indians on the opposite shore of the gulf.   Since the abandonment of

---

[7]Sauer, *Early Spanish Main*, pp. 223-228.

[8]Ibid., pp. 278-280.   El Real de Santa María, a mining camp founded at a later date on the Río Tuira across the continental divide on the Pacific versant, has sometimes been confused in the literature with the original Santa María de la Antigua.

[9]Quoted in Severino de Santa Teresa, *Historia documentada*, 3:420.

the short-lived San Sebastián de Urabá in 1510, this coast and its bellicose natives had been largely avoided except for two abortive entradas launched in 1515 by encomenderos of Castilla del Oro seeking the fabled El Sinú and the legendary mines of Tarufi and Mocri, the reputed source of its gold.[10] The Urabá coast seemed a logical doorway to the Sinú and a counterbalance to the developing claims of other Spaniards working out of Cartagena.[11]

Between 1532 and 1538 Gutiérrez conducted seven separate voyages to the Urabá coast, maintaining the friendliest of relations with the natives.[12] On his initial probe he was accompanied by several Urabá Indians who earlier had been captured and brought to Acla. One of these was Isabel Canal, the sister of the principal cacique of Urabá, who served as interpreter to the party and who later became Gutiérrez' wife. it was through her that he won the sympathy and friendship of the other caciques. The efforts of the Acla Spaniards to colonize the Urabá shore met resistance not from the natives but from Pedro de Heredia, founder of Cartagena, who claimed jurisdiction to the entire coast between the Río Magdalena and the Río Grande del Darién (Atrato), thus including the east shore of the Gulf of Urabá. On hearing of Gutiérrez' presence therefore, Pedro de Heredia sent his brother Alonso to exercise his claim by founding a town on this coast. Established in June, 1535, at the foot of a hill on the site of the modern village of Necoclí, San Sebastián de Buenavista, as it was known, is not to be confused

---

[10]The long delay in the pacification and control of the populous lands across the gulf was explained in a letter dated August 15, 1532, in Panamá by Licienciado Espinosa: "porque por ser como son caribes, y que tienen hierba, nunca se ha podido ni pueden sojuzgar, antes han muerto todos los gobernadores y capitánes que allí han ido a poblar y conquistar. Lo otro porque es tierra muy rica.... " Juan Friede (comp.), *Documentos inéditos para la historia de Colombia* (1955-1960), 2:286-287.

[11]To the Spaniards' practiced eyes the Urabá coast looked like superior country for stock-raising "por ser tierra de buena disposición y haber en ella manera para criar ganados vacunos y ovejunos y puercos y hacer cristianos españolas estancias para tener sus labranzas." Letter to the king from officials of the province of Cartagena, April 5, 1536, in Friede, *Documentos inéditos*, 4:92.

[12]Antonio Matilla Tascón, "Los viajes de Julián Gutiérrez al Golfo de Urabá," *Anuario de Estudios Americanos* (1945), 2:181-264. Most of the documentation on this territorial conflict and the ensuing entradas may be found in Friede, *Documentos inéditos*, especially vols. 4 and 5.

with Hojeda's earlier short-lived settlement of San Sebastián de Urabá which probably had lain a few kilometers to the north.[13]

As the representative of the Gobernación of Castilla del Oro (Panamá), which claimed jurisdiction over both shores of the Gulf of Urabá, Gutiérrez protested the new settlement. The dispute was adjudicated by a *real cédula* (royal order) signed in Madrid in 1536, which gave Urabá definitively to Cartagena and the forces of Heredia. The rival town that Gutiérrez had built four leagues to the south near the mouth of the Río Caimán Nuevo was abandoned on the orders of the Oidor Badillo. Gutiérrez good offices were deemed necessary to keep peace with the natives. Their poisoned arrows made them seem to the Spaniards "the most warlike to the entire province [of Cartagena]." Gutiérrez was retained as intendente of Urabá, a title he held until he left for Perú and Chile where, according to Fray Pedro Simón, he won many new honors.[14]

Port of Entry to Antioquia

San Sebastián de Buenavista, its numbers augmented by the Acla colonists, became for a time a town of some substance. It was the point of entry into the interior and to the fabled treasures of the Sinú, Buriticá, and Dabeiba. The graves of the Sinú, in particular, offered rich rewards in worked gold. From this fortified coastal base camp were mounted a half dozen expeditions which penetrated into the mountains of Antioquia and to the middle Río Cauca drainage, beginning with that of Francisco César in 1536 or 1537 which routed the cacique Nutibara in the valley of Gauca (the upper Sinú) and plundered gold from the sepulchers of the region.[15] It was with César as his guide and the 19-year-old Pedro Cieza de León as chronicler that the Oidor Badillo himself entered Antioquia in the first months of 1538 by the same route. it was later twice used by Pedro de Heredia in entradas into the middle Cauca country. When Jorge Robledo, after founding the original Santa Fé de Antioquia in December 1541, headed for Spain to report to the Crown, he followed in reverse the route of these entradas, coming onto the coast

---

[13]Severino de Santa Teresa, *Historia documentada*, 3:460-462 and end paper map, Vol. 5. Also, Antonio J. Gómez, *Monografías de Antioquia* (1952), p. 736.

[14]Severino de Santa Teresa, *Historia documentada*, 3:378-380.

[15]"Resumen en extenso de la carta de licenciado Vadillo, Cartagena, 15 de septiembre de 1537," in Friede, *Documentos inéditos*, 4:342-345; see also, Emilio Robledo, *La Vida del Mariscal Jorge Robledo* (Bogotá, 1945).

88

at San Sebastián de Buenavista. Heredia, charging that Robledo had usurped his jurisdiction, sent him in chains to Spain. When Robledo returned 3 years later, cleared of all charges and accompanied by a retinue which included his wife and more than a dozen ladies-in-waiting, he came to San Sebastián de Buenavista to organize his return expedition, again by the same route, to take position of the lands newly granted to him as the Mariscal de Antioquia.[16]

The route from San Sebastián to the interior--early Antioquia's umbilical cord to the sea--was not the present one followed by the Carretera al Mar between Turbo and the Río Cauca. Although the trail most commonly employed is not described in detail by any of the early chroniclers, it almost certainly cut across the northernmost outliers of the Sarranía de Abibe to the headwaters of the upper Sinú. It was probably a ridgetop route for at least part of the way and as such much to be preferred by foot soldiers, carriers, and horses to the more direct modern route along the western margin of the Atrato depression with its numerous river crossings and threats of floods. Although the Río León or Río Atrato-Río Sucio routes from the Gulf of Urabá to Antioquia would have cut much rugged topography from the trail journey, they seem not to have been known or employed in the sixteenth century.

Antioquia was placed definitively under the jurisdiction of Popayán and the Audiencia of Quito with the award for Robledo, who was acting as a lieutenant of Sebastián Benalcázar. Thereafter, San Sebastián ceased to function as its gateway and port of entry. Indian uprisings had blocked the road; according to one *probanza* (inquiry) in October, 1548, no Spaniards had left Cartagena for Santa Fé de Antioquia in fourteen months because of fear of Indian troubles.[17] But Pedro de Heredia had not easily given up his hopes that San Sebastián might become the coastal emporium for the trade of Antioquia and Popayán. In a letter to the king in 1551 he was still pleading, as governor of Cartagena, for jurisdiction over Antioquia and its mines.[18] These, he argued, could be exploited only with much difficulty by the Popayán government but easily by him from the Gulf of Urabá, where he had "established a settlement of Span-

---

[16]"Fragmento de la probanza del clérigo Diego de Campo, Cartagena, 5 de octubre de 1548," Friede, *Documentos inéditos*, 9:243-245.

[17]"Tres cartas desconocidas de D. Pedro de Heredia en las que acusa a Robledo," *Crónica Municipal* (Medellín, agosto, 1963), pp. 56-57.

[18]José María Restrepo Saenz, *Gobernadores de Antioquia, 1579-1819* (1944), I:2-3.

iards called San Sebastián de Buenavista, at the most 40 leagues away and in one of the best ports in the Indies, from which that rich land can be developed without further loss, the Royal Fifth being much increased from its mines." Heredia explained that he had maintained the town of San Sebastián in anticipation that one day his suit with Sebastián Benalcázar of Popayán over the boundaries of their jurisdictions would be favorably settled, and that with the latter's death there now seemed no reason why Antioquia should not be formally adjudicated to him. But the Crown turned a deaf ear and Antioquia remained under the secular jurisdiction of the province of Popayán. In 1569 it was finally detached and created into an independent entity when Andrés de Valdivia, like Robledo a native if Ubeda, was named first governor and captain general of "Antioquia and its provinces and districts as far as the port of Urabá and to the North Sea." The new province was under the legal jurisdiction of the Audiencia of Bogotá, established in 1550, but its geographical isolation made it, in fact, for many years a more or less autonomous unit. Thus, politics, reinforced by recurrent Indian uprisings in the mountains of Abibe and in the upper Sinú, effectively sealed off Antioquia from its closest outlet to the sea on the Gulf of Urabá, a route that was to remain closed for nearly four centuries.[19]

With the opening of the Antioquia gold placers at Zaragoza and Cáceres in the lower Cauca district after 1580, the Magdalena River came to be the front door of Antioquia, and its direct link with Spain.[20] The long and tedious back entry through Quito and Popayán became progressively less important. The Magdalena route to and from the coast had several variants, all of them longer in distance and probably in time than the overland route of the original entradas from Urabá through the territory of the Gobernación of Cartagena. Travelers or goods destined for the capital city of Santa Fé de Antioquia generally landed at Cartagena, ascending the Río Magdalena and the Río Cauca to the head of navigable water at Puerto Espíritu Santo (Fig. 7.1), deep in the folds of the Antioquia mountains. From there it was a ten-day overland trip to Santa Fé

---

[19]In 1775 Lieutenant Antonio de la Torre Miranda of Cartagena unsuccessfully attempted to open a trade route from the coast to Antioquia and the Chocó by way of the Río Sinú, Quebrada Nain, and the Real de Minas de Pavarandó on the Río Sucio. "Noticia individual de las poblaciones nuevamente fundadas en la provincia de Cartagena....178," in José P. Ureta (ed.), *Documentos para la historia de Cartagena* (1890), 4:33-78.

[20]James J. Parsons, *Antioqueño Colonization in Western Colombia* (1949), pp. 44-46.

90

de Antioquia through some of the most rugged terrain in all of Nueva Granada. Later, with the rise in importance of the settlements of the Antioquia *meseta* (plateau) such as Medellín, Rionegro, and Marinilla, it became more common to continue up the Magdalena to the port of Nare, above present-day Puerto Berrío, whence several routes fanned out into the highlands.[21] Whichever way was taken, the trip from the coast was a difficult and hazardous journey of a month or more, contributing much to the isolation of Antioquia, an isolation strikingly reflected in its later cultural and economic history.

The shortcut linking the highland interior with the Gulf of Urabá was apparently used a few times after 1547, but the abandonment of San Sebastián de Buenavista, coupled with mounting Indian troubles, made the route progressively impractical. Depredations against coastal shipping by raiding canoe parties were apparently widespread and land travelers venturing into the area between the gulf and the Río Sinú fared even worse. In a 1561 *interrogatorio* (interrogation)[22] several witnesses testified that Spaniards going from Santa Fé de Antioquia to Cartagena by way of San Sebastián and the Caribana coast had been attacked and robbed of much gold, for which reason the route had been abandoned. Most troublesome were the Indians under the caciques Diego, Damaquiel, Carate, and Cayba. One witness told of the recent death of a *vecino* (citizen) of Cartagena, his wife, child, and two other Spaniards who had gone to reestablish the pueblo de Urabá in spite of warnings from friends. They may have been responding to the request made the previous year by the *regidores* (councilmen) of Cartagena for volunteers to participate in the "conquista y reducción" of the Urabáes or Caribanas, but if so their approach to the task was disastrously casual. The many machetes and copper tools they had brought as gifts to the Indians had been of no avail.

Refugees from these and other later disturbances retreated to the Sinú village of the cacique El Viento, probably at the site of the modern village of San Bernardo del Viento (Fig. 7.1), the closest pacified settlement towards Cartagena.[23] The settlement of San

---

[21]Ibid., pp. 154 *ff.*

[22]Archivo Nacional, Bogotá, "Caciques y Indios," tomo 16, folios 686-694.

[23]San Bernardo continued to serve as a refuge for many years. Thus, the Fidalgo expedition (1793-1801) reported that the town had been invaded by Cuna Indians from the west who burned buildings and killed some of the inhabitants before fleeing in the dead of the night. Antonio B. Cuervo (ed.), *Colección de documen-*

Sebastián de Urabá founded on the lower Río Sinú in the early eighteenth century by both Spaniards and Indians fleeing from later uprisings along the gulf was another such refugee establishment. It has been at times confused with the early settlement of the same name on the gulf.

8

The Carretera al Mar: Medellín-Urabá*

As the Colombian economy pulled itself together in the years following World War I, enthusiasm mounted within Antioquia for an automobile route to the sea (Fig. 8.1). No longer would a mere horse trail be acceptable, and a railroad seemed increasingly impractical and unnecessary. The paralysis of Magdalena river traffic for several weeks in 1924 and 1925 caused by critically low water served to heighten interest in an alternative route to the coast.

It was a Medellín businessman and visionary named Gonzalo Mejía who roused the community to action. A Junta Propulsadora para la Carretera al Mar was organized, meetings were called, pamphlets were published, and a large map was placed on display in downtown Medellín showing the route of the proposed road to Urabá.[1] From Urabá members of the Carmelite mission came to urge that the road be built, as did groups from Frontino, Dabeiba, and other communities in the Occidente.

In a wave of enthusiasm the Departmental Assembly in 1926 ordered the initiation of the projected road and appropriated 8 million pesos, to be raised by the sale of new bonds, for the purpose. The R.W. Hebard Company of New York was awarded the contract from Medellín to Dabeiba (140 kilometers) and was further

---

*Reprinted from *Antioquia's Corridor to the Sea: An Historical Geography of the Settlement of Urabá*, Ibero-Americana: 49, pp. 52-65, University of California Press, Berkeley (1967).

[1]*Album de la Carretera al Mar*, p. 38. On the background to this highway construction project, see the special edition of *El Colombiano* (Medellín), 12 junio, 1954.

94

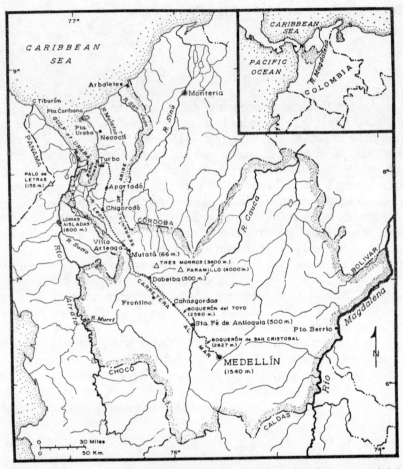

Figure 8.1 The Department of Antioquia and the Carretera al Mar.

authorized to carry out route studies for the additional 210 kilometers to the coast.[2]   A German concern, Siemens-Baunion, was
commissioned to make a study of the projected port at Necoclí, the
mangrove-lined bay at Turbo being judged too shoal and subject to
sedimentation to serve as an effective terminus to the road.

Work is Initiated (1926-1930)

Work was inaugurated with elaborate fanfare on June 10, 1926,
with the Bishop of Antioquia blessing a crowbar at a ceremony at
the end of the streetcar line in San Cristobal, a village across the
valley from Medellín where the work commenced.   The new road,
proclaimed an *obra redentadora* (work of salvation) promising the
emancipation of Antioquia from the Río Magdalena, was called the
most audacious engineering project that Colombia had yet known.[3]
At times as many as 7,000 workers would be employed on it,
together with great gangs of mules and considerable heavy equipment.   The first bridges and concrete retaining walls (*obras de arte*
in the Antioquia vernacular) were to be built with cement imported
from Italy.
The contractor, who had had extensive previous road-building
experience in Latin America, was to be paid from a Department of
Antioquia $12-million-dollar bond issue ("Antioquia External Gold
7's of 1927"), secured by a first lien on the income from the departmental liquor monopoly.   It was said to have been the first such
issue ever made by a South American provincial government.   The
bonds were marketed on the New York market, and just in time.
The Great Depression was soon to drive the quotation on these
Antioquia bonds from a high of 96 to a low of 460   in 1932.[4]
The route to be followed by the highway was approximately
that that had been recommended by Juan Enrique White for Henry
Granger's railroad more than 20 years earlier.   In 1927 a group of
engineers, led by Gonzalo Mejía, had succeeded in making the round
trip from Medellín to Turbo in 5 weeks, traveling by car, horse, and

---

[2]*Album...*, p. 74.

[3]*Album...*, p. 38.

[4]When the provincial debts were later absorbed by the national government some
years later they were being quoted at 18 on the New York bond market.

96

boat.[5] The going was easy enough through the mountains, but on the plains beyond Mutatá they followed the telegraph line through the selva with some difficulty due to fallen trees, mud, and numerous stream crossings. From Mutatá the country was flat and "inviting to settlers," reminiscent, Mejía wrote in his diary, of the United States Middle West of 60 years earlier. The party returned by launch up the Atrato and the Río Sucio to Pavarandocito, thence overland to Medellín, where they proclaimed that although the road was difficult "the benign climate and fertile soils of Urabá" would make the trip worthwhile for any colonists interested in settling there. The reputedly impassible gorges and swamps, it was insisted, were pure fantasies, based on unsubstantiated and exaggerated rumors that had been building up for four centuries. Dabeiba was the half-way point, but the general public still erroneously imagined that even with a road constructed that far, 99 percent of the job would remain to be done. The barrier to Urabá, he seemed to demonstrate, was more psychological than geographical.

Although in the beginning the Carretera al Mar was strictly a departmental project the participation of the national government was not long in coming. In 1927 the Congress agreed to provide a subvention of $20,000 for each kilometer completed, approximately one-third of the total estimated cost.[6] Virtually the entire distance from Medellín to the Urabá plains involved extremely rugged topography, with first a drop of the Boquerón de San Cristobal to the arid canyon of the Río Cauca, then an abrupt climb to the Boquerón de Toyo and a more gradual descent down the upper Río Sucio gorge to the forest-choked lowlands stretching northward to the Caribbean. Grades up to 5 percent were authorized. Retaining walls were eliminated beyond Santa Fé de Antioquia as an economy move, and a 4-meter-wide roadbed was authorized rather than the original 5-meter one. The Hebard contract was modified in 1928 to cover only the Boquerón de San Cristobal-Cañasgordas section of the road; from June 1929, the department took over direction of the entire project. Some 43 engineers--11 from the United States and 32 from Colombia--were engaged in the work at the peak. There were 4 different chief engineers in the first 30 months, and this had caused some delays, but there were also organizational problems and, it was complained, a general lack of planning.

[5]*El Colombiano* (Medellín), 12 junio, 1954; Gonzalo Mejía, *De Medellín a Turbo: Mis impressiones sobre la ruta que ha de seguir la Carretera al Mar* (1927).

[6]*Album...*, pp. 76-79.

Opposition and the Replies

An Assembly subcommittee in 1929 had answered complaints that further investment in the Carretera al Mar threatened to siphon funds from other needed road projects in the department and bring economic ruin to the departmental railroad recently completed between the Río Magdalena and Medellín.[7] It held to the position that an outlet to the sea lying entirely within Antioquia's jurisdiction was vital to the department, providing detailed economic justification of the Carretera al Mar in terms of projected traffic densities and earnings. The project was seen not only as catering to Antioquia's regional interests, but as part of a highway link between Bogotá and the Atlantic and eventually of the Pan American Highway.

Of the $15 million estimated as necessary to complete the work, the $3 million for the construction of the port would come from the national government. Bogotá would continue to provide a $20,000 per kilometer subsidy ($6 million) and Antioquia had been authorized by Congress to collect tolls from users which optimistically might yield as much as $4.3 million a year. The rest of the funds would come from the sale of departmental bonds in the United States. With the initiation of a second front of construction on the gulf and the generally easier topography of the coastal zone, costs were expected to be well below the $40,000 per kilometer allowed for the earlier sections. It was proposed that tolls be limited to 5 cents per ton/kilometer, which would be a charge on top of truckers' estimated operating costs of 10 cents per ton/kilometer.[8] Nowhere, however, was mention made of the cost of road maintenance, which in later years was to become such an important consideration.

The optimism of the road's supporters surprisingly centered especially on the cotton-growing potentialities of the area to be served. The possibilities of growing high-quality cotton had been sufficiently demonstrated for the Dabeiba district in a rain-shadow of one of the Andean spurs, but the idea that cotton would be a suitable crop for the extremely wet llanuras that lay beyond could hardly have been more erroneous. It had even been suggested that the government appoint a cotton expert when the road reached Dabeiba, along with a planner to lay out the projected new port of Neococlí. The suggestion that the giant textile mills of Medellín might have been supplied from the Occidente is difficult to conceive today,

---

[7]*Carretera al Mar, la salvación de Antioquia: Informe de la Comisión que estudió un memorial de D. Emilio Restrepo Callejas* (Medellín, 1930).

[8]Ibid.

when Colombia's cotton comes almost entirely from the vast alluvial plains of the Magdalena, Sinú, and César valleys, but the argument seems to have been one of the most important ones for justifying the construction of the new road. Modern Dabeiba (municipio population 23,000 in 1964) is known for its kidney beans; cotton is no longer a commercial crop there.

The Carretera al Mar was seen as opening a vast new zone of the country to settlement, supplying products to both domestic and foreign markets. Here were "some 35,000 square kilometers of selva awaiting the hand and intelligence of man to be converted into productive coffee plantations, fields of maize, rice and cacao, and into *cañadas* of tagua. Its forested slopes would support productive cattle farms, its subsoil lucrative gold mines and oil fields."[9] Had not this been the area selected by Pedrarias and Balboa for the first Spanish settlement on the mainland? What did it lack today? Only the Antioqueño *alma* or spirit! The 5,000 Antioqueños who each year emigrated to other departments in search of new land could here be provided with land at home. The road-building project, by providing work for a growing number of unemployed, could at the same time help to resolve a serious unemployment problem. "Colombia," it was said, "urgently needs to assert its sovereignty over this coveted part of the national territory, at least as important as Catatumbo, to which Congress has in the past given so much preferential attention."[10] Antioquia was compared with landlocked Bolivia, which had developed an access to the sea under much more difficult conditions. The honor and reputation of both the department and the country was at stake.

Why, asked Emilio Robledo, had the colonizing spirit of the Antioqueños permitted these lands to be so long unoccupied?[11] The true "matriz colonizadora" of Antioquia had been the *Oriente*, the high plateau country south of Medellín. It was a general principle of colonization that emigrants seek environments similar to those from whence they have come, in this case higher lands with healthy climate and fertile soil, without an aboriginal population, and with no full-flowing rivers to interrupt their movements but rather quiet streams that could easily be crossed by country people unaccustomed to swimming. Although the Antioqueños had moved first to the south, then across the Cauca to the southwest, he observed, the

---

[9]*Album...*, p. 17.

[10]Ibid., pp. 17.

[11]Ibid., pp. 94-95.

fiebre colonizadora (colonizing fever) was not yet extinguished and with the growing shortage of land they could be expected to move into the Occidente and towards Urabá once adequate access was provided.

It was a time for stirring rhetoric. Robledo, a physician, historian, botanist, and politician, had spoken of the "Mare Nostrum," the vindication of Balboa's judgment, and the need of the Antioqueño people for an open window to the world on their own coast.[12] A letter signed by 11 former governors of Antioquia and addressed to the president of the Republic declared that the Carretera al Mar was "a life and death matter" for Antioquia.[13] It was, they said, "as the cry of a people asphyxiating in a rockbound natural prison asking the public powers to save them that they might serve Colombia."

A Long Hiatus

Such eloquence, however, seems to have been without avail. The Great Depression was setting in and further financing of the project seemed out of the question. The work had been spread out over 270 kilometers between Medellín and Mutatá when it had stopped at the end of 1929.[14] Vehicles could reach to a point 14 kilometers beyond Santa Fé de Antioquia and with completion of the cut at the Boquerón de Toyo would soon be able to reach Cañasgordas. Some $8.4 million had been spent, chiefly between Medellín and Cañasgordas. Beyond Cañasgordas there was an improved horse trail to Pavarandocito. An early attempt to bring heavy construction equipment in from Pavarandocito to Dabeiba over what was known as the *camino industrial* had been abandoned, but the time required to travel from Dabeiba to Pavarandocito had been cut from three days to one.

Although the financial crisis had all but halted further work on the highway, local interests apparently continued to advance the project as time and money permitted. His unbridled enthusiasm for "la promesa de Urabá" had led Gonzalo Mejía to offer a prize of 5,000 pesos for any car reaching Turbo from the interior. On April 21, 1932, two Model A Fords, driven by three Brazilian adventurers under the patronage of Henry Ford, arrived from Medel-

---

[12]Ibid., p. 91.

[13]Ibid., p. 81.

[14]*Informes del Gerente de la Carretera al Mar* (Medellín, 1930).

lín after a trip of 47 days and with the support of a brigade of 25 assistants to help ferry them across the rivers and to carry them through the intransitable sections and around the landslides.[15]   They had come from Patagonia and continued on by boat to Panamá, thence resuming their overland trip.   They eventually reached New York City, reputedly the first to perform such a feat.

The long hiatus in work on the Carretera al Mar seems to have coincided approximately with the return to power of the Liberal government in Colombia after 30 years of Conservative rule. Antioquia, politically Conservative and traditionally the object of jealousy and even resentment in Bogotá, seems not to have shared significantly in the highway developments associated with the reforms of 1931.[16]   During the period 1930 to 1946 the country's highway system expanded from 9,200 to 28,700 kilometers, but among the multiplicity of projects supported by the national government the Carretera al Mar was noticeably absent.   The department, hopelessly mired in railroad debts, was unable to proceed with the work.

Colonization Along the Route

Much attention continued to be given to encouraging settlement along the route of the Carretera al Mar even after construction work had been suspended.   In contrast to the vigorous and spontaneous colonization in other areas, inducements here seemed to be necessary.   A Departmental Assembly bill in 1930[17] to promote "the colonization of Urabá" provided for the establishment of an agricultural colony at the Río Apurrumiandó (km. 277) to be known as Villa Arteaga, after the Carmelite priest from Turbo who had been an active proponent of the highway project.   The site was at the terminus of road construction at the time and was said to be healthful and malaria-free, but some thought that such a colony might better have been established on the coast, at Necoclí.[18]   At intervals of 5 kilometers beyond Villa Arteaga way-houses were to be con-

---

[15]*El Colombiano*, (Medellín), 12 junio, 1954.

[16]Donald S. Barnhart, "Colombian Transport and the Reforms of 1931," *Hispanic-American Historical Review* (1958), 38:12 ff.

[17]Decreto 33.   On this see also *Album...*, pp. 27-31 and Luis M. Gaviría, **Urabá** (1930), pp. 148-152.

[18]Muñoz, *Problemas de Urabá*, p. 71.

structed, with the buildings and land to be given to settlers with the provision that they should provide shelter to any colonists who might pass by. Tools, food, and financial aid were given to homesteaders. A 1931 law promised the Villa Arteaga settlers a house, medical services, 50 hectares of land, cacao and banana plants for 3 hectares, and *jaragua* (*Hyparrhenia rufa*) or Guinea grass (*Panicum maximum*) seeds, together with the loan of a milch cow whenever pasturage might be available. It was stipulated that 5 of the 50 hectares must be cleared within the first year. Revised lists of provisions and privileges for new colonists were issued in 1936[19] and again in 1939,[20] but relatively few settlers seem to have come to take advantage of the opportunities. Of those who did as many may have been from the Sinú and the Chocó as from the interior of Antioquia. One observer of the time saw Urabá as "a land of Negroes, Indians and even whites who, far from considering themselves Antioqueños, heartily dislike them."[21] The new generation of frontiersmen, reminders of "that glorious legend that colonized southwestern Antioquia in the last century," was disappointingly slow in making an appearance. Now the attraction of empty lands had to compete with the jobs and bright lights of industrializing Medellín.[22]

Such interest as there was in Urabá lands seems to have been along the coast, by persons from the Montería area with lumbering and livestock interests. Through purchase of government bonds it was possible to gain title to baldíos, and beginning in 1911, with a 1,209-hectare grant to an immigrant Lebanese, Nezir Yabur, the municipio of Turbo was one of the most active areas in the country for such land transactions. More than 100 such "purchases" were recorded for Turbo land in the following decade, some of them in 2,500-hectare blocks.[23] Some, in the Río San Juan district behind Arboletes, reflected the expanding Sinuano settlement frontier; others, as those behind Necoclí and Turbo, involved "leap-frogging" across an intervening forested wilderness to the little nuclei of settlement and livestock-fattening potreros on the gulf shore.

---

[19]Ordenanza 1.

[20]Ordenanza 34.

[21]*El Colombiano* (Medellín), 12 junio, 1954.

[22]According to the census returns the population of the municipio of Turbo actually declined slightly between 1938 and 1951, from 10,489 to 10,434.

[23]*Memoria*, Ministerio de Industrias (Bogotá, 1931), Vol. 3.

In 1923 the town of Turbo requested, and 3 years later it received, a grant of 5,120 hectares of baldíos (La Trinidad) near Apartadó as an "in lieu" award for that given it in 1840 but never distributed.[24] Another 4,000 hectares was shortly thereafter given to the municipio for allocation to "qualified heads of families" in the San Juan-Arboletes district. the records of distribution of such grants have not been found; lands not distributed within a few years apparently returned to the public domain of the nation.

The departmental government, too, participated in the largesse when, in 1930, it was given title to 100,000 hectares of unsurveyed land in the Necoclí area, bounded on the south by the Cuna Reserve and on the east by the Río Mulatos.[25] The grant was to be used not only to promote agricultural settlement but to encourage the establishment of new towns near the proposed terminus of the Carretera al Mar, which was then pushing northward from Medellín. A maximum of 200 hectares was to be allowed each colono, 500 hectares if the land was to be employed for stock raising. But there seem to have been previous conflicting grants in the area, including subsoil rights to coal and petroleum, and the survey and adjudication of these lands was long delayed. Indeed, it is unclear that they were ever carried out.[26]

The plantation of *Hevea* rubber established during World War II at Villa Arteaga with the aid of the United States Rubber Development Corporation failed to live up to expectations. It seems to have had little influence in the economic development of the area, although *"El Cauchero,"* as the plantation is known, was for some years the terminus of the uncompleted Carretera al Mar. After a long period of administrative abandonment its 65,000 trees, less than a third of which continued to be tapped, were placed under the administration of the Sociedad Antioqueña de Agricultores in 1966.

Beginning in 1944 the Fonda de Fomento Agrícola provided farm supplies at cost and also administered crop-purchase programs to protect small growers from unscrupulous middlemen at Mutatá, Pavarandocito, Turbo, Necoclí, Arboletes, and other sites. Most recently the Instituto Colombiano de Reforma Agraria (INCORA)

---

[24]Ibid., 4:32.

[25]Ibid, 3:536 and Ley 5, 1930. This land had originally been reserved some six years earlier, apparently as a hydrocarbon reserve. See Lay 72, 1925, and Resolución Executivo 50, 15 octubre, 1924; also, *Diario Oficial* (Bogotá), No. 20028, 25 octubre, 1925.

[26]Ordenanza 43, 1938, ordered the survey of the 100,000 hectares.

has been providing support to new and established settlers, chiefly by providing credit for livestock purchases, building access roads, and aiding in the registry of land titles. Crop-purchase programs continue, now under the Instituto Nacional de Abastecimiento (INA).

The Highway Completed

Completion of the last stretch of the Carretera al Mar, topographically the easiest, had to await the end of World War II. The return to power of a Conservative national government coincided with the initiation of work, but whether this was a consideration of significance is by no means clear. It was nearly 10 years, in 1954, before the first vehicles got through to Turbo from Medellín. A shipment of 15 tons of German barbed wire was waiting in the gulf ready to provide the first foreign imports into the interior of Antioquia on the highway that had been 28 years in building.[27] There seems to have been no rush to take advantage of the new route. The proposal to extend the work to Necoclí was shelved. Turbo would do for now, and it was hoped that the diversion of the lower Río Turbo to an artificial channel slightly to the north would substantially reduce the silting in Turbo bay as well as protect the townsite of Turbo from the periodic flooding to which it had always been subject.

The failure of the national government to create a deep-water port at Urabá has been much criticized in Antioquia, but the shoalness of the gulf waters and their rapidly shifting bottom sediments have posed disheartening barriers to all such developments. Juan Enrique White had proposed a port development at the mouth of the Río León which, unlike the Atrato, is building no delta and has a relatively stable, tide-scoured mouth with depths of 10 to 12 meters behind its bar for some 4 kilometers up river. It was here that the Granger interests had planned to construct the terminus for their railroad.[28] The Consorcio Albingia a few years later was to opt for a long wharf on the open cost to the north. Others were to urge the dredging of the bay at Turbo or the construction of a mile-long pier at Punta de Vacas. Extension of the Medellín-Turbo road to deep

---

[27] *El Colombiano* (Medellín), 12 junio, 1954.

[28] In 1911, when congress adopted a measure to promote the navigation of the Río Atrato, an unsuccessful attempt was made to include a small appropriation for the improvement of the Río León. The rejection of this proposal, together with a proposed ordinance to encourage colonization along the León, has been laid to regional rivalries (Juan Enrique White, *Historia del camino nacional...*, p. 14).

water at Necoclí and erection of a modern port there is inevitable in the long run. Engineering studies in 1967 put the cost of such a port at $4.2 million (U.S.). A car-ferry service to Panamá was also being contemplated.

As the shortest route from the coffee-growing district of interior Antioquia and Caldas to the Caribbean coast, the Urabá corridor would seem to offer logical outlet for at least some of Colombia's coffee exports. But the warehouse at Punta de Vacas built by the coffee-growers' federation has never been used for that crop. The big ships will not call at Turbo until there is a guarantee of cargo and of adequate wharfage facilities; only the banana and lumber ships, which load from lighters, enter the Gulf of Urabá.[29] Meanwhile, Colombia's principal export crop continues to move out either by the much longer highway to Cartagena and Barranquilla or by truck and rail to Buenaventura on the Pacific.

In the first years after the opening of the Carretera al Mar stock-raising on potreros hewn out from the rain forest continued to be the most important land use, especially on the outwash piedmont plain between Turbo and Mutatá. Settlements along the route grew in size, but rather slowly. There was no market at the end of the road. It was, in effect, a very long "vía de penetración," and costs of transporting crop surpluses to interior markets absorbed most or all of the potential profits. Places bypassed, such as Frontino, Murindó, and Pavarandocito, stagnated or declined in population. In the case of Frontino the shutting down of the English-owned mine was equally responsible. The town of Pavarandocito, inhabited mostly by Negroes who were part-time tagua-nut collectors, was burned in 1951 in connection with the political *violencia* (violence) and the offices of the municipio moved to Mutatá on the highway.

From the beginning road maintenance proved difficult and costly beyond expectation. Although landslides and washouts still

---

[29]The complexity of the hydrology of the Gulf of Urabá is associated with the enormous amounts of fresh water and sediment that debouches into it. The Siemens-Baunion Survey of 1924 estimated the average daily flow into the gulf from the Atrato at 144 million cubic meters, and from the León at 13 million cubic meters. *Esbozo de un plan de desarrollo para la región de Urabá*, Planeación Departamental de Antioquia (Medellín, 1964?), p. 78. Most of the suspended sediment, estimated at the equivalent of 23,000 cubic meters daily, is carried out to sea by tidal currents and the northward-flowing surface flow that this great volume of water produces. During the first months of 1966 when the rivers were at an exceptionally low stage United Fruit Company banana boats were reported unable to use their accustomed anchorage in Bahía de Colombia at the southernmost end of the gulf, but were instead forced to stand for loading well to the north and west. The increased time required to deliver the fruit alongside forced the company to obtain the services of extra barges and an extra tugboat.

regularly interrupt traffic through the 9-month rainy season, sometimes for weeks at a time, the mobile bulldozer units based at Dabeiba have proven remarkably effective in keeping traffic moving. Bridges have had a high mortality rate; there are 38 of them between Mutatá and Turbo. Their original specifications were in no way adequate for the more than 500 heavy vehicles that traverse the route daily. This traffic is certain to increase substantially in the years immediately ahead if the road can be maintained in a passable condition. Major realignments, which would involve the virtual rebuilding of the mountainous sections, were being planned in 1966 with financial aid being sought from international development agencies. The Boquerón de Toyo and the 50-kilometer stretch between Pegadó (near Dabeiba) and Mutatá were to receive top priorities.

The Pan American Highway Controversy and the Atrato Route

There has been much controversy and uncertainty both in Panamá and Colombia regarding the route to be followed by the proposed Pan American Highway link between the two countries. Completion of the "Darién Gap" (Tapón del Darién), the last remaining break in the road system that will eventually link the Americas from Alaska to Patagonia, is of much more than local interest. The original agreement to join the highway at the border point of Aspavé, near the Pacific Coast, was modified in 1959 when Palo de Letras, farther to the east, was adopted as the border crossing. Early explorations had eliminated the idea of a route directly across the extensive swamp areas of the Río Atrato valley in Colombia from consideration. Subsequent investigations were generally confined to the Pacific or western coast of the Colombian Darién. Eventually the most southern of the locations considered was recommended for the route of the Pan American Highway. This Colombia *ruta del sur* (southern route), now under final survey, will be a 540-kilometer road from Caldas across the Atrato headwaters to the Pacific at Bahía Solano and thence northward to the Panamanian border. Almost its entire distance is through uninhabited rain forest, making this internationally financed highway project a true "vía de penetración" for the opening of the Chocó.

Antioquia has strongly contested this circuitous official routing, arguing instead for a 96-kilometer short-cut across the Atrato swamps that would branch off from the Carretera al Mar near Chigorodó, ferrying the lower Atrato at Sautatá to reach Palo de

Letras (Fig. 8.1).[30] A 10-kilometer canal for crossing the worst of the swamps has been proposed on which the same ferry employed for the Atrato crossing might be used. This northern route might eventually become a part of the proposed Caribbean Circuit (Transversal del Caribe), a branch of the Pan American Highway that would link, through Turbo, with Barranquilla, Santa Marta, and eventually Caracas. (In early 1966 INCORA initiated work on a road that will link Turbo with El Carmelo [Arboletes] and so with Montería and Barranquilla.)

The Colombian Congress in 1959 (Ley 121) agreed to give equal priorities to the two routes hinging on Palo de Letras insofar as its own appropriations are concerned, at the same time supporting the ruta del sur as the "official" route. Antioquia has vigorously protested that the Ministry of Public Works in Bogotá has consistently ignored Ley 121 and continued to support only the much longer Bahía Solano route.[31] It has been charged, too, that the exclusion of the Carretera al Mar from participation in gasoline-tax monies is another example of the prevalent bias against Antioquia among national government agencies.

The practicality of the Atrato crossing has long been doubted. However, an engineering study undertaken in 1964 and 1965 by the United States Bureau of Public Roads, in cooperation with the Colombian Ministry of Public Works, has indicated the feasibility of an earth-fill viaduct across the entire breadth of the swamps between the Río León and the Río Atrato.[32] It would take advantage of the high ground of the flanks of the Lomas Aisladas, the forest-covered andesitic hills that lie 36 kilometers south of the southern end of the gulf and midway between the León and Atrato. These deeply-weathered hills would provide the fill material for the viaduct, which would reach the Atrato opposite the mouth of the Río Cacarica, 10 kilometers above Sautatá. Soil probes and electrical conductivity tests show a surprisingly and consistently firm sand zone, impregnated with salt, at depths of 7 to 10 meters below the surface layer

[30]Jorge Restrepo Uribe. *Antioquia: Olvidada, marginada y resentida* (1964), pp. 5-50. It was estimated that the project could be completed in three years at a cost of some $3 million (U.S.).

[31]Ibid.

[32]Organization of American States, Pan American Highway Congresses Permanent Secretariat, *Final Act and Appendices, Eighth Meeting, October 12-22, 1965*, Washington, D.C. (Pan American Union, Washington, D.C., 1965), "Río Atrato Reconnaissance and Route Location Survey," pp. 159-253.

of water-soaked organic muck and peat. This sand, not found in earlier tests further to the north, is interpreted as representing the old sea floor, dating from a time when the gulf was much larger than it is today.

The first 9 kilometers has been completed from the Carretera al Mar at Guapá to the Río León. Beyond colonos have already invaded the route of the proposed right-of-way for at least 20 kilometers beyond the León, which has not yet been bridged. In 1966 all work on the project was in suspension for lack of funds.

The Panamanian government has shown little disposition to push construction of the remaining 300 kilometers of the highway on their side, in part because of the uncertainty regarding both the proposed Río Bayano reservoir and the second interoceanic canal, for which the Sasardi route in eastern Panamá is a strong candidate. In Colombia surveys for the ruta del sur are well advanced. Both countries await international financing of this last and most difficult section of the Pan American Highway. The Antioqueño interest in completion of the Atrato "short-cut" to link with the Carretera al Mar seems to derive in part from regional pride and map logic, in part from the suspicion that only through its incorporation into the country's network of Class I roads in this way will funds for the badly needed realignment and paving of the Medellín-Turbo road be forthcoming from Bogotá.[33]

---

[33]Editor's note. Road development since 1967 has been minimal; however in 1988 the Urabá region, with a population well in excess of 100,000 and growing, is one of Latin America's more important banana-growing areas.

9

Seventeenth-Century Colonization of San Andrés and Providencia and the Caribbean Coast of Central America*

Introduction

The coral-girt islands of San Andrés and Providencia stand alone in the vastness of the Caribbean Sea, 300 miles from the Colombian coast, 110 miles from the mainland of Central America, and 250 miles southwest of Jamaica (Fig. 9.1). On a clear day the towering peaks of Providencia can be seen from San Andrés, 48 miles to the south.

First settled in 1629 by English Puritans and later by Jamaica planters and woodcutters with their Negro slaves, both islands came under Spanish rule by a convention signed in London in 1786. When, a few years later, Spain's New World empire went to pieces these islands fell unnoticed and almost by default to the new Republic of Colombia (New Granada). Their position suggests that they should belong to Nicaragua; their cultural affinities are with the British West Indies and North America; but in political reality the 6,000 English-speaking Protestant islanders still remain, after 130 years, the more or less contented subjects of the third most populous of the South American republics.

San Andrés, the larger and more populous of the two (population 3,705 in 1951), is one continuous coconut garden 8 miles long and from 2 to 3 miles wide. From the sea it has the appearance of a cresting green whale, its 300-foot high backbone smooth and

*Reprinted from *San Andrés and Providencia: English-Speaking Islands in the Western Caribbean*, University of California Publications in Geography, Vol. 12, No. 1, pp. 1-2, 4-13, 55-57, Berkeley (1956).

110

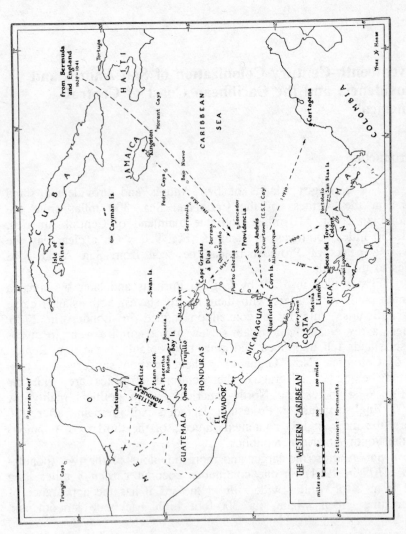

Figure 9.1 Location of San Andrés and Providencia

unbroken until it terminates abruptly at a high, cavernous limestone cliff toward the north. At the foot of the cliff lie the well-populated North End flats, covered with coconut palms but interrupted here and there by small areas of mangrove swamp, now largely cut over for firewood. The west coast of San Andrés is fringed with a scarped ironshore platform, a dark gray lithified marl with a bare, metallic-ringing surface, etched by solution into jagged, karstic[1] forms. On the opposite, windward side brilliant white sandy beaches are lapped by the sun-warmed waters of the shallow coral lagoon which provides shelter to ships and fish for island tables. Off the northeast shore, but within the protection of the fringing reef, are several islets planted to coconut palms.

A rugged interior lends interest and diversity to the landscape of Providencia (population 1,970 in 1951). In appearance it has been likened to some of the Marquesas group.[2] From its 1,190-foot summit, covered with bracken and tree ferns, is seen a jumble of lesser peaks from which spurs radiate toward the sea to terminate in precipitous, sometimes cliffed, coasts. Most of the agricultural land lies either within the small valleys tucked into the folds of these spurs or in a swale of lower-lying country across the southern third of the island, between Bottom House and Southwest Bay. The rocky headland of Santa Catalina to the north, separated from the main island mass by a tidal channel, is wooded and unused except for a few coconut gardens on the gentle south slope, which faces the harbor. The yellow-flowered cockspur bush (*Acacia costarricense*), its ripe pods characteristically overrun by black ants, is still found in extensive stands as an English visitor saw it 120 years ago, but no longer are there the giant fustic, ironwood, or machineel trees, or the

---

[1]The ironshore is swept by waves only during periods of high seas, but its fretted surface is completely devoid of unconsolidated sediment or vegetation, so that it is extremely difficult to walk over. Its origin may be associated with uplift or with a recent eustatic lowering of sea level, or it may develop simply from the action of waves on outcropping edges of limestone. Where waves attack the edges they may undercut the hardened zone into the marl, the upper part calves off, and the typical scarp is produced. This same shore phenomenon, widely associated with limestone islands within tropical seas, is called "promenade rock" by Steers, who observed it on Morant and Pedro Cays and on the Low Wooded Islands off Queensland (Steers, 1940a:29-30; 1940b:309-310). It has recently been described as the dominant shore form of the Cayman Islands (Doran, unpublished Ph.D. dissertation, 1953). Steers noted that it is confined to windward coasts, but on San Andrés it is on the lee side, which is also the side unprotected by a fringing reef.

[2]Fowler, 1944:122

"cedars which will square 20-24 inches."[3]   In their place are pastures of planted Para and Guinea grass which reach to the crests of all but the highest and rockiest slopes.   McBean's Lagoon on the northwest coast is the only considerable area of mangrove swamp....

The low-lying, reef-strewn, and rainy Caribbean coast of Central America held few attractions for the Spaniards in the six-teenth century.   They were already fully engaged to the north in New Spain, to the south in Peru, and in the volcanic uplands that lie between.   During most of the colonial period the only permanent Spanish establishments between Yucatan and Portobelo were the fortified ports of Omoal and Trujillo on the Bay of Honduras, ports of entry into the interior highlands where there were large and tractable Indian populations, a more attractive climate, and mines of precious metals.

The hazards of a shoal coast, the absence of good harbors, and the dishearteningly heavy rainfall must have contributed to the Spaniards' disinterest.   Ships from Cartagena or Portobelo destined for Havana or Veracruz, while keeping well out to sea, still had to maintain a constant lookout for the shoals of Roncador, Serrana, and Serranilla, which were feared at least as much as the English, French, and such privateers.   The isolated limestone mass of San Andrés and the neighboring volcanic peak then known as Santa Catalina must have been familiar and welcome landmarks to seamen, helping to guide them through dangerous and poorly charted waters. To an occasional vessel in distress they may have offered shelter, fuel wood, and fresh water, yet Spain first expressed an interest in occupying the islands only after the English had established a colony there in the seventeenth century and had begun successfully to harass Spanish shipping from them.

Just when these lonely islands were first discovered and by whom is not recorded.   The popular notion that they were visited and named by Columbus is patently erroneous.   If the Spanish custom of naming places after the saint's day on which they were discovered is recalled, it may be reasonably presumed that both islands were first visited by the same expedition, for on the church calendar Saint Catherine's Day falls on November 25 and Saint Andrew's Day only 5 days later.[4]   That they had been noted and

---

[3]Collett, 1837:207.

[4]The islands can scarcely fail to have been known to the Spanish captains whose vessels were carrying *pan de cassava* from Jamaica to the Ojeda-Nicuesa expedition on Tierra Firme beginning in 1510. Jamaica was originally granted to Ojeda and Nicuesa as a supply base for their isthmian operations, it being easier to reach

named by 1527 is certain, for they appear upon the anonymous *Carta Universal* of that date as "S.:catalina" and "S.:andrés."[5] Serrana Bank also appears as "la serrana" on the same map and in its approximately correct position. The same three names are also found on the Jean Rotz manuscript world chart of 1542, although San Andrés is rendered "Santades."[6] The Corn Islands, off the coast of Nicaragua, appear as "Manglares" on the Cornelius Wytfliet map of 1597, and by 1601, Roncador, Quitasueño Bank, and San Millán (Swan Island) are also placed and named on the Herrera map.[7]

"Old Providence," as Santa Catalina came to be known, was the first of the three English Providences. There has been a curious and widespread confusion in the records between it and the island of New Providence in the Bahamas (Columbus's "Abacoúä), so named in 1666 to distinguish it from the lately abandoned Caribbean island and the Rhode Island settlement of the same name.[8]

English Puritans on Providence

To the English and Dutch freebooters, who were roving about the western Caribbean in increasing numbers at the beginning of the seventeenth century, San Andrés and Santa Catalina must have been conspicuous landmarks. When the first English colonists were set down on them, in 1629, they found several Dutch smugglers and

---

Panama from there than from the others of the Greater Antilles. Morales Padró, 1952:65.

[5]Kohl, 1860. The original of this map, in the Grand Ducal Library at Weimar, Kohl believed to be the work of Hernando Colón. A 1529 edition of the same map bears the name of Diego Ribiero, Cosmographer to the King. It is reproduced in Academia Real de História (Madrid), 1951:29ff.

[6]This handsomely executed manuscript chart rests in the Map Room of the British Library (Royal MS. 20 E.XI, f.23[b]). Gerald Bonner, Assistant Keeper, has kindly checked the names on the original for me. A part of it is reproduced in Lynam, 1953:119.

[7]All these early maps are reproduced in an atlas published by the Guatemala Comisión de Limites, 1929.

[8]Wilkinson, 1933:332. For two hundred and fifty years the records of the Providence company were lost. They were discovered in 1876, erroneously catalogued under "Bahamas" in the Public Record Office, London (Sainsbury, 1877:148-149).

114

privateers already on the islands.[9]   One of them was a Captain
Blauvelt (Bluefields) who first suggested the feasibility of fortifying
the more northerly island.   For this he offered the assistance of his
Dutch comrades as well as his allies on the mainland, the Miskito
Indians, who were later to prove such faithful friends to the British.

The settlement of the islands followed by only 4 years the
issuance of the first crown letters patent for British colonists in the
Caribbean, on St. Kitts, Nevis, Montserrat, and Barbados.   Their
strategic position, lying deep within the Spanish seas and athwart the
trade routes of the galleons, was evident.   Yet the immediate factor
promoting the opening of this new colony appears to have been the
disappointing returns from tobacco on Bermuda, known since its
settlement in 1612 as "Somer's Island."   In the summer of 1629 the
London backers of the Somer's Island enterprise had a report from
the colony's governor that a group of his men had returned from a
privateering voyage through the Caribbean and that "Captain Camock
with 30 odd men is left upon an island called San Andreas, which is
a very fertile and hopeful place."[10]   A prior familiarity with the
islands is certain, for it was actually intended to occupy the more
readily defended "nearby island of Kathalina" which, the report
stated, ". . . differs much [from San Andreas] both in pleasantness
and the rich fertility of the soil."   These islands, the report continued, although they lay "in the heart of the Indies and in the
mouth of the Spaniards . . . in a short time could be made more
rich and more bountiful either by tobacco or any other commodities
. . . even if there are no gold or silver mines (which is very hopeful)."   One year here, it contended, would be more profitable than
seven in Bermuda.

Many of the same influential Londoners who had organized
the settlement of Massachusetts established, in 1629, "The Company
of Adventurers of the City of Westminster for the Plantation of the
Islands of Providence or Catalina, Henrietta or Andrea, and the

---

[9]The account of the Providence Company's activities in the following pages is
largely abstracted from Newton, 1914.   This exemplary study is based on the
manuscript copy of the Company's "Journal" and "Book of Entry" which fill two
thick folio volumes in the Public Record office, London.   They were copied in
1649 as an exhibit in a court case involving the company.   A microfilm copy of
this material has been placed on file in the Bancroft Library, University of
California, Berkeley.

[10]Capt. Phillip Bell to Sir Nathaniel Rich, April 28, 1629, quoted in Newton,
1914:31-34.

adjacent islands lying upon the Coast of America."[11]   These were businessmen intent on financial gain, either from legitimate commerce or speculation in privateering; they were also devout Puritans who saw here an opportunity to establish a refuge in the tropical seas at a time when the fear of encroaching Catholicism in England was high.   At the same time the islands offered a home for the discontented Bermuda settlers.   From the tone of the company's correspondence it appears that the project was judged more likely to succeed than the settlements being undertaken at the same time by John Winthrop in Massachusetts; yet these small islands lay more than 1,100 miles from the nearest English settlements on St. Kitts and Nevis.

During the next 12 years an enormous investment of money and effort was expended on the venture.   The first main body of colonists came from Bermuda directly to Providence.   Others soon arrived from Barbados, St. Kitts, and Tortuga.   The last named, a small island off the north coast of Hispaniola, had been specifically included under the company's charter because of its dyewood resources.[12]   In May, 1631, the first shipload of settlers to come directly from England arrived in the *Seaflower*.   Others followed. By the beginning of 1635 there were 500 white men, including several Dutchmen, 40 white women, and a few children living on Providence.

The role of the Dutch is as intriguing as it is obscure.   They were so numerous and influential that the London company felt obliged to order any Dutch place names on either of the islands replaced by others of English origin.   "Be careful," the directors wrote to the governor, "that you give them no interest in any land whatsoever, otherwise than as occupiers and manurers.   And, being of another nation you will do well to have a care what letters they send out of the island."[13]   Dutch vessels called frequently at Provi-

---

[11]Newton, 1914:86-87.   The limits within which the company's activities were originally confined were 1-20° N latitude and 68-88° W longitude.   The patent was later enlarged to 6-24° N so as to be certain to include Tortuga (Association); it included "all islands not being in possession of any other Christian prince" within this area.   This was to provide the legal basis for the later occupation of the Bay Islands and, perhaps, the Caymans.   Great Britain, Public Record Office, I:123; IX:72, 1860.

[12]By 1634, "Association," as the English called Tortuga, had become a rendezvous for rovers of all nations.   The plan to recruit English dyewood cutters from St. Kitts and Nevis had failed.   Newton, 1914:105-108.

[13]Newton, 1914:97.

dence throughout the Puritan occupation, and their infringement on the trade was a constant concern of the company directors. In 1637 a Dutch offer to purchase the island for 70,000 pounds was received, but after some deliberation was refused.

From the outset and by company decree the English called the more northerly, volcanic island Providence, a name which it has retained to the present day. In contrast the Puritan name for San Andrés, Henrietta, after the then reigning English Queen, was soon forgotten. (Although the official names are "Providencia" and "San Andrés," the islands still use the English forms "Providence" and "Saint Andrews," and it is as such that they are frequently described in the non-Colombian literature. I have preferred the Spanish spelling except in this chapter describing the seventeenth-century Puritan activities.) Actually, the original name for Providence, Santa Catalina, is still retained, but is applied only to the rugged northern headland separated from the main island by a tidal channel known as "the Bridge." Newton has shown that the two islands were originally linked by a neck of land.[14] In 1634 it had been advised that this be pierced in order to make Santa Catalina peninsula "a citadel." When the channel was finally dug and by whom is not clear, but it seems likely to have been by Spaniards some time after the Puritan departure from the island in 1641.[15] The English buccaneer Mansveldt is said to have linked Santa Catalina and Providence with a bridge about 1666, "intending to raise provisions on them for his whole fleet."[16] If another bridge was built in a later day it has long since disappeared. In 1809 the channel was described as being 8 *varas* (yards) wide.[17] Tidal scour has widened it nearly ten-fold since that date, although it is still reputed to be fordable at very low tide by a man on foot.

Although Henrietta (San Andrés) had been the first settled, the more easily fortified Providence soon became the focal point of Puritan activities. Here not only were the soils superior to those on Henrietta, but in addition there were several small streams that flowed throughout the year. After 1632 Henrietta was virtually abandoned except for transient woodcutters and boatbuilders who were attracted by the island's find stands of cedar. Yet the island

---

[14]Newton, 1914:53.

[15]Rowland, 1935:301-302, footnote.

[16]Jeffreys, 1775:16.

[17]Rivas, 1914:302.

had produced at least one good crop of tobacco.[18]   Later proposals
to resettle the island were not looked upon with enthusiasm by the
directors, who apparently considered it undefensible.   In 1635 a few
escaped servants from Providence were living there, and some salt
was being made for curing turtle meat.[19]

On Providence the settlers had dispersed around the entire
margin of the island as they are today.   For a time there were three
clergymen, each with his own church.   The principal settlement was
on the northwest coast opposite Catalina Harbor at the site of the
present Old Town.   Named New Westminster, it had a cluster of 30
wooden houses together with a brick church and a governor's house.
All trace of these structures has been obliterated; and the very existence of a Puritan colony on the island more than 300 years ago
remains unknown to all but a handful of the present-day inhabitants.

The scruples of some of the company's directors notwithstanding, tobacco was from the outset the principal export crop grown on
the islands.[20]   Some cotton was also shipped,[21] and there were
continuing experiments with other crops such as madder and indigo
in an attempt to find a high-value agricultural commodity marketable
in Europe.   The fertility of the lower volcanic slopes of Providence
seems to have particularly impressed the newcomers.   Among the
subsistence crops Indian corn, sweet potatoes, and "peas" (possibly
pigeon peas [*Cajanus indicus*], a prominent food crop on the island
today) were of principal importance.   In some cases three crops of
corn were taken during the course of a year.   The company's share
of all the provision crops was allotted to the fortifications workers,
but on at least one occasion it was necessary to bring surplus corn
from Tortuga.   For some reason cattle did poorly, but turtle meat
and fish were in abundant supply.

Financially the venture was a complete disappointment to its
backers.   The very isolation of Providence from the other English
settlements in America made communication difficult.   Company
ships which came laden with settlers and supplies could not always

---

[18]Newton, 1914:11.

[19]Newton, 1914:227-228.

[20]Newton, 1914:148-149.

[21]Two types of "wild cotton," one with short staple and one with long staple, were
found growing on the island. Seeds of each were ordered sent to England in 1635
(Great Britain, Public Record Office, I:302, 1860). Both of these varieties, as well
as others from Barbados and St. Kitts, seem to have been cultivated.

obtain a full cargo for the homeward journey, in part because of the illicit trade between the settlers and the Dutch vessels that visited the islands. There was, moreover, a labor shortage, for at times many hands were engaged in the construction of defenses. Emigrants recruited in England were divided by the company into three classes: the planters, who shared the product of their thirty- to fifty-acre plots equally with the company; the artisans, usually fortification workers, who labored for wages; and the indentured servants or apprentices who were allotted to the planters, the company supplying them with meat and drink[22]. Absentee landlordism was successfully avoided on Providence, for definitive land titles seem not to have been given. The company's control was absolute; all purchases had to be made in company stores; military service was obligatory for all settlers.

Although at the start a white yeoman colony was planned, Negro slaves soon began to appear on Providence, the first ones being introduced in 1633 from the company's dyewood works at Tortuga.[23] Four years later there were reported to be "nearly as many blacks as whites" on the island, most of whom had either been captured in the course of privateering expeditions against Spanish shipping or purchased from Dutch vessels that frequented Catalina Harbor.[24] The London directors cautioned that too many slaves would inevitably cheapen the white man's labor, and attempted without success to require the planters to take two white apprentices for each new slave imported. In 1638 a serious slave revolt occurred, which was put down only with difficulty. Three years later, when the Spaniards took the island, they listed 381 slaves among their captives.[25] Others undoubtedly escaped.

As English customs regulations increasingly interfered with the trade of the company, commercial relations with Massachusetts and Virginia became more and more important. Toward the end of the colony's brief history several shiploads of settlers arrived from Massachusetts. With one of these came 15 Pequot Indian boys and

---

[22]Newton, 1914:89.

[23]Newton, 1914:149. At least one colonist, Samuel Rishworth, began to promote abolition almost at once. He was reprimanded for assisting Negroes to escape.

[24]Newton, 1914:258.

[25]Rowland, 1935:300. The English accounts list close to 600 Negroes, together with much gold, indigo, and cochineal, as being taken (Newton, 1914:303).

2 Pequot women.[26] These Algonkian-speaking natives undoubtedly found other Indians already on Providence. The absence of any archaeological finds on either San Andrés or Providence suggests that neither of these islands was inhabited in pre-Columbian times, but during the Puritan occupation Miskito Indians from the adjacent mainland coast of Central America were accustomed to visit the islands at certain times of the year to fish and to hunt turtles. The company showed much concern that these visitors, skilled boastsmen by tradition, should be well treated and that no firearms or metal should fall into their hands. Although a request for permission "to procure Indian children from the Main, and a few men" was granted by the directors in 1633, no women were permitted to come over.[27]

Almost from the beginning of the colony the temptation to prey on Spanish shipping proved irresistible. Gradually the company directors came to recognize that profits and prizes to be won by privateering offered the only hope of balancing the books of the enterprise. As a result more and more effort went into the building of fortifications and less and less into agricultural and community activities. Slowly Providence was converted into a fortified base from which privateering warfare could be waged against all comers.[28] Open permission was finally granted by the directors in 1636 for "the taking of reprisals." A year earlier the Spaniards, recognizing the threat that Providence posed to their shipping, had made a first unsuccessful attempt to dislodge the English from the island.[29]

A second Spanish assault in 1640 was also repulsed, but in May of the following year a 12-vessel armada from Cartagena under the command of the distinguished admiral Francisco Díaz de Pimienta effected a beachhead on the lightly defended southeast shore of

---

[26]Newton, 1914:260.

[27]Great Britain, Public Record Office, I:148, 1860.

[28]Newton, 1914:121-122. The respect in which the English raiders were held is indicated by the account of the friar Thomas Gage, who traveled from Suerre (Costa Rica) to Portobelo and Panama in 1637. He wrote: "The greatest fear that I perceived possessed the Spaniards in this voyage was about the Island of Providence, called by them Santa Catalina or St. Catherine, from which they feared lest some English ships should come out against them with great strength. They cursed the English in it and called the island a den of thieves and pirates, wishing that their King of Spain would take some course with it." At Cartagena he reported seeing many Englishmen from Providence, presumably captives (Gage, 1928:370).

[29]Newton, 1914:187-208.

Providence. After a brief skirmish the force of some 600 soldiers marched upon New Westminster and two days later obtained the surrender of the garrison. The 500 captured defenders were sent as prisoners to Spain, the women and children were placed on board an English ship and dispatched to England, and the Negroes remained at the disposition of the invaders. When John Humphrey of Massachusetts, the last governor sent to Providence, arrived a few weeks later with a party of immigrants, he found the Spaniards in possession of the island and he could only return to New England.[30]

Although a financial failure, the Providence Company had continued the Elizabethan tradition of hostility toward Spain and exposed that country's weakness in the western Caribbean. It had also laid the foundations for British Honduras and set the stage for the occupation of Jamaica in 1655. In England it was much regretted that Providence was not available as a base from which to launch the "Western Design" of Warwick and Cromwell.[31] The latter was much influenced by the Providence Company directors, who looked upon war against Spain as revenge for their personal losses as well as a moral duty. Of the settlers who had escaped from the Spaniards at Providence, a substantial number had gone with Captain Samuel Axe to St. Kitts, from where they were later to play an important role in the capture of Jamaica. The remainder had dispersed either to Warwick's Tobago colony or to the Bay of Honduras and the Miskito Shore.[32] (The spelling Miskito [Miskito Shore, Miskito Keys, Miskito Indians] has been preferred here over the more common English usage, "Mosquito." The people from whom the geographical names derive were Miskito Indians [Conzemius, 1932]; confusion with the noxious insect has helped to give the area an undeserved reputation.)

---

[30]Wilkinson, 1933:258. Two shiploads of recruits from Boston were the last to arrive at Providence (Newton, 1914:292-293).

[31]Barbados was used in its place as a training and recruitment center for the ill-fated Santo Domingo campaign and the bloodless occupation of Jamaica that ensued.

[32]Newton, 1914:315.

Spanish Occupation and the Jamaica Buccaneers

For nearly 30 years after the ousting of the Puritans from Providence, Spain maintained a presidio there.[33] This was the only period in the island's history in which it was occupied by a predominantly Spanish-speaking, Catholic population. Instead of dismantling the English fortifications, as he had been instructed to do, Admiral Pimienta further strengthened them. It was clear that the strategically placed and readily defensible volcanic island would continue to be coveted by Spain's enemies. Moreover, he reported to his superiors, the island seemed to possess "great natural riches . . . including even a quicksilver mine." [sic][34]

The occupation force consisted of 150 Spanish and Portuguese soldiers under Governor Gerónimo de Ojeda, together with the Negro slaves who had been captured from the English.[35] There were bitter complaints that the garrison had been abandoned by the authorities in Cartagena. Supplies and reinforcement were regularly requested but rarely received. There seems to have been no policy of troop rotation, nor were the free colonists, slaves, and lewd women who were promised ever sent. After the English occupation of Jamaica the fear of attack from that quarter increased. In 1659 a Cartagena *junta* even considered abandonment of the island and the transfer of its depleted garrison to "San Martín" (possibly San Millán ?) as "a better base for the defense against the enemies of Spain,"[36] but the proposed move was not made.

The recapture of Providence was long an English ambition. The terms propounded by General Vanables to the Spaniards on Jamaica had been the same as were given "our English upon Providence," which was that all should leave the island.[37] But Jamaica's capture was considered only partial revenge for the humiliation of 1641. Cromwell wrote to the island's commander in 1655:

We think, and it is much designed amongst us, to strive with the Spaniards for the mastery of all those seas; and therefore

---

[33]Rowland, 1935.

[34]Rowland, 1935:300.

[35]Rowland, 1935:300.

[36]Rowland, 1935:304.12

[37]Newton, 1914:324.

122

we would heartily wish that the Island of Providence were in
our hands again, believing that it lies so advantageously in
reference to the Main, and especially for the hindrance of the
Peru trade and Cartagena, and that you might not only have
great advantage thereby of intelligence and surprise, but even
block up the same.[38]

Later Henry Morgan listed the island, together with Havana, Portobelo, Maracaibo, Cartagena, and Veracruz, as holding the key to the
control of the Caribbean.[39]   He dreamed of Providence, writes his
biographer, Adolphe Roberts, as a sort of pistol held perpetually at
the breast of colonial Spain, threatening as it would the vital line of
communications between the North and the South Seas.[40]
    Finally, on May 25, 1666, a substantial fleet of English
vessels from Jamaica under the old freebooter, Edward Mansveldt,
entered Catalina Harbor and after a brief encounter took the well-
fortified island.   At the time the English were at war with the
United Provinces, and the recapture of Providence seems to have
been in part a face-saving gesture resorted to after a plan to take
Dutch-held Curaçao had failed.[41]   Requests to Jamaica, Massachusetts, and Virginia for colonists brought only a small response,
and when a Spanish expedition from Cartagena recaptured the island
15 months later they found but 52 English there and the defenses
only partly rehabilitated.   The new Spanish garrison numbered about
450 persons, including soldiers, civilians and Negro slaves, but pleas
for food, ammunition, and more women settlers once more went un-
heeded.   Morale was such that when Morgan and his Port Royal
buccaneers approached the island in 1670, intent on taking it as a
base from which to launch an attack against Panama, the Spanish
commander surrendered without a fight.[42]   This time it was occupied

---

[38]Newton, 1914:323.

[39]Roberts, 1933:68.

[40]Roberts, 1933:6.

[41]Rowland, 1935:309.

[42]The Dutch physician Esquemeling is the best source for the action against Old
Providence.   An eyewitness, he described it as an arsenal with nine fortresses and
a total of 49 guns.   A stone castle called Santa Teresa was said to have thick
walls buttressed by earthworks, a dry moat 20 feet deep, and five separate
platforms for its 20 cannons.   Of the island he wrote: "Here is no trade or
commerce exercised by the inhabitants; neither do they plant more fruits than are

but briefly by the English. Then, for nearly 70 years, it was abandoned by both nations. In 1688 a Spanish expedition sent from Cartagena to reconnoiter the island and to subdue and populate it if such were deemed wise, reported that there were no signs of recent habitation either there or on San Andrés. The latter, low-lying and difficult to defend, appears to have been unoccupied since the departure of the Puritans a half-century previously.[43]

English Settlement on the Main and the Beginnings of British Honduras

The neighboring coasts of Central America, although visited by Columbus on his third voyage and later reconnoitered by occasional coasting expeditions, were left alone by the Spaniards. As early as 1633, on the other hand, English Puritans from Providence, under Sussex Camock, had established trade relations with the Miskito Indians, first on the Miskito Cays and at Cape Gracias á Dios and soon all along this low and swampy shore between Bluefields Bay and Trujillo.[44] The extensive natural stands of the long-leafed bromeliad *Aechmea magdalenensis* (pita floja) found here received much of their early attention. The first samples of the fiber sent to London were well received, and plans were formulated to undertake the large-scale exploitation of this "silk grass" or "Camock's flax." However, the initial enthusiasm soon waned, both because of the lack of interest of British weavers and because of the technical difficulties of separating the long, silk-like fibers from the fleshy pulp of the leaf.[45] A long list of minor trade items, such as

---

necessary for human life, though the country would make very good plantations of tobacco of considerable profit were it cultivated." Quoted in Roberts, 1933:148.

[43]Rowland, 1935:311.

[44]Newton, 1914:140-142; Great Britain, Public Record Office, I;163-64, 1860. The initial plan seems to have been to initiate trade with the Indians of Darién (Panama), who were known to possess gold. The expedition being organized for this purpose was instructed "to labour to possess them with the natural goodness of the English nation, restraining any boisterous carriage to the women...." At Darién they found three Dutch ships at anchor. There had been scuffles with the Indians so that the Puritans thought it out of the question at the moment to establish peaceful trade relations. It was this fact that led to the diversion of their interest to Cape Gracias á Dios (Newton, 1914:133).

[45]Newton, 1914:148. The directors wrote to Governor Bell that this silk grass is "vendible in greater abundance than you shall be able to send it to us and at a price that exceeds our hopes...." So promising did the business seem that in 1634

sarsaparilla (*Smilax*), lignum vitae (*Guaiacum*), cassia fistula, and animal and bird skins were also obtained, but there were, disappointingly, "no bezoar stones or manatee stones." Live birds and monkeys held a special attraction, the Providence Company directors even feeling obliged to order seamen to pay ten shillings for each parrot brought to England "so that the ships will not be unnecessarily pestered."[46] To the northward, on the coast of modern British Honduras, logwood was found growing in abundance, and this dyestuff soon became the primary concern of the Providence men who had gone to "the Bay" to trade and to raid.

The Providence Company in 1638 granted a formal patent to William Claibourne of Virginia to establish a colony on Ruatan (Roatán) Island, almost within sight of the Spanish fortress at Trujillo.[47] This short-lived, Puritan-sponsored settlement (Ruatan was abandoned in 1642) marked the beginning of English interest in the Bay Islands of Honduras, which continued for more than 200 years. At the same time trading stands ("stanns") were being established along the Coxcomb Coast of what is today British Honduras, at Stann Creek, Point Placentia, and on several of the off-shore cays. In 1638 as many as 600 Puritan seamen and colonists, with 200 Miskito Indians and 100 Negro slaves, were reported living on the coast.[48] Providence is the springboard from which the British occupation and claims to modern Belize originate.

As familiarity with these shoal waters of the Gulf of Honduras grew, the Providence men were augmented by buccaneers and traders from the other British settlements in America. Scotch and English adventurers from Nevis, reinforced by others from Providence, seem to have accompanied Captain Wallace (Willis ?) when he established the first settlement at the site of modern Belize in

---

a fresh patent was applied for and received. This patent granted exclusive rights to trade on the coast and to exploit the "Camock's flax," which was to pay duty "at the rate of the best wrought flax now brought into the Kingdom" (Newton:168). This fiber plant was planted, and with great hopes, on both Henrietta and Providence. In at least one instance it was "eaten by the cattle," a fact which the directors bemoaned in a letter to the governor (Great Britain, Public Record Office, I:237, 1860).

[46]Great Britain, Public Record Office, I:189, 1860).

[47]Newton, 1914:267. Winzerling, 1946:63, mentions the existence of Ruatan of the ruins of the fort built in 640-1641 by Captain Axe of Providence.

[48]Caiger, 1951:29; Winzerling, 1946:45. Unfortunately the original documentation is not given by either of these authors.

1640.[49] Wallace himself may have been a Providence Puritan; at least his expedition rendezvoused and organized there. Later, on the Main, he was apparently joined by others, including refugees from both Providence and Ruatan.

An indication of the extent of the Puritan activity on the Coxcomb Coast of Honduras is to be found in the numerous place names that have been traced to the activities of Providence men and their Miskito auxiliaries.[50] Such names as Silk Gradd Creek, Commis (Camock's) Bight, Tobacco Cay, Stann Creek, and The Bugles have been attributed to the Puritans; Miskito terms include Sittee River, Ranguana Cay, and Cape Piuta. Winzerling says that Swallow Cay, Point Jonathan, and Point Placentia (Patience) are all named for Puritan ships. The very terms "Bayman" and "Shoreman" appear also to have been of Providence origin, as do many of the names on the map of the Miskito Shore of modern Spanish Honduras and Nicaragua.

On the matter of the Englishmen's relations with the Indians the directors of the Providence Company had been explicit. "You are to endear yourselves with the Indians and their commanders," their instructions read, "and we conjure you to be friendly and to cause no jealousy."[51] The Indians were not to be provided with gunpowder; on the one occasion of a fight with the natives near Cape Gracias á Dios severe reproof was meted out from London. The friendship of the English with the Miskito Indians of the pine savanna country between Bluefields and Black River was to prove especially profitable. "Perhaps never," observes Newton, "has so lasting a friendship existed between Englishmen and a native race as that which . . . has subsisted between Englishmen and the Indian tribes of the Miskito coast."[52]

The London directors warned that if mainland Indians were to be employed by the settlers "it must be as free men drawn to work by reward and they must be entertained by king usage and be at

---

[49]Caiger, 1951:35-36.

[50]Winzerling, 1946:39-47, 81.

[51]Newton, 1914:142.

[52]Newton, 1914:143. The English had early persuaded the Miskito chief, whom they always were to refer to as "King," to send his son to England for three years, the first of many members of the "Royal Family" who were to be "educated" in London or Jamaica.

liberty to return at pleasure."[53]   According to Hans Sloane, many of
them learned only the Lord's Prayer, the Creed, and the Ten Com-
mandments while there, but for others English became a sort of
second tongue.[54]   Many shipped out on buccaneering expeditions as
"strikers" to supply fish or turtle for the mess table.[55]   On several
occasions in later years contingents of Miskitos were taken to
Jamaica, where they were employed in putting down slave revolts.

Only casual farmers, the Miskitos were superior boatmen and
fishermen, and their skills were soon put to use by the English to
raid the ill-manned Spanish establishments all the way from Yucatan
to Panama. For more than a century the harassed Spanish colonies
of Central America schemed and plotted to eliminate the "zambo and
Miskito scourge" and their English prompters, but an all-out effort
was never made. In the shallow waters of this exposed coast it was
clear that the Spaniards' lumbering galleons would be no ·match for
the fleet Miskito *canoas*, each manned by a dozen men. Even after
the suppression of English buccaneering, when all attention in the
north was focused on the profitable logwood trade, the Miskito raids
continued. A favored objective was the Matina cacao district of
Costa Rica, raided so regularly and with such success that the
government in San José at least once sued for peace by offering
substantial bribes to the Indian leaders if they would leave the
coastal plantations alone.[56]   Cacao, gold, Negro slaves, and even
Talamanca Indians were taken by the Miskitos, who carried them to
the English traders at Bluefields or Cape Gracias á Dios where they
were exchanged for rum and gunpowder.

The English settlers along this inside coast of Central America
were dependents of Jamaica in a loose and indefinite way from the
time when that island was occupied in 1655. The Governor of
Jamaica wrote to the Duke of Newcastle in 1739 that there were
about 100 Englishmen on the Miskito Shore, "mostly those such as

---

[53]Newton, 1914:144.

[54]Sloane, 1709, I:lxxvii.

[55]Dampier relates how, in 1681, a Miskito crew member had been inadvertently
left on uninhabited Juan Fernández Island off the coast of Chile by an English
vessel and how, three years later, when another ship stopped off there the first
man ashore was another Miskito Indian "striker" who, of course, greeted his
Robinson Crusoe countryman in the Miskito tongue. Dampier, 1927:65.

[56]Fernández, 1881-1907, X:304-307. The Miskitos ranged as far south as the San
Blas Islands, as the modern name for the waters off the north coast of Panama
(Mosquito Gulf) suggests.

could live nowhere else."[57] He proposed to bring all of them together into one settlement, hopeful that with the help of the Miskitos a general revolt against Spain might be induced. Accordingly, in 1740, he appointed Captain Robert Hodgson of Jamaica to the post of "Superintendent" of the Shore and shortly thereafter a formal cession of their lands to the jurisdiction of England was obtained from the Miskito chiefs.[58] Black River (Río Negro) became the principal English settlement on the coast. It was the only place where there were any English agricultural activities, and even here they were confined to five apparently small and unimportant sugar estates.[59] Other establishments were at Cape Gracias á Dios, Bragman's Bluff (Puerto Cabezas), Bluefields, the Corn Islands, Bonacca, and Ruatan. Tortoise shell, sarsaparilla, vanilla, and mahogany were the principal items of export. To the north the Baymen were cutting logwood and mahogany and, as the occasion permitted, harassing Spanish shipping and the ports of Omoa and Trujillo. The lagoons and estuaries of the Miskito Shore provided an accessible and friendly refuge for those woodcutters whenever the Spaniards launched one of their periodic campaigns to clear the English from Belize and Yucatan. Only in 1798, with the repulse of the Spaniards from St. George Cay off the mouth of the Belize River, was the English right to establish "plantations" in modern British Honduras at last clearly defined.[60]

In view of the strength of the long-established English position on the Shore, their neglect of the Nicaragua route to the Pacific is surprising.[61] It had quite clearly been a consideration in the original establishment of a formal government under Captain Hodgson, yet it was not until 1780 that the abortive attack on the Spanish *castillo* on the Río San Juan was finally launched. Six years later Spain obtained England's promise to evacuate their Miskito Shore and Bay Island settlements. It must have been conditions in Europe rather than any precariousness of the English toehold on the Central

---

[57]Manning, 1936:373.

[58]Manning, 1936:373.

[59]Kemble, 1884:45-46.

[60]Carey Jones, 1953.

[61]This failure to capitalize on the Nicaragua route was deplored by both Edward Long and Bryan Edwards, the two distinguished eighteenth-century historians of Jamaica.

American coast that dictated the 1783 Treaty of Versailles and the clarifying amendments of the Convention of 1786. In the final withdrawal, completed in 1788, there were 2,214 persons, including 537 free whites and 1,677 slaves, who were taken to Belize. With a lesser number of the descendants of the Providence and Jamaica logwood cutters already there, they formed the nucleus of the later colony of British Honduras.[62] Others appear to have gone to Jamaica, Grand Cayman, Providence, and San Andrés.

Thereafter the Miskito Shore was to remain abandoned to the Indians for nearly 30 years despite several unsuccessful attempts by Spain to establish settlers there. Meanwhile, San Andrés and Providence were slowly emerging from obscurity.

Literature Cited

Academia Real de História, Madrid
  1951. *Mapas españoles de América, siglos XV-XVII* (Madrid).

Burdon, Sir John (ed.)
  1931-1935. *The Archives of British Honduras*, 3 vols. London.

Caiger, S. L.
  1951. *British Honduras, Past and Present.* London.

Carey Jones, N. S.
  1953. *The Pattern of a Dependent Economy: the National Income of British Honduras.* Cambridge.

Collett, C. F.
  1937. On the Island of Old Providence. *Journal of the Royal Geographical Society* (London), 7:303-310.

Conzemius, Eduardo
  1932. *Ethnological Survey of the Miskito and Sumu Indians of Honduras and Nicaragua.* Smithsonian Inst., Bur. of American Ethnology, Bull. 106. Washington, D.C.

---

[62]Burdon, 1931-1935, I;4.

Dampier, William
1927. *A New Voyage Round the World [1697]*. London.

Doran, Edwin B., Jr.
1953. Physical and Cultural Geography of the Cayman Islands. Unpublished Ph.D. thesis, University of California, Berkeley.

Fernández, León (comp.)
1881-1907. *Colección de documentos para la história de Costa Rica*, 10 vols. San José.

Fowler, Henry W.
1944. *Results of the Fifth George Vanderbilt Expedition (1941): The Fishes*. Monographs, Academy of Natural Sciences of Philadelphia, 6:69-93.

Gage, Thomas
1928. *The English American; a New Survey of the West Indies, 1648*. A. P. Newton, ed. London.

Great Britain
1860-. Public Record Office. Calendar of State Papers, Colonial Series (America and West Indies). Vols. 1,9.

Guatemala (Republic)
1929. *Comisión de Limites. Cartografía de la América Central*.

Jeffreys, Thomas
1775. *The West India Atlas*. London.

Kemble, Stephen
1884. *Journals of Lt. Col. Stephen Kemble, Brigadier-General in Command of the Expedition in Nicaragua, 1780-81*. Coll. of the New York Historical Society, vol. 17.

Kohl, J. G., ed.
1860. *Die beiden altesten General-Karten von Amerika ausgefuhrt in den Jahren 1527 auf Befehl Kaiser Karl V. Weimer*.

Lynam, Edward
    1952. *The Mapmaker's Art. Essays on the History of Maps.* London.

Manning, W. R., ed.
    1963. *Diplomatic Correspondence of the United States; Inter-American Affairs, 1831-60.* Vol. 6, Washington, D.C.

Morales Padrón, Francisco
    1952. *Jamaica español.* Sevilla.

Newton, Arthur Percival
    1914. *The Colonizing Activities of the English Puritans.* New Haven.

Rivas, Raimundo
    1914. Algunos datos nuevos sobre las islas de San Andrés, Magles y Costa de Mosquitos. *Boletín*, Min. de Relaciones Extreiores (Bogotá), 7:301-320.

Roberts, W. Adolphe
    1933. *Sir Henry Morgan, Buccaneer and Governor.* New York.

Rowland, Donald
    1935. The Spanish Occupation of the Island of Old Providence. *Hispanic American Historical Review*, 15:297-331.

Sainsbury, Noel
    1877. "The Two Providence Islands," *Proceedings Royal Geographical Society* (London), 22:148-149

Sloane, Hans
    1709 *A Voyage to the Islands of Madera, Barbados, Nieves, S. Christophers and Jamaica*, 2 vols. London.

Steers, J. A.
    1940a. "The Coral Cays of Jamaica," *Geographical Journal*, 95:30-41.

    1940b. "Sand Cays and Mangroves in Jamaica," *Geographical Journal*, 96:305-323.

Wilkerson, Henry
    1933.   *The Adventurers of Bermuda.*   Oxford.

Winzerling, E. O.
    1946.   *The Beginnings of British Honduras.* New York.

10

Medellín Reconsidered[*]

It was more than a quarter of a century ago that I returned from my first trip to South America with a suitcase full of dissertation notes from field study in Colombia, especially the department of Antioquia and its capital city, Medellín. I had gone there with the idea of learning what I could about the coffee economy of the northern Andes but had been diverted, instead, to the phenomenon of the Antioqueños--the people of Antioquia--and to the configuration of their distinctive culture and the mark it had left on the land (Parsons, 1949).

The Antioqueños stand apart from other Colombians not only for the predominance of Spanish blood (although legend makes them Jewish, or Basque), but for their food, their dress, their language, their politics (traditionally Conservative), and their religion (profoundly Catholic). They are a culturally cohesive mountain people living in a very rugged part of the Andes, and their special breed of cattle, their ridge-top rural settlements, their fondness for tobacco and rum, are all part of the legend and folklore of the *paisas*, as they like to call themselves. Their distinctive surnames and the tendency to large and patriarchal families also tends to set them apart from other Colombians. So does their reputation for hard work, frugality and commercial acumen. These qualities were reflected initially (after 1790) in the moving frontier of colonization that carried them--with coffee later as the main cash crop--onto the steep, unoccupied volcanic slopes to the south, into Caldas, Tolima, the Quindío district and onto the slopes above the Valle del Cauca.

[*]Reprinted from Proceedings of the Conference of Latin Americanist Geographers, Vol. 5, pp. 119-124 (1976). (Originally titled: "The Historical Preconditions of Industrialization: Medellín Reconsidered.")

Most recently their attention has been equally directed towards the warmer lowlands of the Medio Magdalena, to the Bajo Cauca, the Sinú Valley, and Urabá.

They were derived from a relatively small band of early immigrants come from Spain in search of gold, who were from the first isolated by the rest of New Granada by barriers of mountains and rain forests and remained so until well into this century. An almost Puritanical work ethic was blended over the years into a certain entrepreneurial genius, widely recognized in Colombia, which eventually earned the Antioqueños the nickname "The Yankees of South America." In the nineteenth century they were associated first with mining and pioneer land clearing and then, in the early twentieth century, with a remarkable surge towards industrialization-- against all the odds of geography and economics--which was to make the mile-high valley of Medellín the first manufacturing city of the Republic. Most remarkably, it was a process begun when the city's only access to the outside world was by pack mule.

The obvious question was why and how this distinctive, energetic and innovative culture, in many ways so un-Latin, should have evolved when and where it did. After the initial boom in placer gold the Antioquia highlands had gone through two centuries of stagnation. In 1780 they were still being described as the most backward, poverty-stricken and isolated part of New Granada. But they were largely malaria-free, and racial conflict was at a minimum. There were few Indian survivors of the Conquista, and Negro slaves had been confined to the warmer, lower river valleys where the placer gold tended to be concentrated. The soils of the granitic batholith of Antioquia were thin and unproductive, and the slopes were inordinately steep, so that there was little interest in accumulating land and the resultant latifundia so characteristic elsewhere in Latin America. There were few large land grants made or sought. When capital did accumulate, there was no thought of putting it into land. Instead, it went into trade and, eventually, into manufacturing industry. Mining in particular fostered technological innovation and with coffee brought in a certain amount of foreign capital and technology and, most importantly, led to the establishment of credit institutions, accounting practices, and systems of business organization not previously known. Finally, although there were no local raw materials to support industrialization, there was an abundance of hydroelectric power potential and, perhaps, a willingness born of a miner's background for individuals to take the calculated risk. The result was an early and remarkably successful move towards industrialization that has attracted the attention of historians and social scientists seeking to understand how modernization comes to a predominantly peasant society in the face of imposing economic and geographic disadvantages.

The Antioqueño "Modo de Ser"

I was fortunate to have been one of the first to look at this phenomenon which in subsequent years has become a kind of *cause celèbre* among students of economic development. I owed much in my interpretation to the London-trained Colombian economist, Luis Ospina Vásquez, whose scholarly study *Industria y Protección en Colombia*, published in 1955, carried the analysis much further than I as a geographer had been able to do. Dr. Ospina's cultural and humanistic bias, together with his deep understanding of Antioquia and Colombia society, is revealed in a personal letter addressed to William McGreevey (3 December 1964):

I find myself in a certain impossibility of very clearly visualizing a purely theoretical solution of the problem of industrial development in Colombia in the decisive phase and local (in Antioquia, from the first years of this century). I saw it happen, I have known most of the people who had something to do with it, and several of them quite well....It sounds eerie to me to substitute some impersonal force for their actions, or to make them obey any very abstract call....There were certain necessary conditions--and promptings and stimuli--for the actions of these people--necessary for their action to take place, and for its success (even if at first it were a rather qualified success); these factors were financial, political, moral, mental, there was a great variety of them--but I cannot bring myself to think that they, or anything but the actions of the men who actually had the factories erected, "caused industrialization....That they did act and react in a certain manner, and a somewhat unexpected one, would then seem to depend on a peculiarity of the *"modo de ser."* Some rather similar circumstances, in other places, at the same time, or at other times, would not have elicited the same acts and responses.

After noting the importance of a favorable political climate and an adequate protective tariff, he goes on to observe:

That those men existed, that they found followers and collaborators, that they found acquiescence and even support from the many in Antioquia, more readily than elsewhere, was, I think, due to some "peculiarity of the [Antioqueño] *modo de ser,"* fostered, sharpened, among other factors, by the experience in mining ventures, the relatively large success in extending coffee planting....At bottom, nothing can explain why a man acts the way he acts better than his moral and mental make-up. And a phenomenon such as industrialization is an act of man, not the result of abstract forces.

It was one of these acts of man that the MIT economist Everett Hagan sought to explain in *On the Theory of Social Change*, published in 1962. In his widely cited chapter on the Antioqueños he attributes the entrepreneurial bent among their elite, on somewhat shaky evidence, to the high incidence of persons of Basque ancestry. Growth, he observes, began in spite of the supposed economic barriers, not because those barriers were removed. His explanation of the successful industrial take-off of Antioquia is a sternly psychological one. For him it was a response to the presumed "status deprivation" suffered by the Antioqueños until well into the nineteenth century. Smarting under an inferior social status, scoffed at, ridiculed, and disparaged by the aristocracy of Bogotá, he sees them reacting aggressively to seek status and to prove their worth in the only way that was open to them, through economic prowess in commerce and in industry.

A few years later, Frank Safford, Northwestern University historian, convincingly refuted the idea that nineteenth century Antioquia was either impoverished or burdened by a degrading stereotype (Safford, 1967). By the late colonial period, he showed, there was already a dynamic Antioqueño elite, active in commerce and gold mining, and, far from being snubbed and ignored by the ruling classes in Bogotá, that by the 1840s they controlled the major commercial houses there and were well integrated into the capital's society. The Magdalena River trade and the emerging tobacco monopoly was also in their grasp. From 1820 to 1870 Medellín was Bogotá's banker.

McGreevey, in his admirable *Economic History of Colombia, 1845-1920* (1971), took issue with previous interpretations, questioning that Antioquia benefited much from the rising gold production in the late colonial and early Republican period. Instead, he emphasized the critical role of the new coffee economy especially after 1880 in the origin of entrepreneurial leadership among the Antioqueños and the rapid development of manufacturing that began in the first years of the twentieth century. He also paid considerable attention to the transportation developments, especially railroad building, which was itself in substantial measure associated inextricably with the coffee boom.

Colombian students have given the case relatively little attention (Orlando Melo, 1969). Ospina Vásquez stands as a conspicuous exception. Two other Colombians, Luis Fajardo (1968) and Luis López Toro (1968), have recently reviewed the literature. In particular, they have refuted the suggestion that the Antioqueños reflected a kind of Weberian Protestant ethic, pointing out that instead they were the most devoutly Catholic of all Colombians. For example, the department produces more than half of the country's ordained priests, and mass is regularly attended by men and women in all classes of society.

Recent Antioqueño Studies

Recently French scholars, too, have plunged into the Antioqueño controversy. One group of priests, in an essentially Marxist interpretation, has emphasized the classic stratification and class conflicts within Antioquia, refusing resolutely to reach down to the level of individual human action. François Chevalier (1973), well known for his work on the Mexican hacienda, has also addressed the question in a perceptive essay on Medellín as a "pole of industrial development" in which, without rejecting the various hypotheses already cited, he places additional emphasis on agricultural development and the role of smaller-holder food producers in establishing the base from which the industry of the metropolis might arise. Other French workers have concentrated on the more recent aspects of the economic development of Medellín and its satellites (Herrero, 1970; Revel-Mouroz, 1973), including the impact of industrialization on the rest of the department. A cooperative research program on "Les villes et Regions en Amerique Latine" under the *Centre National de la Recerche Scientifique* has chosen Medellín and Antioquia as one of its principal examples.

The Medellín metropolitan area today accounts for about one-fourth of Colombia's value added in manufacturing. Although its isolation has ended, it has lost some ground in recent years in the face of intensified competition from Cali, Barranquilla, Cartagena, and especially Bogotá. The mile-high Valle de Aburrá is almost completely urbanized and decentralization to the near high valleys of the granitic plateau of the *Oriente* around Rionegro, and Marinilla is underway. Up to the present the benefits of industrialization have not spread significantly beyond the urbanized metropolitan area. The rural population of Antioquia (pop. 3.3 million), the largest and most populous of Colombia's departments, remains backwards and impoverished. A plan to develop secondary centers of industry in four regional sub-centers of the department, designed to spread more widely through rural areas such benefits as industrialization may bring (Gilbert, 1973; Ibiza de Restrepo, 1973), appears to face almost insurmountable odds.

Most recently we have the first results of the meticulous archival research of Ann Twinam (1973a, 1973b), a Ph.D. candidate in history at Yale University working under the urban historian Richard Morse, and it is the insight generated by her work, and recent discussions concerning it, that has led me back to this theme. Through genealogical research she has conclusively established that Basques were no more numerous among the early elite in Antioquia than were other groups. She shows further that there were numerous Antioqueño capitalists in the late eighteenth century, almost always merchants who received goods on consignment for sale to miners, though in some instances mine owners too. Between 1760 and 1790, imports into the province of Antioquia increased six-fold, clear evidence, she holds, of a healthy and expansive economy. The unique character of the placer mines, small and widely scattered, together with the shortage of both good agricultural land and cheap labor, are seen to set the conditions for the rise of a merchant elite-- as opposed to the landowner elite so common elsewhere in Latin America. She shows, for example, that from early times the members of the Medellín *cabildo* were almost exclusively merchants, who might also be mine owners but who almost never held any significant amounts of land. She sees it as significant that the origin of the Jewish myth of the Antioqueños first surfaced in the late colonial and early Republican period, at the same time when Antioqueño merchants were extending their entrepreneurial activities to other areas of Colombia. It is this expanding mercantile activity, based first on gold-mining and later on coffee, combined with the distinctive Antioqueño character, that set the stage for modern development.

Thus, Twinam suggests, it is not so frivolous as it may sound when Ospina Vásquez suggests that there came a time when the Antioqueño leaders "decided to industrialize." There was a well established elite, with access to capital and technology. They were experienced in joint venture capitalism, they had a flexible attitude towards the use of capital, and they had contacts with the outside world, not only with Bogotá but with Europe (especially through the coffee trade). When the time came they were ready to move decisively, first into cotton textiles and very soon into a broad spectrum of manufacturing activities both to supply the domestic market and now increasingly that for export.

So we are back to a kind of multiple hypothesis for Medellín's industrialization, including cultural, economic, and geographic factors, but emphasizing above all what Ospina Vásquez calls the *"modo de ser,"* the Antioqueño cultural particularism or "way of life," including their rather special attitude towards risk taking. The case has become a classic among students of the theory of economic development, not because it fits a pattern but because it is different--involving the very uniqueness that so many social scientists have of late seemed so cautious to avoid. But to understand better how economic development begins it seems clear that we ought to know more about people who are different in places that are different--such as the Antioqueños of Antioquia. And they are still at it. Medellín, as it celebrates the tricentennial of its founding, seems full of the ebullient confidence that sometimes has so irritated other Colombians. Bumper stickers and *carteles* proclaim *"Los Antioqueños podemos hacer mas"* and one senses that they can and will.

References

Chevalier, FranÇois. "Les Origines d'un pole de developpment industriel: pour une étude global de cas de Medellín, Colombie." in *Mélanges de la Casa Velasquez*, IX. Madrid, 1973, pp. 633-651.

Fajardo, Luis H. *The Protestant ethic of the Antioqueños.* Cali, 1968.

Gilbert, Alan. "The spatial distribution of social variables in Antioquia, Colombia." Discussion Paper No.38, Department of Geography, London School of Economics, 1973.

Hagen, Everett. *On the theory of social change.* Homewood, Ill., 1962. Chapter 15, "The transition in Colombia."

Herrero, Daniel. "Medellín au XXe siecle: essai d'analyses de la croissance economique." In *Villes et regions en Amerique Latine*, Cahier No. 1, CNRS-Institut de Hautes Etudes de l'Amerique Latine. Paris, 1970.

Ibiza de Restrepo, Ghislaine. "Impact de l'industrialisation de Medellín sur le development socio-economique du department d'Antioquia, en Colombie" (ms). Reviewed by O. Dollfus in *Cahiers des Amerique Latine*, No. 7, 1973, pp. 419-420.

140

López Toro, Alvaro. *Migración y cambio social en Antioquia durante el siglo diez y nueve.* Bogotá, 1968.

McGreevey, William P. *An economic history of Colombia, 1845-1920.* New York, 1971.

Orlando Melo, Jorge. "Los estudios históricos en Colombia: situación actual y tendencias predominantes." *Revista de la Dirección de Divulgación Cultural,* Univ. Nacional de Colombia, No. 2, Enero-Marzo, 1961, pp. 1-27.

Ospina Vásquez, Luis. *Industria y protección en Colombia, 1810-1930.* Medellín, 1955.

Parsons, James J. "Antioqueño colonization in western Colombia." *Ibero-Americana,* 32, Berkeley & Los Angeles. 1949. (Revised ed., University of California Press, 1968).

Revel-Mouroz, Jean. "Industries, Villes, Regions." *Cahiers des Amerique Latine,* No. 7, 1973, pp. 137-181. (This is a comparative analysis of industrialization in Medellín, Guadalajara, and Monterrey, cities of similar size, and the relationship between capital and region. It cites additional studies on the economy of Medellín and Antioquia by Claude Collin-Delavaud, Daniel Pecant and Milton Santos.)

Safford, Frank. *Significación de los Antioqueños en el desarrollo económico colombiano.* Inst. of International Studies, Univ. of California, Berkeley,

Twinam, Ann. "Antioqueño entrepreneurship, the myth and the reality," *Proceedings from S.U.L.A.* (State University Latin Americanists), Vol. 2, pp. 184-207, Council on International Studies, SUNY Buffalo, 1973.

_____. "The Medellín elite, 1780-1810." Paper given at meeting of the American Historical Association, San Francisco, December, 1973.

_____. *Miners, Merchants and Farmers in Colonial Colombia,* Austin, 1982.

PART THREE

Transient Colonial Imprints

11

The Topia Road: A Trans-Sierran Trail of Colonial Mexico[*]

The Sierra Madre Occidental presents one of the most formidable obstacles to land transportation in Mexico. Throughout its length of 750 miles, from a point near the United States-Mexico boundary in the north to the Santiago River in the south (Fig. 11.1), no railroad, auto road, or cart trail has ever traversed this barrier. Since colonial days only a few pack trails across the Sierra have served as direct lines of land contact between the Pacific coastal areas and the interior plateau of northern Mexico.

The Sierra Madre is a plateau, 100 to 150 miles wide, with a steep western escarpment. It represents the higher western edge of the great Mexican plateau. Outflows of Tertiary extrusives, accompanied by uplift, have raised the Sierra to a general altitude of 8,000 feet above the sea, and some 1,500 to 2,000 feet above the adjacent parts of the interior plateau; only isolated sections reach altitudes above 10,000 feet. The eastern part is characterized by a slightly rolling surface dotted with mountain meadows occupying the shallow north-northwest-south-southeast structural depressions. This part presents few difficulties to land transportation. To the west, however, the headward erosion of the streams flowing to the Pacific has cut deep box canyons into some parts of the plateau surface. These precipitous canyons, 800 to 1,000 feet deep, are more numerous near the western edge of the highlands and impose serious handicaps on even mule transport. However, the most formidable barrier is the steep western escarpment, known as the *barrancas*. Scores of large westward-flowing streams have frayed this escarpment with enormous canyons, or barrancas, 2,000 to 3,000 feet deep, producing

[*]By Robert C. West and James J. Parsons. Reprinted from *The Geographical Review*, Vol. 31, pp. 406-413 (1941).

some of the most rugged terrain in Mexico. Pack trails must follow either the rough summits of the interfluve ridges or the narrow, boulder-strewn canyon bottoms, where constant fording and refording of rushing streams are necessary.

The deep water of the torrents usually makes travel along the barrancas impossible during the height of the rainy season, from July to October. During this period travel must turn to the wet-season trails along the interfluve ridges. Even in the early part of the dry season, during December, January, and February, occasional rains (*equipatas*) may make travel difficult through the barrancas. Moreover, in the northern half of the Sierra heavy snows are not infrequent.

Routes Across the Sierra Madre

The routes for wheeled vehicles between the west coast and the interior plateau have avoided the Sierra Madre. The most important of these rounds the southern end of the Sierra, using the pass now traversed by the Southern Pacific Railroad through the barranca country of eastern Nayarit and western Jalisco to Guadalajara. This road has been in continual use by Europeans since 1530. Another route, significant in pre-railroad days, skirts the northern end of the Sierra, leading from the Casas Grandes area, in northwestern Chihuahua, by way of the Carretas Plains and the Púlpito Pass to Fronteras, in northeastern Sonora.

Only two trans-Sierran routes have ever become significant. One, which attained importance in the nineteenth century, crosses the Sierra from Durango City to Mazatlán, on the Pacific coast. The other, an old colonial *camino real* (a main route of travel), proceeds across the highlands from the mission pueblo of Tepehuanes, 125 miles northwest of Durango City, passing through the mining town of Topia, to Culiacán, on the coastal plain of Sinaloa (Fig. 11.2). This trail is known as the Topia Road. Other trails have been used in colonial and modern times; but the antiquity of the Topia Road and the volume of traffic carried over it have made it the most outstanding of the trans-Sierran trails.

The Topia Road in Colonial Times

The establishment and maintenance of the Topia Road in the last quarter of the sixteenth century were closely associated with the search for, and exploitation of, precious metals in the Sierra Madre. In 1563 rumors of silver and gold deposits lured Francisco de Ibarra, explorer and first governor of Nueva Vizcaya, into the Sierra to the

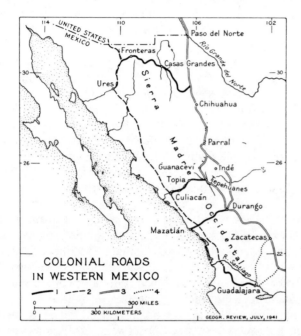

Figure 11.1   Colonial Roads in Western Mexico.   Key: 1. West coast-interior plateau connections; 2. West coast road; 3. Western interior plateau road; 4. Connections northward from Gaudalajara.

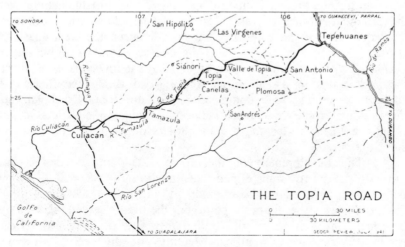

Figure 11.2   The Topia Road.

Acaxee Indian village of Topia. From this point, at which indications of silver were found, Ibarra and his forces continued westward to the coastal plain and the frontier settlement of Culiacán, thereby establishing a route across the high plateau.

Exploitation of the rich silver deposits around Topia probably did not begin until the 1580s. The *real de minas* (a mining community founded by official sanction) of Santa Cruz de Topia (altitude 5,800 feet) was founded near the site of the Acaxee village on the edge of the western escarpment, midway between the mining settlements of the interior plateau and the tropical agricultural districts of the Pacific coastal plain. It was the eastern section of the Topia Road that, as an outlet for the silver production of the new real de minas, first became significant. Bar silver from the crude Spanish smelting furnaces and amalgamation patios of Topia was taken by mule trains eastward across the mountain plateau to the royal countinghouse in Durango. By the beginning of the seventeenth century, as the population and mineral production of Topia had increased and contact with the coastal plain had become more frequent, the Topia Road had developed into a trans-Sierran artery between the lowland and the interior plateau.

Throughout the colonial period products such as *panocha* (raw cane sugar), bananas, oranges, beeswax, lard, and salt were carried from Sinaloa by way of the Topia Road to the northern interior mining centers, of which Indé, Guanacaví, and Parral were among the most important. Bar silver and gold from the Sierra mining camps as well as from the *reales* of Sinaloa to Sonora found their way to Durango over the Topia Road. Luxury goods, cloth, and mining equipment, including quicksilver for amalgamation, were the principal articles of trade carried on the return trip. Although the larger part of the colonial commerce between the west coast and central Mexican markets followed the coastal camino real by way of Guadalajara, the swampy nature of the Nayarit lowlands often forced the pack trains to use the drier Topia Road across the Sierra. In addition to serving as a commercial trail, the Topia Road was also the principal route of contact between Durango, the official capital of Nueva Vizcaya, and the distant outliers of its jurisdiction, Sinaloa and Sonora.

The development of the Topia Road into a trans-Sierran camino real partly transformed the function of the real of Topia. Although it retained its most important role as a producer of silver, this settlement, the midway point on the road, served also as the principal way station on the trail. *Posadas*, or inns for *arrieros* (mule drivers), were significant features of the real. Moreover, Topia, like all other Spanish mining towns, was organized along military lines and served as a garrison protecting mule towns from frequent Indian raids along the trail. Mineral discoveries were continually being made in the Sierra in the closing decade of the sixteenth century and the first decades of the seventeenth century; and new reales, such as San Andrés, San Hipólito, Las Vírgenes, and Siánori, were established near Topia. Topia served as the commercial distribution center for most of these surrounding camps; and as early as 1604 ten merchants, a number larger than that found in many larger reales, had established headquarters in Topia. At that date, according to a document in the Archivo General de Indias (Audiencia de Guadalajara), the population of Topia included only 47 male Spaniards.

Bulky food staples, such as maize, beans, and wheat flour, did not enter significantly into the trade over the Topia Road in colonial days. Instead, small settlements of Spanish farmers were established near the mining camps of the Topia area to supply food for the mine laborers. Two farming communities, Valle de Topia (altitude 5,000 feet) and Canelas (4,600 feet), both situated on alluvial valley floors near the head of barrancas, supplied, as they do today, the bulk of the food for the men at the surrounding mines. Parenthetically it may be noted that documents in the municipal archives of Parral, Chihuahua, indicate that Indian uprisings during the first half of the seventeenth century led to the periodic abandonment of Valle de Topia. The isolation and the relatively rapid extermination of the local Indian population played a part in the maintenance of pure Spanish blood in these highland agricultural communities. Even today Canelas is, in its dominantly white population, outstanding among the agricultural settlements of Mexico. Coffee, oranges, sweet limes, cherimoyas, and sugar cane mature in the vicinity, and the honey from the hives of Canelas has an exceptionally fine flavor. The maize, known locally as "ocho," is noteworthy in being a straight-rowed dent type with only eight rows to the ear and in having unusually large kernels.

Physical Characteristics of the Topia Road

The distance from Culiacán to Tepehuanes, the eastern terminus of the trail on the interior plateau, is about 140 miles; the time required for a mule train to travel that distance over the Topia Road is usually 8 to 10 days. From Culiacán caravans destined for Tepehuanes and beyond crossed the rolling, scrub-covered inner coastal plain to Tamazula, an agricultural village at the foot of the barrancas. Through the barrancas the trail followed the narrow, rocky stream bottom of the Quebrada de Topia for 34 miles to the real of Topia. This section of the route is known locally as "el camino de pura agua," since the rushing stream, 3 to 4 feet deep in the dry season, must be forded more than 300 times in that distance. In the rainy season trans-Sierran traffic practically ceased, since it was impossible to use the barranca section of the trail. However, a wet-season road that followed the crest of a ridge directly north of the quebrada was sometimes utilized. From Topia, located near the head of the Quebrada de Topia on an alluvial terrace 1,000 feet above the stream, the trail proceeded eastward across the pine and oak-covered plateau, where occasional grassy meadows afforded abundant pasturage for the pack animals. Today many of these meadows are sites of small agricultural settlements, in which notched log cabins are the characteristic house type. However, along this section of the road several deep quebradas, including the Quebrada del Valle de Topia, had to be crossed before Tepehuanes was reached. In 350 years the hoofs of mules and burros have worn narrow ruts, one to 2 feet deep, in the andesite and rhyolite rocks; and on the canyon slopes erosion has aided in gouging out the trail in places to a depth of 4 or 5 feet. In the rainy season these troughs are filled with veritable torrents; and to avoid them, the trail has constantly shifted like a braided stream over a considerable width of territory.

The Decline of the Topia Road

The construction of the Mexican Central Railway in the 1880s from Mexico City and Guadalajara northward to the mining areas of Durango and Chihuahua caused the Topia Road to lose its importance as a trans-Sierran route. The influx of American capital into Mexico during the Díaz regime (1877-1911), however, brought about a revival of mining activity in the Topia region. During this period the eastern section of the Topia Road was crowded with mule trains carrying ore concentrates to the rail connections on the interior plateau. By 1902 a branch rail line had been completed to Tepehuanes. It was even proposed to extend the line across the Sierra Madre to Culiacán; and a survey of the route was actually made in 1910, though construction work has never been attempted.

The Topia mining boom collapsed after 1910 as a result of political upheavals and the depletion of the supply of high-grade ores. In 1937 operations at Topia had ceased. Thus the old Topia Road is rarely used today; and the settlements of Topia (population 1,000) and Valle de Topia (about 600) are among the most isolated in all Mexico. At least a third of the adobe structures of Topia are in ruins, and its rarely visited 15-room hotel is reminiscent of better days.

Traffic in the plateau section of the Sierra has not disappeared entirely, however. A newer trail between Tepehuanes and Canelas, south of the old Topia Road, has been in use for many years.[1] Silver and gold concentrates from numerous small mines in the region compose the bulk of the mule-borne traffic along this route. In October 1939, a new gold strike was made at Plomosa, about 10 miles south of the through trail. Within a year three thousand people had arrived at the mines, and a sharp increase followed in pack-train traffic carrying gold ore to the railhead at Tepehuanes. In January 1941, more than 2,000 mules and burros were engaged in this service.

Present-day trade between either Topia or Canelas and the coast down the barrancas is confined to a few products such as cherimoyas and panocha. The agricultural community of Canelas has exceeded decaying Topia in size and is now the most thriving settlement in that part of the Sierra. From Tamazula a "truck" road leads to Culiacán; but as the daily truck requires 7 hours to make the 34-mile trip, much of the produce is still carried by pack train.

---

[1] Luis Zubiría y Campa: Mi expedición a Canelas, Durango, *Bol. Soc. Mexicana de Geogr. y Estadística*, Vol. 43, 1931-1934, pp. 73-97.

12

Realejo: A Forgotten Colonial Port and Shipbuilding Center in Nicaragua*

Colonial Nicaragua was an important source of Indian slaves, timber, dyewood, naval stores, and foodstuffs for the Viceroyalty of Peru. The great bulk of this traffic moved through the port and *villa* of Realejo, at the head of a mangrove-lined estuary some 8 kilometers up river from the modern Pacific coast port of Corinto. Today Realejo is an almost forgotten village of thatch-roofed cane houses, shrouded by giant mango trees and reached not by ship, but by a rutted dirt turnoff from the modern paved Corinto-Chinandega highway. The road lies deep in mud during the rainy season, is choked with dust during the dry season, and can hardly be distinguished from private access paths through surrounding fields of cotton.

Once called, perhaps with only modest hyperbole, "the best natural harbor within the Spanish monarchy"[1] this large estuary consists of the drowned confluence of the mouths of several rivers which cross the León-Chinandega Plain of Nicaragua to reach the Pacific Ocean. It could safely have accommodated a fleet of several hundred Spanish men-of-war within its spacious confines. The entrance is well protected from strong winds and swells, both of which are common along this stretch of Central American coastline.[2]

---

*By David R. Radell and James J. Parsons. Reprinted by permission of the publishers from *The Hispanic American Historical Review*, Vol. 51, pp. 295-312 (May 1971), copyright 1971 by Duke University Press. See original publication for maps.

[1]Domingo Juarros, *A Statistical and Commercial History of the Kingdom of Guatemala*, trans. by J. Baily (London, 1823), p. 337.

[2]The coastal shelf is shallow off this section of the Nicaraguan coast and at several points between the Gulf of Fonseca and Corinto offshore reefs or islands are aligned parallel to the coast. Mentioned in the 1904 U.S. Hydrographic Office

152

Paso Caballos estuary, a mangrove-lined creek that presently separates the mainland from the beach ridge on which Corinto stands, had an outlet to the sea 12 kilometers northwest of the harbor according to the Juan Bautista de Jáuregui plan of 1819.[3] Early used by small vessels for entry into the harbor, it has long been sealed off by sand accretion. In colonial times this broad beach, known as Isla Aserradores, was a source of fine timber as well as a favored nesting beach for sea turtles. Ocelots and jaguars from the interior came here during the nesting period to hunt female turtles as they came ashore to deposit their eggs.[4]

Protecting the mouth of the harbor is the small Isla del Cardón (on early maps Isla Maese Antonko), a barren rocky islet named for the abundance of *Cereus aragoni* which grew there.[5] It was early the site of a battery of guns and a lighthouse. Navigable channels enter the harbor from both the east and west of Isla del Cardón so that the harbor could be entered by sailing vessels in almost all weather and at all times of year regardless of wind direction.[6]

Bulletin 84 (*West Coasts of Mexico and Central America*, 3rd edition) are Speck Rock and Shoal and Limón Island. The entire coast was considered a graveyard for ships. Such long-shore bars may readily build to the surface to become new beaches where there is a sufficient rate of sediment supply and favorable wave action. This may have been the origin of the original Isla Corinto (Isla Aserradores), since anchored to the mainland at various points by the vagaries of beach erosion and deposition.

[3]Reproduced in E. Pérez-Valle, "El puerto de el Realejo dos años antes de la Independencia," *La Prensa* (Managua), 27 Nov., 1960.

[4]"Descripción de Realejo," c. 1791 (Museo Naval, Madrid 570 (Virreinato de Méjico, IV), Expediente No. 6.17 ff.) in Sauer Collection, Vol. 51, Department of Geography, University of California, Berkeley.

[5]Antonio Morel de Santa Cruz, "Carta al Rey" 1752, in Sofonías Salvatierra, *Contribución a la historia de Centroamérica* (Managua, 1939), I, 381-383. Isla Limón, 12 kilometers northwest of Corinto harbor, is referred to on Hydrographic Office charts as False Cardón, apparently because it has been confused in the past with the island at the entrance to the port. Recent maps suggest that Isla Limón may have been incorporated into the mainland by sand accretion. Similar shifts in the configuration of the coastline are seen south of the Realejo bar, especially on the peninsula of Castañon, where a high cliffed headland now attached to the mainland is shown on earlier maps to have been an island ("Mapas de las coasts de la Nueva España en el mar del Sur," c. 1650 (Biblioteca Nacional, Madrid, MS 2959, folio 75) in Sauer Collection, Vol. 61, Department of Geography, University of California, Berkeley.)

[6]R.G. Dunlop, *Travels in Central America* (London, 1847), p. 26.

The western entrance, El Cardón Channel (also called Barra del Cardón), has long been the principal entrance to the harbor. It is about half a kilometer wide and can accommodate merchant ships of deep draught. The bottom is sandy, and there are few hazards. On the island of Cardón a large rock overlooks this passage. The freebooter Reveneau de Lussan, on his way to sack the town of Realejo in 1685, noted that although Cardón Channel lay unprotected, the Spaniards had once considered building an outer fortification on this rock to protect the passage.[7] This site was later fortified, as is mentioned by Morel de Santa Cruz in his 1752 description of Nicaragua.[8] The narrower eastern channel, Boca Falsa (also called False Bar Channel), was used extensively during the sixteenth and seventeenth centuries. However, as early as 1740 it was already known as La Barra Vieja, presumably because it had not been important for many years. Only on the occasion of winds from the south did eighteenth century vessels venture into this channel, which had long since become dangerously narrow and shoal.

Entering the harbor and doubling Punta Icacos, which lay on the left, vessels found fully protected anchorage in seven fathoms. Across the channel, to the north, at Jaguey, an opening in the mangrove-lined beach, large ships from Peru were careened. Barracks had been established there for guarding port provisions and equipment. Smaller vessels were careened further up the estuary at Borrachos (five fathoms), Cadavera, or the parish of Espanta de Negros, where sentinels for the defense of the *villa* of Realejo were stationed.[9]

The narrow, meandering tidal creek known as Río del Realejo was bordered by stilt-rooted mangrove almost to the edge of town. Towards the end of the colonial period silting of the channel appears to have become a problem, with larger vessels no longer being able to reach the port. Encroaching mangrove along with the deposition of sand and silt by tidal currents seem to have contributed to the

---

[7]Raveneau de Lussan, *A Journal of a Voyage made into the South Sea, by the Bucaniers or Freebooters of America from the year 1684 to 1689* (London, 1704), p. 48.

[8]Morel de Santa Cruz, "Carta al Rey," I, 381-383.

[9]Felipe Gómez y Messia, Corregidor "Autos y Relación...de la Villa y Puerto de Realejo y Pueblos de su jurisdicción," 1740, Archivo de Guatemala (hereinafter cited as AG), (MS) Al.17(14) 5014-210.

shoaling.[10] The waters of the harbor, furthermore, were infested with *teredo*, the shipworm which feasted on wooden sailing ships and which often caused their hulls to be riddled with holes.[11]

Settlers and travelers alike found the natural environment of the port and *villa* quite unpleasant. It was hot, humid, and unhealthy although the adjacent area was well endowed with fine alluvial soils and fruit trees of every description.

Realejo, for three centuries one of the most active shipbuilding and commercial ports on the South Sea coast, first assumed its commercial role in 1533, some 10 years after the initial settlement of Nicaragua. Prior to that time all Spanish commerce entered and left Nicaragua by way of the Gulf of Nicoya in modern Costa Rica. To accommodate this trade the port city of Brusélas had been founded on the east shore of the Gulf of Nicoya by Hernández de Córdoba in 1524.[12] Brusélas was forcibly depopulated twice for political reasons, initially during the time of Hernández de Córdoba and again only a few years later, in 1527, when it was dismantled completely by Diego López de Salcedo.[13] It was never again rebuilt.

Following the abandonment of Brusélas, ships arriving from Castillo de Oro (Panama) anchored off the island of Chira and from there longboats and native canoes carried commodities and passengers up the Río Tempisque to the province of Nicoya. The friendly cacique, Nicoya, supplied food, water, and Indian porters for the 35 league overland journey through almost uninhabited territory to the Indian city of Nicaragua (Rivas).[14] From there the journey to Granada and then León, through a well-populated country, was adequately supplied with food, water, and resting places.

An excellent Pacific harbor, situated scarcely fifteen leagues northwest of the city of León, had been discovered by sea during the initial voyage of Gil González and Andrés Niño to Nicaragua in

---

[10]"Descripción de Realejo," c. 1791.

[11]Antonio Vásquez de Espinosa, *Compendio y descripción de las Indias Occidentales* [1628], Smithsonian Miscellaneous Collections (Washington, D.C., 1948), pp. 108, 232-233.

[12]Hubert Howe Bancroft, *History of Central America* (San Francisco, 1883), I, 512.

[13]"Carta con documentos de Licenciado Francisco Casteñeda a S.M.," León, March 30, 1529, Archivo General de Indias, Sevilla (hereinafter cited as AGI), Patronato 180, Ramo 27 in *Colección Somoza*, I, 479-508.

[14]*Ibid.*

1523. They traveled into the harbor and up a large tidal river and at the head of navigation took possession of Nicaragua in the name of the King of Spain, calling the port "Puerto de la Posesión" and the river "Río de la Posesión."[15] The settlement that grew up at the head of navigation was later to gain fame as the port and *villa* of Realejo.

Although discovered and explored before any Spanish cities were founded in Nicaragua, this harbor was not frequented until Spanish navigators had learned to sail safely past the Gulf of Papagayos, northwest of the Nicoya Peninsula. Here very strong offshore winds called *papagayos* prevail, accompanied by turbulent ocean currents. This treacherous area seriously impeded coastal navigation in the 1520s because skilled pilots had not yet become completely familiar with these anomalous sailing conditions. Even after this navigation had been mastered and Realejo had been opened to trade, the Gulf of Nicoya remained an important alternate route for Nicaraguan commerce.[16]

The first Spanish ships constructed on the Pacific shores of the New World had been built on the Gulf of San Miguel in Panama in the first years after Balboa's crossing of the isthmus to explore the newly found South Sea.[17] The initial stimulus for the development of a Central American shipbuilding industry came in part from the demand for ships to carry Indian slaves from Nicaragua to Panama and the new mines of Peru. The settlers of León and Granada early had turned to slaving among the densely settled and sedentary aboriginal population. As early as 1526 at least one shipload of Nicaragua Indians had arrived at Panama. After Pedrarias Dávila moved to Nicaragua 2 years later the trade expanded rapidly, with slaving expeditions ranging far into the interior to supply the insatiable demands of the traders. Following the death of Pedrarias in

[15]Francisco López de Gómara, *Historia general de las Indias* (1554) in Biblioteca de Autores Españoles, 1946, XXII, 280-281.

[16]"Carta con documentos de Licenciado Francisco Castañeda a S.M.," *Colección Somoza*, I, 479-508.

[17]Woodrow Borah, "Early Colonial Trade and Navigation Between Mexico and Peru," *Ibero-Americana*, 38 (Berkeley and Los Angeles, 1954). Borah's reconstruction of early Pacific shipbuilding and trade is followed in this and the following paragraph. On the Nicaragua Indian slave trade see also David R. Radell, *Historical Geography of Western Nicaragua: the Spheres of Influence of León, Granada, and Managua, 1519-1965*, Nonr-3656 (03), Project NR 388 067, Department of Geography, University of California (Berkeley, 1969), especially Chapter 4.

1531 the colonists were allowed to build ships and engage in slaving virtually without restraint so that by 1533 or early 1534 between 15 and 20 caravels were reported exclusively engaged in the Nicaraguan slave trade. Between them, Nicaragua and Panama supplied the overwhelming majority of vessels, trained seamen, and pilots then operating in the Pacific.

Within the next decades modest shipbuilding enterprises were to spring up at Alanje in Veragua, Iztapa in Guatemala, Acajutla in El Salvador, and in New Spain at Acapulco, Huatulco, Tehuantepec, and La Navidad, as well as on the Gulf of Guayaquil in the Audiencia of Quito. But it was Nicaragua that dominated the industry, producing ships not only for the coastwise trade southward, but the bulk of those in the Mexico-Peru traffic and significant numbers of Manila galleons.

The port of Realejo first attracted attention in connection with Pedro de Alvarado's plan to invade Peru.[18] In 1533 Alvarado was in the process of assembling a small fleet in the Gulf of Fonseca for an exploratory expedition to Peru. He heard that three ships were being constructed on the Río del Realejo under the supervision of governor Francisco de Castañeda for the purpose of sending reinforcements to Francisco Pizarro, the conqueror of Peru. Immediately Alvarado dispatched a band of well-armed men, along with a few ships outfitted for battle, to attack the shipbuilding yard. This party successfully seized two completed ships and from the remaining vessel which had not yet been completed and still lay on the slip, took the anchors, cables, and sails. According to complaints filed by Nicaragua officials, Alvarado not only seized the ships but also inveigled a substantial number of Spanish settlers from the province of Nicaragua to man his expeditionary force.

In the years following the departure of the Alvarado expedition shipbuilding activity increased; Nicaragua emerged as a leading supplier of Spanish soldiers, Indian slaves, and agricultural supplies for the Peruvian conquest, and Realejo developed into the principal port for this inter-colonial trade.

The port's hinterland provided abundant raw materials suited to ship construction. Indeed, it was claimed that few places in the New World were so well endowed with the resources required for the development of a shipbuilding industry. From the upland pine forests of the Central Highlands of Nicaragua, the southernmost natural stand of the genus *Pinus* in the New World, lumber, pitch,

---

[18]"Información Legalizada en la Ciudad de Panamá, ante el Gobernador de Castilla del Oro," San Miguel, Perú, October 24, 1533, AGI, Justicia, Leg. 1,051 in *Colección Somoza*, III, 283-305.

and resins were carried to the port of Realejo by Indian porters. The amount of pine lumber transported overland for shipbuilding was so great that Las Casas ranked the rigors of hauling timbers as one of the chief causes of death and misery among the Indians of Nicaragua.[19] The supply of masts in the pine forests of the adjacent highlands were said to be "inexhaustible."[20] Hardwood species useful in ship fabrication also were numerous. Among the most important local timbers available for maritime use were *cedro* (*Cedrela*), *Caoba* (*Swietenia*), *guácimo* (*Guazumo*), *madero negro* (*Gliricidia sepium*), which was a durable "underwater" timber, *palo cuadrado* (*Macrocnemum glabresceus*), a very hard wood for levers and rudders, and *sapodilla* (*Achras sapota*), famed for its resistance to teredo.

Cotton, grown by the Indians throughout the Pacific coastal area of Nicaragua, was plentiful and from the beginning had been one of the most important commodities collected as tribute. In addition, the weaving of cotton was one of the chief handicrafts in the province,[21] so that native talents were easily turned to the weaving of much needed sail cloth as well as other fabrics considered useful by the Spaniards. Rope-making, based on local raw materials, was another important handicraft industry. Maguey (*Agave*) and *cabuya* (*Furcraea cabuya*) were the principal sources of fiber for cordage manufacture in Nicaragua.[22]

Of all major necessities for ship construction only iron, used primarily for anchors on colonial ships, was not produced within the province of Nicaragua. Anchors usually were brought directly from Spain by ship over the Río San Juan route from the North Sea to Granada and from there were carried overland to Realejo.

Notwithstanding the abundant availability of raw materials, early ship construction at Realejo appears to have suffered from serious mismanagement. Unscrupulous practices by contractors sapped gold from the royal treasury as well as sweat and blood from Indian workers. In 1578 a report was made informing the Crown of

---

[19]Bartolomé de Las Casas, *Destrucción de las Indias* (1552), (Puebla, 1821), p. 37.

[20]Juarros, *Statistical and Commercial History*, p. 337.

[21]"Diligencias de la Distribución de los Tributos de los Pueblos de Nicaragua, practicadas por los Oidores de la Real Audiencia de los Confines," San Salvador, November-December, 1548. AGI, Audiencia de Guatemala, Leg. 128, in *Colección Somoza*, XIV, 357-385.

[22]Vásquez de Espinosa, *Compendio y descripción*, p. 236.

developments at the shipyards of Realejo.[23] One galleon had recently been completed and another was under construction. Although
these two ships were reputed to be the best vessels in the South
Seas, their cost to the Crown and to the Indian workers was excessive. The 1578 report estimated that the ships could have been built
for one-fourth the price actually charged the royal treasury.[24] Shipyard owners, dissatisfied with handsome profits wrung from the
Crown, apparently also short-changed the Indians for their labor.
Shipbuilding contractors were paid in gold for their finished product,
but Indian workers usually were promised only cacao beans. It was
said that the quantity of cacao beans promised the Indians for 20
reales worth of work could be purchased on the open market by
their employers for not more than 15 *reales*. If payment were to be
made in silver, the workers were paid one peso for 10 *reales* worth
of work instead of the standard rate of exchange, 1 for 8. These
practices were said to have netted contractors an additional 20 to 25
percent profit at the expense of the Indians. Of 300,000 *tostones*
paid by the Crown for ship construction under one contract, only
5,000 *tostones* were allocated to be paid to the Indian workers.[25]
Even this meager amount was not necessarily received by the
Indians, for they often received worthless promises of future payment instead of hard cash. Rather than work in the shipyards
without pay, natives fled the country, abandoning their wives and
children, thus contributing to the province's serious depopulation.

In partial solution to the problem of labor in the shipyards, the
Crown was implored by the clergy to import Negro slaves.[26] Although not much is known about their importation to Western
Nicaragua, the recommendation appears to have been implemented;
for, when Vásquez de Espinoza visited Nicaragua in the early years
of the seventeenth century, he could report that many laborers in
Realejo's shipyard were Negro slaves, Negro freemen, or mulattos.[27]
Mestizos also must have worked in the yards, for there was evidence
of an incipient organized labor movement. In 1674, for example, a

---

[23]"Fray Pedro Ortiz a S.M. el Rey," February 6, 1583, in *Manual María de
Peralta, Costa Rica, Nicaragua y Panamá en el siglo XVI*, pp. 623-625.

[24]*Ibid.*

[25]*Ibid.*

[26]*Ibid.*

[27]Vásquez de Espinoza, *Compendio y descripción*, p. 236.

Calker's Union felt strong enough to demand the dismissal of a *calafate mayor* or supervisor on the ways.[28]

Most of the ships built at Realejo after the first years were for Peruvian merchants and the Peru trade. Until 1585 Manila galleons also were constructed at Realejo.[29] Two such vessels of 350 tons each were completed there in 1579, for example, for trans-Pacific use.[30] Another Realejo-built vessel of 700 tons, seized by Cavendish in 1587, was also on the Philippine run.[31] The original link of the Nicaragua port with the Manila trade was through Acapulco, the northern terminus of the Mexico-Peru trade, for which Realejo served as a frequent port-of-call. In later years, a cabotage trade with other Central American ports such as Iztapa, Acajutla, and Panama became increasingly important.

During the last half of the sixteenth century and the early seventeenth century pine pitch (*brea*) was the most important product shipped from Realejo to Peru. As the viceroyalty to the south solidified its territorial control and became less dependent on agricultural imports, naval stores from the Nueva Segovia region of the northern Nicaraguan highlands became progressively more important in the trade. First used in ship construction at Realejo, pine tar and resins had become the primary export of this port to Callao as early as the 1540s.[32] With illicit Oriental trade goods, smuggled overland from Mexico for transshipment to Peru, and illegal wine shipments bound from Peru to New Spain, they dominated the commerce of the port.

The intercolonial naval stores trade was especially profitable to the Nicaraguan merchants. By the early seventeenth century it was reported that a kindle (100 pounds) of Nueva Segovia pine tar could be delivered at Realejo for two pesos. From Realejo transportation

---

[28]"Los calafates del puerto y villa de Realejo pretenden la supresión del officio de Calafate Mayor de la provincia de Nicaragua," AG, (MS) A 3.10, 3140-164, folio 76.

[29]Peter Gerhard, *Pirates on the West Coast of New Spain* (Glendale, California, 1960), p. 29.

[30]Sofonías Salvatierra, *Contribución a la historia de Centroamerica*, I, 299.

[31]Borah, "Early Colonial Trade," p. 66.

[32]See William M. Denevan, "The Upland Pine Forests of Nicaragua: A Study in Cultural Plant Geography," *University of California Publications in Geography* (Berkeley and Los Angeles, 1961), 12 (4), 251-320, esp. 298-300, for references on the *brea* trade.

by ship to Callao cost three pesos more, including duty. Yet at Callao merchants received no less than 12 pesos and as much as 30 pesos per kindle.[33] The pitch was used not only for caulking ships but also for treating wine containers in the wine producing districts of the Peruvian coast. But by the end of the seventeenth century the supply seems to have been largely depleted.

By 1540 activity generated by the shipbuilding and the prospering Peru trade had enabled Realejo's population to grow to more than 50 Spanish *vecinos*, exclusive of sailors, persons in transit, and merchants.[34] Although most merchants controlling trade at Realejo were residents of León (León Viejo), that town was too distant to handle all of Realejo's affairs conveniently. Many grave crimes and illicit activities are said to have gone unpunished for lack of local peace officers and adequate law enforcement from León, situated 12 leagues to the southeast across the volcanic Pacific outwash plain on the shores of Lake Managua. About the only law enforced during the 1540s was a governor's restriction on Realejo's trade which declared that all Peruvian imports unloaded at Realejo could be traded only at León.[35] Residents of Realejo complained bitterly, and as a result this restriction was subsequently revoked.[36] The official status of "*villa*" was granted to Realejo during the late 1540s and with it an increase in local authority. In 1560, with the Peru trade very active, the resident European population of Realejo was listed as 30. Interestingly, almost all of these were said to have been Genoese, although there were also a few Spaniards in residence.[37]

Realejo's port and shipyards were unmolested by pirates until 1578 when Sir Francis Drake passed through the Straits of Magellan and entered the Pacific Ocean. He quickly moved northward, attacking shipping and coastal settlements and taking the Spaniards by surprise. Word of his approach often preceded him. Yet, so rapid was his progress that the colonists had little time to prepare adequate defenses.

---

[33]Vásquez de Espinosa, *Compendio y descripción*, p. 233. Also pp. 484, 499.

[34]"Capítulos de cargas formulados por Francisco Sánchez contra Rodrigo de Contreras," Panamá, July 1, 1540, AGI, Indiferente General, Leg. 1206 in *Colección Somoza*, VI, 103.

[35]*Ibid.*, 108.

[36]*Colección Somoza*, VI, 108.

[37]Salvatierra, *Contribución a la historia*, I, 301-302.

On April 6, 1579, Realejo received news of Drake's approach. The port was fortified as quickly as possible. A breastwork was laid near the Río del Realejo's mouth, and a log chain was stretched across the stream to prevent a river assault on the *villa*. However, fate intervened; Drake, unable to induce his captured pilot to guide him past the Isla Cardón into the harbor, simply bypassed the port and proceeded northward along the coast.[38] Drake had traveled up the coast so quickly that Cardón had been bypassed before the Spaniards had even begun to fortify the river. Nevertheless, these fortifications were maintained for a few years in fear of his return. The presence of pirates who infested the South Sea after Drake's initial voyage seriously depressed business at Realejo for the remainder of the sixteenth century. Although the port was not attacked, the mere presence of pirates had an adverse effect on Pacific Coast commerce, and Realejo's trade diminished along with that of other Pacific ports.

By the late sixteenth century the increasing advantages of building ships in the Philippines to meet Pacific commercial needs were having their effect on Realejo's shipyards. In 1585 Padre Alonso Sánchez of the Compañía de Jesús reported on the situation.[39] He observed that construction of ships at Realejo and other ports of New Spain was inefficient and expensive when compared to similar work done in the Philippines. Sánchez estimated that four ships could be built in the Philippines in the time required to build one in New Spain, and a 500-600 ton ship costing 50,000 to 60,000 pesos in New Spain could be built for only 6,000 to 8,000 pesos at Manila. The low cost was attributable to three factors: (1) excellent wood; (2) low priced iron, costing only 8 to 10 *reales* per kindle; and (3) artisans skilled in carpentry and iron work. In addition, a concentrate of coconut oil could be used for caulking, lead was available for weights, and local rope was of the highest quality.

Above all, however, Realejo's commercial function was most seriously undermined by the relocation of León in 1610 to its present site at the foot of Volcán Cerro Negro and only 3 leagues from the port. As a consequence, by 1620 most of Realejo's official functions had been assumed by the nearby capital. León's more convenient new site induced many of Realejo's successful merchants to abandon the hot, humid, unhealthy coast for the comparative

---

[38]Gerhard, *Pirates on the West Coast*, pp. 67-68.

[39]Ricardo Cappa, *Estudio críticos acerca de la dominación española en América* (Madrid, 1894), III, 47-49.

comfort of the interior city. Realejo, as a consequence, not only lost administrative power, but also her most influential citizens. Recurrent attempts thereafter to breathe new life into its economy were largely ineffective.

In the early seventeenth century, sometime after the height of its affluence, Realejo claimed nearly 100 Spanish *vecinos*, not to mention mulattos, free Negroes, slaves, and a few Indians.[40] One of the four corregidors appointed by the President of the Audiencia of Guatemala to administer justice in Nicaragua had his headquarters in Realejo; his jurisdiction extended to the province of El Viejo, which included among its twelve villages Chinandega, Chichigalpa, and Posoltega.[41] A few decades later, with León firmly established in its new site, there remained in Realejo only a few Spaniards. When Thomas Gage visited the *villa* in 1637, he described its vulnerability to attack:

> But neither this creek or arm of the sea is fortified (which might be done with one or two pieces of ordnance at most placed at the mouth of the sea's entrance) neither is the Realejo strong with ammunition, nor with people, for it consists not of above two hundred families, the most of them are Indians and mestizos, a people of no courage, and unfit to defend such an open passage to Guatemala and Nicaragua.[42]

Perhaps inspired by Gage's description of both Nicaragua's commercial wealth and the weakness of its defenses, the pirate John Davis traveled from the Caribbean Sea up the Río San Juan to Lake Nicaragua in 1665 and proceeded successfully to sack Granada, León, and Realejo. After another pirate attack followed the same back-door route, the Río San Juan was fortified. Pirates then turned to direct attacks on Nicaragua from the Pacific Coast. Although the Spaniards were well aware of the threat posed by the filibusters, defense measures taken against them appear to have been of a very limited nature.

In 1684, apparently hoping to find Realejo in a state of unpreparedness as described by Gage, a group of English freebooters made an abortive attempt to take the port by surprise. After Captain

[40]Vásquez de Espinosa, *Compendio y descripción*, p. 252.

[41]*Ibid.*

[42]Thomas Gage, *The English-American: A New Survey of the West Indies, 1648.* Edited by A. P. Newton (London, 1928).

Edmund Cook's death off Nicoya Peninsula earlier that year, Edward Davis had taken command of Cook's three ships and set sail for Realejo. When, on August second, the little armada arrived at Isla del Cardón and entered the harbor, they found the river approaches to Realejo fortified by breastworks. Rather than fight the well-entrenched Spaniards, Davis decided to pirate elsewhere and put to sea bound for Amapala in the Gulf of Fonseca.[43]

The next year Davis returned in the company of the freebooters Townby, Swan, and Knite with 8 ships and a combined force of 640 men. The ships anchored in the harbor and a raiding force of 470 marched inland, by-passing Realejo to attack León, a day's march inland.[44] After looting and burning the city, they returned to sack Realejo. They were too late, however; the residents of the villa had heard of their approach and had abandoned their homes. Finding the place vacant, the freebooters gathered whatever naval stores, rigging, and supplies had been left at the port, put the town to torch, and sailed away on September 7, 1685. It probably would have pleased the Nicaraguans somewhat had they known that the free-booters suffered for this attack by contracting a "spotted fever" which, while at sea, considerably thinned their numbers.[45]

Nicaragua's troubles for the year were not over. On November first, a French buccaneer, FranÇois Grogniet, entered the harbor of Realejo, where his men found the breastworks along the river unmanned and the partially burned *villa* of Realejo deserted.[46] After raiding a large sugar estate and local cattle ranches, Grogniet's force of 120 men attempted to attack León but found the city too heavily defended. Before leaving Nicaragua the buccaneers did raid the pueblo of El Viejo, on a navigable tributary of the Gulf of Fonseca near Chinandega, there securing much-needed supplies.

After this visit to Nicaragua, Grogniet's force sailed back and forth along the West Coast of Central America, raiding Spanish settlements. Granada also suffered at his hands. Grogniet returned to Realejo, found it still vacant, captured El Viejo again, and also burned Chinandega before putting to sea on May 19th, 1686. Once again, 8 months later, Grogniet returned to sack El Viejo for a third

---

[43]William Dampier, *A New Voyage Round the World* (London, 1927), pp. 85-90.

[44]*Ibid.*, pp. 152-157.

[45]*Ibid.*

[46]Lussan, *Voyage into the South Sea*, pp. 47-49.

time before making a hasty retreat.[47]   According to Lussan, people did not begin to resettle Realejo again until December, 1687, when the Spanish warship "San Lorenzo," mounted with 30 cannon and manned by 400 hands, provided protection by anchoring at the entrance to the port.[48]

With the departure of Grogniet's buccaneers, shipbuilding resumed at Realejo.   Gerhard provides a description of two small galleys being built there at this time to protect Mexican shipping and coastal settlements from pirate attack.

> The flagship had the breath-taking name of "Jesús Nazareno Santo Domingo y San Gaspar." The smaller "Nuestra Señora de la Soledad y San Francisco de Paula" had a keel of 33 *codos* (46 feet), twenty-eight oars, and a normal complement of fifty soldiers in addition to the rowers.   The armament of these vessels must have been quite small, probably a few light swivel guns, but their maneuverability would make them useful in a hit-and-run engagement.   The first of the galiots reached Acapulco in December, 1690, and the second in March, 1691.   For the next few years they patrolled the coast from Huatulco to Lower California, investigating rumors of pirates and serving as convoys to the Manila galleon.[49]

Although pirate attacks declined on the Pacific Coast of Central America after the beginning of the eighteenth century, incidents were still common.   In 1704, John Clipperton sailed into the harbor of Realejo and captured two ships.[50]   In the same year William Dampier captured an 80-ton ship bound for Realejo from Zihuatanejo. Fear of raids from the Atlantic persisted.   Documents in the Guatemala archives show that more than of the port taxes levied on ships

---

[47]*Ibid.*, pp. 69-71.

[48]*Ibid.*, 151-152.

[49]Gerhard, *Pirates on the West Coast*, pp. 198-199.

[50]William Funnell, *A Voyage Round the World Containing an Account of Captain Dampier's Expedition into the South Seas in the Ship St. George, in the Years 1703 and 1704* (London, 1707), pp. 47-68.

at Realejo from Panama in the 1720s were for the "Castillo de San Juan" fund for building defenses on that river.[51]

Throughout most of the eighteenth century Realejo's contact with the French, Dutch, and British involved the exchange of contraband. Shipbuilding for colonial commerce also continued. As late as 1742, the shipbuilding facility at Realejo was still capable of launching one 300-ton ship each year for the Callao trade.[52]

There were 15 Spanish *vecinos* living in the *villa* in 1740, together with 108 other families, mostly mulattos.[53] At least two of the latter were of sufficient substance to occupy tile-roof houses, as did all the Spaniards, but most of the structures were of cane and straw. Several of the *vecinos*, as well as the *cura* and the *corregidor*, owned small sugar mills and livestock *hatillos*. The town garden plots (*chacaras*) were dominated by plantains, as they are today, while the adjacent fields were planted to maize, cotton, and, in good years, indigo. Port activity was said to be in decline "because of the prohibition of *suertos* from both Guatemala and Peru," but ships still came from Peru to load lumber, naval stores, cacao, indigo, hides, dried beef, and brazilwood, as well as occasional cargoes of maize and sugar. Panamá, Guayaquil, Acajutla, and Acapulco also sent vessels, and ships in the Acapulco-Callao trade frequently stopped off for supplies and to fill out their manifests. To stem the declining trade a royal order in 1796 exempted from all taxes ships in the Acapulco-Realejo trade, but it was without effect.

By 1752, it was reported that Realejo's fortifications had been considerably improved.[54] El Cardón channel was guarded by an outpost. The town, three leagues up the estuary, was protected on three sides by strong palisades and a moat. In the center of the settlement a building, 20 paces long and 14 paces wide, held the town's arms. These consisted of four cannons and six mortars of bronze, along with gun carriages, munitions, gunners' ladles, and other defensive equipment. In case of sudden attack, a company of local militia was armed with 40 muskets. Within the palisades were

---

[51] "Registro de entradas y salidas de embarcaciones, Villa de Realejo, año 1721," AG, (MS) A 3.6 2200-120.

[52] Fernando de Echeverz, *Ensayos mercantiles para adelantar por medio del establecimiento de una compañía del comercio de los fructos de el reyno de Guatemala* (Guatemala, 1742).

[53] Gómez y Messia, "Autos y Relación," (see Note 9).

[54] Morel de Santa Cruz, "Carta al Rey," I, 381-383.

87 houses of straw and 13 of masonry, serving a population of 320 persons "of confession and communion."[55] There was also one parochial church and two convents, one Franciscan and the other of the order of La Merced. The ruins of the town's hospital, destroyed in 1685, were still evident. Since the attack all patients had been sent to the hospital at León.

In the mid-eighteenth century ship construction at Realejo was compared with that at Guayaquil:[56]

> The woods at Realejo suck in nails without splitting whereas those of Guayaquil split easily. The woods of Realejo are much superior to those of Guayaquil. They do not discharge splinters, and they are lighter and more flexible, the result being that fewer planks are needed and the ships are therefore stronger.[57]

Whereas a ship's frame at Guayaquil might be fitted with nine planks, one of comparable size at Realejo required only five, and it was easier to get the lumber of Realejo to port than it was at Guayaquil.[58] Whereas ships built at Guayaquil were said to have lasted 40 or 50 years, those of Realejo were reputed to have lasted much longer. The ship "Santa Cruz de León," built in 1682, was still in sound condition in 1746, and other ships which were only 30 years old showed almost no signs of wear.[59] But despite the natural advantages of Realejo for ship construction, by 1752 the shipyard had begun to deteriorate, apparently owing in good measure to incompetence and mismanagement.[60]

Realejo never again regained its earlier prominence as a ship-building center although the port continued to export Nicaraguan products until 1859 (Table 12.1). The deeper drought sailing vessels of the eighteenth and nineteenth centuries could not easily ride the tides up the Río del Realejo and increasingly they were forced to anchor in the harbor behind Punta Icacos while lighters served the

---

[55]*Ibid.*

[56]*Ibid.*

[57]Cappa, *Estudios críticos,* pp. 100-101.

[58]*Ibid.*

[59]*Ibid.,* 110.

[60]Morel de Santa Cruz, "Carta al Rey," I, 381-383.

upstream port. A careenage on the opposite shore at Jaguey attracted ships in need of minor repairs to the lower harbor.

TABLE 12.1

Export from Realejo--1852

Item	Amount	Item	Amount
Boards	71,764	Sugar	1,664 Quintales
Brazilwood	22,845 Cwt.	Beans	100 Quintales
Cedar	20,000 Sq. yds.	Egg	600 Dozen
Mahogany	21,000 Sq. yds.	Cotton	1,000 Cwt.
Honey	11,000 Gallons	Hides	12,870
Limes	50,000	Cigars	120,000
Maize	16,155 Bags	Coyol Oil	615 Gallons
Rice	7,627 Cwt.		

Source: A. Boucard, *Travels of a Naturalist* (London, 1894), p. 109. Other exports included mules, cattle, horses, pigs, indigo, fruits, hammocks, shoes, and miscellaneous manufactured goods.

As its fortunes declined Realejo apparently became increasingly a mulatto town. The 272 adults censused in 1791 were said to be nearly all "gente de color, zambos y motallos."[61] The women were appreciatively described as slender, erect and fine-featured with "los pechos muy bien conformados, recojidos, semiglobosos, con los pezones horizontales y crecidos."[62] By this time only the church was of *mamapostería* (plaster), many ruins in the town being described as "reminiscent of the cruelty of the filibusters." In neighboring pueblos, however, Indians were in the majority. Chinandega had become the principal settlement of the region with some 400 houses hidden among trees, their yards fenced with *pita*, which yielded *cabuya* fiber. Agricultural activity continued to be centered on maize, cotton, and indigo, along with the ubiquitous plantains. In the wet season locusts frequently ravaged the cotton crop; in the dry season "fevers" laid men low.

---

[61]"Descripción de Realejo," c. 1791 (see Note 4).

[62]*Ibid.*

Towards the end of the century Acajutla (Sonsonate) in modern El Salvador replaced Realejo as the major Pacific port of Central America. More and more Nicaraguan commerce, especially with Guatemala, moved in small boats north from El Viejo through Puerto Real and the Estero Real to the Gulf of Fonseca. After independence El Viejo replaced Realejo as the district capital, under the Intendencia of León. Realejo continued to handle the largest share of Nicaragua's export trade (see Table 12.1), but the ship-building industry had disappeared. In 1831 an English entrepreneur proposed installation of new sawmill equipment at Realejo to revive shipbuilding if the government of the Central American states would permit the machinery duty-free entry, but apparently nothing came of it.[63]

Finally, in 1859, the port of Corinto was established at Punta Icacos near the deepest part of the harbor, and the *villa* of Realejo was relegated to the role of an insignificant backwater village. In contrast, Corinto continued to gain importance, diverting trade especially from the Río San Juan Caribbean gateway. By 1878 three-fourths of Nicaragua's foreign trade, including the growing coffee and cacao exports, was moving through Corinto. In that year construction was begun on the railroad from Corinto to the interior. Eight years later it had reached Lake Managua at the port of Momotombo, 93 kilometers distant. After another 17 years, in 1903, Managua was finally linked directly to Corinto by rail.[64]

The early rise of Realejo as a major port and shipyard on the Pacific Coast of Central America was facilitated by its superior resources, its dense and relatively docile Indian population, and the superior shelter afforded by the mangrove-lined estuary of the Río del Realejo. From the beginning it proved an attractive target for the pirates of the several European nations bent on embarrassing the Spanish presence. Their persistent threats, coupled with the relative shallowness of the river, a gradual depletion of nearby timber and naval stores, and apparent mismanagement of the shipyards, led to the decline of shipbuilding in the eighteenth century and the port's eventual abandonment. In its place the modern, mechanized port of Corinto, linked by rail and highway with the interior of the republic, serves today as Nicaragua's principal Pacific gateway through which

---

[63]Robert S. Smith, "Financing the Central American Federation, 1821-1838," *Hispanic American Historical Review*, 48 (1963), 509.

[64]Radell, *Historical Geography of Western Nicaragua*, p. 195; Mariano Barreto, *Recuerdos históricos de Chichigalpa, Corinto, Chinandega, y León* (León, Nicaragua, 1921), pp. 131-132.

most of its imports and exports flow. All that is left of the former port and *villa* of Realejo is a forlorn and forgotten cluster of thatched-roofed houses huddled at the head of a minor tidal estuary on the margin of the vast new fields of cotton and planted pasture grass that cover the fertile Chinandega volcanic outwash plain--mute evidence of the effect of time and of changing technology on the evaluation of site and situation.

13

Santa María la Antigua del Darién[*]

It is one of the more extraordinary facts of history that the site of the first European settlement and administrative center on the American mainland lies on what today is one of the continent's least known, most isolated, and inhospitable coasts. The rain-drenched shores of Darién, facing the Caribbean along the present-day border between Colombia and Panama, were densely settled in aboriginal times. Disease and forced labor decimated the native population in the first years of the Spanish Conquest. After 14 difficult years the Spaniards abandoned the area for a drier, more healthful, and strategically better located site on the Pacific coast near Panama City.

Santa María la Antigua del Darién, the first permanent Spanish settlement, functioned as the seat of authority of the Crown in northwestern South America from 1510 until its abandonment in 1524. It superseded the short-lived establishment called San Sebastián de Urabá, founded by Ojeda in 1509 on the opposite side of the Gulf of Urabá and abandoned to hostile Indians and their poisonous arrows a few months later. Las Casas gives Balboa the major role in the decision to move westward across the gulf, where there were good lands, a large and apparently friendly Indian population, and mountain streams that the natives described as being paved with gold.

Despite its early importance and considerable size, there has been uncertainty about the precise site of Santa María la Antigua. The descriptions of the chroniclers, especially Oviedo, Balboa, and Peter Martyr, suggest that it was located some miles inland on a small stream known as the Río Darién, which then entered directly into the Caribbean a few miles west of the Atrato delta. However,

---

[*]Reprinted from *The Geographical Review*, Vol. 50, pp. 274-276 (1960).

no positive identification could be made because no stream seemed to fit the descriptions and, moreover, the entire area had become overgrown with rank second-growth rain forest. Two Colombian scholars who independently studied the problem in the field made tentative identifications, but their findings were not widely disseminated (Eduardo Acevedo Latorre: Breve noticia sobre los lugares donde existieron San Sebastián de Urabá y Santa María la Antigua del Darién, *Bol. de Historia y Antigüedades*, Vol. 30, Bogotá, 1943, pp. 1096-1102; Graciliano Arcila Vélez: Acerca de Santamaría de la Antigua del Darién, *Bol. Inst. de Antropol., Univ. de Antioquia*, Vol. 1, Medellín, 1956, pp. 375-376). Early in 1956, an expedition under the leadership of Leopold III of Belgium, with logistic support that included two helicopters, visited this northwesternmost corner of Colombia and identified and excavated what is beyond doubt the site of the original Spanish *villa* (C. Verlinden, J. Mertens, and G. Reichel-Dolmatoff: Santa María la Antigua del Darién, première "ville" coloniale de la Terre Ferme américaine, *Rev. de Historia de América*, No. 45, México, D.F., 1958, pp. 1-48).

Aided by aerial photographs and using the helicopters for reconnaissance, the Belgians located the extensive ruins of Santa María 7.5 kilometers from the coast and directly south of the high, wooded island of La Gloria (Isla Tarena) and its protected port (Acla). At this point a chain of low mountains comes down to the sea, the first protection encountered by ships approaching from the northeast across the Gulf of Urabá and past the Atrato delta. The beach behind La Gloria, it seems clear, formed the port for the ancient villa, rather than that opposite an island a few miles to the northwest, as Kathleen Romoli has suggested in her brilliant biography of Balboa (*Balboa of Darién: Discoverer of the Pacific* [Garden City, N.Y., 1953], pp. 56-57). This is demonstrated by the historian Verlinden (Verlinden, Mertens, and Reichel-Dolmatoff, *op. cit.*, pp. 3-5) on the basis of the early documents and seems corroborated by the sixteenth-century cannon emplacements found in the tangled forest on the summit of the island. Leopold's party, following the lead of the Colombian investigators earlier cited, concluded that the Río Darién (now the Río Tanela), beside which the settlement stood, formerly debouched directly northward into the gulf a few kilometers southeast of La Gloria. Aerial photographs are said to reveal clearly the course of the former stream, which may be traced by the vegetation. Arcila Vélez, who earlier had made a similar conjecture, was told by old settlers that as recently as 60 years ago the Tanela had flowed directly to the sea, but an earthquake, accompanied by landslides, had blocked its course and diverted it to the east. The Belgians report that the Tanela now flows eastward and parallel to the coast through a marshy area, draining into the Río Tislo near its junction with the Atrato a few miles from the mouth of this great river. The Río Tislo is identified on the Barranquilla sheet of the American Geographical Society's Millionth Map of Hispanic America as the Caño de Tarena, of which the Río Tanela is now apparently the major left-bank tributary.

The site of the capital where the aged Pedrarias ruled with an iron hand and whence the ill-fated Balboa set out for his historic crossing of the isthmus was crisscrossed with 23 trenches by the Belgian archaeologists in a period of 18 days. They found a fairly large Indian habitation site below the bronze, iron, glazed brick, and porcelain left by the Spaniards. On its northern and eastern margins the archaeological zone, 650 meters by 350 meters, extends into a swampy area that is very wet in the dry season and completely inundated during the heavy rains. Artifacts were found on the higher ground to a depth of 1.5 meters. Although there was conclusive evidence of a street pattern in the Spanish settlement, there was a general absence of durable construction materials. The Europeans, like the Indians, built of wood and thatch. The site of Santa María is on a forested eminence whose summit stands some 15 meters above the surrounding swamps, through which the waters of the Río Tanela meander sluggishly eastward. It lies some 2.5 kilometers east of the modern Negro settlement of Tanela, to whose inhabitants the place is known as "La Antigua." Its marshy, malarial environment makes it seem one of the least attractive of all possible locations for a frontier establishment, but to the sixteenth-century Spaniards it may have offered compelling military advantages. Low hills hid it from ships approaching from the northeast, yet southward and eastward it had a clear view of the Atrato delta and the Gulf of Darién. Thus Santa María controlled the entrance into the Atrato Valley as well as into the adjacent Panamanian highlands. In its prime it was no mean town, with a church, a Franciscan convent, government buildings, and well-constructed residences. Fernández de Oviedo valued his home there at 6,000 ducats. No population census seems to exist, but an expedition that arrived in 1514 brought more than 2,000 Spanish soldiers and settlers, some with their wives. In addition to Balboa, Pedrarias, and the chronicler Oviedo, here lived such men as Pizarro, Almagro, Pascual de Andagoya, Hernando de Soto, and others who figured prominently in the Conquest.

It was the promise of gold that lured the Spaniards to Darién, together with the large Indian population available to work the stream placers. Today the gold is forgotten, and the Indians have been replaced by a sparse population of shifting cultivators, descendants of escaped slaves, who carry the same culture as the people to the south recently described with such discernment by Robert C. West (The Pacific Lowlands of Colombia: A Negroid Area of the American Tropics, *Louisiana State Univ. Studies, Social Sci. Ser. No. 8*, Baton Rouge, 1957). The place that Balboa thought the most suitable location for the first Spanish settlement on Tierra Firme lies smothered under the tropical forest, another reminder of the impermanence of the works of man and his changing evaluation of geographic site and situation.

PART FOUR

Prehistoric Ridged Fields

14

Ancient Ridged Fields of the San Jorge River Floodplain, Colombia[*]

For more than half of every year the lower Magdalena Valley of Colombia is a vast aquatic landscape. Where the Magdalena is joined by its first major tributary, the San Jorge, some 150 miles from the Caribbean coast, this seasonally flooded plain, a bewildering and constantly changing complex of shallow lakes, swamps, and sloughs, flares out to a width of nearly 100 miles. With the aid of aerial photographs and low-flying reconnaissance aircraft, we have identified along the western margin of this floodplain an extensive area of ridged fields that apparently were constructed by Indian agriculturists well before the arrival of Europeans in the New World. It is remarkable that these conspicuous patterns on the land have never attracted the attention of travelers or scholars; for they lie in readily accessible country directly below the main airline route between Colombia's coastal cities and Bogotá and Medellín.

The mesopotamian zone of swamps, of *ciénagas*, in which these extraordinary man-made features are found is blocked off on the north by the Tertiary hill lands of the Sabanas de Bolívar and to the east of the Magdalena by outliers of the Sierra Nevada de Santa Marta. In this great settling basin, sometimes known as the Mompós Depression (Depresión Monposina), the muddy waters of the

[*]By James J. Parsons and William A. Bowen. Reprinted from *The Geographical Review*, Vol. 56, pp. 317-343 (1966). Fieldwork was supported by The Geography Branch, Office of Naval Research. The authors are grateful to the Instituto Geográfico "Agustín Codazzi" in Bogotá for free access to its splendid collection of aerial photographs and to the many people in Colombia who assisted them in other ways. Gerardo Reichel-Dolmatoff, Universidad de los Andes, Bogotá, and William M. Denevan, University of Wisconsin, Madison, read the manuscript and made constructive suggestions.

Ríos San Jorge, Cauca, and César converge with those of the Magdalena. Here are found probably the maximum rates of alluvial deposition in the Magdalena system.[1] Virtually the entire area lies less than 8 feet (25 meters) above sea level according to the new 1:100,000 topographic maps of the Instituto Geográfico "Agustín Codazzi." When not covered with water, the area serves as the rich pasture reserve of the departments of Bolívar and Córdoba, Colombia's two leading livestock states, but its human population is sparse.

The seasonality of precipitation strongly influences the rhythm of life in northern Colombia today, as it must have done for the unknown people who built these ridges. The dry season, from December to late April, is progressively less marked from north to south. The transition is particularly sharp south of Ayapel. Thus the annual precipitation on the lower San Jorge (1,600-1,800 millimeters) is less than half that on the lower Cauca (Pato Mines, 4,400 millometers), where even the driest month (February) normally receives more than 2 inches (60 millometers), and the rain forest reaches optimal development. But it is the regimes of the rivers, controlled by the march of annual precipitation in their headwater areas, that largely determine patterns of land use and human occupancy in the floodplains.

The west side of the Mompós Depression, where the waters of the San Jorge and the Cauca mingle before joining the Magdalena, has long been famed for the gold taken from its countless Indian mounds, which were the objects of Spanish looters following the initial *entradas* into the equally rich graveyards of the adjacent Sinú country. Except for the Reichel-Dolmatoffs' hearsay mention in 1953 of "grandes extensiones de montes inundadizo atravesadas por diques, canals y surcos paralelos" near Ayapel,[2] these artificially

---

[1]Ernesto Guhl: Ambiente geográfico-humano de la costa del Atlántico, *Revista Geográfica* (Universidad del Atlántico, Barranquilla), Vol. 1, No. 1, 1952, pp. 137-172; reference on pp. 168-169.

[2]Gerardo and Alicia Reichel-Dolmatoff: Investigaciones arqueológicas en el Depto. del Magdalena 1946-1950: Parte III, Arqueología del Bajo Magdalena, *Divulgaciones Etnológicas* (Universidad del Atlantico, Barranquilla), Vol. 3, No. 4, 1953, pp. 1-123: "En la región de Ayapel . . . se dicen existir grandes extensiones de montes inundadizo atravesadas por diques, canales y surcos paralelos de 100 metros de largo por un metro de ancho. Se trata de extensiones de unas diez hectáres cada una y en las elevaciones vecinas se encuentran abundantes fragmentos cerámicos y líticos. Estos datos, obtenidas de personas fidedignas de la región, son de valor especial . . ." (p. 14). Gerardo Reichel-Dolmatoff mentions the San Jorge ridges again in "Colombia" (Ancient Peoples and Places, Vol. 44; New York, 1965), p. 127: "In many parts of the San Jorge valley one can still observe hundreds of acres covered with parallel ridges separated by furrows,

corrugated surfaces, reminiscent of giant washboards when seen from the air, have received no attention either in travel accounts or in the scholarly literature. They are indicative of a hitherto unexpectedly dense aboriginal population of considerable social and technological sophistication. They take the form of groups of parallel ridges arranged in various patterns over an area some 70 miles long by 20 miles wide on the San Jorge floodplain within the *municipios* of Ayapel (Córdoba), San Marcos (Bolívar), Sucre (Bolívar), and San Benito Abad (Bolívar). Forest clearing in recent decades has exposed them in much the same manner that the medieval open-field landscapes of ridges and furrows were earlier unveiled in Denmark and in the British Isles.[3]

When the San Jorge old fields are partly inundated by floodwater, modest relief contrasts can be clearly distinguished, and our reconnaissance visit in mid-June 1965, was especially well timed in this respect. At that time, in the first days of the rainy season, the humped backs of the ridges were still accentuated by parched grass, while the depressions between them, not yet inundated, remained green. From the ground, however, they are not always easy to detect and may sometimes be unrecognized by a person who is not familiar with them; from a dugout canoe, the commonest means of travel in the area, they are rarely visible. Moreover, these old fields (*lomillas*) are not always recognized by the local inhabitants as man-made. It has remained for air photography and low-level air reconnaissance to make known their extent and nature. Much work, however, remains to be done to clarify their age and significance.

The Extent of the San Jorge Old Fields

From aerial photography we have been able to delimit some 160,000 acres in the San Jorge floodplain where these old fields are well developed, from Tierra Santa downstream almost to the junction with the Magdalena. The original extent of the ridging was probably much greater than is now discernible. From a low-flying plane we could distinguish vestiges of old fields that were invisible on vertical air photography, including a considerable area that could be seen through the extensive shallow waters of the Ciénaga de Ayapel. Of the 160,000 acres of land and water surface mapped as old fields

---

providing well-drained fields for maize and other crops."

[3]See, for example, M.W. Beresford and J.K.S. St. Joseph: Medieval England: An Aerial Survey (Cambridge Air Surveys, Vol. 2; Cambridge, 1958).

(Fig. 14.1), perhaps half is covered by specifically identifiable ridged surfaces.

The system of land use that produced these ridges and swales appears to have been a culture trait of continuous and sharply delimited distribution. Although similar ecologic environments exist along the lower Cauca and on both sides of the Magdalena from at least Barrancabermeja to its mouth (including the Isla de Mompós and the extensive Ciénaga Zapatosa on the lower Río César), careful inspection of air photography has failed to reveal any evidence of such labor-intensive agricultural engineering. The floodplain of the Río Sinú, inhabited by a people of similar cultural attainments at the time of first contact with Europeans, also lacks indications of such features, except, possibly, for one small area with suggestively parallel lines on the land immediately north of the famous Indian necropolis of Betancí (Cenú). There the floodplain of the Sinú is only 30 miles from that of the San Jorge.

The Sabanas de Bolívar

The surfaces of the rolling Tertiary hill lands between the Sinú and the San Jorge, known as the Sabanas de Bolívar (Sabanas de Ayapel, Sabanas de San Marcos), show no evidence of such old fields, although burial mounds are conspicuous along the margins. These upland surfaces, 100 to 300 feet above sea level, overlooking the San Jorge floodplain, were apparently nearly treeless when first seen by the Spaniards, whence the name *Sabanas*. Gordon[4] has convincingly explained this by the pressures of an expanding population and the destructive exploitation of a slash-and-burn agriculture that was leading to progressive deterioration of these shale-and-sandstone-derived soils, the formation of iron concretions and subsoil hardpans, and the replacement of the original forest cover by coarse bunchgrasses[5] and fire-resistant savanna trees (*Curatella, Byrsonima*). The San Marcos airport stands on one such savanna remnant today, and another, known as the *sabanas* comunales de Ayapel, lies behind the town of that name.

---

[4]B. LeRoy Gordon: Human Geography and Ecology in the Sinú Country of Colombia, *Ibero-Americana*, No. 39, 1957; see also James J. Parsons: The Settlement of the Sinú Valley of Colombia, *Geogr. Rev.*, Vol. 42, 1952, pp. 67-86.

[5]The principal native grass species are *Paspalum carinatum, Axonopus purpusii*, and *Andropogon leucostachylus*; sedges are also plentiful. Identification by Jason R. Swallen, United States National Herbarium.

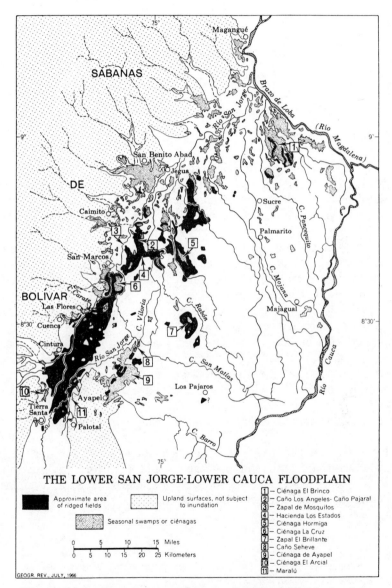

THE LOWER SAN JORGE-LOWER CAUCA FLOODPLAIN

■ Approximate area of ridged fields	▦ Upland surfaces, not subject to inundation	1 – Ciénaga El Brinco 2 – Caño Los Angeles- Caño Pajaral 3 – Zapal de Mosquitos 4 – Hacienda Los Estados 5 – Ciénaga Hormiga 6 – Ciénaga La Cruz 7 – Zapal El Brillante 8 – Caño Seheve 9 – Ciénaga de Ayapel 10 – Ciénaga El Arcial 11 – Maralú
	▨ Seasonal swamps or ciénagas	

0   5   10   15 Miles
0 5 10 15 20 25 Kilometers

GEOGR. REV., JULY, 1966

Figure 14.1 Approximate Extent of Ridged Fields in the Río San Jorge Floodplain.

The process of savanna extension seems to have been inter-rupted by the Conquest and the resultant catastrophic decrease in native populations, but not before large areas of degraded grassland vegetation had been established, encouraged by annual burning. These areas support a considerable number of livestock during the rainy half of the year but are abandoned during the dry season when the stock are moved to the still-green ciénagas of the San Jorge or the Sinú.[6]   A similar complementarity between upland and lowland may well have attracted Indian populations to this area in pre-Columbian times.

The Spanish Entradas

In early accounts the lower San Jorge area was known as Penzenú. Its native population, cultural kin to the Cenú, suffered a similar fate of social disorganization and rapid demographic decline.[7] Early in 1535 the Spaniards under Alonso de Heredia, having looted the graves at Cenú, advanced eastward to the drainage of the Río San Jorge and entered the savannas of a *gran señor y cacique* called Yapel or Yapé, whence the name Ayapel.   After a costly confronta-tion with more than 2,000 brightly plumed warriors armed with bows and clubs, the Spaniards reached Yapel's town, on a height of land, probably not far from the present town of Ayapel overlooking the beautiful ciénaga of that name.   It reminded them of Cenú, being laid out in straight streets and plazas, with well-built, clean houses, and surrounded by extensive fields and gardens.[8]   Gold objects worth some 6,000 pesos were taken from the houses, and more from settlements within 1 or 2 leagues inhabited by vassals of Yapel.   When Heredia ordered the soldiers to refrain from excavating the numerous grave mounds to avoid further arousing the natives, there were murmurs of mutiny. He argued that the graves could wait, that the dry season invited them to search for larger prizes toward the east, and that they could ill afford to lose time, especially since they had encountered no maize there, a food they had come to consider practically indispensable.

---

[6]Herbert Wilhelmy: Die Weidewirtschaft im heissen Tiefland Nordkolumbiens, *Gregr. Rundschau*, Vol. 6, 1954, pp. 41-54.

[7]Gordon, *op. cit* [see footnote 4 above], pp. 33 ff.

[8]Juan de Castellanos: Elegías de varones ilustres de Indias (3rd edit.; Madrid, 1874), p. 382.

To the east they found other towns but no evidence of maize. According to Castellanos, they were forced to live on the fish that the natives, having no salt for preserving them, customarily smoked *en barbacoa* along the streams where they were caught. The Spaniards reached the Cauca before hunger forced them to return to the *pueblo grande* of Yapel. They arrived there with 300 fewer soldiers than had set out,[9] an indication that this was indeed a major expedition, the feeding of which could well have presented serious problems. They found that in their absence the graves had been cleaned out of all gold, presumably by the suspicious natives, who were well aware of what had happened earlier at Cenú. Frustrated, the Spaniards abandoned the area and turned their attention increasingly to the presumed source area of the gold, the mountains and mines of Antioquia to the south. In the following year a party of 180 Spaniards from Cenú in search of the fabled province of Urute happened on the headwaters of the San Jorge, but they were lost and did not linger.[10] In 1539 the governor of Cartagena sent an expedition to search out additional rich graves reported on the San Jorge, but it returned with a disappointing 1,500 pesos and the report that there were many graves but they were all *sepulturas pobres.*[11]

The San Jorge area, to which the *gobernación* of Santa Marta also laid claim,[12] early became a refuge for runaway slaves and rebellious Indians. It was within the province of Jegua of the cacique Talacigua, whose raids had long plagued navigation on the Magdalena.[13] Talacigua controlled the Indian labor supply of the *villa* of Mompós as well as the river traffic. Numerous reports on his activities and the Spanish strategy for his containment are given in the "Documentos inéditos" recently brought together by Juan Friede, but in none of these is there any specific reference to the agricultural system or earthworks of the San Jorge.

Most of the Indians not killed off by disease or warfare were eventually settled in new towns toward the coast or along the Magdalena. The Indians of Jegua who refused to serve the Span-

---

[9]Castellanos, *loc. cit.*

[10]Juan Friede, comp.: Documentos inéditos para la historia de Colombia, 1509-1550 (9 vols.; Bogotá, 1955-1960), Vol. 5, p. 50.

[11]*Ibid.*, Vol. 7, p. 331; and Vol. 5, p. 231.

[12]*Ibid.*, Vol. 5, p. 180.

[13]*Ibid.*, Vol. 8, pp. 55, 67, and 105.

iards took final refuge at Tamalameque, farther up the Magdalena, where they continued to inflict much damage on passing shipping.[14] As early as 1536 runaway Negro slaves had been loose in the area, terrorizing Indians and Christians alike. A report of their activities by the governor of Cartagena in 1545[15] refers to a Negro raid on the settlement of Tofeme (Caimito) in which 20 persons were killed and more than 250 taken prisoners with much cruelty. The whole province was said to be terrified, and several Indian towns were abandoned through fear of further raids. In these first years following the Conquest the modern tri-ethnic population of the area had already begun to evolve.

Later Settlement History

The villa of Ayapel, the one durable Spanish settlement on the lower San Jorge, apparently dates from 1582, when the villa of San Gerónimo del Monte, a mining camp founded 12 years earlier by the governor of Antioquia on the upper reaches of the San Jorge, was removed to the site of the modern town on the shore of the ciénaga.[16] But it was isolated and was soon all but forgotten. A few *hacendados* from Mompós sent their cattle to graze on the grasses of the ciénaga, which during the dry season shrank to a relatively small pond. In 1776 construction of a stock trail was begun from Ayapel to Medellín to bring Ayapeleño cattle overland to the mining centers of Antioquia.[17] This later became an important trade.

The intensification of missionary and town-founding activities in Nueva Granada in the late eighteenth century had its impact on the San Jorge area. It is recounted in the diary of Padre Joseph

---

[14]*Ibid.*, p. 69.

[15]*Ibid.*, pp. 67-69.

[16]Dimas Badel: Diccionario histórico geográfico de Bolívar (Corozal, 1943), p. 27. However, according to another source (Tulio Ospina and others: Informe sobre límites del departamento de Antioquia [Medellín, 1912]) the actual transfer of the villa was not effected until 1642, "to a place called Sejevé belonging to *vecinos* of Antioquia." Antioquia's claim to Ayapel, reiterated from time to time, was never validated.

[17]Francisco Silvestre: Informe sobre la apertura del camino desde Antioquia hasta Ayapel, y sobre la distancia que hay desde la propia ciudad al Paso del Río San Jorge, 4 Junio, 1776, *Archivo Historial*, Manizales, July, 1919, pp. 560-568.

Palacios de la Vega,[18] who was charged with the conversion of the Indians and Negros of the San Jorge and with bringing the families dispersed through the forests and along the rivers into established towns, where they might come under the civil and ecclesiastical authorities. In this he seems to have been singularly successful. In March, 1786, he was at the mission outpost of San Cipriano, deep in the forests of the upper San Jorge, administering to Chocó and Chimila Indians. The next year he shifted his base to Ayapel, five days downstream, where one of his first tasks was to induce the 135 families of the *palenque de Carate*, who had "rebelled," to resettle in the villa of Ayapel. The *palenque*, a fortified Negro village, must have been somewhere along Caño Carate, one of the best-developed areas of old fields in the San Jorge region. In the following months Padre Palacios brought several hundred additional persons from the dispersed settlements along the San Jorge and the lower Cauca and their distributaries into Ayapel and Majagual, "people so lost that they appear men only in physical aspect, but wild animals in condition and custom." The physical and moral misery of these naked, hungry, incestuous, polygamous, malaria-infested vagabonds, as described by the padre, may well be exaggerated, but by bringing groups that had lived in almost complete isolation as subsistence fishermen and farmers into social contact he apparently opened the way for the establishment of the modern society of the region. Plantains, maize, yuca, yams, and rice, and contraband tobacco and sugarcane for *aguardiente*, were the principal agricultural products. This valorous Franciscan, whom Reichel-Dolmatoff calls "the last conquistador of the Nuevo Reino de Granada," must have passed over and through many of these old fields, but no reference to them appears in his diary.

When the Alsatian mining engineer Luis Striffler was in the San Jorge country a century later, it was in the process of being opened up by stockmen from the Sabanas.[19] Clearing and settlement extended upstream as far as Maralú, 6 miles west of Ayapel; beyond that point the forest was unbroken. Sabana-margin towns such as Ayapel, Las Flores, San Marcos, and San Benito Abad, on navigable ciénagas yet high enough to escape the floods, were prosperous labor-contracting points and trade centers, linking two contrasting but complementary environments. The collecting of *Castilloa* rubber,

---

[18]G. Reichel-Dolmatoff, edit.: Diario de viaje del Padre Joseph Palacios de la Vega entre los indios y negros de la provincia de Cartagena en el Nuevo Reino de Granada 1787-1788 (Bogotá, 1955).

[19]Luis Striffler: *El río San Jorge* (Cartagena, 1886).

ipecac root, pita fiber, and bird feathers was a commercial activity of some importance. The September trade fair at San Bentio was famed throughout the region. San Marcos was the traditional fish market, with buyers from the Sabanas congregating there, especially during the Lenten season. The forests of the floodplains were being converted into pastures of Pará grass (*Panicum barbinode*) or native species. Clearing must have revealed the corrugated surfaces of many old fields, but they seem to have escaped Striffler's attention. Only the *zapales*, the swamp forests that mark the permanently inundated backwater depressions, were free from attack by the ax.

Hydrology and Alluvial Morphology

The alluvial morphology of the Mompós Depression is in continuous evolution, evidenced by its countless abandoned channels (*caños*), natural levees, oxbow lakes, and ciénagas. One of the most spectacular recent changes occurred at the end of the nineteenth century when the Magdalena shifted its main course westward into the Brazo de Loba, leaving the colonial villa of Mompós stranded.[20] The resultant increased volume of the Brazo de Loba, which also receives the Cauca and San Jorge discharges before rejoining the Brazo de Mompós below Magangué, must have had a blocking effect on the San Jorge and may have led to increased flooding in the old-field area toward San Marcos and Ayapel. It should have had a similar effect on the Cauca, which at flood stage discharges part of its flow into the lower San Jorge through half a dozen left-bank distributaries. Caño Mojana is the largest of these and apparently is the only one that carries moving water throughout the year. Because of its well-developed natural levees, its banks are densely peopled; the towns of Majugual, Palmarito, and Sucre are on its east bank. In the time of Padre Palacios de la Vega, Cauca waters moved into the Ciénaga de Ayapel through Caño Barro[21] and then northward into the San Jorge or Caño Vilorio through Caño Seheve. This still happens when the Cauca reaches bank-full stage. More commonly the Ciénaga de Ayapel is fed by San Jorge flood-waters flowing southward from Boca de Seheve. Caño Seheve reverses its flow as the waters subside and the ciénaga begins to

---

[20]Helmuth Seidel: Der Abflussvorgang im Rio Magdalena, *Zeitschr. Gesell. für Erdkunde zu Berlin*, 1934, pp. 284-302.

[21]Reichel-Dolmatoff, Diario de viaje del Padre Joseph Palacios de la Vega [see footnote 18 above], p. 37.

drain. The gradient between the Cauca and the San Jorge is slight, not more than a foot to a mile.[22]

As the San Jorge heads in the forested, rain-drenched Serranía de San Jerónimo along the Antioquia-Córdoba border scarcely 70 miles southwest of Ayapel, its flood crest is normally well in advance of that of the Cauca, which in turn usually reaches its maximum height before the December crest of the Magdalena.   Local residents affirm that the ridged fields in front of San Marcos did not regularly flood in times past, before clearing of the forests had begun in the San Jorge headwaters.   Accelerated erosion in the last 40 years is said to have led to the silting up of the beds of the river and its distributaries to the point that flooding has become more widespread and more prolonged.   In late June 1965, when flooding of the old fields on both sides of Caño Carate was already well advanced, we could see marks on the trunks of trees along the banks which indicated high-water lines at least 6 feet above the level at that time.   This would have assured the total inundation of the natural levees and the ridges built on them.   It is the Cauca, however, that is responsible for the exceptional high waters along the lower San Jorge, especially when its flood stage coincides with the Magdalena's.   The Magdalena Valley Development Commission has accepted the 1916 high water as the norm for the "50 year" flood;[23] Striffler[24] refers to the exceptional San Jorge flood of 1879, which inundated the Zapal de Mosquitos, opposite San Marcos, for the first time since 1819.

Man's activities have influenced the drainage within the San Jorge-Cauca mesopotamia in yet another way.   Landowners along some of the north-flowing distributaries of the Cauca have damned them off to protect their *potreros* from flooding, and this has worsened flood conditions along the left-bank channels farther downstream, especially Caño Mojana.   Local feuding, retributive raids, and nighttime dynamiting parties are said to have resulted. The reduction in the flow of the Cauca waters into the San Jorge old-field area, for whatever reason, should lead not only to a reduction of flooding there but also to reduced sedimentation.   Unfortunately, no data exist on streamflow, flood stages, and sediment load for either river.

---

[22]"Programa de desarrollo económico de Valle del Magdalena y norte de Colombia: Informe de una misión dirigida por Lauchlin Currie" (Bogotá, 1960), p. 273.

[23]*Ibid.*, p. 275.

[24]*Op. cit.* [see footnote 19 above], p. 74.

Isostatic subsidence, too, may have strongly influenced the drainage history of the Cauca-San Jorge floodplain. Continued sinking of the land surface could account for the prolonged flooding of ridged fields that in times past may have been relatively dry. Such subsidence has been well established for most of the great river valleys and deltas of the world, and it seems reasonable to assume that it is also occurring in the Mompós Depression. If so, it may even have led to the obliteration of additional old fields of unknown extent. At least a suggestion of this lies in the fact that the ridges seem in general best preserved along the margins of the Sabanas and are progressively indistinct eastward toward the axis of the depression. But further checking in the field will be necessary to confirm this hypothesis. Also, through laboratory analysis of sediment cores, rates of subsidence may eventually be established and the source areas of the sediments determined.

A 3,000-year pollen diagram, as yet unpublished, from a ciénaga in the lower Magdalena Valley between Magangué and El Banco reveals clear fluctuations of water level, interpreted as climatic, with the drier periods showing small maxima of the savanna xerophytes *Curatella* and *Byrsonima*. A major dry period has been dated by carbon 14 as about A.D. 700-800, and others occurred earlier.[25] If these do indeed represent significant climatic variation within the past few thousand years, yet another consideration is added to the problem of the ridges. An environment more arid than that of the present might, at least in some instances, make it possible to postulate irrigation as a rational objective of their builders.

Classification of Ridge Patterns

The San Jorge old fields may be classified into three distinctive types: (1) a "caño" pattern, in which the ridges and swales extend back at right or slightly oblique angles from the higher ground (natural levees) on each side of abandoned channels (Fig. 14.2); (2) a "checkerboard" pattern, in which blocks of short parallel ridges, from 10 to 30 yards on a side, are arrayed irregularly but more or less at right angles to one another; and (3) a clustering of loosely parallel ridges, many of considerable length and without evident orientation to natural levees, which often gives a "combed" or "grained" appearance to the surface when viewed from the air.

The most striking, and perhaps most extensive, of the field types is what we have termed the "caño" pattern. Here the associa-

[25]Personal communication from Thomas van der Hammen, Rijksmuseum van Geologie en Mineralogie, Leiden.

tion of the ridged fields with the high ground of the natural levees strongly suggests that drainage improvement was the primary consideration in their construction. Depending on the microrelief, these ridges and swales may run back from the old channels for only a few yards or for nearly a mile before being lost or inundated in the backswamps. The sinuous channel, choked with water hyacinths, of the abandoned Caño Los Angeles-Caño Pajaral system, northeast of San Marcos, provides the classic example (Fig. 14.3). For more than 10 miles it is continuously bordered with parallel ridges, most of them about 1,200 feet long and perhaps 20 feet wide, that run in straight lines down the gentle backslopes of its natural levees, much as closely spaced property lines run back from the banks of the Mississippi River in French Louisiana. The trees growing on the ridges (probably *mangle, Symmeria panicalata*) give a striking orchard-like appearance to the landscape. A more recent distributary, Caño Pimienta, itself sealed off and abandoned, has broken across the ridged and furrowed axis of Caño Pajaral near Hacienda Los Estados, blurring but not obliterating the old-field patterns as seen from air photographs. Although veneered with the levee silts from the new Caño Pimienta, which overlies it almost at right angles, the striated surface vegetation pattern, oriented to the old axis of Caño Pajaral like metal filings to a magnet, clearly betrays the buried clay ridges. Nearby caños of about the same size and importance as Caño Pajaral have no ridges associated with them. Could this particular channel have had some sort of special, perhaps even religious, attraction for these people? Or maybe the unoccupied caños have originated since the period of ridge-building activity? In the latter case the ridged levees may be the oldest ones, as the photographs have strongly suggested to alluvial morphologists who have examined them.

Another conspicuous example of this association of ridges and swales with particular channels is found along Caño Carate, for several miles upstream from its mouth, near San Marcos. This is a live channel, a major tributary of the San Jorge, which in Striffler's time was used at flood stage as a shortcut to the upper river.[26] It is no longer so used, but it is navigable for most of the year for at least 20 miles upstream, as far as Ciénaga El Arcial, and serves the Sabana-margin towns of Las Flores, Cuenca, and Cintura. During flood stage all but the highest points on the levees, usually artificial mounds or house platforms, are inundated. Under present conditions some of the ridges radiating back from Caño Carate into the Ciénaga

---

[26]Striffler, *op. cit.* [see footnote 19 above], p. 67.

190

Figure 14.2   Ridges or planting platforms at right, partly flooded, appear at right angles to an abandoned channel. Those on wooded point at upper left are of lesser relief and may be of greater antiquity. Photo: William A. Bowen.

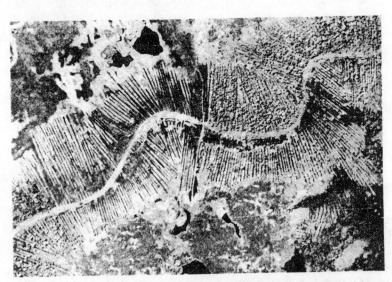

Figure 14.3   Section of vermiform Caño Pajaral with ridges on natural levees oriented at right angles to channel like iron filings to a magnet. Photo: Instituto Geográfico Austín, July 1954.

San Marcos and the Ciénaga La Cruz may be under water for more than 6 months of the year. This may be attributable in part to subsidence, but it also reflects changes in the drainage system. Until some 20 years ago Caño Carate apparently debouched directly into the San Jorge, but it has since breached its levee and opened a new channel (Boca Nueva), which flows into the Ciénaga San Marcos and thence to the river.

The checkerboard pattern of blocks of short ridges, usually set at right angles to one another, is widely dispersed, especially on somewhat better drained lands where there are no well-developed natural levees. Occasionally one may detect in the air photographs a faint pattern of ridges that is oriented in "herringbone" fashion to old crevasse breaks in the natural levees of distributaries. A particularly intricate pattern can be seen northeast of the Ciénaga de Ayapel between Zapal El Brillante and Caño Rabón, and again back from the left bank of the San Jorge opposite Maralú. The same pattern is found in the backwater swamps, as in the Ciénaga La Cruz, where photographs taken in June 1965 show an aquatic grass (probably *Hymenachne amplexicaulis*) outlining the crazy quilt of fields with remarkable clarity. Although these patchworks of grouped parallel ridges are remarkably suggestive of medieval European open fields, they can hardly have been associated with the same scattered pattern of ownership and occupancy. The English "furlong" was technically such a block of plowed furrows and ridges, each ridge having a different owner. If the communal land tenure so widespread in aboriginal America existed in the San Jorge, as we tend to assume, why are these blocks of ridges and ditches of such varying size and alignment? Sometimes even a single ridge is broken by a series of very short ridges set at right angles to it. We have no hint as to the rationale that lay behind this intricate but seemingly nonfunctional organization of agricultural surfaces.

Some of the best-preserved and more clearly visible ridges show a relief of 3 feet or more, possibly as much as 5 feet. In many situations, however, the relief may be so slight as to be invisible except for a faint texture or color contrast in the vegetation or by irregularities in the margins of shallow sheets of standing water. These may be discernible only on enlargements of the available 1:60,000 air photographs. No ridges and swales are found on the natural levees of the present-day San Jorge, nor are they found along the presently active distributaries of the Cauca such as Caño Mojana, Caño San Matías, and Caño Rabón. These channels and levees could, of course, post-date the period of ridge building, or the levees may have been sufficiently high to obviate the need for such earthworks.

The ridges are normally wide enough to have supported at least four or five rows of root crops or maize. The Caño Carate fields are about 45 feet from ridge crest to ridge crest, and this seems to be a reasonably representative figure. Some are more closely spaced, a few more widely so. The slightly rounded crowns of most of the ridges range from 15 to 20 feet in width. The separating ditches are usually about twice as wide as the ridges, but they may be up to four or five times as wide, when the area takes on the aspect of a flooded Oriental rice landscape (Fig. 14.2).

Many of the ridge soils are heavy clays, reddish yellow and mottled with iron stains. Others are a more friable clay loam. The material from which the ridges were constructed, dug from the adjacent borrow ditches, would originally have been darker in color and richer in organic matter. Mixing of soil with vegetable matter in the process of their construction doubtless added fertility and improved soil structure. The mottling of the tough clays of the ridges, and their sometimes hard concretionary structure when dried, would be indicative of oxidation associated with alternate periods of desiccation and flooding. On the radial ridges running back from Caño Carate we found well-formed iron concretions on the surface of a 6-foot-high ridge under a clump of spiny *lata* palms. Surficial digging exposed no pottery in the ridges, though it is abundant on the higher house mounds and burial sites often associated with the old fields. Small pieces of black gritty material found at a depth of 8 inches under a giant *Ficus* on a ridge some 200 yards back from Caño Carate have not yet been positively identified.

Burial Mounds and House Platforms

Artificial earth mounds, either settlement sites or graves (*túmulos*), are associated with most of the caños that lace the San Jorge floodplain. Normally they are from 5 to 15 feet in height; exceptionally they reach 25 feet. A few covering several acres indicate major settlement concentrations. All are littered with potsherds, and most have been superficially excavated by grave robbers in search of gold. Some objects of impressive worth have been recovered, but in this matter exaggeration is undoubtedly rife. A piece of filigree gold reportedly found in 1923 near Ayapel, said in a Colombian publication to be "the most valuable archaeological treasure" exhibited in the Chicago Field Museum,[27] is not even

---

[27]Badel, *op. cit.* [see footnote 16 above], p. 28. There are illustrations of San Jorge gold ornaments in Wm. Curtis Farabee: Ancient American Gold, *Museum Journ.*, Vol. 11, Philadelphia, 1920, pp. 92-129, Figs. 67 (p. 119) and 68 (p. 121).

known to the museum's curator! During high water, when even the higher ridges are flooded, these house mounds and túmulos provide refuge for cattle. The trampling of their hooves often exposes clay and gold objects, especially when the surface has been washed clean by heavy rains. Where these mounds are adjacent to navigable water, they are still occupied. Virtually every house on the flood-plain is built on such an eminence, and potsherds are everywhere under foot.

Gerardo Reichel-Dolmatoff, who has excavated mounds near Maralú and on Caño Viloria, has shown that many of them were occupied at the time of the Conquest, the pottery being of a homo-geneous, late-contact type similar to that of the Sinú and other coastal areas. Earlier horizons suggest a relationship, not yet clearly defined, with sites excavated at Momil and Puerto Hormiga, on the north coast. Both of these are situated in ecological niches similar to those of the San Jorge, adjacent to seasonally flooded lowlands. They have proved to have extraordinary time depths. The carbon 14 date for the Puerto Hormiga shell mound, near Cartagena, is 4050 ±70 years from the present (1950), or 3090 B.C., the oldest date yet recorded for a site with pottery in the New World.[28] The bases of these earliest village sites are several feet below the present high-water level, and this is also true for most of the mounds in the San Jorge area. This may mean subsidence, but equally it may be interpreted as evidence for a rising sea level and associated marine transgression and change in base level since the first settlement.

The pottery found on the surface of the house mounds does not suggest the antiquity that on other grounds may be attributed to the ridged fields that surround them. It is possible that the mound builders and the ridge builders in the San Jorge were not always the same people. Although many of the mounds are in close association with ridged fields, as along Caño Carate, the areas with the greatest concentrations of mounds are to be found where ridged fields are either inconspicuous or absent. Thus along Caño Viloria and Caño Rabón, at Isla de Coco, and in the area of Hacienda Los Pájores there are large numbers of mounds but few ridged fields. These assemblages of mounds are often conspicuous from the air, usually worn bare by the trampling of cattle or the excavations of grave

---

According to Gerardo Reichel-Dolmatoff (personal communication) they are mislabeled as being from Antioquia.

[28]G. Reichel-Dolmatoff: Excavaciones arqueológicas en Puerto Hormiga (Departa-mento de Bolívar), *Ediciones Univ. de los Andes: Antropología 2*, Bogotá, 1965, p. 46.

194

robbers.   Some *fincas* on Caño Viloria apparently contain several
hundred such mounds.   One mound that we inspected at Finca Mata
Corozo covered an area 100 by 200 yards.   A map of the distribution of these mounds might reveal unsuspected relationships.
Their numbers run into the thousands; their ages are unknown.

Possible Agricultural Uses of the Old Fields

It is presumed that the earliest farmers of coastal Colombia
and Venezuela were root-crop cultivators, growing yuca (*Manihot*
spp.) and perhaps sweet potatoes, malanga (*Xanthosoma* spp.), and
the yampee (*Dioscorea trifida*).   Archaeological evidence suggests
that maize may have arrived here relatively late, but by 700 B.C. it
was well established, as is evidenced archaeologically by changes in
food-preparation implements.[29]   It may be postulated that maize gave
a new flexibility to settlement, which to then had been closely tied
to the fish and game of the rivers and the ciénagas.   To the extent
that starchy root crops were replaced by this fairly high-protein
cereal, the protein resources readily accessible in the ciénagas would
have lost some of their strategic importance.   Thus the Sabanas may
have become inhabited.

If the San Jorge ridges were for agricultural use, as we assume, and if their siting and orientation are rightly interpreted as
designed to provide improved drainage, then yuca (sweet manioc)
seems the most likely crop to have been grown on them.   It was
apparently the staple starchy food for the people of Ayapel at the
time of the Conquest.   The early chroniclers were impressed by the
abundance of gardens of avocado, *guamo, caimito*, and other fruit
trees, and by the extensive fields of yuca, sweet potatoes, and other
tubers that gave the country its open aspect.   Castellanos,[30] in
particular, comments repeatedly on the absence of maize.   Gordon
has interpreted this to mean that the people of Panzenú, along with
those of Cenú, were essentially yuca cultivators.   He points to the
few maize varieties in this part of Colombia today, as compared

---

[29]Reichel-Dolmatoff, Colombia [see footnote 2 above], pp. 74 ff.

[30]*Op. cit.* [see footnote 8 above], p. 383: "...era raiz la principal comyda, sin que
hallasen de maiz un grano." This observation, however, must be interpreted with
caution. The *Bachiller* Enciso wrote in 1519 in his "Suma de geografía" (Sevilla,
1519), referring to the Sinú, "el pan y el vino es de harina de mayz como en
Cartagena." Enciso, however, knew only the coast personally, since Ojeda's
expedition did not penetrate into the interior.

with the many varieties of yuca grown there.[31] Yuca, propagated by stem cuttings, normally at the beginning of the rainy season, requires good drainage. More than other crops, it would seem to provide a rationale for the effort of building raised beds in seasonally inundated lands. The heaviness of the soils of some of these ridges today would seem to make them poorly suited to yuca, but they were probably much lighter when originally thrown up. When in use they may also have been greatly improved by the regular addition of organic matter, much as is done today in the New Guinea highlands, where suggestively similar raised fields are found.

Yuca grown in the San Jorge area today generally requires 6 to 7 months to mature. Under the present condition and duration of flooding, large parts of the ridges and swales would be under water too much of every year to permit cropping, even during the dry season. Maize, requiring half as much time, would make out better, but it too is properly a wet-season crop, and many of the ridged areas are completely inundated throughout the period of the rains. There can be no question that the floods on the San Jorge are much higher and more prolonged today than they were when the ridged fields were constructed.

It is not impossible, though it seems unlikely, that the swales or ditches were of at least as much utility to the old-field occupants as the ridges were. Under some circumstances they might have been used during rising waters for fish drives. And they might have been utilized for the growing of a swamp plant such as the elephant-eared aroid *Xanthosoma*. Castellanos[32] wrote of "grandísimas labranzas de yucales, y otras raices dellos estimados, como batatas, ajes, himaconas..." at Ayapel. The *batatas* and *ajes* would have been varieties of sweet potatoes. *Himacona* (*imacona*) was the term used for the narrow-leafed form of *Xanthosoma* (*X. sagittifolium*), still grown in parts of northern Colombia as a wet-land plant. It might have prospered, even during the dry season, in the furrows or lower beds between the ridges and could explain why these are sometimes as much as four times the width of the ridges associated with them.

---

[31]Gordon, *op. cit.* [see footnote 4 above], p. 40. Reichel-Dolmatoff, on the other hand (Colombia [see footnote 2 above], p. 127), seems to believe that maize cultivation furnished the economic basis for the occupance of the fertile floodplains, a judgment apparently based largely on archaeological evidence. Perhaps the ridges date from a time before the introduction of maize! This would be in line with the suggestion, deriving from recent pollen analysis, that about 700 B.C. the prevailing dry and continental climate of the coast turned more humid with increasing rainfall (*ibid.*, p. 74, based on the studies of Thomas van der Hammen).

[32]*Op. cit.* [see footnote 8 above], p. 383.

Digging down to moist soil for planting beds (*hoyas*) was a well-established practice on the desert coast of Peru. Conceivably it could have been an adaptation to the rigorous 5-month dry season of the San Jorge region, if the heavy floodplain soils remained moist at a foot or two below the surface.

Although there is no direct evidence that irrigation was practiced in these ridged fields, some arrangement for lifting water at low-water stage from the rivers into the ditches would not necessarily have been beyond the technological competence of these people. A detailed mapping of the ridges in relation to existing and abandoned channels and to the microrelief of the natural levees and basins might provide evidence of water control, perhaps aimed at gaining two crops a year, one in the wet season and one in the dry season. In this connection the long, parallel, canal-like features east of the Ciénaga El Arcial especially deserve closer attention.

Protein Resources of Rivers and Sabanas

It may be significant that the San Jorge old fields are nowhere more than a dozen miles or so from the upland Sabanas surfaces. It is where the higher ground of the Sabanas crowds against the San Jorge that the best-developed or best-preserved field patterns are found. One might surmise that the same people who were taking a wet-season crop from the sandy upland soils may have moved to the floodplains during the months of drought to fish, and perhaps to take a second crop from the heavier, wetter soils there.

The productivity of the freshwater fishery of the Magdalena and its tributaries is extraordinary, above all in the San Jorge.[33] Fishing is best during the dry season, when the enormous fish populations leave the vanishing ciénagas for the spectacular ascent, *subienda*, of the main rivers to the spawning grounds. During the subienda, which lasts for several months, the *bocachico* (*Prochilodus reticulatus magdalenae*) constitutes the favored food of the valley population, and large quantities are shipped both fresh and salted to the markets of interior cities. The fish at this season are very fat and thus provide an important source of animal fat in the diet. Since the bocachicos are vegetarians, they are usually taken in large nets, which, drying in the sun, are a characteristic feature of every fishing camp along the San Jorge today. The numerous species of catfish, on the other hand, are almost always taken with hook and line. In addition to a wide diversity of fish, the ciénaga landscape

---

[33]Georg Dahl: Peces y pesca, in *Programa de desarrollo ecónomico*...[see footnote 22 above], Chap. 7.

produces an abundance of water turtles (*Podocnemis lewyana*), land turtles (*Pseudemis scripta callirostris*), manatees, iguanas, and crocodiles (*caimán*), the true cayman (*babilla*), and such aquatic rodents as the capybara, the paca, and the agouti. This richness of river and lagoon resources, along with the prodigious waterfowl population, could have made sedentary village life possible in northern Colombia, and along the San Jorge, long before the advent of agriculture. In the earliest riparian settlements, Reichel-Dolmatoff suggests, systematic agriculture would at best have played only a minor role.[34] Like Sauer for Southeast Asia,[35] he postulates that freshwater fishing and reptile hunting may first have given stability to society here, with agriculture a later addition. He draws attention to the siting of the early compact villages, not on the banks of the main rivers but, rather, on the shores of large lagoons, backswamps, or oxbow lakes which were connected to the rivers by channels. For a yuca-eating population especially, the attraction of this abundant protein supply could have been sufficient to induce a riverine orientation of settlement, particularly during the dry season, when the upland Sabanas were seared with drought.

Of course, food was to be had on the Sabanas, too. Yuca and maize would have yielded an acceptable wet-season harvest. Padre Simón noted that the Sabanas supported "innumerable deer, rabbits, small rodents, doves, and quail."[36] Peccary were numerous. Much of the Sabanas surface was apparently burned every year, probably for the same reason that stockmen burn it today, to improve pasturage. Striffler[37] mentions the practice of burning the grass, perhaps in the floodplains as well as on the Sabanas, to drive turtles (*tortugas*), noting that despite the many taken in this way their numbers did not decrease. During the dry season much of the game of the Sabanas must have migrated to the ciénaga margins, as men and livestock do today. And for men on the move the ease of travel by dugout canoes on the interlacing caños and ciénagas must have provided a

---

[34]G. Reichel-Dolmatoff: The Formative Stage: An Appraisal from the Colombian Perspective, *Actas XXXIII Congreso Internacional de Americanistas, San José, 1958*, Vol. 1, San José, Costa Rica, 1959, pp. 152-164; reference on pp. 156-157.

[35]Carl O. Sauer: Agricultural Origins and Dispersals, *Amer. Geogr. Soc. Bowman Memorial Lectures Ser. Two*, New York, 1952, pp. 22 ff.

[36]Pedro Simón: *Noticias historiales de las conquistas de Tierra Firme en las Indias Occidentales* (5 vols.; Bogotá, 1882-1892), Vol. 4, p. 56.

[37]*Op. cit.* [see footnote 19 above], p. 70.

welcome relief from the warm overland marches, often without drinking water, across the Sabanas surface. Fruits from such wild trees as the caimito and several palms would have furnished a dietary supplement in the floodplains as well as on the uplands.

Other Areas of Indian Old Fields in South America

The only other area of Colombia where there is evidence of extensive ridged-field agriculture lies more than 200 miles to the south on rolling to steep upland surfaces. In the Quindío basin of Caldas, in the Calima district (Valle del Cauca), and farther south in the departments of Cauca, Huila, and Nariño, remnants of somewhat similar old fields, there termed *eras*, have been exposed by the forest-felling activities of modern agriculturists. These ridges and swales, which give grassy surfaces a peculiar corrugated appearance, run up and down slopes and are often divided into blocks by transverse furrows. The ridges are narrower (5 to 6 feet) than those of the San Jorge floodplain but are otherwise somewhat suggestive of them. They were observed in the 1540s by Cieza de León, who thought they had already been long abandoned at that time. According to Robert West, a more closely spaced ridge is still used by mestizos and Indians in the vicinity of Popayán and Pasto for growing root crops. He saw them being prepared in new, grass-covered fields around Pasto by cutting parallel furrows with a special kind of hoe and placing the blocks of sod, grass down, on the intervening strips in such a manner as to form planting ridges. Such "lazybed" farming is also practiced in the highlands of Peru and Bolivia, where it is a common method of potato culture in the *puna* above 10,000 feet. The ridges in highland Colombia are usually cropped for 1 or 2 years, then fallowed for 2 or 3 years. After several years of alternate cropping and fallowing the field may be converted into grass.[38]

Remarkably, the closest parallel to the San Jorge old fields seem to be found in the seasonally inundated Llanos de Mojos of the department of Beni in northeastern Bolivia, some 2,000 miles to the south. Denevan[39] and Plafker[40] have recently described these

---

[38]Robert C. West: Ridge or "Era" Agriculture in the Colombian Andes, *Actas XXXIII Congreso Internacional de Americanistas, San José, 1958*, Vol. 1, San José, 1959, pp. 279-282.

[39]William M. Denevan: Additional Comments on the Earthworks of Mojos in Northeastern Bolivia, *Amer. Antiquity*, Vol. 28, 1963, pp. 540-545.

features. They consist of closely spaced ridges and swales, widely spaced rectangular platforms as much as 1,000 feet long, and orderly rows of small planting mounds. There is no evidence that they were in use when the Spaniards arrived, and their age remains uncertain. Although they extend over an area several times larger than that of the San Jorge old fields, they are more widely dispersed. Denevan[41] estimates the total extent of ridges and platforms in Beni at not less than 15,000 acres (23 square miles), whereas our estimate for the San Jorge is four times as great, perhaps as much as 80,000 acres. However, as Denevan's figures refer to the higher "planting" surfaces only and do not include the ditches between them, the total area may be comparable with that of the San Jorge old fields. From the photographs the closely spaced ridges of Beni could readily be mistaken for those of the San Jorge, but they tend to be narrower (5 to 20 feet) and probably on the average have less relief. The widely spaced platforms lie in an area 100 miles north of the ridges and swales and may have been the work of a different people. They have no counterpart in the San Jorge. Neither do the mound fields, which are of smaller extent. The Beni ridges and furrows are 6 to 24 inches high, which is substantially less relief than we observed in the better-defined San Jorge old fields. Perhaps for this reason there has been little invasion by second-growth forests, such as occurs widely in the San Jorge, where the orchardlike arrangement of trees reflects the better-drained soils of the ridges. In Bolivia the ridges and furrows occupy savanna surfaces of poor drainage, on which grass is apparently maintained by annual burning. In the San Jorge most of the old fields were apparently forested until clearing was initiated by stockmen in the nineteenth century. In both areas the ridges are inundated in periods of high water.

Causeways and artificial canals designed as navigation short-cuts are other impressive features of the Bolivian area, but these are of minor importance along the San Jorge. Cruxent[42] has described causeways in the Venezuelan llanos near Barinas that are 25 and 80 feet wide, 1 to 6 feet high, and several miles long. Both there and

[40]George Plafker: Observations on Archaeological Remains in Northeastern Bolivia, *Amer. Antiquity*, Vol. 28, 1963, pp. 372-378.

[41]William M. Denevan: The Aboriginal Cultural Geography of the Llanos de Mojos of Bolivia, *Ibero-Americana*, No. 48, 1966:90.

[42]J.M. Cruxent: Notes on Venezuelan Archaeology, in Indian Tribes of Aboriginal America, *Selected Papers XXIXth Internatl. Congr. of Americanists, New York, 1949*, Vol. 3, Chicago, 1952, pp. 280-294; reference on pp. 280-286.

in Bolivia the causeways seem to have linked points of higher ground, often wooded "islands," and are presumed to have been used for local foot travel. For a people so well adapted to boat travel, a pedestrian causeway would seem a rather extravagant investment of effort, but no better explanation is at hand. In the San Jorge there are some long, narrow ridges--for example, southeast of the Ciénaga El Arcial and north of Palotal--that might be interpreted as causeways. Where two of them run side by side, they appear almost like canals. Extensive causeways are said to occur in the vicinity of hacienda Los Pájaros, but they are not discernible on available air photography.

Cruxent does not seem to have observed old-field vestiges in the Venezuelan llanos, but he calls attention to the sixteenth-century reference to them of Juan de Castellanos. Castellanos wrote, in his tortured verse, that the conquistador Cedeño had seen "prolijisimo calzada que fue mas de cien leguas duradera con señales de antiguas poblaciones y de labranzas viejos camellones."[43] The term *camellones* is good Castilian for "agricultural ridges." The text is vague about locations and dimensions, but the reference to them as *labranzas viejos*, "old fields," indicates that they were not in use at the time of the Conquest. Cruxent notes that the native population of this part of the llanos was at a very low cultural level in Cedeño's time (*ca.* 1536) and scarcely capable of the organization of labor necessary for constructing such earthworks or raised fields with the available technology. This was a time, however, of considerable disruption from intertribal warfare as well as from the effects of the Conquest.

Raised fields have also been reported near Wageningen, Nickerie District, on the coast of Surinam. They apparently are more like rectangular platforms, less elongated than the San Jorge ridges. A large artificial mound in the center of the area of raised fields has been dated *ca.* A.D. 700;[44] a report on the archaeology and palynology is forthcoming.

Such a remarkably disjunct distribution--the Magdalena Valley, Surinam, the Orinoco llanos, and northeastern Bolivia--of what would appear to be a rather sophisticated way of utilizing an environment subject to high flood risk, and certainly one requiring a high degree of social organization and work-force coordination, opens a Pandora's box of questions relating to cultural origins and the process of dispersal.

---

[43]Castellanos, *op. cit.* [see footnote 8 above], p. 136.

[44]Personal communication from Thomas van der Hammen.

It is almost impossible to conceive that the observant Spanish chroniclers would not have commented on these unusual surface features had they seen them under cultivation. None did. It seems likely that in none of the seasonally inundated lands under discussion were the ridged fields in use at the time of the white man's arrival.

The extent of the San Jorge old fields, the massive and organized human effort represented in their construction, and the potential productivity of the area in starch and protein suggest that the aboriginal population evaluated the seasonally flooded tropical lowlands of northern Colombia quite differently from contemporary man. It is difficult to imagine that for people lacking iron tools and draft animals the practical advantages to be gained by the construction of the ridges and swales could have been worth the effort. Conceivably the builders may have had some non-utilitarian purpose, but there seems to be no systematic regularity or alignment to the earthworks of the sort that one would expect from a religiously motivated society. How much time may have been required for their construction, or how intensively they may have been employed, we cannot know. On the assumption of a conservative 2 acres of land and water surface to a person, or 320 persons to a square mile, some 80,000 persons might have been supported within the old-fields as delimited on Figure 14.1. If the ridges were fallowed this figure might have been reduced by half or more, but the supplementary food derived from the rivers and the Sabanas should have balanced that loss. We do not know, of course, that more than a small percentage of the fields were ever in cultivation at one time, though it seems reasonable to assume that they would have been.

This new evidence from northern Colombia substantially reinforces the growing argument that the pre-Columbian population densities of the American tropical lowlands have been grossly underestimated. Today, with the promised control of malaria and the introduction of large-scale mechanized farming, Colombia is turning once more toward its lowland areas as sources of food and fiber for the rapidly increasing populations of the over-taxed highlands. Ambitious plans have recently been proposed for the diking off of the great interfluve between the lower Cauca and the San Jorge, including a part of the San Jorge old-field area, to reclaim it for rice growing and artificial pasture.[45] Yet this would mean moving only a small fraction of the volume of earth moved with primitive hand implements in the construction of the San Jorge

---

[45]"Programa de desarrollo económico..." [see footnote 22 above], pp. 272-279.

ridges and swales. Clearly, other men at other times have found other ways of living in this tropical floodplain environment with tools inferior to ours. We may yet be able to learn from their experience.

15

Ridged Fields in the Río Guayas Valley, Ecuador*

Attention has been called in recent years to the existence of extensive tracts of pre-Columbian ridged fields and planting beds in the seasonally flooded lowlands of eastern Bolivia (Denevan 1963, 1966; Plafker 1963) and northern Colombia (Parsons and Bowen 1966). In the summer of 1965, while on a commercial flight approaching the airport at Guayaquil, Ecuador, I observed and photographed raised platforms and ridges in the Río Guayas floodplain that were strikingly similar to the Colombian old fields that I had only recently been mapping. Further investigation, both on the ground and in a low-flying reconnaissance aircraft, established at least two concentrations of these vestiges of an ancient, labor-intensive, agricultural system. In one, on the low-lying land immediately across the Río Guayas from the airport, long parallel systems of ridges and furrows predominate, while more or less rectangular planting platforms are characteristic (Fig. 15.1) of the other, which is under the flight path of approaching aircraft some 14 to 16 kilometers to the northeast of the airport, near the head of Estero El Rosario, a right bank tributary of the Río Babahoyo.

The former area, characterized by the linear pattern of ridges, some up to 2 miles long, is swamp and overflow land lying behind the natural levee of the left bank of the Río Guayas. It is drained by several short *esteros* that are navigable in the rainy season, of which the Estero Matanzas and Estero Las Alforjas are the most important. This corrugated surface extends northward from the

*Reprinted from *American Antiquity*, Vol. 34, No. 1, pp. 76-80 (1969). Reproduction by permission of The Society for American Archaeology. Field work was supported by the Geography Branch, Office of Naval Research and the Center for Latin American Studies, University of California, Berkeley.

204

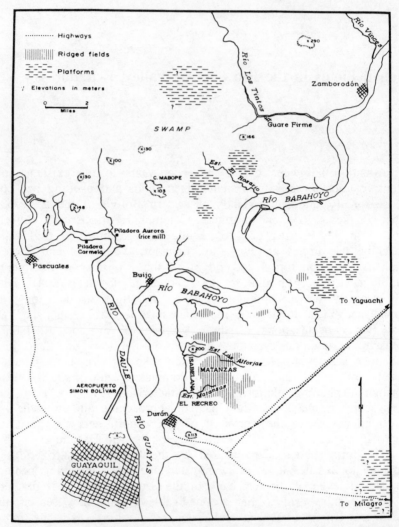

Figure 15.1 Map of Guayaquil Region Showing Areas of Ridged Fields and Platforms. [Additional areas of fields have been discovered since 1969 - editor.]

railroad town of Durán for about 8 to 10 kilometers to the first great bend of the Babahoyo (Fig. 15.1). Air photographs reveal an area of at least 4,000 acres of parallel ridges and swales, usually with a north-south orientation, that gives the land a distinctive combed appearance. The original extent of the ridges was almost certainly greater than is now identifiable, for silting has obliterated them in some areas and has left them barely discernible in others. Most of the ridges, which rise from 2 to 4 feet above the adjacent swales, support a luxuriant second-growth forest, while the lower land on either side of them is delineated by aquatic grass and reed. The raised liner features, locally known as *bancos*, are for the most part still covered with large trees, but the area has recently come under the axe of charcoal-burners and share-croppers. After clearing the forest in the dry season, the settlers plant maize, beans, or cotton on the better-drained *bancos* that are uncovered in the clearing process while rice is transplanted from seed beds onto the heavier soils of the lower surface. The ridges average 10 to 12 meters across, the swales between them being up to 16 meters, significantly wider than their counterparts in Colombia and Bolivia. When cleared and planted, they have something of the aspect of great bowling alleys. The dead skeletons of giant forest trees, recently girdled, may still stand here and there as witness to the recency of modern man's appreciation of these rich but poorly drained lowland soils.

These ridged field patterns, so conspicuous from the air, never seem to have been described in any of the archaeological or geographical literature on the Guayas basin (e.g., Estrada 1957; Meggers 1966; Anonymous 1964). The Milagro-Quevedo culture, noted for its abundance of artificial mounds (*tolas*) and its elaborate gold and copper working, represents the last archaeological occupancy of this area, from about A.D. 500 on. Estrada and Meggers both comment on the abundance of artificial "platform mounds" of the Milagro phase in the seasonally inundated lands of the southern Guayas basin, but they see them only as habitation sites and burial mounds. A few groups of larger mounds or *tolas* (up to 100 meters long, 30 meters wide, and 10 meters high) appear to them to represent centers of administrative or religious activity.

The conspicuous linear ridges north of Durán contain little or no pottery or refuse and seem explicable only in terms of agriculturalists seeking better drainage for such dry-land crops as maize and manioc. The rich aquatic resources of the nearby rivers and fresh-water swamps would have provided an abundant protein supplement to their diet. Early chroniclers in the area do not seem to have commented on this distinctive form of farming, which may indicate, as it seems to in Colombia and Bolivia, that it was no longer being

206

practiced at the arrival of the Spaniards. In all three areas the ridged fields occur in juxtaposition with raised house sites and burial and ceremonial mounds, but whether they were always built by the same people is by no means clear. In Ecuador the concentration of *tolas* reaches its maximum at areas rather far removed from the ridged fields or raised planting beds, as around Milagro and Duale. It is clear that these linear earthworks are old, almost entirely pre-Columbian, and that they could only have been built by a socially and politically sophisticated folk with a substantial degree of central authority. Such a laborious adaptation to a difficult environment by peoples lacking both iron tools and draft animals suggests either a rather extreme pressure or an addiction (one might almost say a mania) for earth-moving and regimented labor directed toward ends that would at best seem to have been only marginally functional.

Another type of raised field occurs along the Durán-Milagro highway, in the vicinity of Kilometer 13 (Fig. 15.2), where there are extensive tracts of roughly rectangular raised beds, separated by lower-lying borrow pits of various shapes. While some of these are higher *tolas* which obviously served as habitation or burial sites, the vast majority are relatively low lying, like the parallel ridges closer to the river rising perhaps 1 meter above the surrounding depressions. Some of this artificially mounded land along the road has been recently cleared for farming, the low ground (*aguajes*) being planted to rice, the higher surfaces to maize, or sometimes to an off-season crop of rice. For the mechanized farming envisioned in the Milagro Development Scheme these rough surfaces promise to present substantial difficulties. Their extent has not been established. In most instances they may be identified on air photos by the vegetation pattern. Trees delimit the better-drained platforms, reed and grass the low-lying land between them.

The fields observable on the approach pattern to the Guayaquil airport, in seasonally flooded lands lying immediately west of the Río Babayoho and south of the Río Los Tintos and the village of Saborondón, are mostly of this same rectangular platform type (Fig. 15.3), but they also include, less conspicuously, some groups of relatively short parallel ridges. Here the land has almost all been cleared and planted to rice, an export crop in Ecuador, but because of annual floods permanent settlement in the area is impractical. The higher platform or ridge surfaces produce the wet-season crop while the more extensive areas of lower land between them produce the dry-season harvest.

It may seem surprising that these distinctive man-made features of the microrelief of the Guayas basin so close to Guayaquil have never been described. But from the ground they are not easy to

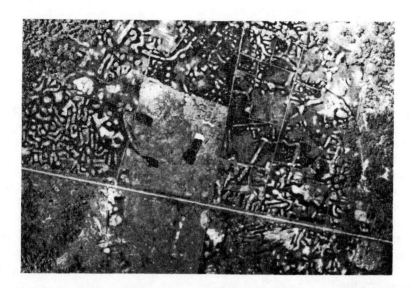

Figure 15.2 Rectangular platforms of planting beds, planted to rice, at kilometer 13 on Durán-Milagro Highway. Photo: Instituto Geográfico Militar, July 24, 1966.

Figure 15.3 Raised planting platforms near Estero Las Carolinas west of the Rió Babahoyo. The lower ground (darker areas) was covered with a growing rice crop when this photo was taken in mid-August, at the beginning of the dry season. Photo: James J. Parsons.

detect, and they may be unrecognized by persons not familiar with them. The local inhabitants usually attribute them to the natural processes of flood-plain sedimentation, except for *tolas* identifiable as habitation or burial mounds. It has remained for air photographs and low-flying reconnaissance flights to make possible their ready identification and mapping.

Another area where raised agricultural planting surfaces are known to exist on seasonally flooded lowlands in tropical South America is Surinam (Laeyendecker-Roosenberg 1966; Parsons and Denevan 1967). Somewhat similar features have also been observed recently on poorly drained inter-Andean highland surfaces of the Sabana de Bogotá (Sylvia Broadbent, pers. comm.) and along the shores of Lake Titicaca (William Denevan, pers. comm.). The sunken planting beds or *mahamaes* (Spanish: *hoyas*) of the Peruvian coastal desert fringe (Jeffrey Parsons 1968) may be thought of in one sense as "inverted ridges," the construction of which must have involved comparable amounts of earth movement with similarly primitive tools.

The whole idea of the large-scale raising of ridges or platforms for farming on flood plains and, by extension, on the surrounding uplands, has intriguing cultural and ecological connotations. The South American fields have a close parallel in the blocks of narrower linear "planting beds" described more than a century ago in the upper Mississippi Valley and around the southern end of Lake Michigan (Schoolcraft 1860; Fox 1959), and again in such southern counterparts as the Ocmulgee old fields near Macon, Georgia (Kelly 1938). The possibility, however remote, of cultural relationships between the earth-movers of the north and their tropical American counterparts seems worthy of consideration.

References

Anonymous
    1964.   *Survey for the Development of the Guayas River Basin of Ecuador, An Integrated Natural Resource Evaluation.* Pan American Union, Department of Economic Affairs, Washington.

Denevan, William M.
    1963.   Additional Comments on the Earthworks of Mojos in Northeastern Bolivia, *American Antiquity*, Vol. 28, pp. 540-5.

1966.   *The Aboriginal Cultural Geography of the Llanos de
Mojos of Bolivia.* Ibero-American, No. 48, Berkeley.

Estrada, Emilio
1957.   Ultimas civilizaciones pre-históricas de la cuenca del
Río Guayas. *Museo Victor Emilio Estrada, Publicación No. 2.* Guayaquil.

Fox, George R.
1959.   The Prehistoric Garden Beds of Wisconsin and
Michigan and the Fox Indians. *The Wisconsin Archaeologist,* Vol. 40, pp. 1-19.

Kelly, A.R.
1938.   A Preliminary Report on Archaeological Explorations
at Macon, Georgia. *Bureau of American Ethnology,
Bulletin 119.* Washington.

Laeyendecker-Roosenburg, D.M.
1966.   A Palynological Investigation of Some Archaeologically Interesting Sections in Northwestern Surinam.
Leidse Geologische Mededelingen, Vol. 38, pp. 31-6.
Leiden.

Meggers, Betty
1966.   *Ecuador.* Praeger, New York.

Parsons, James J. and William A. Bowen
1966.   Ancient Ridged Fields of the San Jorge River Floodplain, Colombia. *Geographical Review,* Vol. 56,
No. 3, pp. 317-43.

Parsons, James J. and William M. Denevan
1967.   Pre-Columbian Ridged Fields. *Scientific American,*
Vol. 217, No. 1, pp. 92-101.

Parsons, Jeffrey R.
1968.   The Archaeological Significance of Mahamaes
Cultivation on the Coast of Peru. *American Antiquity,* Vol. 33, pp. 80-5.

210

Plafker, George
    1963.   Observations on Archaeological Remains in Northeastern Bolivia. *American Antiquity*, Vol. 28, pp. 372-8.

Schoolcraft, Henry Rowe
    1860.   *Archives of Aboriginal Knowledge*, Vol. 1, pp. 58-61. Philadelphia.

16

Pre-Columbian Ridged Fields*

In South America thousands of square miles of tropical lowlands are submerged in shallow floodwaters for weeks or months during the rainy season and are parched by drought during the dry season. Covered either with savanna grasses or with forest, these poorly drained river floodplains have generally been considered unfit for agriculture since the Spanish Conquest. When they are exploited at all, it is usually as cattle range. In the open savanna the grass is renewed by annual burning; in some wooded areas today the trees are being cleared to make way for planted pasture.

Recently the surprising discovery has been made that areas in several such regions were once intensively farmed. The pre-Columbian farmers had a specialized system of agriculture that physically reshaped large parts of the South American continent. Aerial reconnaissance and surface exploration have now located the intricate earthworks required by this system in the tropical lowlands of four widely separated regions: eastern Bolivia, western Ecuador, northern Colombia and coastal Surinam (Dutch Guiana) (Fig. 16.1). Similar earthworks exist in other parts of the continent. Here we shall describe the earthworks in the four lowland areas in South America that have been identified and mapped thus far, review what is known about prehistoric earthmoving for agricultural purpose elsewhere in the Americas (both lowland and highland), and then examine the implications of these early works with respect to the rise of civilization in the New World.

---

*By James J. Parsons and William M. Denevan. Reprinted from *Scientific American*, Vol. 217, No. 1, pp. 92-100 (1967).

212

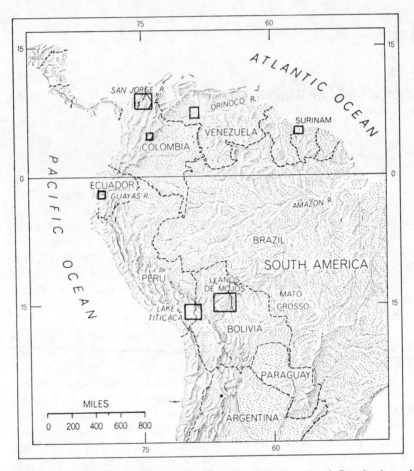

Figure 16.1 Four regions in the tropical lowlands of South America have pre-Columbian earthworks built so that lands subject to seasonal flood and drought could be utilized for farming (Mojos, Guayas, San Jorge, and Surinam). Similar earthworks were also built in the Andean highlands at Lake Titicaca. [Since 1967 additional ridged (raised) fields have been discovered in the Orinoco Llanos of Venezuela, the Bogotá Basin of Colombia, and in several other highland and coastal areas of Colombia, Ecuador, and Peru - editor.]

Except for two brief references in early chronicles, the first mention of agricultural earthworks in South America was made in the 1900s by the Swedish ethnographer Erland Nordenskiöld, in connection with his studies in the Llanos de Mojos (Plains of Mojos) of northeastern Bolivia. Located in the heart of the South American continent, between the Andes and the Brazilian highlands, most of the Mojos plains area is less than 800 feet above sea level. Bounded by the Beni and Mamoré rivers, these broad lowlands are a sea of grass in which occasional islands of forest mark the higher, better-drained ground; indeed, the vegetation is locally known as *pampa isla*. Here, for as much as 7 months of the year, floods cover the grasslands with a sheet of water ranging in depth from a few inches to several feet.

Faced with a hostile environment of this kind, people everywhere usually adapt their lives to the circumstances; a commonplace example in areas subject to flooding is the building of houses on stilts. The modern cattle ranchers of the Llanos de Mojos do much the same: they simply select high ground for building sites. The pre-Columbian inhabitants of the area chose instead to modify the landscape. They raised mounds, causeways and serried ridges for their crops, all of which stood high enough to surmount the flood-waters. To this day the wet savannas are crisscrossed with narrow causeways that connect the natural islands of high ground. The causeways are as much as 7 miles long; their total length in the Llanos de Mojos, as measured on aerial photographs, exceeds 1,000 miles. Also visible in the area are many artificial mounds that served as sites for burials, for houses, and even for small villages.

The agricultural earthworks in the area cover at least 50,000 acres. They are of three kinds. West of the town of Trinidad the prevailing pattern is narrow, closely spaced ridges. South of Lake Rogoaguado the ridges are much larger: as much as 80 feet wide and 1,000 feet long. In other areas there are rows of small circular mounds 6 to 8 feet in diameter. Whatever their form, most of the earthworks are less than 2 feet high. Originally they were doubtless high enough to stand above the average flood level.

In 1908 and 1909 Nordenskiöld excavated several burial mounds east of the Mamoré River that were associated with some of the Mojos causeways. Within the mounds he found fragments of elaborately decorated pottery, which he attributed to the ancestors of the region's Arawak Indians. This work of half a century ago is the only serious archaeology that has been undertaken in the area. Early Jesuit accounts of the region imply that the socioeconomic development of the Indians was advanced enough to enable them to construct the kinds of earthworks found there, but such literature, some

of which is quite detailed, makes no mention of any agricultural
ridges. Indeed, the extent of the ridges was not realized until 1960,
when swamp buggies engaged in petroleum exploration encountered
seemingly endless ridges near the town of Trinidad. Thereafter the
ridge system was examined on aerial photographs. Here in Bolivia,
however, the lack of archaeological investigation makes it impossible
to determine exactly when the ridges and other earthworks were
raised.

A second ridged area is in northern Colombia some 150 miles
inland from the Caribbean coast. There the waters of the San Jorge
and Cauca rivers join with those of the Magdalena in a great interior
basin that is less than 80 feet above sea level. Known as the
Mompos Depression, this seasonally flooded alluvial plain is covered
with a constantly changing complex of lakes and swamps. When it
is not covered with water, it is a rich reserve of pasturage for
Colombia's two leading beef-producing provinces, Córdoba and
Bolívar.

Since the Spaniards entered the region in the sixteenth century
the western part of the Mompos Depression has also been famous
for its Indian mounds and their content of gold. Neither the early
settlers nor today's *colonos*, however, seem to have been aware that
some 80,000 acres along the San Jorge are covered by a pre-
Columbian ridged-field system.

The San Jorge ridges, like those of the Llanos de Mojos, are
not easily perceived on the ground. From a dugout canoe, a common means of travel in the area, they are virtually invisible. The
local people are aware of the ridges, but few recognize them as
man-made features. From the air the ridges are clearly distinguish-
able. When the Mompos Depression is partly inundated, slight
differences in relief are emphasized, and the ridge pattern is sharply
outlined by the floodwaters. Moreover, both before and after the
rains the color of the grass reflects the difference between the dry
ridge crests and the damp ditches between them; for several weeks
the pattern is clearly painted in tan and green.

The San Jorge fields are of three kinds. In one type the
ridges are on the natural levees of old stream channels and are
perpendicular to the channels. In the second type short ridges are
arrayed in a checkerboard pattern. In the third type the ridges are
in clusters, generally parallel but unoriented with respect to the
higher ground of the levees. Averaging about 20 feet in width, the
ridges vary in length from a few feet to almost a mile; the ditches
between them are in some places wider than the ridges and in some
places narrower. The majority of the ridges are 2 to 3 feet high; a
few are nearly 5 feet. Most of the San Jorge fields have been

invaded by forest since they were abandoned. Where the trees have been cleared and the area has been planted with pasture grass the ancient ridge system gives the landscape a distinctive corrugated appearance.

A third ridged area is immediately north and east of the airport for Guayaquil in Ecuador. To the east of the Guayas River, opposite Guayaquil and just north of the town of Durán, an extensive system of parallel ridges is visible that looks almost exactly like the ones at San Jorge and Mojos. Another zone of earthworks lies some 15 miles north of Guayaquil, in the lowlands between the Babahoyo and Daule rivers, where rectangular mounds predominate. These relics of pre-Columbian agriculture in Ecuador seem not to have been recognized for what they are until we observed them in 1966. We might not have noticed them ourselves if it had not been for our familiarity with the earthworks of Bolivia and Colombia.

The ridged fields of the Guayaquil area cover substantially less ground than those of San Jorge and Mojos; the floodplain and swampland they occupy probably total some 10,000 acres. The system of ridges near Durán is currently being cleared of second-growth forest and sharecroppers are planting it mainly with rice and maize. Rice seedlings are transplanted from seedbeds into the ditches, the soil of which is heavier than that of the better-drained ridges. The ridges, which are 30 to 40 feet wide and as much as 2 miles long, are being planted with maize, squash, beans, sugarcane, and cotton.

As in Bolivia and Colombia, serious archaeological investigation that could identify the peoples who raised the Guayaquil earthworks has yet to be undertaken. The Guayas floodplains are known to have been occupied from about A.D. 500 to the time of the Spanish Conquest by people of the Milagro culture, noted for its elaborate work in gold. The low-lying countryside is dotted with thousands of *tolas*, or artificial mounds, built by the Milagro people for burial places and house sites. Some of the *tolas* appear to be associated with ridge systems and others with the rectangular earthworks. It is possible that the same culture made both. Only investigation can prove or disprove the association.

The coast of Surinam, the site of our fourth example of ridged-field agriculture, is a low-lying plain consisting of a series of ancient beaches running parallel to the present shoreline. Between these fossil beaches are swampy stripes of clayey soil that support savanna vegetation. At a number of places along the coast ridged fields have been noted in these grassy swamps. The most extensive system of ridges is associated with an artificial mound known as Hertenrits, which is about 800 feet in diameter and rises 6 to 7 feet above the level of the surrounding swamp. Hertenrits is 3 miles from the coast between Nieuw Nickerie and Caroní, in the middle of a long-uninhabited savanna belt that is now being reclaimed as part of a government rice-growing project. The mound is being investigated by the Dutch archaeologist, D. C. Geyskes, and the Dutch pollen analyst, D. M. Laeyendecker-Roosenburg.

The Hertenrits ridges are short--perhaps three times as long as they are wide--and haphazardly arrayed. Some stand alone; others are clumped together like sausages in a pan. The aerial photographs indicate that the ridges rise 2 to 3 feet and that in many places they support vegetation distinctly different from that of the surrounding savanna.

Analysis of pollen contained in peat taken from the Hertenrits mound and from an adjacent swamp indicates that the mound was raised not long after A.D. 700. At that time the sea had encroached on the area; the evidence for the encroachment is a marked increase in the abundance of mangrove pollen in the samples. The Dutch investigators suggest that, in order to continue living in the area under these conditions, the local people were obliged to build the mound as a village site and presumably also to make ridges for their crops. They calculate that the mound was occupied until at least A.D. 900 and probably later.

The pollens identified at Hertenrits do not include those of any cultivated plants such as maize. Although the evidence is admittedly negative, this fact suggests that the ridges were devoted to growing manioc, a plant that rarely flowers and is propagated not by seed but by stem cuttings. Manioc was a staple crop in much of tropical South America at the time of the Spanish Conquest, and it is still widely grown today. The cuttings are usually planted at the start of the rainy season and require good drainage. More than most crops, manioc would call for artificially raised ground in areas subject to flooding. It is probably that not only here but also in Bolivia, Colombia, and Ecuador the people who made mile after mile of ridges were growers of manioc. It seems possible, although it is by no means proved, that the oldest earthworks in some of these areas may date back to a period before maize had arrived from Middle America.

In the absence of archaeological investigation making possible carbon 14 dating or other age determinations, one can only speculate on the antiquity of most of these early agricultural works. The ridged-field system in the Mompos Depression of Colombia appears to be associated with the Indian mounds there, and the mounds seem to have been more or less continuously occupied for a long time before the Spaniards arrived. A hundred miles or so to the north, near the Caribbean coast, there are mounds of shells that have been dated by the carbon 14 method. These dates range from 800 B.C. at Momil to about 3000 B.C. at Puerto Hormiga, making the latter the oldest-known site in the New World where pottery is found. There is no evidence that the San Jorge fields are equally old, but it is interesting that some of the shell mounds occupy a similar ecological niche, being located on the margin of seasonally flooded lands.

One possible means of determining the age of the San Jorge earthworks arises from the fact that there the ridge pattern is often oriented at right angles to old stream channels. A reconstruction of the district's history of sedimentation might provide a key to the question of age. Many of the ridges appear to be related to the oldest and longest-abandoned channels, which are now choked with water hyacinths when they contain any water at all.

Although many other lowland regions of tropical South America have terrain suited to ridged-field agriculture, our investigations up to now have produced concrete evidence of their existence only in the four areas described here. Nonetheless, promising conditions for the discovery of similar earthworks exist over huge areas: the Orinoco delta, Marajó Island at the mouth of the Amazon, the Pantanal region of the western Mato Grosso in Brazil, and the broad llanos of Venezuela and Colombia.

South of the old colonial city of Barinas in the Venezuelan llanos a complex of man-made causeways as much as 6 feet high, 20 feet wide and 3 miles long has been described by the Venezuelan archaeologist J. M. Cruxent. Both in Bolivia and Surinam similar causeways, possibly used as footpaths during periods of flooding, are associated with ridged fields. Our inspection of the available aerial photographs of the grassy Venezuelan plains has failed to reveal any ancient agricultural earthworks, but the area deserves more intensive examination. The sixteenth-century Spanish chronicler Juan de Castellanos, writing of the plains country, mentions "old cultivation ridges" (*labranzas, viejas camellones*), an indication that the agricultural areas of this kind he had seen or heard about had been abandoned at the time of his observations. Yet some 200 years later the author of *Orinoco Ilustrado*, Father José Gumilla, clearly described the continuing use of ridged fields. "In poorly drained sites," he wrote, the Indians "without burning the grass...lift the earth from ditches on either side, mixing the grass with the earth and then planting their maize, manioc and other root crops, along with pimento."

Father Gumilla does not say exactly where he observed this practice. It could have been anywhere in the llanos of Colombia or

Venezuela, but visible remnants of this farming system must still persist. Bush pilots, if they are on the lookout for such ridges, may find them on the lower floodplains of such major tributaries of the Orinoco as the Apure, the Arauca, and the Meta. [Ridged fields were discovered in 1968 near the Río Apure - editor.]

Several parallels to the ridged fields of the tropical lowlands are found in the highlands of South and Central America. It seems likely that the earth-moving practices in both environments were related in function, if not always in form. One of the closest approximations in both form and function are the ridged fields recently discovered along the western shore of Lake Titicaca, at an altitude of 12,000 feet in the Andes. These fields, covering some 200,000 acres, are found over a distance of more than 160 miles, from north of Lake Arapa in Peru to the Straits of Tiquina in Bolivia. Today the ditches are encrusted with alkali and the ridges are highly saline, so that cultivation is usually impossible. The fields still serve as grazing land, however, particularly during the dry season. At that time the upland pastures are parched and brown, but the high water table along the shore of the lake serves to keep the grass among the ancient earthworks green.

The Titicaca ridges are from 15 to 40 feet wide and range up to hundreds of feet in length. The height from ditch bottom to ridge crest is usually 3 to 4 feet. Most of the ridged fields are on the poorly drained margin of the lake plain and are subject to flooding in years of high water. The fields form checkerboard or ladder-like patterns or are irregular; their resemblance to the ridged fields in the Mojos area nearby in lowland Bolivia is striking.

Another form of agricultural earthworks in the Andean highlands consists of narrower parallel ridges, often built on sloping ground and running straight downhill rather than across the slope. Some of these ridge systems are old but others are new. Called *huachos* in Peru and Bolivia, they help to aerate heavy sod, to channel excess water from parts of a slope, and to improve drainage on slopes so gentle that they are subject to waterlogging. In Colombia's central mountains, where old second-growth forest is being cleared to establish coffee plantations and pasture, the ancient ridge systems are so abundant that the hillsides in places give the appearance of having been combed. These pre-Columbian ridges are 5 to 6 feet wide, as much as twice the width of the *huachos* that are built today.

Huachos are usually confined to hillsides but are also found on level plains. Near Lake Titicaca, for example, recently dug *huachos* can be found overlying the pre-Columbian ridge systems. Above 10,000 feet in the central Andes *huachos* are planted mainly with potatoes. To the north in the Colombian Andes, where the earthworks have been raised at much lower altitudes, they are used to grow maize, manioc, and the white carrot-like root known as *arracacha*.

The well-known chinampas, or artificial islands, of the Valley of Mexico have some characteristics in common with the various drainage-promoting earthworks that are found in South America. Although many chinampas were built up in shallow lake waters, others served to convert swampy ground into useful fields. Still others were evidently formed on lake margins subject to seasonal flooding. At Xochimilco, the classic chinampas site, the planting areas are quite large. They are squares 100 yards or more on a side, surrounded by navigable canals edged with alders and willows. In the poorly drained basin at the headwaters of the Balsas River in the nearby state of Tlaxcala another example of artificial-island agriculture is found; it is apparently a variation on the Valley of Mexico pattern. [Since 1969, large numbers of raised fields and drainage canals have been discovered in the Maya lowlands of Mexico and Belize - editor.]

Raised fields built to avoid the hazards of floodplain agriculture are not confined to Latin America. Henry Schoolcraft, a pioneer ethnographer who worked in the U.S. Middle West in the middle of the nineteenth century, described agricultural earthworks or "planting beds" in valley bottoms extending from the vicinity of Fort Wayne, Indiana, to the St. Joseph, Kalamazoo, and Grand rivers in Michigan. Parallel ridges were laid out in rectangles with "paths" between them; some were as much as 300 acres in extent. Similar tracts existed in Illinois, Wisconsin, and Missouri. Observing that the contemporary Indian inhabitants of the region cultivated maize only by "hilling," Schoolcraft concluded that the ridged fields were the work of an earlier culture, perhaps the then little-known Mound Builders. The possibility of some link between these garden farmers of the Mississippi valley and the ridged-field farmers of Latin America invites further study, particularly by those who are reluctant to accept the idea that similar environmental adaptations are independently invented again and again.

Putting together all our evidence concerning pre-Columbian agriculture in the seasonally flooded lowlands of tropical South America, we find that remarkably little is known other than what can be deduced from studying the ridged fields themselves. In the absence of any but the scantiest of early accounts, the means used to build the earthworks, the crops raised on them, and the ways in which the crops were fertilized and rotated remain matters for speculation. It is especially difficult to attempt a projection of the number of people who could have supported themselves on the produce of the ridged fields, although some useful insights can be gained by examining the populations of areas where similar agricultural systems are used today.

Before considering this question it is only fair to mention several explanations of the earthworks that deny them any agricultural function, or at least rule out the role of improving drainage. Some observers have suggested that they might be fortifications, others that they might be the remnants of sluice-mining systems. They have been called fishponds, irrigation channels, or enclosures for the culture of freshwater mussels. They have even been declared to be the result of natural sedimentation processes and not the works of man at all. The last is the easiest of the alternative claims to disprove. The evidence of the aerial photographs--in particular the variety of intermingled patterns they reveal--makes it clear that man is responsible for the raised ground. The tremendous extent of the works may seem to present a puzzle. What we know from the construction of contemporary chinampas in Mexico and from gardening practices in New Guinea indicates, however, that simple digging sticks and wooden spades are the only tools needed for similar earth-moving projects today.

What are the advantages that floodplain rivers and their associated swamps offer as a habitat for a settled people? For one thing, the rich protein resources of such an environment would have allowed a settled way of life even before the development of agriculture. In the tropical lowlands of South America the rivers, swamps, and even the flooded grasslands harbor abundant fishes, turtles (both land and water), iguanas, manatees, and large rodents such as capybaras, pacas, and agoutis. There is also a large and diverse population of waterfowl. Even after farming had become an established way of life, tropical agriculturists whose main food was a starchy root crop such as manioc would have valued the animal protein available in this environment.

A dual economy of this kind--ridged-field agriculture supplemented by hunting and fishing--should have been able to support far larger populations than the ones that scratch a living from the tropical forests today. Estimates of population density based on the extent of the ridged fields, however, are risky. For one thing, we do not know what fraction of the fields in a given area were under cultivation at any one time. The fields along the San Jorge River in Colombia, if they were all cultivated at the same time, could have supported as many as 400 people per square mile. In 1690 the Llanos de Mojos of Bolivia had a population of about 100,000 Indians. A century earlier, before the first contacts with Europeans resulted in deadly epidemics of Old World diseases, the population very likely numbered several hundred thousand. There is no reason to believe it was any smaller when the pre-Columbian ridged fields were under cultivation.

New archaeological evidence and new analyses of historical records attest to the existence of a surprisingly large aboriginal population in many parts of tropical South America. Both the extent of the seasonally flooded tropical farming areas and the evidence for a massive human effort that they provide suggest that the early lowland cultures had achieved a highly complex adjustment to their environment. The direction of flow of early cultural influences between the highlands and the lowlands of South America is a matter of continuing controversy. Those students of the question who contend that major cultural elements moved upstream from the lowlands of the Amazon, Orinoco, and Magdalena regions into the Andean highlands in the past 2,000 or 3,000 years may find their arguments supported by the evidence for a complex, socially strati- fied lowland culture in pre-Columbian South America presented here. It is certain that future archaeological studies of South America's tropical lowlands and the complex ecological relations worked out by the region's early farmers should contribute much toward a more precise reconstruction of New World culture history.

Parsons "in the field" with Carl Sauer in Costa Rica, 1968.

Parsons holding the Livingston Medal from the American Geographical Society, with John Leighly holding the Wahlberg Medal from the Swedish Society of Anthropology and Geography, in Berkeley, 1985.

Parsons leading a geography field class in northern California, 1967.

Parsons "passing the word" to a field class in Marin County, California, 1967.

PART FIVE

The Human Impact

17

The Miskito Pine Savanna of Nicaragua and Honduras[*]

The genus *Pinus*, the most widely distributed and most valuable member of the temperate zone forests of the Northern Hemisphere, extends well into tropical latitudes both in the Old World and in the New World. Natural stands of *P. merkusii* form a part of the man-induced highland savanna association which reaches to within a few miles of the equator in northern Sumatra. This pine has an even more extensive distribution on the Shan Plateau of Burma and Siam, in Indo-China, and on the islands of Luzon and Mindoro in the Philippines. Related species (*P. khaysa, P. insularis*) occupy somewhat higher elevations both on the mainland and in the Benguet hill country of northern Luzon.

The most extensive stands of pines within the tropics, however, are found in Middle America. At least a dozen distinct species are represented among the highland pines which cover much of the more arid portions of interior southern Mexico, Guatemala, Honduras, and northernmost Nicaragua. There are three species of pines on Cuba and Hispaniola. One of these, *P. caribaea*, also occurs extensively in open stands with grass and sedge on the low sand and gravel plains of the rainy British Honduras coast and again on the Miskito (Mosquito) coast of Nicaragua and Honduras, separated from the highland pine forests by a belt of broadleaf high tropical forest.[1]

[*]Excerpted (pp. 36-51, 56-58, 63) from *Annals of the Association of American Geographers*, Vol. 45, pp. 36-63 (1955). The field reconnaissance for this study, carried out in Central America during the spring of 1953, was supported by the Geography Branch, Office of Naval Research.

[1]This three-needled Caribbean pine, which also is found on the Bay Islands (Guanaja), the Isle of Pines, in western Cuba, the Bahamas, and in the Petén

The Extent of the Savanna

The pine savanna of eastern Nicaragua and Honduras seems never before to have been mapped and its very existence has been unknown to many geographers. Interspersed with saw palmettos and scrub hardwoods such as are found along the Gulf Coast and South Atlantic seaboard of the United States, it covers an extensive area of deeply weathered quartz gravels stretching southward from Cape Camarón, Honduras, for some 300 miles to a point a few miles north of Bluefields, Nicaragua, where the southernmost natural stand of pine trees in the New World occurs (Fig. 17.1). Commercial exploitation of the softwood lumber resource of this coast has only recently been initiated. The designation "Miskito pine savanna" seems appropriate for this particular plant association as its limits approximate closely those of the territory originally occupied by the Miskito Indians.[2] Their descendants, with a generous admixture of Negro and White blood, are still the most numerous inhabitants of this thinly-settled coast of Central America where both the English and the Miskito languages are more commonly heard than Spanish.

At its most westerly extension on the north bank of the Río Coco (Río Wanks) the Miskito pine savanna reaches more than 100 miles inland from the cost, but its average width is closer to 30 miles. Gallery forests mark the courses of each of the several rivers which cut across the savanna in slightly entrenched channels of

---

district of Guatemala, has only recently been recognized by foresters as botanically distinct from the larger-coned slash pine of the southeastern United States. The latter has not been restored to *P. elliottii* as Englemann originally distinguished it from *P. caribaea* from the Isle of Pines type locality in 1880. Elbert L. Little, Jr. and Keith W. Dorman, "Slash Pine (Pinus Caribaea), Its Nomenclature and Varieties," *Journal of Forestry*, XC (1952):918-23.

[2]Eduard Conzemius, "Ethnographical Survey of the Miskito and Sumu Indians of Honduras and Nicaragua," *Bureau of American Ethnology Bulletin 106* (Washington, 1932). "Mosquito" (Mosquito Coast, Mosquito Territory) has been the spelling generally adopted by the English, originally under the erroneous assumption that the name owed its origin to the insects. I have here adopted the alternative spelling "Miskito" which avoids that confusion. The Spaniards called the Indians "Moscos" and the area "Mosquitia" or "Costa de Mosquita." In general mosquitos are neither particularly numerous nor bothersome in this area today.

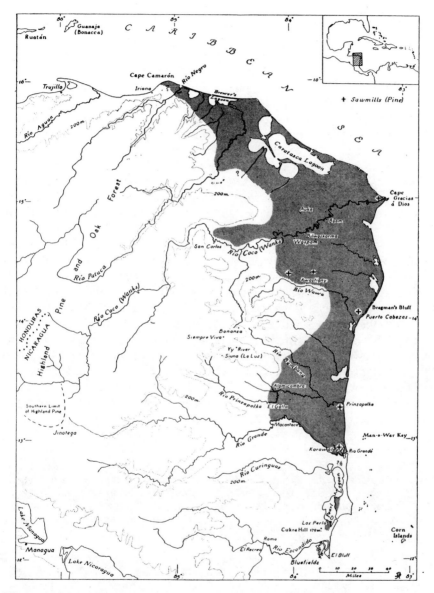

Figure 17.1   The Extent of the Miskito Savanna (Shaded).   Map drawn by Brigham Arnold.

which the larger, the Río Patuca, Río Coco, Río Prinzapolca, and Río Grande, are all navigable deep into the interior. Pines occur chiefly on the higher, better drained surfaces interspersed with palmettos and scrub hardwoods which often occur as islands in the savanna. Extensive tracts of seasonally inundated land along the coasts, as behind Cape Gracias á Dios, are treeless marshes. Mangroves and freshwater swamp trees fringe the coastal lagoons and estuaries. Even toward the interior, where pine-covered gravel ridges reach elevations of 500 feet or more, there are fairly extensive, ill-drained flats of grey-blue clay soils supporting only sedges and palmettos.[3] The total area mapped as savanna south of the Río Coco in Nicaragua approximates 2.5 million acres, but of this nearly one-third may be "hardwood islands," gallery, and swamp forests. An area almost as large lies to the north, most of which is within the so-called "disputed territory" which is claimed by both Nicaragua and Honduras, but, except for the immediate banks of the Río Coco, actually administered by the latter.[4]

The northern and southern limits of the coastal Miskito savanna are clearly edaphically conditioned. On the north, below low-lying Cape Camarón, the rugged Sierra de Esperanza comes down to the sea to pinch out the gravel shelf. These gravels are not to be found on Banacca (Guanaja) Island, 60 miles northwest of the cape, where there is a small stand of Caribbean pine. To the south, high forest replaces the pine beyond Pearl Lagoon as the quartz sands and gravels give way to the striking red, friable clays of the Cukra Hill mafic igneous complex and the basalt flow at El Bluff (elevation 200 feet) which protects the entrance to Bluefields Bay.

The interior boundary or "bush line" between pine savanna and high evergreen forest (a dense tropical *monte* as much as 120 feet

---

[3]There is an early recognition of the association of pines with better drained savanna soils in the remarkable report by a German commission appointed by Prince Carl of Prussia and the Duke of Schoenburg-Waldenburg to investigate the colonization possibilities of the Miskito Coast. A. Fellechner, Dr. Muller, and C.L.C. Hesse, *Bericht über die im hochsten Auftrage....bewirkte Untersuchung einiger Theile des Mosquitolandes.* Berlin, 1845.

[4]Although the Río Coco was made the boundary under the King of Spain's 1906 arbitration award it was never accepted by Nicaragua. In 1953 Nicaragua police exercised jurisdiction for a few miles north of the Río Coco and there were Nicaraguan schools on both sides of the river. However the only Nicaraguan military post north of the river was at Cape Gracias á Dios, a Nicaraguan settlement which was moved from the mouth of the river to a site upstream on the north bank following the hurricane of 1941. The nearest point clearly under Honduras was Auka, 18 miles from the Río Coco, where there was a Honduran mayor, Honduran money, and people who considered themselves Hondureños.

tall) is almost everywhere sharp. Silicous sand and gravel soils, often containing a mottled, impervious subsoil with iron concretions, characteristically support a savanna vegetation; the high forest occurs on the crumb-structured humic clays of superior water-holding capacities which are found towards the interior.[5] The "bush line" seems not to be related to topography (save possibly near Cape Camarón), and it is some distance inland from it that the land rises above the 700-foot contour. *P. caribaea* stops abruptly with the savanna at the margin of the high broadleaf forest, but is said to recur locally in the arid hill lands of interior Honduras. There, however, the *ocote* pine (*P. oocarpa*) is the dominant conifer.[6] In British Honduras, too, the Caribbean pine occurs not only on the coastal "pine ridges," but also at elevations of more than 3,000 feet on Mountain Pine Ridge along the Guatemala frontier....[7]

Climate

The Miskito Coast is drenched with rain throughout most of the year. Average annual rainfall probably exceeds 100 inches everywhere within the pine-grassland area, reaching 150 inches to the south in the neighborhood of Bluefields. Average daily temperatures range narrowly between 76°F (January-February) and 81°F

---

[5]This relationship seems to have been first noted by Hugh Bennett, "The Soils of Central America and Northern South America," *American Soil Survey Association Bulletin*, I, No. 6 (1925): 69-81. Karl Sapper also recognized the soil as the factor determining the boundary of pine savanna and high forest on the Miskito Coast in "Klimakunde von Mittelamerika," *Handbuch der Klimatologie*, IIH, W. Köppen and R. Geiger, eds. Berlin, 1932, p. 58.

[6]Paul J. Shank, "Forest Resources of Honduras," *Proceedings of the Inter-American Conference on the Conservation of Renewable Resources, Denver, 1948.* Washington, 1959, pp. 559-63. Frederick H. Vogel, *Forestry in Honduras.* Institute of Inter-American Affairs, Washington, 1952, 18 pp. The taxonomy of the pines of Honduras remains to be worked out. There is a possibility that there is more than one species on the Miskito savanna. Francisco Altschul, "Informe sobre Territorio de la Mosquitia," *Revista del Archivo y Bibliografía Nacional* (Tegucigalpa), XV (1927):576-79, 657-60, mentions two distinct types of pines on the Honduras savannas along the lower Río Patuca, one the "common Baltimore pine," the other "a Rosemary or shortleaf pine" which branches closer to the ground (p. 658). This may refer, however, only to the often-observed correlation between needle length and growing site.

[7]A.F.A. Lamb, "Pine Forests of British Honduras," *Empire Forestry Review*, September 1950:219-26. E.E.M. Loock, "The Pines of Mexico and British Honduras," *Union of South Africa Department of Forestry Bulletin 35*, Pretoria, 1950.

232

(May-June) with sensible temperatures being lowest during the spring months when Trade Winds blow most steadily. Despite the high annual rainfall there is a marked dry season which usually sets in about mid-February and continues into the first week of May. March and April are the driest months, but protracted drought is rare. At Bluefields, for example, over a 21-year period there has never been a rainless month. The average 2-month precipitation for March and April at Puerto Cabezas is 4.38 inches; for Bluefields, 5.79 inches; for Iriona, at the northern margin of the savanna in Honduras, 2.44 inches. Critical levels of soil moisture are reached, however, in these months when the herbaceous cover withers and dies and low fires smoulder the length and breadth of the savanna. The occasional showers that fall during March and April, together with the heavy dews, are usually sufficient to induce sprouting in the recently burned savanna grasses and sedges, the roots of which are undamaged by the light burns.

Precipitation values at Puerto Cabezas, on the coast, are remarkably similar to those recorded at the gold mining camps inland 60 to 70 miles within the high evergreen forest. The annual average for Puerto Cabezas is 129.15 inches; for Siempre Viva Gauging Station (elevation 1,050 feet), 116.22 inches; for Bonanza (elevation 760 feet), 117.13 inches; for Yy River Power House (elevation 900 feet), 130.60 inches; for El Gallo (elevation 100 feet), 123.32 inches. All of these are from records of 10 to 19 years length. A rain-shadow location probably explains the lower figure of 80.56 inches for the 16-year record at Siuna (elevation 575 feet) although there is a suggestion that the rainfall values in the southern interior foothills are somewhat lower than those along the immediate coast. At the El Recreo Agricultural Experiment Station the 5-year average is 122 inches, or 30 inches less than either Bluefields or Cukra Hill for the same period, both of which lie due east near the coast. On the other hand, recent 12-month records from Karawala (135.46 inches) and Macantaca (144.97 inches) show somewhat higher precipitation for the more interior location.[8]

Throughout the length of the coast precipitation is highly local in character and a wet year in one season may be a dry year elsewhere. The driest year in the Puerto Cabezas record (1931, 94.81

---

[8]Rainfall data cited have been obtained from the following sources: Standard Fruit & Steamship Co. and U.S. Weather Bureau (Puerto Cabezas); Neptune Gold Mining Co. (Bonanza, Siempre Viva); La Luz Mines, Ltd. (Siuna, Yy River); Empresas Nolen, S.A. (Karawala, Macantaca); Cukra Development Co. (Bluefields, El Gallo); U.S.D.A. (Cukra Hill, El Recreo); Köppen-Geiger, *Handbuch der Klimatologie*, II H (Iriona).

inches) was followed by a record-breaking 184.93 inches in 1932. In the longer record for Bluefields, extremes of 60.19 inches (1935) and 200.11 inches (1927) have been recorded, the former figure being less than half that for the next driest year, 1939, with 126.40 inches. Extremes at Bonanza have been 95.32 inches and 141.50 inches; at Siuna, 57.51 inches and 101.53 inches. In general, annual rainfall increases southward along the coast, a fact which must contribute to the more rapid growth of pines and wider spacing of tree rings in the southern extremity of the savanna. A 3-year record for Iriona, Honduras, averages 98.78 inches, which compares with 129 inches for Puerto Cabezas and 155 inches for Bluefields. South of Bluefields, where the mountains come down to the sea, the annual precipitation is even greater, exceeding 250 inches at San Juan del Norte on the Costa Rican frontier.

A single precipitation maximum which usually occurs in July (at Bonanza and Siuna in June) is characteristic throughout the savanna. In contrast, on the "banana coast" of Honduras beyond Iriona, pronounced November maximums are registered at all stations.

Although hurricanes occur with much less frequency than in the Antilles, they are nevertheless a conspicuous climatological feature of the Miskito Coast. Most tropical disturbances occur in late September and October, at the end of the Caribbean hurricane season. Occasionally one strikes at the beginning of the season, in late May or early June. From mid-June to mid-September hurricane development centers much further eastward in the Atlantic Ocean, and the tracks of those storms which enter the Caribbean area lie well to the north of Cape Gracias á Dios.

Savanna and Forest Soils

The Miskito Coast is probably the rainiest area of its size in the New World with a savanna-type vegetation. For so extensive a tropical grassland, either with or without trees, to occur under an average rainfall of 100 to 150 inches with so abbreviated a dry season clearly contradicts once more the traditional concept of the "savanna climate."[9] Pines have been described from widely separated areas in the temperate latitudes as being far less demanding of nutrient values than broadleaf trees, but it is by no means certain that this holds true in the tropical pine savannas. Existence of islands of hardwoods within the Miskito savanna on sites similar to

---

[9]Carl O. Sauer, "Grassland Climax, Fire and Man," *Journal of Range Management*, III (1950):16-21.

those occupied by pine and grass suggest that geology alone does not hold the key to the distribution of vegetation types here.

For the most part, the surface soils of the savanna are a light grey in color, becoming darker where drainage is poorest. Wherever gully erosion has been active, or where ant-hills or hurricane-uprooted pine trees are found, yellow-red subsoil is characteristically exposed at the surface. Neither tree roots nor percolating rainwater can easily penetrate this B horizon, a poorly aerated and mottled gravelly clay. While the quartz gravels in the top layers of the soil are little weathered, being white and hard, they become increasingly iron-stained and crummy with depth. Irregular-shaped iron concretions are sometimes found within a top 4 to 5 feet of gravels; with the quartz pebbles they frequently accumulate on the surface like "desert pavement."

The micro-climate at ground level is very distinct as between forest and savanna. The hot tropical sun gets directly to the exposed savanna soils, so raising the surface temperatures as to increase greatly the rate of evaporation, of humus combustion, and of soil development. The breakdown of silicates to clays is accelerated and the clay particles, which under forest conditions would tend to be flocculated by humus, are free to move downward and to accumulate with the subsoil, this process being most rapid in coarse textured soils.[10] With increasing impedance of soil drainage the impermeable horizon would gradually extend upward. Such colloid accumulation would be especially favored on relatively level sites where there is a marked fluctuation in the water table between wet and dry periods or where sheet erosion has clogged the original drainage channels.

---

[10]It would be instructive to know more about the relative fertility and composition of savanna and forest soils where found side by side. Samples of six savanna and two forest soils from the Nicaragua side were subject to laboratory analysis by Dr. Frank Harradine, Division of Soils, University of California, Berkeley. The soils were acid, but not extremely so, the pH ranging from 5.0 to 6.0 (determined by Beckman pH meter glass electrode at saturation). Organic matter (Cx1.742 per cent) content of the surface soil was surprisingly high, in contrast to the classical relationship within the temperature zone, higher in the forest soils (5.80 and 8.35 per cent) than in the grassland soils (1.67 to 5.00 per cent). Nitrogen content of the two forest soils (0.37 and 0.57 per cent) was much higher than in samples taken a few yards away across the "bush line" within the pine savanna (0.06 and 0.07 per cent). The carbon-nitrogen (C:N) ratio was relatively high (14.5 to 21.9 on pine savanna soils; 8.4 and 9.0 on forest soils), suggesting that the decomposition of humus here may be less rapid than has commonly been supposed under tropical conditions. However, any charcoal particles in the soil would have added to the carbon values so that the evidence for organic matter accumulation is not entirely convincing.

While the micro-climate is not a cause, but an effect, of the vegetation cover it must have an important influence on the rate and nature of soil formation and on the perpetuation of a savanna vegetation once that has been established. The basic questions would seem to be "which came first, pine savanna or impeded soil drainage" and, in either case, "to what extent may man and fire have been involved?"

The Case for a Fire-Savanna

Where soils have been used for some time, have become depleted and have been given up, pines are known to establish themselves where few other trees can survive. O.F. Cook long ago suggested that the pine forests of the highlands of Central America with their characteristic herbaceous understory usually are a secondary formation, the aftermath of clearing and burning of mixed montane forests by native agriculturists.[11] It seems highly improbable that the Miskito savanna surfaces were ever farmed extensively, at least in their present highly leached state. Moreover, the native Indians of the region were at best casual farmers who took their living chiefly from the sea and the hunt. Although their cultivations have probably always been restricted to the narrow strips of alluvium along the streams and behind the coastal beach ridges, it appears that they have habitually burned the savannas for as long as anyone can remember, whether to aid in hunting, to improve grazing, or simply for excitement. In more recent times foreign adventurers and lumbermen have followed their example. Such fires have not only suppressed the encroachment of broadleaf forest trees, but have also sharply restricted the regeneration of the pines themselves until, with the added pressures from the logging operations, there is a very real concern for the perpetuation of the pines as an element in the savanna association.

These coarse textured Pleistocene surfaces with their low water-holding capacity may always have supported a vegetation quite distinct from that of the primary soils developed on the tertiary rocks of the interior hill lands. Occasional clumps of scrub hardwoods standing as islands in the midst of the pine savannas are possibly remnants of what may once have been a xerophytic broadleaf forest which at one time covered the whole extent of this low

---

[11]O. F. Cook, "Vegetation Affected by Agriculture in Central America," *U.S.D.A. Bureau of Plant Industry Bulletin 145*, Washington, 1909.

and rainy coast.[12]   Relative to the "fireproof" high evergreen forest, one can imagine that this lower scrub forest on the gravel surfaces might have been highly combustible.   During the dry season, and especially during occasional years of prolonged spring drought, such a forest would have been extremely vulnerable to fire, which, while used by early man as a tool for both hunting and agriculture, must have been quite beyond his control.

Hurricanes, too, must have played an important role in opening up what may have been originally a dense canopy of forest trees, thus increasing susceptibility to recurrent burning.[13]   Flames spreading through wind-thrown forest trees or through a standing, but combustible, scrub forest during the dry season would have bared the surface soil and inhibited regeneration of the primary forest dominants.   Repeated with sufficient frequency such fires, fanned by the steady on-shore winds of this coast, would have contributed to the eventual degradation and impoverishment of the surface soil through accelerated sheet wash, humus destruction, and leaching with consequent development of clay accumulations under a sand and travel topsoil.   These ill-drained senile soils, so characteristic of the Miskito savannas, may thus be envisioned as the product of forest removal through recurring burning and subsequent acid soil hydrolysis, the breaking down of silicates to clays, and the interruption of the cycle of mineral nutrients crucial to the maintenance of tropical forest growth.   As the soils became progressively degraded, fire-resistant and sun-loving grasses, sedges, and pines, probably less demanding of mineral nutrients, would have colonized the more

---

[12]Professor Robert L. Pendleton of The Johns Hopkins University who has visited the Miskito Coast offers another possible explanation of the origin of these interesting hardwood islands which deserves further investigation.   He writes (personal communication, March 26, 1954): "These islands had been studied by a man who described them to me when I was there.   They were believed to be the site of former camps of the Miskito Indians, for such sites would be protected from fire, and the soil had been enriched by wastes defecated, ashes, and other refuse.   It was considered that when the growth got too dense, cutting off the breeze which was depended upon to blow the mosquitoes and other insects away, the camp was moved to an open part of the savanna.   There seemed to be no difference in the texture of the soil, but the color was darker in the 'islands,' as one would expect, and the reaction according to my informant was nearer neutral. The 'island' forest is kaingined, so the soil is useful."

[13]The puzzling occurrence of extensive areas in the uninhabited rain forest behind Pearl Lagoon with single-specie dominants is tentatively attributed by Archie Carr, *High Jungle and Low*,   Gainesville, Florida, 1963, to hurricane blow-downs which have opened up the forest canopy and permitted the establishment of a sun-loving secondary vegetation.

vigorously, to the eventual exclusion of the more fire-vulnerable growth.[14]

Woodsmen familiar with the area report the existence of occasional pockets of mature pine along the margins of the savanna which are surrounded or nearly surrounded by scrub monte. This suggests to them that the hardwood forest may now be in the process of shading out pine and grass and recolonizing the savanna wherever fire is suppressed. I regret that I was unable to verify this and to observe more closely the relationship of soil to vegetation along the "bush line" during my visit to the Nicaraguan portion of the savanna. Therein undoubtedly lies the answers to many of the questions raised in these pages.

The Role of Drainage Impediment

J. S. Beard, in his general survey of the savannas of northern tropical America,[15] considers the lack of aeration, for which brilliant mottling is sure evidence, to be crucial in the differentiation between forest and savanna soils together with the alternate water-logging and dessication which this poor drainage promotes. In the rainy months water collects in the sandy surface horizon over the clay, and the soil becomes saturated; whereas during the dry season the surface completely dries out, and the grass and trees, having no deep roots, are subjected to severe dessication. While such drainage impediment is not found everywhere, it is at least widespread within the Miskito savanna. One of the striking characteristics of the pines on the more level sites is the apparent absence of tap roots, indicated by the great number of blow-downs as well as the radial, pad-like root system which is frequently exposed on the surface. For the development of such impervious horizons the acceleration of laterization and

---

[14]A similar argument that succession here has been from evergreen forest to pine savanna is to be found in J. B. Kinloch, *Brief Review of the Forest Resources of Nicaragua*, Managua, February, 1950, an unpublished 12-page manuscript in the Library of the U.S. Department of Agriculture, Washington. See also Felix Rawitscher, "Die Erschopfung Tropischer Boden infolge die Entwaldung," *Acta Tropica* (Basle), III (1946):211-247. A partially analogous case may be that described by Frank E. Egler, "Southeast Saline Everglades Vegetation, Florida, and its Management," *Vegetatio* (Den Haag), III (1952):213-265 in which it is convincingly contended that "the herbaceous Everglades and the surrounding pinelands were born in fires; that they can survive only with fires; that they are dying today because of fires" (p. 227).

[15]J. S. Beard, "The Savanna Vegetation of Northern Tropical America," *Ecological Monographs*, XXIII (1953):149-215. Beard, however, was not personally familiar with any of the Caribbean area pine savannas.

238

the downward migration of clays which the removal of an original broadleaf forest would have promoted can quite reasonably be called upon in explanation.

These impermeable clay horizons actually need not always be considered the normal product of soil weathering under high rainfall and constantly high surface soil temperatures. Occasional beds of dirty white volcanic tuff (dacite-andesite pumice, degraded almost to bentonite) also occur within the travels, and where these are at or near the surface (e.g., at the Waspam airstrip) mottling and impeded drainage are frequently conspicuous.

In British Honduras, Charter[16] has envisioned *P. caribaea* as a successional species which becomes established only as alluvial soils age and drainage becomes progressively impeded, but which eventually dies out with further impediment of drainage to be replaced by treeless grass and sedge savanna. The implication here seems to be that, given time, all tropical forest soils become degraded sufficiently no longer to support a high forest. This thesis seems highly questionable in view of the known antiquity of the tropical forest of the Amazon and Congo basins.[17] In any event, the Miskito pine savanna, developed on Pleistocene gravels, can scarcely have the great age which would seem to be required to support this argument. We obviously need to know much more about the time factor in tropical soil formation as well as the effect of forest removal on micro-climate and rates of soil development to speak with any assurance here. It appears well established, however, that the tropical high forest is self-perpetuating until man destroys the cycle and the forest-soil system and dissipates the nutrients.

The Pine-Savanna Plant Association

In general aspect the open, park-like Miskito savanna bears an extraordinary resemblance to the pine flats of Louisiana or Florida.

---

[16]C. G. Charter, *Reconnaissance Survey of the Soils of British Honduras.* Port-au-Spain, Trinidad, 1941.

[17]Louis Lauvaudan represents a view widely held by European foresters when, with reference to the rain forest of central Africa, he argues that "there is no connection whatsoever between the quality of the soil and the distribution or luxuriance of the primeval forest which grows on it;" that the soil owes its fertility to the existence of the forest and disappears with it. "The Equatorial Forest of Tropical Africa: Its Past, Present and Future," *Journal of the Royal African Society*, Supplement, XXXVI, 1937. See also P. W. Richards, *The Tropical Rain Forest: An Ecological Study*, London, 1952, and R.L. Pendleton, "Agricultural and Forestry Potentialities of the Tropics," *Agronomy Journal*, XLII (1950):115-123.

Where pines occur they are usually widely spaced and straight boled with few low branches. Average diameters for mature trees are probably not much over 16 inches, with heights of from 60 to 100 feet. Merchantable stands average from 3,000 to 5,000 board feet to the acre, reaching maximums of 10,000.[18] On the inner margins of the savannas where fires are probably less frequent and soil conditions perhaps more favorable, stumps of up to 36 inches in diameter may be seen. However, the slow-growing timber of the poorly drained soils is more highly prized in the European export market where a knotless, high density, high tensile strength wood is required. The "four-lining" of logs measuring upwards to 20 by 20 inches by 30 feet for the overseas market rather than the sawmill operations has made operations profitable for foreign lumbermen here in the past. Only the coarser-grained wood is sawn into lumber. Most of the pines being cut commercially carry from 80 to 100 tree rings, with 125 rings being close to the maximum reported. Probably more than one ring is produced in some years. In general, the heartwood is a reddish brown, the sapwood lighter colored. Termite damage occurs in about one-third of the trees, some of the worst infected often being left to re-seed cut-over lands, as is done in mahogany operations. Some trees 60 years or more of age may still be under the minimum diameter of 12 inches, yet mature and past their prime and unlikely ever to reach legal size.

The resin content varies greatly from tree to tree, but it is generally quite high. Early English accounts indicate a greater interest in the pines as a source of pitch for the Royal Navy than as a source of lumber. Commercial turpentining ventures were inaugurated in both Honduras and Nicaragua some 30 years ago but the ventures failed, perhaps more because of labor difficulties, theft of containers, fire losses, and transport difficulties than to any lack of resin flow.[19]

In some areas the only non-herbaceous species is the pine, but for the most part the pines are mingled with a sparse orchard vegetation of large, stiff, leathery-leaved brush and low gnarled trees with thick bark, especially *Curatella americana, Micronia* spp., *Byrsonima crassifolia, Calliandra houstoniana* and, less commonly,

[18]G. R. Fahnestock and G. A. Garrett, "Nicaraguan Pine (Pinus Caribaea Mor.)," *Tropical Woods*, LV (1938):1-16.

Quercus, Crescentia and *Mimosa.*[20] Clumps of palmetto (*Acoelor-raphe?*) may occur with them, but they are most common on poorly drained soils in the flats and adjacent to the mangrove-fringed coastal lagoons.

Most of the genera of herbaceous plants found in the Nicaraguan portion of the savanna are also represented in the piney woods flora of the southeastern United States. As there, they are characteristically arranged in scattered clumps with bare soil between. *Cyperaceae* are sufficiently widespread that the designation "sedge savanna," which Beard associates with high rainfall areas, would seem to be appropriate.[21] They occur even on well-drained slopes, especially *Rhynchospora barbata* and *Bulbostylis paradoxus* (*Stenophyllus paradoxus*), the latter a peculiar little upright sedge locally called "niggerhead" whose fire-blackened aerial rhizome sheathed with old leaf bases give it something of the appearance of a shaving brush. It occurs most conspicuously on hill slopes where a white quartz pebble pavement mantles the soil surface.

Among the bunch grasses the genera most conspicuously represented are *Trachypogon, Andropogon, Paspalum (grama), Aristida,* and *Leptocoryphium,* possibly in that order. The sward-like gramas are especially common on the better soils. Along the margins of the high forest, in the "tension zone" between savanna and monte, these shorter grasses give way to the tall *Arundinella deppennae, Ischaemum latifolium,* and a species of *Tripsacum* locally known as "*teocinte.*" These head-high grasses of superior grazing value may well be pioneers in the process of invasion of the savanna by the monte. It would be useful to know in detail the nature of the soil transition from low grass savanna to high grass savanna to forest. The pines which occur with these tall grasses along the "bush line" characteristically are superior specimens of larger than average diameter, perhaps because fires are less frequent here than in the short grass-sedge areas.

Everywhere the high forest environment, damp, dark and insect-infested, contrasts sharply with the open sunny landscape of the pine-bunch grass-sedge savannas where monkeys and parrots chatter incongruously amidst the upper branches of orchid-festooned

---

[20]Botanical determinations of species and genera cited in this section have been made by Jason R. Swallen and Lyman Smith of the U.S. National Herbarium, Washington, D.C.

[21]Beard, *op. cit.*, p. 195, considers a sedge savanna as characteristic of swampy conditions of relatively small extent which alternate rapidly with forest and woodland. This does not fit the Miskito Coast situation well.

pine trees. Within the monte or "mahogany bush" there is an extreme diversity of species. Palms and bamboos are prominently represented as are such economically significant rain forest genera as *Swietenia* (mahogany), *Cedrela* (Spanish cedar), *Calophyllum* (Maria), *Carapa* (*cedro macho*), *Hieronyma* (*nancito*), *Dalium* (*comenegro*), and *Castilla* (*caucho*)....[22]

The Pine Resource

Modern commercial pine lumbering dates from 1921 when a group of New Orleans and Slidell, Louisiana, lumbermen joined forced with the Vaccaro Brothers (who were later to found the Standard Fruit and Steamship Company) to establish the Bragman's Bluff Lumber Company, purchasing timber rights to 80,000 acres of land behind Bragman's Bluff "adapted to cattle raising or on which there are pine trees." Although there were conflicts with Indian Reserve land claims, the American company poured some $5 million into the development, establishing the new town of Puerto Cabezas (named for a Nicaraguan patriot) and building deep-water port facilities and some 100 miles of railroad to service both the lumber operations and the new banana plantings along the alluvial bottoms of the Río Wawa.[23] A modern sawmill was moved here intact from Louisiana and a planing mill established. Exports of sawn lumber began in 1925. Revolutions and civil war greatly disturbed operations, more particularly in the banana business, and after 1931 banana plantings were abandoned.[24] In recent years the pine lands held in fee simple have been leased on a stumpage basis to the Robinson interests of New Orleans who have built an extensive network of logging roads throughout the savanna to the banks of the Río Coco at Waspam and Bilwaskarma....

The life expectancy of the coastal pine forests of the Miskito Shore cannot exceed a very few years. While the lumbermen have

---

[22]For an extraordinarily vivid description of this forest as it exists behind Pearl Lagoon, Nicaragua, see Archie Carr, *op. cit.*

[23]"A Magnificent Pine Operation in Nicaragua," *The Lumber Trade Journal* (New Orleans), Jan. 15, 1928:22-23.

[24]The annual report of the Nicaragua Customs Service for 1929 referred to the Standard Fruit banana operations as follows: "The lands have not proven so fertile as supposed, the heavy rains washed out the bridges, the banana disease appeared and the production of bananas was very small for the acreage planted." *Report of the Collector-General of Customs*, Republic of Nicaragua, Administrator of Customs, Managa, 1930.

been cutting as much as 40 million board feet annually, termites, beetles, windfall, and especially fire have continued to take their toll. The importance of wind-fall is evidenced by the traces of large numbers of uprooted trees, all similarly aligned, that are seen in many areas. There is little fire damage to mature trees, for crown fires are apparently unknown although root and basal trunk scars from burning grass may provide access to termites. The most serious effect of the fires is the killing of the young pine seedlings on which the regeneration of the forest depends. In many cut-over areas, moreover, only a very few small, non-merchantable trees have been left standing as seed stock for the future. Replanting, although required by law, is unnecessary, for the pines are prolific seed producers. What is needed is complete fire protection of cut-over areas for from 5 to 10 years or until the natural regeneration has reached 8 to 10 feet in height. A simple system of firebreaks would accomplish much towards this end, for often a narrow foot trail is sufficient to stop the flames.

At present there is no forester, no fire prevention crew, and no inventory of the merchantable timber still standing on this low-lying Caribbean coast of Nicaragua and Honduras. Like sarsaparilla, turtle, rubber, mahogany, and bananas before, pine lumbering, which has revived the economy of the coast in recent years, will soon drop off to insignificant levels. Under some semblance of a management program, a second crop of timber trees might be ready in another 50 to 75 years. The alternative would seem to be continued destructive fires and continued impoverishment of the pine resource.[25] A few small protected areas, as around the Moravian Church's mission hospital at Bilwaskarma, offer abundant evidence of the pine tree's capacity to reproduce itself here when given the chance....

Conclusion

An English- and Miskito-speaking Protestant enclave within a Spanish-speaking Catholic world, the Miskito Coast of Nicaragua and Honduras with its 80,000 inhabitants has been until very recently a land of mystery for which Managua and Tegucigalpa have had little understanding or concern. Until the establishment of regular airline service from Managua to Bluefields, Puertos Cabezas, and the gold

---

[25]Report of the FAO Mission for Nicaragua (United Nations Food and Agriculture Organization), Washington & Rome, 1950, and The Economic Development of Nicaragua (International Bank for Reconstruction and Development), Baltimore, 1952, both strongly urge the introduction of modern forest management principles to the wasting pine forest asset of the Caribbean coast.

camps, it was easier to get to the Miskito Shore from New Orleans than from the interior capitals, but now that is all changed, at least for the country south of the Río Coco. The opening of the often-delayed truck road from Managua to Rama may likewise stimulate further economic development and settlement by Spanish-speaking peoples, especially along the Río Escondido. But economic prospects are at best modest.

The United Fruit Company's 1,400 acres of African oil palm and 2,500 acres of mahogany, cedar, and teak plantations on abandoned banana lands along the Río Escondido represent the first serious attempts at tree-farming in this tropical high-rainfall area where tree crops may provide one of the few possibilities for a really permanent agriculture. Perhaps, too, the planting of introduced pasture grasses on forest soils behind the "bush line" may one day be dove-tailed with a beef cattle industry on the savannas. A better knowledge of tropical soils, their potentialities and limitations, is obviously necessary. The understanding of the causes underlying the presence here of an extensive pine savanna, for which a tentative theory has been suggested above, would be an important step in this direction.

18

Europeanization of the Savanna Lands of Northern South America[*]

The prevailing easterly air flow along the Caribbean coast of the South American continent produces atmospheric divergence and subsidence that makes a near desert of much of the immediate littoral of Venezuela and Colombia. A short distance inland heavy summer rains occur in association with the passage of the Intertropical Convergence Zone, but from December to April the *llanos* of the Orinoco, and the coastal lowlands of Colombia from the Magdalena River westward almost to the Gulf of Urabá, lie under cloudless skies. The area of alternate wet and dry seasons is continuous in a band some 300-400 kilometers wide across northern South America and includes the northern Colombian cordilleras, the Sierra Nevada de Santa Marta, and the eastward trending Venezuelan Andes that stand between the llanos and the sea. The diversity of micro-environments in these mountains, which attain heights of more than 5,000 meters and reach into the zone of perpetual snow, contrasts sharply with the uniformity and vastness of the adjacent lowland plains with their predominantly herbaceous vegetation. European man's past and present place in these lowland savannas is the concern of this chapter. Aboriginal occupation of these savanna lands, and aspects of their plant and animal ecology, are discussed elsewhere by Hammond (1980) and Medina (1980).

The Distinctiveness of Tropical American Savannas

---

[*]Reprinted from *The Human Ecology of Savanna Environments*, David R. Harris, editor, Academic Press, New York, pp. 267-289 (1980). Copyright (c) 1980 by Academic Press Ltd. (London).

246

several units, of which the llanos and the coastal *sabanas* of Colombia are only the most extensive and most clearly differentiated. Unlike the savanna landscapes of Africa, Australia, Brazil, and the Guiana highlands, these plains in northern South America are built up from recent and sub-recent outwash from the youthful Andes. The older, dissected alluvial surfaces tend to be deeply weathered, with leached soils that are extremely low in exchangeable bases. They contrast with the younger fans and lower floodplains, which, although of superior fertility, are subject to prolonged seasonal inundation.

Medina (1980) differentiates between the grassy savannas of the annually flooded riverine and basin lands, which are either treeless or include scattered palms, and the more wooded *cerrado* savannas on the higher, non-flooded surfaces where shrubs and trees (most commonly fire-tolerant species of *Curatella*, *Byrsonima*, and *Bowdichia*) often grow within the grass matrix.[1] Water is the main constraint on the human occupancy of both types of savanna: in the former there is too much of it in the rainy, high-sun months; in the latter there is too little of it during the long, dry season (*verano*). The numerous rivers that head in the better watered highlands and then cross the savannas have provided attractive stream-side habitats for both aboriginal and modern man, with their rich resources of aquatic protein and their gallery forests growing on relatively fertile, easily tilled alluvial soils.

The savanna lands of the New World are generally wetter than those of the Old World. They fall almost entirely within the humid-savanna category, with 1,000-2,000 millimeters average annual rainfall and a short, dry season of 2.5-5.0 months (Harris 1980). They are also differentiated both by the relative recency of human occupancy and by the present absence of large herbivores (Harris 1980, Medina 1980), as well as by the lack of domesticated herd animals among the pre-Columbian Amerindian populations. They are accordingly much less "worn" than their African counterparts, the

---

[1]The vegetation of the northern tropical American savannas, however, is very different from that of the classical cerrado of Brazil. The latter has a much more diversified population of vascular plants and includes almost the whole continuum of structural types from closed-canopy forest to grass with or without scattered trees and shrubs. According to one estimate, in 70% of the total cerrado area of Brazil, which covers 40% of the country excluding Amazonia, the woody plants are too dense to permit passage of a jeep (Eiten 1972). Cerrado is used in two senses. It refers either to the cerrado region or province as a whole, with its many structural types of vegetation, or to a part only of the structural continuum. The confusion that this entails is not unlike the ambiguity associated with the term savanna itself (Harris 1980).

impact of man-set fires and grazing animals being of much briefer duration. Yet fire, a pervasive force in all savanna environments (Harris 1980), clearly has modified the vegetation cover from the moment of man's arrival in the New World, most probably during the last interglacial (Sauer 1958, 1961, 1975). Natural lightning fires, of course, have a much longer history (Budowski 1959). Only since the arrival of Europeans has grazing by domestic livestock been a significant factor in the ecology of tropical American savannas.

The introduction and spread of African grasses into the American tropics has been a seldom recognized but important component of the ongoing biotic interchange between the Old World and the New World. The palatability and nutritiousness of the numerous introduced African grasses contrast sharply with that of most of the native American species. The adaptability of the former to grazing is probably related to their co-evolution with large herbivores in their area of origin. In the American tropics these African grasses have proved to be remarkably aggressive, naturalizing themselves wherever they have received minimal human support (Sternberg 1968, Parsons 1970). Six species of grasses have been principally involved to date in this African invasion that is still in progress: Guinea grass (*Panicum maximum*), Pará grass (*Brachiaria mutica*), molasses grass (*Melinis minutiflora*), jaraguá (*Hyparrhenia rufa*), Pangola (*Digitaria decumbens*), and pasto peludo (*Brachiaria decumbens*), together with a seventh species, the vigorous Kikuyu grass (*Pennisetum clandestinum*) of higher elevations. The first two have been longest in the Americas and are probably best known and valued, although some of the later arrivals have become more aggressive colonizers.

Derived savannas produced by repeated forest clearing and burning have been much discussed (Budowski 1956, 1959, Johannessen 1963, Sauer 1958, 1975, Scott 1977). They are certainly less extensive in the American than in the Old World tropics. In both hemispheres man probably has become more influential in extending existing grasslands than in originating new ones. In recent times the ubiquitous chainsaw, and heavy land-clearing and road-building equipment, has been increasingly threatening the remaining tropical American rain forest (selva) in an unprecedented epidemic of *potreroismo* (pasteurization). The long-term ecological consequences of this "pasture revolution," which is producing vast new areas of derived savanna, are of increasing concern. Yet forest clearance continues to find support from the FAO, the World Bank, the AID, and from national and local governments, as well, of course, as from the large landowners who raise cattle (Parsons 1976).

The distribution of the major long-established or "natural" savanna areas of tropical America is shown in Figure 18.1. They include the vast cerrado region of the interior of Brazil, although, except locally, its ancient, gently undulating peneplain surfaces tend to be dominated by xerophytic scrub rather than by grass (see footnote 1 and Eiten 1972). Next most extensive are the Orinoco llanos (some 480,000 square kilometers), stretching for 3,000 kilometers in a lozenge-shaped swathe of grassland across Venezuela and Colombia. The less well defined and more diverse savannas of the north-coastal plain of Colombia consist of a mosaic of woodland, natural grassland, and improved pasture. Other savanna areas, less affected by modern developments, include the Miskito pine savanna of Nicaragua-Honduras (Parsons 1955), the Rupununi-Rio Branco savannas of the Brazil-Guyana boundary (Eden 1964), the Gran Sabana of the Guiana highlands, and the coastal Guianan savanna belt. Additional small tracts of grassland (*campos*) or cerrado are scattered throughout the Amazonian rain forest. They are now believed to be remnants of previously more extensive savanna environments of the Pleistocene period (Prance 1978, Vuilleumier 1971).

The absence of large herbivores and domestic herd animals in the Americas seems to have precluded the development of the parasites and vector-borne disease organisms that evolved through the millennia of man-animal relationships in tropical Africa (McNeill 1976). It was rather the infectious diseases of the Old World brought by the Spaniards, and later by African slaves, that were to decimate what Desowitz has referred to (in discussion at the Savanna Environments symposium) as the "immunologically virgin" lowland populations. The humid lowlands, especially, became a demographic void within a few decades of discovery, thus leaving a niche open to occupation by Europeans and their livestock. As was the case three centuries later on the island of New Caledonia, "Europeans could not see these grasslands without immediately thinking of cattle," the herds of which often multiplied in a semi-wild state without human intervention (Barrau 1980:257).

Lacking precious metals and a native labor force, the savanna lowlands of Venezuela and Colombia remained a cultural backwater that until recently participated only minimally in the economic and social development of their respective countries. Malaria, probably introduced by the Europeans, has been the principal barrier to effective savanna occupancy, together with cattle ticks, hoof-and-mouth disease, and similar livestock-related infestations. Such great scourges of Africa as onchocerciasis and trypanosomiasis, described by Desowitz (1980), had no, or only a late and local, effect on

Figure 18.1 Major Savanna Areas in Tropical America (after Sarmiento and Monasterio 1975:225).

tropical American populations. Chagas' disease, an endemic form of trypanosomiasis transmitted by a blood-sucking insect, seems to stand as the single exception.

In recent decades all tropical American savanna areas have been affected in varying degree both by the great advances in public health that have brought malaria largely under control, and by the revolution in transportation that has brought the jeep and air taxi to the doorstep of even the most remote cattle ranch (*hato*). The grasslands of northern South America, where the traditional way of life has been so closely tied to livestock ranching, are beginning to be looked on with fresh eyes as land reserves which, under other management systems, might contribute significantly to the alleviation of the overriding problem of food for an exploding population and of land on which to produce it.

The Orinoco Plains

The Orinoco plains or llanos form an almost unbroken savanna landscape sloping gradually from the base of the Andes, at elevations of from 250 to 500 meters, toward the Orinoco River and the crystalline massif of the Guiana highlands. The frayed southwestern limit of the plains is approximately marked by the Guaviare River of Colombia. Beyond, to the south, lies the Amazonian selva. This open grassland was called the "llanos" by Spanish explorers unfamiliar with the term "sabana" which originated from the Arawak Indian language from the Greater Antilles (Harris 1980). Numerous low-gradient rivers, originating in the Andes, cross the llanos in broad valleys marked by gallery forests. Between the valleys are low, mesa-like, lateritic interfluves or terraces of fluvial origin. The *llanos altos*, closer to the mountains, are dominated by coalescing alluvial fans. Some are still accumulating, and support youthful, fertile soils, while others are older surfaces (*mesas*) with impeded drainage and soils of low nutrient content. Although grasses predominate, especially species of the genus *Trachypogon*, woody growth interdigitates with grassland in many areas. Southward and at lower elevations are the seasonally flooded *llanos bajos* along the Apure-Orinoco axis, where inundation can be expected for several months during the wet season. Here relatively palatable species of *Paspalum* dominate the unbroken grasslands. South of the Arauca River, on both sides of the Colombia-Venezuela border, there are extensive sand dunes aligned northeast-southwest and separated by small basins of interior drainage. West of Barinas unbroken forest prevailed until recently.

The Venezuelan Llanos

The Venezuelan llanos (Fig. 18.2) initially offered little attraction to the Spaniards. They found in the adjacent Andes better soils, a healthier climate and a more abundant and compliant labor force (Schmieder 1932). Yet there were European cattle on the great interior grassland by the 1540s. By the time the first Spanish town was established on the margins of llanos, at Barinas in 1577, there were said to be 12,000-14,000 cattle and half as many horses and asses on the plains of Guárico and Apure to the east and south, and they were multiplying rapidly (Bolívar Coronado 1947). This Andean piedmont became an active frontier in the following years as colonists moved down from the highlands and interior valleys with their *encomienda* Indians.

To control contraband, and to facilitate administration of the Crown tobacco monopoly, a Real Cédula in 1606 had made Barinas the only area of the Capitanía General de Caracas where tobacco could be legally grown. Although the prohibition was lifted a scant 6 years later, the town became increasingly important as a center of high-quality tobacco production and an oasis of prosperity, and such it remained until the last years of the colonial period (Crist and Nissly 1973). Settlers continued to bring Indians from the mountains to grow the leaf for export, as well as cotton, indigo, and maize, and to help round up the semi-wild cattle, which were valued chiefly for their hides.

Humboldt (1969), who was there in the year 1800, wrote that Venezuela was then exporting to the Antilles alone 30,000 mules, 173,000 cow hides, and 140,000 arrobas of dried beef annually. He thought that the estimate of 1.2 million for the country's cattle population was probably too low. Twelve years later there were reported to be 4.8 million head, of which the majority was probably on the llanos. Whatever the precise numbers, they were catastrophically reduced as a result of the general disorders and breakdown in security that occurred during the Wars for Independence. By the end of the fighting the cattle population, according to one account, had dropped to a mere 256,000 (White 1956).

For the rest of the nineteenth century cattle numbers on the llanos rose and fell with the political stability of the country. In 1856, some 350,000 cow hides and another 150,000 skins of the white-tailed llanos deer (Odocoileus virginianus), along with 10,000

252

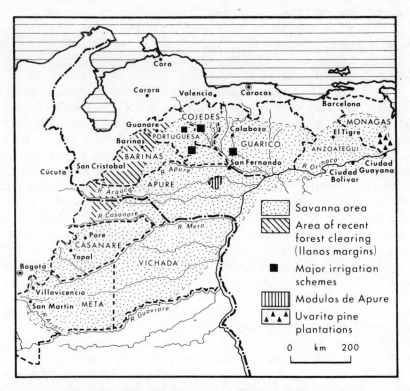

Figure 18.2 The Venezuelan and Colombian Llanos.

live cattle, were being shipped through Angostura on the lower
Orinoco to West Indian markets (Robinson 1970). But exports
fluctuated wildly and the figures were much lower both a few years
before and a few years after that date. During his regime the
dictator Guzman Blanco took a personal interest in the cattle business, introducing improved stock and offering fiscal incentives for
cattle raising (James 1969). By the time of his exile in 1888 the
country's herd had reached an estimated 8.5 million, probably more
than half on the open range of the llanos. But in the anarchy that
followed his exile numbers dropped precipitously.

In 1906 Hiram Bingham (later United States Senator), retracing
the steps of the Liberator Simón Bolívar, described the abandonment
and ruin of what had been once prosperous llanos communities:
Barinas, Guanare, Tucupido (Crist and Nissly 1973). He estimated
the population of the area to be but one-tenth of that at the end of
the colonial period. Lack of security, malaria, and an increased
incidence of hoof-and-mouth disease (*aftosa*) among cattle had
contributed to the decline.

These recurrent fluctuations in livestock numbers undoubtedly
affected the vegetation cover. The German Carl Sachs, who in
1876-77 traversed the same route earlier taken by Humboldt across
the llanos to San Fernando de Apure, observed that the horizon had
a forested appearance, "with green thickets of palm, *chaparro* and
mimosa," (quoted in Johannessen 1969). Sachs was puzzled by the
contrast between what he had observed and the treeless grassland
Humboldt had reported. From conversations with old residents he
became convinced that the apparent increase in woody growth since
the turn of the century could be attributed to a recent reduction in
cattle numbers associated with the civil wars and the high price of
hides. He postulated that fewer cattle meant fewer mouths to eat off
sprouting, broadleaved seedlings and that the woody growth established in an earlier period of high numbers and overgrazing had
subsequently increased in abundance and density. J. G. Myers
(1933) made a similar trip to San Fernando de Apure in 1930-31
and described most of the route as through low deciduous forest.
He reported widespread evidence of overstocking and deterioration of
the range. But such accounts inevitably describe conditions only in
relatively restricted areas and are of doubtful value as the basis for
generalizations about vegetation changes.

When present in modest numbers European cattle may have
had little impact on the annually burned grassland. Set fires, wind-
swept across the flat llanos surface, could destroy or effectively
suppress woody sprouts or seedlings. Only when grazing intensity
became sufficient to reduce significantly the fuel supply, so that dry-

season fires would not carry, did invasions of woody growth occur. Overgrazing would have disturbed the sod to provide openings for seedlings, and reduced numbers of stock would have permitted them to survive. Once established the brush and trees would continue to spread. Johannessen (1959) has argued that such wide fluctuations in livestock numbers, with periodic overstocking, has led to recurrent brush invasion on the llanos, in interior Honduras, in south Texas, and elsewhere. A similar relationship between cattle density and the encroachment of woody plants is apparent in Indian and African savanna environments. Once the woody growth is established it spreads, unless intensive efforts at its suppression are initiated, until eventually it may force a reduction in the cattle population.

The rehabilitation of the llanos frontier began about 1940. In the next 20 years the population of Barinas and Portuguesa states more than doubled (Miller 1968). Only the capital region of Caracas had a greater proportionate increase. A visitor who had been there in 1931 could scarcely believe what he saw when he returned in 1955 (Crist 1956, Crist and Nissly 1973). Forgotten and lifeless villages and hatos were bustling centers of activity. Infant mortality rates were much reduced, as was malaria, diphtheria, and typhoid fever. The automobile, truck, and bicycle had replaced the horse, and asphalt roads and bridges now linked long isolated communities into the national communications network. New, deep wells brought uncontaminated drinking water to every *pueblo*. Rotational grazing on fenced pastures was already replacing the traditional open-range cattle industry. No longer was it necessary to drive the bony range-steers from the llanos on foot to fattening pastures. With the truck as the universal medium of transport it was increasingly profitable to upgrade herds with Brahman or Santa Gertrudis blood. Italian, Spanish, and Portuguese immigrants had settled on new government projects and introduced new techniques and new forms of land use, especially irrigation. An extraordinary intensification of economic activity was apparent on all sides.

With one of the world's most renowned grasslands at its back door Venezuela has long dreamed of developing a meat export trade. Yet today, with a rapidly expanding internal market (estimated population 12.4 million in 1978), the country seems farther than ever from this goal. From 150,000 to 250,000 head of cattle are annually herded across the border from Colombia in a flourishing contraband trade, and the imports are likely to increase still more, given the disparity in prices that exists between the two countries.

Since 1920 the cattle population of the Venezuelan llanos has probably doubled, while being much upgraded in quality, but the national herd may still be no more numerous than a century ago. In

1970 half of Venezuela's 8.4 million livestock (cf. 5.7 million in 1950) were in the llanos states (*e.g.*, Apure 1.3 million, Guárico 1 million, Barinas 700,000). At any time perhaps one-third of these are on improved fattening pastures along the Andean piedmont, often on land recently cleared of forest. These higher quality, fenced *potreros* cover 1.1 million hectares in the three states mentioned (a three-fold increase in 20 years) compared with 7.7 million hectares of "natural" grassland (Venezuela 1973).

The area in grass in the western plains (Barinas, Portuguesa, Cojedes) at the height of the earlier prosperity was significantly greater than it is today (Veillon 1976). Drastic reductions in both human and livestock numbers in the early nineteenth century, and consequent land abandonment, left huge areas open to invasion by secondary forest. The reclamation of these piedmont lands, with their better forest soils, began about 1950. Between that year and 1975 the population of the three western llanos states increased from 254,000 to 683,000 as landless peasants and entrepreneurs alike poured in from the economically depressed minifundia lands of the Andean slopes, seeking new opportunity for economic betterment. With its new highway links with the interior and coast, and malaria seemingly conquered, the image of the plains had become that of a frontier land of opportunity.

Along the western margins of the llanos, the area in grass has been expanded at the expense of forested lands at the rate of 50,000 hectares annually since 1950 (Veillon 1976). In a study area between Barinas and San Cristobal (selva of Ticoporo) the proportion of land in forest was shown to have decreased from 45 percent in 1950 to 30 percent in 1975. And the conversion of the remaining woodland to pasture continues, facilitated by the completion of the Barinas-San Cristobal highway in 1966, the last link in an east-west llanos-margin route across the length of the country. However, the staying power of these grasses and the capacity of such lands to support permanent intensive agriculture without major input of energy, is yet to be established.

Petroleum has financed not only highway and public health developments in modern Venezuela but also numerous planned settlement schemes along the llanos margin. The first one was the Turén project (20,000 hectares) in Portuguesa, begun in 1947 and completed 8 years later. The carefully selected settlers included 56 Italian farm families recruited by an immigration mission sent to Europe. Most ambitious has been the Guárico irrigation scheme near Calabozo, which has created on the Guarico river a reservoir two-thirds the size of Lake Valencia that irrigates some 2,000 holdings and nearly 100,000 hectares. But costs have been high, up to $1,700 per hectare, and as early as 1961 an international bank report questioned the fiscal wisdom of such capital-intensive schemes. Nearly half of Venezuela's rice production (277,000 metric tons in 1976) comes from four such llanos-margin development zones, employing mechanized planting and harvesting and with extensive input of pesticides and chemical fertilizers (Eidt 1975). Government price supports and subsidies have encouraged these developments, as well as research at experiment stations on varieties of rice ecologically adapted to the area. Maize, sesame, and sugar cane are other commercial crops, but the most extensive land use is irrigated pasture on which steers driven in from the llanos are fattened prior to shipment to slaughter houses in Caracas, Valencia, Maracaibo, and other urban centers. The year-round availability of green grass has given a significant boost to the traditional stock-raising economy on the natural savannas to the south.

The llanos clearly are ecologically sensitive. The effect of changing livestock densities on the vegetative cover has been referred to. The ecological equilibrium of the natural grasslands of northern and eastern Guárico was described in 1936 as threatened by overstocking and the careless and excessive use of fire, leading to soil compaction, sheet erosion, and declining productivity (Lasser 1951). Alarming invasions of weedy growth, especially thorny mimosa (*cují*) and cactus (*cardón*), have been reported on what were formerly unbroken *Trachypogon* grasslands, suggesting the approaching "desertification" of the high llanos in much the same way that environmental ruin had earlier come to the dry, north-coastal zone around Coro and Carora (Falcon and Lara states). Dry farming (without irrigation) of upland rice, cotton, peanuts, and sorghum has more recently led to the machine clearing by agri-business firms of extensive areas of sandier soils, as on the Calabozo mesa (Guárico), and the Mesa de Guanipa, near El Tigre. Such activities are dependent on continuing applications of commercial fertilizer. Land so used may be put into artificial pasture on cessation of cropping, or it may revert to weedy secondary growth, often becoming subject to severe soil erosion.

The extensive stock-raising of the heart of the llanos, whether on lateritic mesas or seasonally flooded basins of the llanos bajos, remains more a way of life than an economically motivated activity. The physical and chemical characteristics of the soil in most cases are unfavorable to any intensification of use, and water is either in surfeit or severely in deficit. At certain times stock losses from toxic plants are high; insects and animal parasites are other problems. The sparse pasture of the dry months limits the number of stock, which in turn is insufficient to consume the great quantities of pasture available during the rains (Ramia 1959). Flooding is a serious concern, especially on the llanos bajos south of the Apure (the Capanaparo-Meta zone). It is hoped that earthen dikes designed to retain rainwater through much of the dry season, known as the *módulos de Apure* and designed to increase the quantity and quality of the natural pasture that carries over during the verano, will soon ameliorate drought conditions on as much as 1 million hectares of low-lying land. There is considerable optimism that this experiment may significantly increase the carrying capacity in the cattle-growing state of Apure, although possible ecological side effects are of some concern (Salina 1975). These *módulos* have been compared with the pre-Columbian raised fields discovered in 1968 in the state of Barinas and the much more extensive ones in northern Colombia (see below, Parsons and Bowen 1966, Zucchi 1975, and Hammond (1980).

Fire is almost the only management technique available to llanos stockmen, and its more effective use is a major goal of the Estacíon Experimental de los Llanos at Calabozo. Annual burning increases nutrient uptake and organic matter production, but where grass is protected from fire for as many as 5 years excessive fuel accumulation sets the stage for fire so hot that, when the grassland does burn, perennial grasses are killed off and replaced by a successional flora of dicotyledons (Medina 1980). Fencing, and a rotation of pastures with controlled burns in which small areas are successively grazed as they sprout, may permit an ecologically sounder utilization, but it cannot be expected significantly to increase the carrying capacity of the llanos. To achieve this, wells must be drilled to provide water for both stock and pasture. Supplementary feeding with concentrates during the dry season is another obvious response. But the long-sought technological breakthrough that would permit the curing of native grasses as hay continues to be elusive (Tamayo 1972). Selection and encouragement of palatable, deep-rooted shrubs (especially legumes) has shown promise in northeastern Brazil and might well have applicability to llanos conditions.

A vigorous petroleum industry has played the key role in the economic revitalization of extensive sections of the Venezuelan llanos. The eastern oil province, centering on El Tigre, and with pipeline connections to the coast at Barcelona, produces nearly one-third of the country's oil and there is promise of substantial additional development in the western llanos, especially in Barinas state. Furthermore, the equivalent of at least 200 million barrels of oil is known to lie in the belt of tar stands north of the Orinoco River awaiting only the technology to exploit them. Some geologists speculate that the reserve may be 10 times this figure. This energy cushion far exceeds that of all of the country's oil fields and is further supplemented by the enormous hydroelectric potential of the southern highlands.

Venezuela is modernizing more rapidly than any other country in tropical America and the llanos are inevitably at the crossroads of this development. Increasingly a network of asphalted highways and airports is covering these plains, linking up oil-field and pipeline facilities, but also tying the populated north to the new industrial complexes at Ciudad Guayana and Ciudad Bolívar on the Orinoco as well as to the mining and hydroelectric developments and colonization schemes in the Guiana highlands subsumed under the much propagandized drive for the *Conquista del Sur*. A massive redistribution of population, underway for half a century, is continuing. By the year 2000 there are expected to be 28 million Venezuelans, double the present figure. Smallholders and landless peasants are streaming out of the Andes into urban centers, but also to the margins of the llanos.

The Ministry of Environment and Non-renewable Resources (MENRR) is actively studying the ecology and development possibilities of these sparsely settled grasslands. The optimism regarding the "new frontier" is even reported to have given rise to the suggestion (vetoed by the President) that the capital be moved from Caracas to somewhere in the *llanos centrales*. A rail link between the coast and the industrial complex of Ciudad Guayana has been under study. While much attention is being given to more fully exploiting the product potential of the llanos by such means as irrigation and mechanized dry farming, afforestation with pines (Medina 1980), the introduction of water buffalo, and commercial production of the capybara--a large, native, semi-aquatic rodent (*Hydrochoeris hydrochoeris*)--and the once abundant river turtle (*Podecnemis expansa*), these plains at the back door of the country's crowded capital seem likely to be increasingly valued as ecological and recreational reserves, as open space of limitless horizons, and for their symbolic place in the history of conscience of the country.

The Llanos Orientales of Colombia

The eastward flowing Arauca and Meta rivers mark the historical boundary between Venezuela and Colombia (Fig. 18.2). Although the western margin of the Colombian llanos lies directly under the shadow of the eastern Andean cordillera, traditional center of the pre-Columbian Chibcha culture and the economic and demographic pivot of the modern Colombian state, these grassy plains have always been marginal lands, a "static frontier," symbol of the legendary wealth of El Dorado (Loy 1976). The Casanare and the upper Meta rivers divide these eastern plains into three political units, the department of Meta (earlier San Martín) and the territories of Casanare and Arauca. To the east, toward the Orinoco, lie the seasonally flooded llanos abajos, including most of the Comisaría of Vichada (Goosen 1964).

Aboriginal populations on the savanna lands were largely concentrated along rivers and in the gallery forests. Most of the Amerindians were agriculturalists, but fishing and hunting were significant supplementary activities. The initial impact of the European presence was catastrophic, but later the savannas were to provide a refuge of sorts from outside pressures. Some 20,000 Amerindians, mostly Guahibo, survive to this day in the lower llanos on both sides of the Venezuela-Colombia boundary, principally in Colombia. While many are in a pitifully dependent state, camping at the doorsteps of the white ranchers, others have shown remarkable adaptive capacities as they undergo rapid acculturation. Despite severe persecution, and growing pressures for land, their numbers may now be on the increase (Arcand 1972, Dostal 1972, Morey and Metzger 1974).

As in Venezuela, these native peoples were often heavily dependent for their food on the wild-animal resources of the savannas. Aquatic birds, reptiles, and mammals as well as fish attracted them to riverine habitats. White-tailed deer, peccary, tapir, agouti, capybara, otter, iguana, turtle, and caiman, as well as waterfowl, provided a protein base of abundance and diversity. Today the Amerindians practice a limited agriculture, while continuing their hunting and gathering activities on an increasingly restricted land base. It has been suggested that they might best resist the encroachment of *colonos* by themselves adopting cattle-raising.

Humboldt saw the Meta River as a navigable lifeline that would one day carry the products of the highlands to world markets. But it was not to be. Many have waxed eloquent on the beauty of this seemingly endless sea of grass. Emiliano Restrepo (quoted in Loy 1976) wrote in 1870 that his first impulse on reaching the plain after the tortuous descent from the mountains was to shout "land! land!" as did Columbus' crew on sighting the West Indies. The plains, he said, were "like the ocean on a calm day; like the ocean they make man feel very small before such grandeur and instill in him a desire to conquer." But Colombians have historically had a love-hate relationship with the llanos. Despite much rhetoric, a predilection for the highlands has persisted, supported in part by the recognition of their superior soil, more attractive climate, and better health conditions.

In the early colonial era the focus of Spanish interest was the northern llanos. Jesuit missionaries from Bogotá established the first outposts in the Casanare country in 1589. By the time of their expulsion in 1767 their system of Indian *reducciones* and cattle hatos (15,000 head of livestock were turned over to their Augustinian successors) was second in size only to their operations in Paraguay. Although there were a few early Spanish ranches in the savannas of San Martín, directly east of Bogotá, the difficulties of the trail link with the highland population centers, and of the belt of montane tropical forest it had to traverse, eliminated the Meta area from effective early development.

Pore, now a forlorn village of less than 1,000 inhabitants, was once a city of 20,000 persons and the colonial head of Casanare (Brunnschweiler 1972). Cattle raising was the business both of the missions and of private entrepreneurs. The cattle drives from the Casanare to Labranzagrande, site of a major cattle fair in the Andean foothills, were famous through the eighteenth century.

The Wars of Liberation, in which the llanos played a critical role, brought economic activities to a halt here as in Venezuela. There were few llaneros who did not take part, and few were left after victory was achieved. With the eviction of the Jesuits, the livestock industry of the llanos had suffered a serious organizational breakdown. Civil war in the following years brought even more complete destruction than it had in Venezuela. Royalists and patriots alike confiscated cattle and horses until few were left (Loy 1976).

It was from Pore that Santander had organized the army that Simón Bolívar himself led up a difficult mountain trail in the middle of the rainy season to surprise the Spanish army at the Puente de Boyacá in August 1819. The turning point of the war, it made the llaneros legendary soldier-heroes, but it also plummeted the Casanare into a depression from which it has never recovered. Agustín Codazzi, visiting the Casanare in 1856, contrasted the desolateness of the Colombian llanos with the neighboring Venezuelan plains where there were many more cattle and people. The Colombian llanos were by comparison deserted. Even the Indians seemed to have gone.

The llanos languished, virtually abandoned. Sporadic efforts of successive governments in Bogotá to expand effective settlement westward from the mountain front were ineffective. Loy (1976) has noted that, as long as mules were the means of transport, the people of the llanos could transport their products to the highland markets with some hope of competing. Once steamboats were operating on the Magdalena River, and railroads and highways cut through the cordillera, the llanos could no longer supply anything of value

cheaply to the interior. Booms in rubber, quinine, and lesser medicinal and aromatic products of the forest margin briefly impinged on
an essentially subsistence economy. Of the several new towns
established in the nineteenth century, only Villavicencio, the gateway
to the llanos from Bogotá, proved to be permanent. To the isolation
and unhealthy climate of the llanos was added the continuing threat
of Indian uprisings and stock thefts, which increased as mission
influence waned and white ranchers usurped traditional Indian
hunting grounds. Among most Colombians the llanos developed a
reputation as a place to avoid.

In the last 40 years the Colombian llanos, like their Venezuelan counterpart, have witnessed unprecedented growth of population
and economic expansion, but this has been almost entirely confined
to the piedmont (*pie de monte*) zone of better soils in what became
in 1960 the department of Meta (Brunnschweiler 1972, OAS 1973).
Villavicencio (elevation 500 meters), spectacularly sited on the
Guatiquía River fan at the foot of the Andes, is the focal point for
land and air transport that radiates out across the plains in the east
and north. Meta has recently been the fastest growing department in
Colombia (1978 population estimate 258,000, half of whom were
born outside the department). It was first linked to the highlands by
motor vehicles with the completion of the Bogotá-Villavicencio
highway in 1938. Heavy vehicles today traverse the paved, 122-
kilometer route between the two cities in less than 4 hours. It
remains a spectacular, spine-tingling trip that is still subject to
interruption by washouts. The Quiebraloma slide on June 24, 1974,
which buried 200 persons alive, closed land communications with
the llanos for several weeks. It created pressure for an auxiliary
route to the north, through the Valle de Tenza and Chivor, which
was opened in 1976.

Commercial rice growing, introduced after World War I,
brought the first considerable influx of settlers to the area around
Villavicencio from nearby cordilleran towns. Meta in 1972 produced
17 percent of Colombia's rice, much of it rain-grown on the younger, more fertile soils in the vicinity of Villavicencio. But the rice
bonanza may be of limited duration. Competition has been increasing from new irrigated rice-producing areas in the Magdalena valley,
where dwarf varieties developed in tropical Asia have made possible
the doubling of yields. Oil palm, cacao, sesame, and cotton are
other lesser commercial crops, but as in Venezuela the principal land
use is planted pasture grass, especially the genera *Panicum, Melinis,
Hyparrhenia* and, most recently, *Brachiaria*.

The entire Colombian llanos today holds some 3 million head
of cattle or an estimated 15 percent of the national herd. More than

half of all stock are in the outer llanos where the carrying capacity is extremely low (1 animal/20 hectares). Management practices are primitive in the extreme; the cattle are of poor quality, being small and with poor characteristics for meat production, especially on the extensive hatos of the outer perimeter where the shortage of water and forage during the dry months is a barrier to either range or herd improvement (Kalmanovitz 1972). In the wet season, drowning, or prolonged isolation on areas of slightly higher ground known as *islas* or *bancos*, is always a hazard. Efforts to upgrade stock through introduction of Cebú or Santa Gertrudis crosses suffered a serious setback during the period of political *violencia* following 1948 when lawlessness prevailed in much of the outer llanos.

The planted or improved pastures, which represent an increasing share of Meta's productive grassland, serve as fattening range for 3 to 4-year-old cows and steers that come off the haciendas of the outer llanos. Held here for a few months on fenced pastures, they are eventually trucked to Bogotá for slaughter. In the wet season 40-50 cattle trucks climb to the highlands each day. There is another secondary center of fattening around Yopal in the Casanare piedmont, linked recently to highland markets by a road from Sogamoso (FAO 1966, Kirby 1978). Finally, a new access road (*via de penetración*) into the Arauca district from the cordillera has opened to settlement a substantial tract of forested land on piedmont alluvial fans on the Colombian side of the international border between Saravena and Tame. While a few thousand live cattle move from the border area to Cúcuta each year, a much larger volume moves to Venezuela as contraband. But most llanos cattle go to Bogotá. With new rail and highway links opened between Bogotá and the Caribbean coast the position of the llanos in this market is deteriorating.

The eastern grasslands of Colombia are thus being extended onto the better bordering forest lands of the piedmont, as colonists follow the new penetration roads down from the overcrowded cordillera. These new pastures, mapped by Blydenstein (1967) as a derived *Melinis minutiflora* savanna, are especially conspicuous around Villavicencio and southward, beyond the old colonial settlement of San Martín and across the Ariari River bridge to the base of the isolated Sierra de Macarena. This last separates the eastern llanos from the zone of new land clearings to the south, in the selva of Caquetá and Putumayo in Colombian Amazonia. These active pioneer areas are linked to the interior by difficult mountain roads from the upper Magdalena valley (to Florencia) and from Pasto (to Puerto Asís and the Putumayo oil fields on the Ecuador border).

There remains an encyclopedic ignorance and traditional indifference about the llanos, especially among planners and administrators. Most successful settlement has been spontaneous rather than government directed. The isolated hatos and mission centers scattered across the lower savannas towards the Orinoco are linked to the rest of the country by a remarkably good air service, but cattle must be driven on hoof or barged up river to the head of navigation on the Meta from where they are trucked into the Villavicencio fattening district. At Cravo Norte, on the Casanare, a sportsmen's lodge attracts hunters both from the interior and from overseas.

Historically, the "El Dorado" myth has associated the llanos with the idea of fabulous wealth and has obscured the ecological realities of this tropical lowland savanna environment. Perhaps fortunately, governmental moves to exploit its resources have been tentative and unsure. The absence of petroleum discoveries, and of a Colombian equivalent to the mineral-rich Guiana highlands beyond, such as is facilitating the opening of the Venezuelan llanos, has been a break on development. The llanos of Colombia are a *cul-de-sac*, "East of the Andes and West of Nowhere" in Nancy Bell Bates' (1947) felicitous phrase. A *carretera* marginal will one day link Villavicencio with the Caquetá and Putumayo colonization zones to the south and with Arauca to the north, but it is not likely significantly to stimulate economic development. For the foreseeable future the llanos seem likely to remain the llanos.

Colombia's North-Coastal Plains (Sabanas de Bolívar)

The other principal savanna landscape of northern South America is the north-coastal plain of Colombia (Fig. 18.3). Scarcely one-fifth the size of the Colombian section of the llanos, its strategic location and extensive adjacent tracts of river floodplains have given it an immeasurably more important historical role than its better known counterpart east of the Andes. The three port cities, Cartagena, Barranquilla, and Santa Marta, that front the Caribbean on the northern margins of this ill-defined lowland of sharply contrasting wet and dry seasons, have strongly influenced its development. It comprises the larger share of the old departments of Bolívar, Atlántico, and Magdalena, in late years subdivided into the additional administrative units (with their principal towns) of Córdoba (Montería), Sucre (Sincelejo) and César (Valledupar). These six coastal departments today have a population in excess of 4 million persons or one out of every six Colombians. They contain close to half of

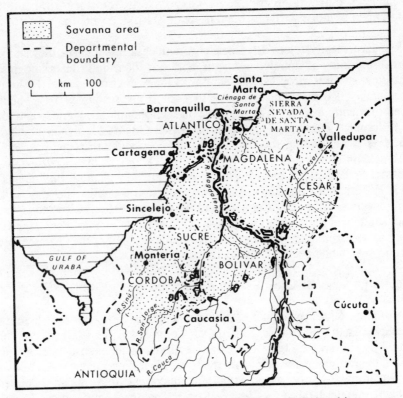

Figure 18.3 The North-Coastal Plain of Colombia.

the country's beef cattle, 10 million head in 1976, or three times the number on the Colombian llanos.

The older, rolling surfaces above the floodplains are the "sabanas" proper, home of the traditional Costeño cattle culture. These are interrupted by the *ciénagas* or overflow lands of the Magdalena River and its tributaries, especially the San Jorge, and the César. To the west the smaller Sinú River, heading in the northern-most spurs of the west Andean cordillera, has built up another floodplain of considerable extent. The seasonally inundated margins of these rivers constitute nearly half of the larger region under consideration, and, although plagued with floods, are increasingly seen as a major potential reserve for future agricultural development. Since World War II new highway and rail routes have supplemented the navigable natural waterways to provide superior accessibility between this extensive *tierra caliente* and the rest of the country. Cut off from the sea by low hills between the mouths of the Sinú and the Magdalena, and again by the Ciénaga lagoon and the Sierra Nevada de Santa Marta to the east, the north-Colombian lowlands are a complex of geographical subunits with little of the uniformity of surface or vegetation associated with the eastern llanos.

This area, rich in aquatic resources, supported a substantial population at the Conquest (Reichel-Dolmatoff 1965). The early designations "sabanas de Tolú," "sabanas de Cenú," or simply "sabana" appears to have reflected the consequence of a long human occupancy (the *conquistadores* of New Granada had staged through Hispaniola and so were familiar with the Arawak term). Gordon (1957) has described how, with the rapid decline of the aboriginal population and the cessation of Indian agriculture and burning, much of the country between the Sinú and the Magdalena, described as "sabanas" in the sixteenth century, reverted to secondary forest. However, some edaphically determined savannas remained in grass.

On the San Jorge plains the density and sophistication of the pre-Columbian occupancy is demonstrated by the extensive tracts of raised or ridged fields, an agricultural adaptation to seasonal flooding that *colonos* and stockmen have uncovered by forest clearance as they have moved onto these long abandoned lands (Parsons and Bowen 1966, Hammond (1980). Following in the wake of an earlier wave of mahogany cutters, these settlers have largely converted the landscape to introduced pasture grasses or, in the less flood-prone areas of good soils in the Sinú and César systems, to cotton, rice, and sesame fields. In popular usage the term "sabanas" or "sabanas de Bolívar" relates especially to the *tierra firme* surfaces beyond the reach of floodwaters, whether in grass, forest, or crops, but more particularly to the higher rolling surfaces between the Magdalena and Sinú rivers.

Today probably more than 80 percent of the surface area of the north-coast plains is in pasture, most of it in fenced potreros of Guinea, Pará, and jaraguá grass established only in the last 20 to 30 years. As on other savanna areas of tropical Latin America, carrying capacity and productivity are low due to inefficient management practices, the poor quality of the pastures, and especially the shortage of feed during the dry season. But cattle are considered of great importance in Colombian agrarian development plans (Rivas Rios 1974), and future livestock expansion is likely to be centered in this area and in the peripheral savanna lands of the Bajo Cauca and the Medio Magdalena.

Since the eighteenth century the livestock industry here has been dependent on a classical system of transhumance in which herds spend the dry season in the overflow lands, where water and grass are abundant, and are trailed to the higher ground of the sabanas during the rainy period when much of the lower lying land becomes a shallow sea (Wilhelmy 1968). During the flood season almost the only dry ground is on the natural levees and on an occasional Indian mound or raised field. Most hacenderos operate two properties, one in the ciénagas and one on the higher surface, spending roughly half of the year with their herds on each. Overland movement is difficult during the dry months, impossible during the rainy season. For most of the year the dugout canoe with attached outboard replaces the horse and jeep.

Studies are under way on a master plan to control and use the waters of the Magdalena-Cauca drainage and to reclaim for more productive use the 2 million hectares in the lower basins that are annually subject to destructive flooding (INDERENA 1974). These fertile alluvial soils near the confluence of the Cauca and Magdalena occupy a privileged geographical position with respect to both markets and transport, and they have already been settled by small communities of campesinos and fishermen.

The original plan for the reclamation of the recent alluvial soils between the lower Cauca and the San Jorge called for the construction of a 110-kilometer levee along the left bank of the Cauca River. More recent studies, by a Dutch-Colombian consortium, indicate such a rapid rate of isostatic subsistence that large-scale earth moving and channel control is now considered impractical. A series of smaller projects is now being planned in which lesser tracts would be poldered for 5 to 10 years, then replaced by others in a kind of rotating reclamation system. The engineering problems remain formidable. They induce new respect for the ingenuity of the aboriginal populations whose raised fields are proof that man can live in considerable numbers in this floodplain environment with a low-energy technology and apparently with minimal ecological risk.

To officials in Bogotá reaching out desperately for ways to close the widening gap between living standards in the cities and in the rural areas, the integrated river-basin planning agency patterned after the American T.V.A. has held much attraction. The 1960 study that led to the establishment of an autonomous regional development corporation for the Magdalena and Sinú valleys looked especially to an export-based livestock industry and the establishment of effective measures of drainage and flood control. The new Ferrocarril del Atlántico, providing the first rail link between the Caribbean coast at Santa Marta and Bogotá, had been completed 5 years earlier and major land use changes were in the offing.

Highway development was to be another important catalyst in the economic development of the north coastal lowlands. Thirty years ago the road north from Medellín reached only as far as the Cauca River above modern Caucasia. Beyond, to the north, lay a patchwork of tropical forest and edaphic savanna, with occasional man-made clearings. The 680-kilometer *Troncal Occidental* highway, linking Medellín with the coast, was completed in 1962. Completely paved, today it carries close to 1,000 trucks daily each way. The population of Antioquia's Bajo Cauca município of Caucasia (35,000) has increased tenfold since the 1951 census. Montería has exploded from a river village, linked with Cartagena only by slow Sinú passenger barge, to a provincial capital of 90,000 people (1973 census). East of the Magdalena there have been similar developments, supported by new highway and rail lines. Valledupar (population 87,000), capital of the new department of César, has in recent years been the fastest growing city in Colombia. Cotton and rice have become major commercial crops, but planted pasture far exceeds all other forms of land use. Pests and floods have been the principal limiting factors in these developments, especially in the Sinú.

What was once a mosaic of forested floodplain and higher surfaces of natural savanna grassland is rapidly becoming again a humanized landscape. No other South American savanna area is economically so well situated nor so well endowed with soil and water (Parsons 1977).

Conclusion

The savanna lands of the American tropics, originally the home of substantial Amerindian populations, have been largely usurped by Spanish-speaking mestizo settlers and their cattle. Traditional stock-raising systems have been but marginally viable in economic terms due to environmental constraints and the low level of technology. Sharply increased demand for food and fiber for exploding populations is leading to new interest in these marginal lowlands on the part both of governments and of private investors. Irrigation and flood-control projects, improved pasture, fending for rotational grazing, improved crop varieties, new credit courses, new energy-intensive systems of farming, more effective disease control, and especially the revolution in transportation that has made the most remote hato accessible both by land and air during most of the year, is encouraging a re-evaluation of tropical American savanna environments. Even the isolated Rupununi-Rio Branco savannas along the Brazil-Guyana boundary are being linked by road to markets both from the north and from the south. Powerful forces of modernization have been unleashed. But the past still hangs heavy over most of these lands. The traditional llanero way of life gives way but slowly, especially in the more remote districts where cattle-raising remains the focus of attention and prestige.

Pre-Columbian man showed great ingenuity in dealing with these intransigent lowlands of alternating extremes of water scarcity and abundance. Today, as the savanna environments of South America attract renewed attention, the opportunities are vastly greater, but so are the ecological uncertainties.

References

Arcand, B. 1972. *The Urgent Condition of the Cuiva Indians of Colombia*. Copenhagen: International Work Group for Indigenous Affairs.

Barrau, Jacques. 1980. Indigenous and colonial land-use systems in Indo-Oceanian savannas: the case of New Caledonia. 253-265 in *Human Ecology in Savanna Environments*, D.R. Harris, ed. London: Academic Press.

Bates, N.B. 1947. *East of the Andes and West of Nowhere*. New York and London: Scribners.

Blydenstein, J. 1967. Tropical savanna vegetation of the llanos of Colombia. *Ecology* 48, 1-15.

Bolívar Coronado, D. 1947. *El Llanero. Ensayo de Sociología Venezolano.* Buenos Aires: Ed. Venezuela.

Brunnschweiler, D. 1972. The llanos frontier of Colombia. *Michigan State University Latin American Studies Monograph 9.*

Budowski, G. 1956. Tropical savannas as a product of repeated forest felling and burning. *Turrialba* 6, 22-3.

Budowski, G. 1959. The ecologic status of fire in tropical American lowlands. *Actas 33°, Congreso Internacional de Americanistas, San José, Costa Rica, 1958.* 1,264-78.

Crist, R. 1956. Along the llanos-Andes border in Venezuela: then and now. *Geographical Review* 46, 187-208.

Crist, R. and Nissly, C.M. 1973. East from the Andes. *University of Florida Social Science Monograph 50.*

Desowitz, R.S. 1980. Epidemiological-ecological interactions in savanna environments. 457-477 in *Human Ecology in Savanna Environments*, D.R. Harris, ed. London: Academic Press.

Dostal, W., ed. 1972. *The Situation of the Indian in South America.* World Council of Churches (Department of Ethnology, University of Berne, Publication 3).

Eden, M.J. 1964. The savanna ecosystem--northern Rupununi, British Guiana. *McGill University Savanna Research Series 1.*

Eidt, R. 1975. Agricultural reform and the growth of new rural settlements in Venezuela. *Erdkunde* 29, 118-33.

Eiten, G. 1972. The *cerrado* vegetation of Brazil. *Botanical Review* 38, 201-341.

FAO. 1966. *Reconocimiento Edafológico de Los Llanos Orientales, Colombia.* 4 vols. Rome: United Nations Food and Agricultural Organization.

Goosen, D. 1964. Geomorphología de los llanos orientales. *Revista de la Academia Colombiana de Ciéncias Exactas, Físicas y Naturales 12*, 129-40.

Gordon, B.L. 1957. The human ecology of the Sinú country of Colombia. *Ibero-Americana 39*.

Hammond, N. 1980. Prehistoric human utilization of the savanna environments of Middle and South America. 73-105 in *Human Ecology in Savanna Environments*, D.R. Harris, ed. London: Academic Press.

Harris, David R. 1980. Tropical savanna environments: definition, distribution, diversity, and development. 3-27 in *Human Ecology in Savanna Environments*, D.R. Harris, ed. London: Academic Press.

Humboldt, A. 1969. *Alejandro de Humboldt por Tierras de Venezuela*. Caracas: Fundación Eugenio Mendoza.

INDERENA. 1974. Plan de regulación fluvial y contrra les inundaciones en la cuenca Magdalena-Cauca. Bogotá: Instituto Desarollo de los Recursos Naturales Renovables (mimeo).

James, P.E. 1969. *Latin America*. 4th ed. New York: Odyssey Press.

Johannessen, C. 1959. The geography of the savannas of interior Honduras. Ph.D. dissertation, University of California, Berkeley, Appendix A:218-28.

Johannessen, C. 1963. The savannas of interior Honduras. *Ibero-Americana 46*.

Kalmanovitz, S. 1972. El desarrollo de la ganadería en Colombia. *Boletín Mensual de Estadística* 253-4, 195-241. Bogotá.

Kirby, J.M. 1978. Colombian land-use change and settlement of the Oriente. *Pacific Viewpoint 19*, 1-25.

Lasser, T. 1951. *La Tragedía de Nuestros Llanos*. Caracas: Ministerio de Agricultura y Cría.

Loy, J. 1976. The llanos in Colombian history. *University of Massachusetts Latin American Studies Occasional Paper 2.*

McNeill, W.H. 1976. *Plagues and People.* Garden City, N.Y.: Anchor/Doubleday.

Medina, Ernesto. 1980. Ecology of tropical American savannas: an ecophysiological approach. 297-319 in *Human Ecology in Savanna Environments*, D.R. Harris, ed. London: Academic Press.

Miller, E. 1968. Population growth and agricultural development in the western llanos of Venezuela. *Revista Geográfica* 69,7-27.

Morey, R. and Metzger, D. 1974. The Guahibo: people of the savanna. *Acta Ethnologica et Linguistica* 31.

Myers, J.G. 1933. Notes on the vegetation of the Venezuelan llanos. *Journal of Ecology* 24, 335-49.

OAS. 1973. *Departamento del Meta: Conservación de Los Recursos Naturales Renovables.* Washington, D.C.: Organización de Estados Americanos.

Parsons, J.J. 1955. The Miskito pine savanna of Nicaragua and Honduras. *Annals of the Association of American Geographers* 45, 36-63.

Parsons, J.J. 1970. The "Africanization" of the New World tropical grasslands. *Tübingen Geographische Studien* 34, 141-53.

Parsons, J.J. 1976. Forest to grassland: development or destruction? *Revista Biológica Tropical* 24 (Suppl. 1), 121-38.

Parsons, J.J. 1977. Geography as exploration and discovery. *Annals of the Association of American Geographers* 67, 1-16.

Parsons, J.J. and Bowen, W. 1966. Ancient ridged fields of the San Jorge river floodplain, Colombia. *Geographical Review* 56, 317-43.

Prance, G.T. 1978. The origin and evolution of the Amazon flora. *Interciencia* 3, 207-22.

Ramia, M. 1959. *Las Sabanas de Apure*. Caracas: Ministerio de Agricultura y Cría.

Reichel-Dolmatoff, G. 1965. *Colombia*. New York: Praeger.

Rivas Rios, L. 1974. Some aspects of the cattle industry of the north coast plains of Colombia. *Centro Internacional de Agricultura Tropical, Cali, Technical Bulletin 3*.

Robinson, D.J. 1970. Evolución en el comercio del Orinoco a mediados del siglo XIX. *Revista Geográfica 72*, 13-43.

Salinas, P.J. 1975. Observaciones ecológicos sobre los módulos de Apure. *Revista Forestal Venezolana 25*, 131-55.

Sarmiento, G. and Monasterio, M. 1975. A critical consideration of the environmental conditions associated with the occurrence of savanna ecosystems in tropical America. 223-50 in *Tropical Ecological Systems. Trends in Terrestrial and Aquatic Research*, Golley, F.B. and Medina, E., eds. New York: Springer-Verlag.

Sauer, C.O. 1958. Fire in the ecology of tropical America. *Proceedings, 9th Pacific Science Congress, Bangkok, 1967*. 20, 104-10.

Sauer, C.O. 1961. Fire and early man. *Paideuma 7*, 339-407.

Sauer, C.O. 1975. Man's dominance by use of fire. *Geoscience and Man 10*, 1-13.

Schmieder, O. 1932. *Länderkunde Südamerikas*. Leipzig and Vienna: Franz Deuticke.

Scott, G. 1977. The role of fire in the creation and maintenance of savanna in the montaña of Peru. *Journal of biogeography 4*, 143-67.

Sternberg, H. O'R. 1968. Man and environmental change in South America. 413-45 in *Biogeography and Ecology in South America*, Junk, W., ed. The Hague: Junk.

Tamayo, F. 1972. *Los Llanos de Venezuela*. 2 vols. Caracas: Monte Avila.

Veillon, J.P. 1976. Deforestation of the western llanos of Venezuela from 1950 to 1975. Appendix IV, 1-17 in *Tropical Rainforest Use and Preservation: A Study of Problems and Practices in Venezuela*, Hamilton, L.S., ed. San Francisco: Sierra Club.

Venezuela. 1973. *Anuario Estadística Agropecuario, 1973.* Caracas.

Vuilleumier, B.S. 1971. Pleistocene changes in the flora and fauna of South America. *Science* 173, 771-80.

White, C.L. 1956. Cattle raising: a way of life in the Venezuelan llanos. *Scientific Monthly* 83, 122-9.

Wilhelmy, H. 1968. La cría de ganado en las costas del Caribe del norte de Colombia. *Revista Geográfica* 68, 63-81.

Zucchi, A. 1975. Campos de cultivos prehispánicos vs. módulos de Apure: datos experimentales modernos para la interpretación arqueológica. *Boletín Indigenista Venezolano* 16, 37-52.

19

Forest to Pasture: Development or Destruction?*

Substantial parts of Central America and Panama have undergone a dramatic change of aspect in recent years, the result of accelerated forest clearing and enormous expansion in the area of artificial or planted pasture (repasto).   At times it seems that the isthmus is on the way to becoming one big stock ranch.   Twenty years ago the Pan American highway route passed through extensive tracts of tropical forest (27).   Today its entire paved length is through cropland and *potrero*, even over its 3,700 meter summit in Costa Rica.   In pre-Columbian times the tropical forest zone was intensively exploited and occupied, as its abundant archaeologic remains illustrate.   But without livestock the American Indians had no interest in the establishment of pasture, so that their agricultural clearings, whenever abandoned, were allowed to revert directly to secondary forest or *rastrojo*.

With the depopulation of the lowlands following the Conquest, settlement became concentrated largely on the better soils of the healthier highlands and on the drier Pacific coast.   This pattern of population distribution persisted more or less undisturbed until the twentieth century.   The fruit companies, so often maligned for their social irresponsibility, first showed that permanent and productive agriculture could be carried on profitably in these rainy lowland environments given capital and management skills, an adequate social infrastructure, and public health facilities.

More recently modern highways and *vias de penetración* have provided increased access to these forested lands which increasingly has attracted the overflow of landless *colonos* from the more densely

---

*Reprinted from *Revista de Biología Tropical*, Vol. 24 (Suppl. 1), pp. 121-138 (1976).

settled rural areas. The growing pressures for new lands, sometimes channeled through government-sponsored colonization schemes but more often as spontaneous colonization onto government *baldios*, have been reflected in the accelerating retreat of the forest margins towards the rainy Atlantic slope. Figure 19.1, adapted from *Sandner* (33), broadly delineates the more active pioneer zones and the extent of the remaining forest.

Conversion of *selva* to grassland continues on many fronts. The southern extension of the Isthmian highway, driving southward from Chepo into Colombia is one such in Panamá; another is along the new road being driven across the flanks of the Volcán de Chiriquí from David to Almirante Bay. The Valle de El General in Costa Rica has been almost completely converted to pasture and crop land in less than 20 years, and the same process is well along in the Coto Brus. Similarly, the cattle people have been moving in on Puriscal and Turrubares, onto the San Carlos, the Sarapiquí and the Arenal fronts, and elsewhere in the more humid parts of Costa Rica (32). In Nicaragua, the opening of the Rama road led inevitably to the establishment of an open corridor through to navigable water on the Atlantic Coast about 1960, and since then the attack on the forest front both northward and southward from it has intensified. Interior Honduras, drier and lacking in volcanic soils, perhaps shows less activity but again in northern Guatemala FYDEP, the official colonization agency, has been vigorously promoting the settlement of Kekchi-speaking Maya Indians from the Vera Paz highlands onto farmlands in the southern portion of the Petén, where they are also pushing large scale cattle ranching on both the scattered natural savannas of that area and into the adjacent forests (25). To acquire legal title the *colono* has often been required to clear and plant half of the area to be claimed. Hence, at the beginning of each dry season, the attack on the uncleared forest is zealously renewed, filling the air with smoke from the *roza* fires that give the familiar amber color to the sunlight at this time of year.

After one or two crops of maize, rice, or yuca are harvested from the forest clearing, declining soil fertility, invasive weeds and noxious insects combine to force the colono to sell out to a second wave of settlers or speculators who follow behind, consolidating small holdings into larger ones for the exclusive purpose of raising beef cattle. In other cases, where the forest is privately held, the colono is given the right to take two or three crops from a *roza* in exchange for leaving the land in planted pasture at the end of that period, much as alfalfa was established under contract by Italian immigrants to the Argentina pampas in an earlier day. Either way

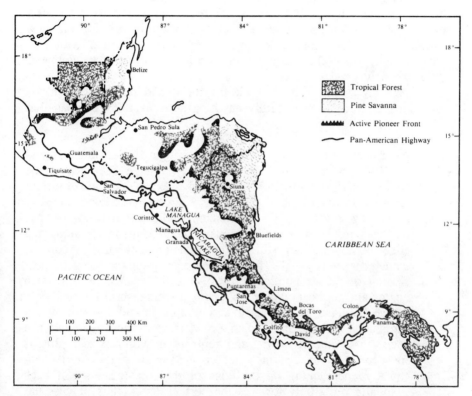

Figure 19.1   Forest Retreat in Central America (From Sandner, 1970:34)

the crops, in effect, pay for the cost of forest clearing. They represent only a transient stage between forest felling and pasture establishment.

At times there seems an almost mindless mania for converting forest to pasture, a kind of *potreroismo* mentality at work here. Yet for the colono who clears the forests and plants in its ashes, enduring countless hardships and difficult living conditions on an isolated and malaria-infested pioneer fringe, it may be the most attractive available alternative. If he does not move on ahead to make new patch clearings in the forest beyond he goes to work for the new owner as a wage laborer, joining the *chapia* gangs that with machetes fight back the *matorral* or secondary forest that competes with the new grass.

This process of driving back the forest and its replacement by grassland and cropland is hardly anything new; in 1873 Thomas Belt (2) wrote:

> After seeing the changes that were wrought during the four and a half years that I was in the country, I have been led to the conclusion that the forest formerly extended much further towards the Pacific, and that it has been beaten back principally by the agency of man. The ancient Indians...cut down patches of the forest and burnt it to plant their corn, as all along the edge of it they do still. The first time (after the corn is gathered) seeds of the forest trees...spring up and regain possession of the ground....After two or three years it is cut down again...and a great variety of weedy looking shrubs found only where the land is cultivated spring up....Should the brushwood ultimately prevail...the Indian or Mestizo comes again after a few years, cuts it down, and replants it with maize. But as most of his old clearings get covered with grass, he is continually encroaching on the edge of the forest, beating it back gradually but surely towards the northeast. As this process has probably been going on for thousands of years, I believe that the edge of the forest is several miles nearer the Atlantic than it was originally. . . .
>
> What would be the result if man were withdrawn from the scene I do not know, but I believe that the forest would slowly, but surely regain the ground that it has lost through the centuries. . . . It is far more likely, however, that man will drive back the forest to the very Atlantic than that he will quit the scene.

In the wake of the advancing frontier come serious social consequences, including unemployment and a declining rural population. Stock-raising provides few jobs and no seasonal or part-time employment. Boserup (3) holds that intensification of agriculture and the adoption of scientific methods of farming are likely to be a consequence of increased densities of rural population, a condition hardly associated with an expanding Central American livestock economy. Sandner (34) sees some indication that there may be a slowing of this process of forest clearing and its replacement by grassland, that the land-seeking population may no longer be quite so willing to endure hardships of pioneering in distant, undeveloped areas as it has been in the past. But in most areas time is running out. Within 10-15 years in Costa Rica, perhaps 20 years in Nicaragua and Guatemala, most of the remaining selva will have been destroyed unless drastic measures are taken to preserve it. And much of this clearing will have been on soils at best only marginal for agricultural use or for pasture.

Road-building has enormously facilitated this rapid replacement of forest by cropland and pasture. The Mexican economist Edmundo Flores observes that "roads create space (resources); they give value to previously worthless land by making it accessible and incorporating it within the market area." Wherever a new road is being built colonos are on hand to establish their claims to the new lands being made accessible. When the route has been dictated by engineering rather than ecological principles, the land it passes through may be ill-adapted for farming. Within a few years, despite large inputs of human labor, such land is often exhausted and left to return to valueless secondary scrub. Budowski (5) has observed that more destruction of landscapes has probably been achieved in tropical countries in recent years through the opening of roads than for any other reason. We are finally learning the critical importance of making ecological surveys, before initiating a road-building program but it has been a lesson slowly learned (9).

The Extent of Pasture Land and Numbers of Cattle

Statistics on the area in planted pasture in Central America and Panama are incomplete and unreliable. Probably better than two-thirds of the agriculturally productive land is devoted to livestock, and the share is increasing (Fig. 19.2). In Panama the land in planted pasture increased 43 percent between the 1960 and 1970 agricultural census to 965,000 hectares; in Nicaragua it increased by 48 percent to 1.7 million hectares between 1953 and 1971; in Costa Rica, a startling 62 percent to 1.5 million hectares in the 10 years

280

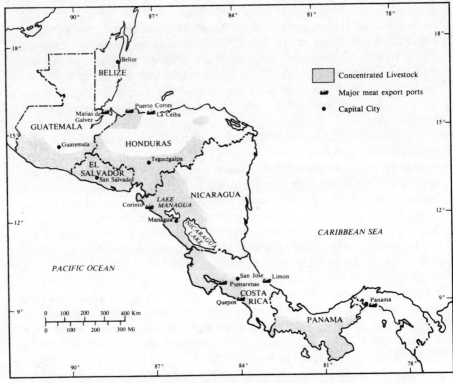

Figure 19.2 Livestock Areas in Central America
(U.S.D.A., 1973).

1963-1973. On the Pacific coastal plains of Guatemala and on the north coast of Honduras, *potreros* have been expanding at comparable rates. Along with the expanded area in pasture there has also been an increase in cattle numbers and an upgrading of herd quality (42). Except in Costa Rica, however, *criollo* stock generally remains dominant. From 1961-64 to 1972 total numbers of cattle in Central America and Panama increased from 7.4 million to 10.3 million and are projected by FAO to reach 12.9 million by 1980 (17). In Costa Rica the present herd of 1.7 million is double what it was 15 years ago. Guatemala's estimated 1.9 million head of cattle in 1973 represented an increase of one-third in only 5 years. The Nicaragua cattle population (2.3 million, largest in the area) was up a remarkable 75 percent in a like period (42). Yet only in Nicaragua do cattle outnumber the human population. That country's herd is roughly the size of the cattle population of Denmark. The lowest rates of herd increase have been in Honduras and El Salvador. In Honduras 80 percent of the cattle are on small farms, few with as many as 50 hectares or 50 head. Only in El Salvador has crop production expanded more rapidly than livestock numbers, but even this smallest and most densely settled of Central American republics aspires to become a cattle country (14). Yet its production of basic cereal foods has scarcely kept up with population growth.

Boneless beef export from Central America to the United States, mostly canner-and-cutter grade, began about 1954 and since has steadily increased. In 1974 it was expected to amount to approximately 210 million pounds (100 million kilograms) or some 15 percent of total U.S. beef imports (42). Honduras, Nicaragua and Costa Rica are all exporting more than half of their annual beef output despite restrictions or quotas imposed from time to time to insure more adequate supplies for local markets. In some years Costa Rica has exported as much as two-thirds of its total slaughter. As this symposium meets, Costa Rica's representatives in Washington are seeking a further 33 percent increase in the country's meat import quota for 1975, to 69 million pounds (31 million kilograms).

But Nicaragua is the number one exporter (86 million pounds or 40 million kilograms in 1972) and seems likely to remain so. Even El Salvador has joined the parade in the last 2 years. FAO (17) projects an export availability of 280 million pounds (127 million kilograms) of beef carcass weight by 1980, an increase of 77 percent above 1970 and even higher figures later.

But what does Central America profit from this "protein flight" to the mid-latitudes? While both the area in pasture and the numbers of beef cattle have been expanding vertiginously the per capita consumption of beef in Central America has been declining. Virtually the entire increase in output has been channeled to the profitable export market. Between 1959-1963 and 1972 per capita consumption of beef appears to have climbed only in Nicaragua and Panama, the two countries with much the highest consumption rates. In Costa Rica it plummeted from 27 to 19 pounds (12 to less than 9 kilograms) per capita during this period despite a doubling of total beef production. Exports absorbed the entire increase in this period. But in Panama, where the surplus goes chiefly to the Canal Zone markets and to sales to U.S. commissaries, the increase in output has gone largely to internal consumption, up from 42 to 52 pounds (19 to 24 kilograms) per capita. The comparable increase in Nicaragua in the same period (1959-1963 to 1972) was from 29 to 32 pounds (13 to 14 kilograms), (Table 19.1).

There may be one mitigating consideration in this seemingly dreary picture. Figures on supplies of beef available for domestic consumption in Central America are based on dubious estimates of the number and average liveweight of the animals slaughtered in a given year (42). It is suspected that the beef consumption figure often excludes the consumption of viscera (entrails).

All of the viscera produced and passed as wholesome, including that from animals slaughtered for export, is consumed locally--heart, liver, kidney, tripe, tongue, brains, etc. Viscera, being priced relatively low, is an important source of animal protein for many consumers who cannot afford red meat. An increase in the level of exports paradoxically may mean increased supplies of protein for the domestic market--although this increase may not show up in official statistics.

Behind the Shift to Grass

Why, in the face of malnutrition and underconsumption of protein, is Central America so enthusiastically exporting it, and to one of the best fed nations on earth? Quite clearly because it is profitable to do so--it brings in much needed foreign exchange--but also because stock raising is an activity congenial to the Latin value system. *Ganadero*, like *caballero*, is a term of respect. It carries prestige, and it implies an attractive way of life that is relatively easily entered. With price ceilings imposed on most basic commodities it has not been attractive to the farmer to intensify his efforts to produce rice, maize, beans or yuca. And the market for the traditional export crops such as coffee, bananas and sugar has been notoriously fickle and unreliable. With beef it is another matter, especially since the opening of the U.S. market some 20

Table 19.1

Central American Beef Production: Consumption and Export
(in Million Pounds)

	Total Production	Exports	Domestically Available	Per Capita Consumption (lb)	Number of Cattle '73 (Millions)
Guatemala					
1959-63 av.	82.3	7.2	75.1	19	
1972	158.9	54.2	104.7	15**	1.9
Honduras					
1959-63 av.	40.7	----	29.7	16	
1972	90.5	51.0	39.5	14	1.6
El Salvador					
1959-63 av.	40.7	----	43.7	17	
1972	52.3	8.5	43.8	12	1.2
Nicaragua					
1959-63 av.	61.2	20.7	40.5	29	
1972	151.1	86.0	65.1	32	2.3
Costa Rico					
1959-63 av.	53.3	17.5	34.8	27	
1972	108.0	73.7	34.2	19	1.7
Panamá					
1959-63 av.	47.9	1.5	46.4	42	
1972	89.5	9.9	79.6	52	1.3
Belize					
1959-63 av.	.9	.1	1.0	10	
1972	1.2	.6	1.8	14	0.4

* USDA, Foreign Agric. Service. "The beef cattle industries of Central America and Panama". Revised, July 1973.

** Livestock and Meat Report, Agricultural Attaché, US Embassy, Guatemala, Sept. 30, 1974. FAS figure of 19 lbs per capita consumption in Guatemala in 1972 apparently included pork.

years ago. Profits have been good and risks low. Moreover, grass is the easiest of crops to grow. It takes less resources in capital and management to develop pasture than to intensify cropping efforts, and it is simply easier, requiring less work and effort. In some cases the shift to cattle may reflect a desire to avoid labor problems, or perhaps recognition that the tired land has been pushed to the limit and needs a rest. In the drive to diversify exports, government has encouraged an expanding cattle industry, and international agencies have given further support. Especially decisive has been the availability of low-cost credit. In Costa Rica, for example, nearly half of all agricultural credit in recent years has been to the livestock industry (36).

The Durability of a Grassland Economy

Can this be a permanent and enduring form of land use? Can beef be produced indefinitely without exhausting the land? Yes, said the late Robert Kleberg of the King Ranch, which in Venezuela and Brazil is spearheading massive, large scale land clearings for just this purpose, provided one takes care of the grass. Yet the United Fruit Company gave up on its efforts at cattle raising at Monkey Ridge near Bluefields, now converted to a modest dairy operation. The Le Tourneau land-opening project at Tourneauvista in the Peruvian *oriente* is another case of well-capitalized failure in tropical pasture development. Clearly there are major problems. Corporate giants like Swift and Co., Volkswagen, Daniel Ludwig, even the Japanese, the Germans, and the Arabs, equipped with the most modern land-clearing equipment but often lacking the most rudimentary ecological understanding, are currently converting large blocks of the Amazon rain forest into pasture. In this process a natural biomass that has maintained a large bulk of nutrients in a living cycle is suddenly reduced to a low biomass with a much reduced storage capacity (12, 37). We may learn much from their experiences in the next few years regarding changes that follow from the conversion of natural vegetation to planted pasture and the potential of the humid tropics for supporting a permanent grass economy.

Such development-oriented international organizations as FAO and IBD seem to foresee a kind of mixed farming as the optimal ultimate use for the better soils for the high rainfall Central American forests. For example, a detailed FAO report on Northeastern Nicaragua (16) identifies some 800,000 hectares of broadleaf forest as eventually adaptable to cattle raising or mixed farming under a 10-year crop-grass rotation in which 4 years of rice or maize would be followed by 6 years in pangola grass pasture. Eventually, it is suggested, the eastern part of Nicaragua should become a major contributor to the country's cereal production, at the same time supporting an additional 1.5 million head of cattle. There is a vision, it seems, of an isthmus converted to cropland and grass from the Pacific to the Atlantic. In Nicaragua a model for this is the 70,000 hectare Colonia Rigoberto Cabezas project on the La Gateada-Nueva Guinea road south of the Rama road, recently funded by an $80 million IBD loan. Another is the Siuna mining district, still without land connections with western Nicaragua, where an efficiently run cooperative and the existence of an established market at the mines has opened the way for successful agricultural development in the heart of the rain forest.

The Adverse Effects of Forest Removal

The belief that the soil that supports the magnificent tropical forest will yield a succession of rich crops has been proven cruelly illusory. Yet the accepted ecological wisdom, that conversion of tropical forest to grassland for domestic herbivores causes serious deterioration of the soil nutrient level and soil structure has been based on largely inferential evidence (4, 18, 23). We lack data on the magnitude and rate of soil change under differing climates and different parent materials. No Rothhamsted exists for the tropics with its century-long history of changing soil productivity under differing types of land use. The effect of forest clearing and grass establishment, including annual burning, on mineral cycling, soil microbiology, organic matter content, erosiveness, permeability and runoff are little understood in the tropics. It is clear, however, that much of the nutrient stock locked up in the virgin forest, reduced to ash in the clearing process, is quickly leached beyond the root zone of the shallow rooted grasses and crop plants (30). Unless carefully managed, and usually fertilized, both planted and natural grasses become sparse or woody with overgrowth, trampling, compaction, and declining soil fertility (41). Hand weeding is costly, and seasonal burning is not always feasible, especially in the wetter areas toward the Atlantic coast. In some situations the sharp reduction in transpiration following forest removal produced such a raise in the water table that agriculture becomes impossible. Commercial fertilizers, scarce and expensive, must be applied with care to minimize wastage by leaching and chemical recombination in the acid soils, for physical processes are much speeded up here as compared to temperate lands. Here too, plant and animal diseases and parasites find their optimal habitat. Much depends on both the length and severity of the dry season and on the character of the underlying parent material. Soils developed on limestone, on volcanic rocks, or on recent alluvium clearly have a much greater inherent fertility than those on older, weathered upland surfaces. It is on the last that most of the remaining forests of Central America are found.

One way to avoid the wastefulness of present systems of tropical land use, wasteful of the original forest and of human labor, would be by replacement of dependence on cereals, roots and grasses by a new diversified tree-crop or multi-storied agriculture (23, 41). By simulating the forest environment and its high biomass productivity (40), production of carbohydrates and protein of both plant and animal origin might be maximized. Tree crops, including browse for cattle, undoubtedly offer much promise, but the plantation system under which most tree crops have been most effectively grown in the past is politically and socially unstable and probably unacceptable. In Costa Rica, at least, dairy farmers have worked out an interesting system of planting fast-growing alter trees (*Alnus jorullensis*), here called "haul," in planted pastures where they provide shade for cattle as well as saw-timber, while by fixing nitrogen in the soil they are supposed to have a beneficial effect on the pasture grass (22).

In drier parts of the tropical lowlands, with a *verano* of 5 months or more duration, the soil is probably better adapted to grassland agriculture, despite the stress caused by seasonal feed shortages, than in wetter areas. Thus, in Guanacaste province, Costa Rica, Daubenmire (10) found little change in the fertility and physical structure of the soil after 22 years in planted pasture. In particular, he found no suggestion of downward movement of clay or other irreversible changes in the profile of the study site near Cañas, as some authorities have suggested, and he doubts that other Guanacaste soils have undergone such deterioration. Erosion between the conspicuously pedestaled bunches of jaragua grass appeared to be the most significant environmental change under pasture in this particular case. Similar paired tests in other life zones are badly needed.

Soil erosion is generally much less under a good stand of grass than on tilled slopes and may not be greatly in excess of that under fully developed tropical forest (1). Still, there is a wide variation in the coefficients of infiltration and runoff. In drier areas tall grass gives the illusion of complete soil cover, an impression that does not survive close inspection. The hydraulic regime is quite likely to be altered drastically, especially on steep slopes, in the year or two following clearing, and this may induce flow irregularities and reservoir sedimentation downstream that can have disastrous effects on hydroelectric power generation (11). But these considerations do not rule out grass. They only remind us of the necessity for caution.

Intensive Tropical Pasture Management

The alternative to the continued expansion of pasture at the expense of the remaining tropical forest is better use of existing grassland. Sternberg (38) observes that livestock production in developing countries is currently among the world's most inefficient industries. One recent report suggests that the present beef cattle population of tropical grassland areas of Latin America could probably be increased four or five times and total marketable meat production up to 10-fold through application of available knowledge to existing pasture and animal resources.

On theoretical grounds the greatest grassland potential in the world ought to lie in the humid tropics where year-round warmth, adequate rainfall and deep porous soils prevail (19, 39, 43). This view finds forceful expression especially in reports of long-term investigations carried out in places like tropical Queensland, Florida and Puerto Rico. It assumes, however, the input of capital and management skills of a fairly high order, as well as economic and political stability. Intensive grassland management practices that have proven effective in a wet-and-dry season tropical environment similar to that of Central America are convincingly detailed in an important recent publication, Bulletin 233 of the Puerto Rican Agricultural Experiment Station (43), and in the journal of the Tropical Grassland Society of Australia, *Tropical Grasslands*. From such well-subsidized centers of tropical grassland studies the general tone is one of confidence and optimism.

But high-yield tropical grassland farming in such areas is closely tied to heavy fertilization in a world and at a time when fertilizers are becoming expensive and in critically short supply, although more from limitation in plant capacity than from any permanent change in supply-demand relationships.

Appropriate levels of fertilization and frequency of its application on different soil types are a major concern of this experiment station literature, for most tropical soils are inherently low in nutrients and there is heavy nutrient loss through forage take-off, leaching and fixation. Nitrogen is the key. With adequate application, both the bulk yield and the protein content of grass increases sharply, especially where organic matter content of the soils is low. It is especially effective in keeping nitrogen content up during the dry season.

There has been some modest success in developing nitrogen-fixing tropical legumes appropriate for grassland farming in Australia, but in general legumes are not able to compete with the vigorous tropical grasses, especially on the acid soils of high rainfall areas. Apparently, however, the recent discovery of nitrogen-fixing strains of *Paspalum notatum* (Bahía) and Transvaal Pangola *(Digitaria decumbens)*, the latter a hybrid developed in Florida, holds out a substantial hope for the future. When the soil is inoculated with appropriate bacteria, these grasses are said to produce up to 80 kilograms per hectare a year of nitrogen, not as root nodules but within the cell structure (Hugh Popenoe, pers. comm.).

The natural cycling of nutrients through grazing cattle is a part of the appeal of a mixed farming system with both crops and livestock in the mid-latitude tradition. About 80 percent of the nitrogen, phosphorus and potassium consumed by cattle is returned to the soil in the form of manure. But grazing animals are not very effective in maintaining pasture fertility, mostly because of poor distribution of this excreta. Even under the best of conditions in Puerto Rico about half of it is lost through volatilization and leaching (43). To be fully effective, urine and feces should be mixed and distributed uniformly in the field, something that is uneconomic in high labor-cost areas but which may be feasible in Central America.

There are other approaches to an intensified grassland farming. Especially effective is the investment in fencing that permits carefully-timed rotational grazing, using individual potreros sufficiently small that the forage is consumed down to the indicated height in not more than 1 week in any individual plot. This practice, well appreciated by dairymen, as on the Meseta of Costa Rica, has not yet been widely adapted by cattlemen. Again, the feeding of supplements during the dry season--little employed to date with Central American beef cattle--awaits improvements in systems of tropical hay curing and in the making of ensilage. Or, by feeding urea--a low cost form of synthetic nitrogen--it is possible to vastly increase the cow's capacity to digest cellulose, whether from coarse tropical grasses, sawdust or corn stalks, and so to concentrate its protein. To do this molasses, usually cheap and abundant in the tropics, is fed to help "prime the pump," to initiate the fermentation process in the cow's rumen.

Such approaches to intensive pasture management, including the continued search for improved higher yielding grasses, offer attractive and probably economically viable alternatives to the continued destruction of forest lands and their conversion into grass. Or, if protein availability becomes the problem, we can even argue the case for the greater efficiency of poultry or hogs as compared to a long-cycle livestock population in which only one-fourth of the herd can be harvested in a given year.

The African Origin of Artificial Pasture Grasses

It is not well appreciated that these new pasture lands are over-whelmingly comprised of grasses of African origin that have only recently been introduced into Central America, usually through Brazil or the United States. Several of them have become naturalized and have spread widely as volunteers, so that we can almost speak of an "Africanization" of the Central American landscape (37). These African grasses are almost invariably more palatable to livestock than the native American species, and more productive. It is impossible to imagine the present level of development of stock raising in Central America without them....**

Towards a Balanced Development

There is little prospect of stemming the process of conversion of forest to pasture so long as government attitudes support the continuing expansion of stock raising. As pasture area expands the annual crops that supply most of the local food requirements are displaced onto increasingly marginal, inaccessible lands while the better areas closer to population centers go under grass, contrary to the classical theory of location of Johann von Thünen. In terms of preservation perhaps the best that can be hoped for now may be the setting aside of some substantial natural reserves of the rapidly disappearing lowland and montane forest habits to preserve for posterity at least some of their enormous floral and faunal diversity. A prerequisite of a successful system of reserves, as Archie Carr (6) has observed, is a land ethic that understands and supports the rationale for it. An economically advanced society can think of welfare in terms of abstract values. To people in much of Central America today, however, such values and that sort of welfare seem overshadowed by problems of nutrition, public health and political change. Still, he says, the time may be approaching when wilderness will also be recognized as wealth. Then, that village with the incomparable quetzal, or a nightingale thrush, in a cloud forest above it, will be blessed among villages. And if carefully planned

---

**Editor's note. The spread of African pasture grasses is covered in Chapter 20.

trails and viewing balconies are constructed, it may find itself with a demonstrably economic asset.

Much emphasis has been placed on the virtues of diversity with relation to tropical environments. Economic diversity should be as much of a consideration as ecologic diversity. A grassland monoculture, carried to extreme, could put the Central American economies at the mercy of the world market for meat in much the same way that bananas and coffee did earlier. A quarantine on Central American beef in the United States as a result of an unanticipated epidemic--or the cutting of quotas, for whatever reason, could have disastrous consequences. Yet mixed farming, however idealized, has not always given the results expected of it either. Settlers on the Coto Brus frontier in Costa Rica, after years of effort, have found themselves once more reduced to a coffee monoculture. No other crops can be produced and marketed competitively. An initial optimism has been reduced to a lean skepticism more closely defined as the need to survive than a will to succeed (8).

Clearly, development must be within the limits of the environment. Can energy-intensive industrial farming realistically be expected to survive in the face of growing scarcities of fertilizers and hydrocarbon fuels? There is no more important question. As a first step we surely need to get off the reckless energy binge we have been enjoying and think about allocating resources to more nearly maximize long-term benefits which should probably be defined in nitrogen-fertilizer units. A fossil-fuel subsidized monoculture, whether it produces beef or commercial export crops, must in the end be replaced by a self-sustaining agroecosystem (21, 23). In this the aboriginal inhabitants of Central America long ago showed the way. Perhaps it was their great blessing, as Skutch (35) has suggested, that they had no livestock and were thus without motivation to create pasture. Still, the cow, itself a product of the tropics, is a magnificent converter of cellulose into protein, the best there is. With perseverance a durable grassland economy based on sound ecological principles is probably within reach. More than enough of the forest resource has been cleared already for this purpose. It is time now to pause in this mad assault on nature, time to think more in terms of saving what is left. We are rapidly running out of both time and the forest.

Literature Cited

1. Alberts, H.W., & O. García-Molinari
   1943. *Pastures of Puerto Rico and their relation to soil conservation.* U.S.D.A. Misc. Pub. No. 613.

2. Belt, T.
   1874. *The Naturalist in Nicaragua.* Everyman's Library, London.

3. Boserup, Ester
   1965. *The conditions of agricultural growth: the economics of agrarian change under population pressure.* Aldine, Chicago.

4. Budowski, G.
   1956. Tropical savannas: a sequence of forest felling and repeated burnings. *Turrialba,* 6:23-33.

5. Budowski, G.
   1970. *The opening of new areas and landscape planning in tropical countries* (with special reference to Latin America). XII Congress of the International Federation of Landscape Architects. Lisbon, Sept., 1970.

6. Carr, A.F.
   1969. Thoughts on wilderness preservation and a Central American land ethic. *Audubon,* 71:52-55.

7. Centro Internacional de Agricultura (CIAT)
   1969. *Annual Report.* Cali, Colombia.

8. Cole, D.G.
   1968. The myth of fertility dooms development plans. *Natl. Observer,* Apr. 22, p. 10.

9. Dasmann, R.F., J.P. Milton, & P.H. Freeman
   1973. *Ecological principles for economic development.* Wiley, London and New York.

10. Daubenmire, R.
    1972. Some ecologic consequences of converting forest to savanna in northwestern Costa Rica. *Trop. Ecol.,* 13:31-51.

292

11. Daugherty, H.F.
    1973. *Conversación ambiental en El Salvador: recomendación para un programa de acción nacional.* The Conservation Foundation, Washington, D.C.

12. Denevan, W.M.
    1973. Development and the imminent demise of the Amazon rain forest. *In* David Hill (ed.), *Latin American Development Issues.* Proceedings of the Conference of Latin Americanist Geographers, 1971, Vol. 3, pp. 80-85.

13. Dickinson, J., III.
    1973. Protein flight from Latin America: some social and ecological considerations, p. 132. In David Hill (ed.), *Latin American Development Issues.* Proceedings of the Conference of Latin Americanist Geographers, 1971, Vol. 3, pp. 127-132.

14. 1971 El Salvador puede y debe ser un país ganadero. *Agric. El Salvador*, enero, 1971.

15. Esponda, J.M.
    1888. *Manual Práctico del nuevo ganadero mexicano.* México.

16. FAO
    1969. *Survey of agricultural and forest resources--Nicaragua. Final Report.* Vol. 1: General. Vol. 2: El desarrollo agrícola. Estudio de los recursos agrícolas y forestales del noreste--Nicaragua. Informe final. Rome.

17. FAO
    1971. *Agricultural commodity projections, 1970-1980.* Rome.

18. Farnsworth, E.G., & F.B. Golley (eds.)
    1974. *Fragile ecosystems: evaluation of research and applications in the neotropics.* The Institute of Ecology. Springer-Verlag, New York.

19. Garst, J.
    1963. *No need for hunger.* Random House, New York.

20. Gordon, B.L.
1967. *Anthropogeography and rain forest ecology of Bocas del Toro Province, Panama.* Department of Geography, University of California, Berkeley (processed).

21. Harper. J.L.
1974. Agricultural ecosystems (Editorial). *Agro-Ecosystems* 1:1-6.

22. Holdridge, L.R.
1955. Costa Rica (Agriculture and forestry, cooperation or co-existence). *Int. J. Agr. Aff.*, 2:94-99.

23. Janzen, D.H.
1973. Tropical agroecosystems. *Science*, 182:1212-1219.

24. 1971. Limitations to dairy production in the tropics. Proceedings of the Conference held at Wollongar, NSW, May 10-14, 1971. *Trop. Grasslands,* Brisbaine, 5(3).

25. Minkel, C.W.
1968. Colonization in the Sebol region in north central Guatemala. *Pacific Viewpoint*, 9:69-73.

26. Ospina Vasquez, L.
1955. *Industria y protección en Colombia, 1810-1930.* Editorial Santafe, Medellín.

27. Parsons, J.J.
1965. Cotton and cattle in the Pacific lowlands of Central America. *J. Interamer. Stud.*, 7:149-159.

28. Parsons, J.J.
1972. Spread of African pasture grasses to the American tropics. *J. Range Managem.*, 25:12-17.

29. Pittier, H.
1957. *Ensayo sobre plantas usuales de Costa Rica*, 2nd. ed. Editorial Universitaria, San José, Costa Rica.

30. Sáenz, A.
1955. *Los forrages de Costa Rica.* Universidad de Costa Rica, Fac. de Agronomía.

31. Sánchez, P.A. (ed.)
    1973. *A review of soils research in tropical Latin America.*
    North Carolina Agric. Exp. Sta. Techn. Bull. 219.

32. Sandner, G.
    1961. Agrakolonisation in Costa Rica. *Schr. Geogr. Inst. Univ. Kiel*, 19.

33. Sandner, G.
    1964. Die Eschliessung der Karibischen Waldregion im Südlichen Zentral Amerika. *Erde*, 95:111-131.

34. Sandner, G.
    1970. Population pressures on resources in Costa Rica. *In* W. Zelinsky *et al.* (eds.). *Symposium on the geography of population pressure on physical and social resources.* International Geographic Union, Pennsylvania State University.

35. Skutch, A.F.
    1971. Naturalist in Costa Rica. Univ. of Florida Press, Gainesville.

36. Spelmann, H.Q.
    1972. *La expansión ganadera en Costa Rica, problemas de desarrollo agropecuario.* Informe semestral, Instituto Geográfico Nacional, San José, Costa Rica, julio a diciembre, 1972:33-57.

37. Sternberg, H.O.
    1968. Man and environmental change in South America. In E.J.Fittkau, *et al.* (eds.), *Biogeography and ecology in South America*, Vol. 1, pp. 413-445. W. Junk N.V., The Hague.

38. Sternberg, H.O.
    1973. Development and conservation. *Erdkunde*, 27:253-265.

39. Tietzel, J.K.
    1974. Beef cattle in the wet tropics. Queensland Agric. J., 100:98.

40. Tosi, J.A.
    1974. *Los recursos forestales de Costa Rica.* 1st National Congress on Renewable National Resources, San José, Costa Rica.

41. Tosi, J.A., & R. Voertmann
    1964. Some environmental factors in the economic development of the tropics. *Econ. Geogr.*, 41:189-205.

42. U.S.D.A. Off. For. Agric.
    1973. *The beef cattle industries of Central America and Panama.* Washington, D.C., revised.

43. Vicente-Chandler, J.
    1974. *Intensive grassland management in the humid tropics of Puerto Rico.* Agric. Exp. Sta., Río Piedras, P.R., Bull. 233.

20

Spread of African Pasture Grasses to the American Tropics*

The once limitless forests of humid tropical America are rapidly being converted to grasslands. Areas newly cleared of *selva* or *montaña* are cropped for a few years, then planted to perennial African grasses to form "artificial" pastures. These generally have been aggressively colonizing species, readily disseminated either by seed or cutting, and they have become widely naturalized. Agriculture is thus but a temporary stage in the process by which forest is being converted to *potreros*, especially where grazing pressure, set fires, and the purposeful cutting or uprooting of aggressive woody species promote the dominance of grasses over second-growth vegetation (*rastrojo*). There is a surge and ebb to the forest-grassland boundaries thus created, but the relentless sweep of the *colonos* axe is producing an ever-widening sea of grass. Where once stood great tracts of lowland forest--along the Pan American Highway in Mexico and Central America, on the north coast of Colombia, on the Andean spurs of eastern Venezuela, in the interior of Brazil, on the islands of the Greater Antilles--today one sees pasture lands stretching to the horizon, interrupted only by scattered palms, remnant woodlots, or linear rows of trees planted originally as live fences. The tropical forest of Latin America, so long considered inviolate, is under serious and sustained attack on countless fronts, and it must now be considered an important question whether it will long endure (Sternberg, 1968).

*Reprinted from *Journal of Range Management*, Vol. 25, pp. 12-17 (1972). Research was supported by the Geography Branch, Office of Naval Research, and the Center for Latin American Studies, University of California, Berkeley.

Tropical Africa--especially Angola, Rhodesia, and the Trans-vaal--has been an independent center of development for a number of sown forage grasses, including virtually all of the important ones that may be considered truly tropical (Hartley and Williams, 1956). Most of these are said to have evolved from woodland or forest margin habitats (Cooper, 1965). Although originally they appear to have had quite restricted distributions in Africa, they are today found over wide areas of 'derived' savanna surface that once supported trees. Introduced into America, these grasses have proven to be explosively aggressive, invading and holding vast areas wherever they have received minimal support by man (Fig. 20.1). For most of them numerous subspecies or ecotypes have been recognized, but little is known regarding their differing ecologic adaptations and the mechanisms for them (Torres, 1954). The role of genetic variability, including polyploidy, in the evolution of these invasive species remains to be investigated. It is noteworthy that all appear to have the ability to respond to higher soil nutrient levels than those en-countered in the regions from which they came. Invariably they are more palatable to livestock than the native American species and more productive. Such adaptability to grazing clearly must be related to their simultaneous evolutionary development with grazing animals in their areas of origin during the late Pliocene and Pleistocene.

There are no data on how much of Tropical America today supports a grass cover. It is a patchwork quilt. Excluding the Amazon basin, it must approach 40 percent. What part of this surface supports naturalized African species is not known. Although the vegetation maps may not show it, grass, whether volunteer, planted, or simply encouraged by man, is the most widespread of all cover types over much of the continent. Most pastures and exten-sive tracts of so-called savanna are, in fact, a mixture of native and introduced grasses.

A half dozen species of *Gramineae* have been principally involved to date in this African invasion: Guinea grass (*Panicum maximum* Jacq.), Pará grass (*Brachiaria mutica* (Forsk.) Stapf), molasses grass (*Melinis minutiflora* Beauv.), jaraguá (*Hyparrhenia rufa* (Nees) Stapf), Kikuyu grass (*Pennisetum clandestinum* Hochst.), and, most recently, pangola grass (*Digitaria decumbens* Stent). The first two have been longest in the Americas and are probably the best known and most valued, although some of the later arrivals have been more aggressive colonizers.

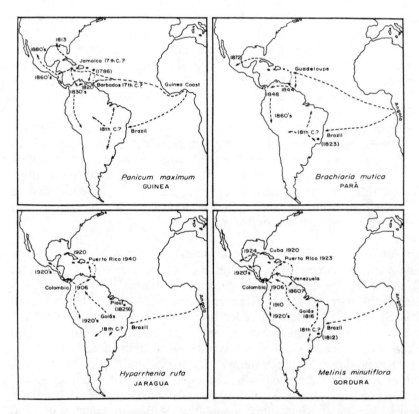

Figure 20.1   The Spread of Some African Pasture Grasses Into the New World Tropics.   *(1823) indicates place of initial collection and date of first scientific description of species.

Guinea Grass

Guinea grass (*Panicum maximum*), a tall growing clump-former that may be propagated either by seeds or cutting, is undoubtedly the most widespread. It is also known as *hierba de India* (Colombia), *privilegio* or *zacatón* (Mexico), and *capim colonio* (Brazil). Its establishment in the West Indies apparently dates from the seventeenth century. In 1684 Hans Sloane, founder of the British Museum, collected and described a "Scotch grass" in Barbados, and later in Jamaica (Sloane, 1707, p. 106). He labeled it *"gramen paniceum maximum* or *paniceum vulgare."* He described it as 4-5 feet tall with thick nodes at 6-inch intervals on the stalk, being:

> Planted in moist ground all over the island for provision for cattle, but grows wild...in the north side [of Jamaica] and in part of Barbadoes called Scotland, whence the name. After its being found very useful in Barbadoes, and had been there planted for some time, it was brought hither [Jamaica] and is now all over the island in the moister land by river sides, planted after the manner of sugar canes.

Such an early English introduction would fit into a pattern of fairly widespread introductions of economic plants to the West Indies from West Africa, for many slave ships made Barbados their first and often only port of call. Alternately the seed might have arrived from Brazil, with which Barbados had fairly close associations at the time. But to be sure that Sloane's grass was indeed *Panicum maximum* we need to examine his collections in London.

Bryan Edwards, the historian of Jamaica, writing prior to 1794, was enormously impressed with the rapid spread of "Guinea grass," but he, like several other observers, attributed its presence in the West Indies to a casual introduction from Africa to Jamaica in 1740 or 1741 by the captain of a slave ship who had intended it for use as bird seed. Multiple introductions seem quite likely. Commenting on the revolutionary impact of the grass, he observed (Edwards, 1801, p. 253):

> ...Most of the grazing and breeding farms, or pens, throughout the island [of Jamaica] were originally created and are still supported by this invaluable herbage....Perhaps the settlement of most of the north-side parishes is wholly owing to the introduction of this excellent grass, which happened by accident about 50 years ago...

Its spread throughout the West Indies was apparently rapid. The first scientific description of the grass, in 1786, was from a specimen collected in Guadeloupe, where it was said to have become naturalized *("In insula Guadeloupe sponte crescit")*. By the end of the century it was described as being "extensively cultivated" in Antigua, where it had been introduced from Jamaica. As early as 1813 it had reached Mississippi, approximately the northern limit of its range in the New World (Weintraub, 1953).

Guinea grass appears to have been introduced to New Granada (Colombia) from Jamaica in 1797 (Restrepo, 1963). Here, too, it is reported to have been looked upon at first as only a curiosity, a source of bird seed. Its large scale cultivation was initiated in the area of Guaduas (Cundinamarca) in the middle Magdalena Valley in the 1930s where it created a major land-use revolution. One observer called it "a true miracle grass," suggesting that the unknown person responsible for its introduction to that region deserved a statue "as high as New York's Statue of Liberty, illuminated by night . . . so as to be visible throughout the vast area of the new haciendas of the *tierra caliente* that it has made productive" (Rivas, 1946). It was also from Jamaica that it reached Central America, apparently sometime around the middle of the nineteenth century. Extensive planted pastures of Guinea grass began to appear in Guatemala about this time, reportedly introduced by way of the Soconusco coast of Chiapas (Esponda, 1888). In 1870 "great zacatón potreros full of fat cattle" were described as one of the principal arms of wealth of that republic. In southern Mexico, too, it provided the basis for a greatly expanded livestock industry. A 15-fold increase in land values in the valley of the Río Grijalva in the 1880s was attributed directly to the establishment of the new Guinea grass potreros. The seed was introduced into Costa Rica in 1885 (Pittier, 1957).

The time and manner of the arrival of Guinea grass into Brazil seems to be undocumented. It was undoubtedly early. Indeed numerous Brazilian observers have mistakenly called it native to that country. The late Agnes Chase, authority on all matters pertaining to grasses, suggested that it was probably introduced as bedding on slave ships, establishing itself wherever such vessels unloaded (Chase, 1944). From Brazil it may have gotten to Venezuela, although the more important implantation to that country seems to have come from Colombia in the early years of the nineteenth century.

Pará Grass

Pará grass (*Brachiaria mutica* [*Panicum purpurascens*]), a lower growing stoloniferous grass spreading chiefly by runners, is to the poorly drained bottom lands of the *tierra caliente* what Guinea grass is to the better drained lower slopes. The name suggests an early connection with the lower Amazon Valley; in the earlier literature it is sometimes referred to as Mauritius grass; in Oaxaca it is known as *Egipto*, in Colombia as *admirable*. It has been so long established in Brazil that it has often been listed as a native, but there it is called *capim Angola*. Like Guinea grass it may have been introduced as bedding in slave ships. It was well established in Brazil at least as early as 1823, for it was first described taxonomically in that year from a specimen collected at Rio de Janeiro. It was in Guadeloupe, French West Indies, sometimes prior to 1844, when it was taken to Venezuela with some fanfare (Official correspondence...1849). From there it was carried to the Santa Marta area of Colombia (Ospina Vásquez, 1955). Its adoption was rapid, especially in Antioquia and the middle Magdalena Valley. It reached the Valle del Cauca in the 1860s. A Colombian observer (Rivas, 1946) at the end of the nineteenth century wrote of the great prosperity that Pará and Guinea grass had brought to that country:

> In the warm and temperate lands where it was so difficult to maintain clean pasture they are now established easily by means of these two grasses, which destroy all other competing plants.

Their introduction has been called (Ospina Vásquez, 1955, p. 447) the most important economic event in Colombia between 1820 and the final establishment of coffee as the country's major commercial crop near the end of the century. The introduction of Pará grass into Central America seems to have been relatively late; it reached Mexico from Cuba in 1872. At that time it was already in Guatemala where it was especially valued for milk production. Today Pará grass is found on moist, poorly drained soils everywhere in the American tropics, including the irrigated pastures of the desert coast of Peru and along the new "penetration roads" reaching down from the Andes into the Amazonian lowlands.

Molasses Grass

Melinis minutiflora or molasses grass (*gordura, melado*), so named for its characteristic sweet odor and the gummy exudations that make its hairy leaves sticky, occurs naturally in two disjunct areas of tropical Africa. The western one extends in an arc from central Angola to Cameroun, while another to the east includes the lower slopes and adjacent areas of the Ruwenzori Range and Mount Kenya (Rattray, 1960). The time and manner of its initial introduction into the New World is unrecorded, but it is clear that molasses grass found here optimal ecologic conditions. The worn and eroded soils of the abandoned coffee lands of the Paraíba Valley, between Rio and Sao Paulo, are almost taken over by this self-sowing grass, which tends to form a thick and impenetrable mat that snuffs out all competition. It seems to thrive best in disturbed areas and on thin soils, especially in the more temperate "coffee climates." Molasses grass is the basis for much of the modern beef cattle industry of Minas Gerais and Goiás; it covers patches of soil on the steep open sides of the Sugar Loaf and other granitic domes around Guanabara Bay.

The first scientific description of *Melinis minutiflora*, published in 1812, was from a specimen collected near Rio de Janeiro; it was not identified in its African homeland until nearly half a century later. St. Hilaire observed it in 1816 in Minas Gerais spreading so rapidly northward that he judged it to be an invader (Anon., 1922). Martius, on the other hand, like many other observers, thought it must be indigenous to Brazil. Gardner (1730) observed:

> It is now everywhere so common in this province (Minas) it is difficult to say which of those excellent botanists is right; [but] all of the agriculturalists I have spoken with on the subject agree with St. Hilaire . . .

St. Hilaire had not observed it beyond 17°40'S, but Gardner met it much further north, especially in the vicinity of houses. He thought that it would soon overrun the mountains on the Goiás-Minas border, its dissemination being greatly aided by cattle.

Despite its early establishment, molasses grass, also known in Latin America as *calinguero*, seems to have been curiously slow in moving beyond Brazil. It is said to have been introduced from there to Venezuela in 1860, but apparently without major consequence. It was not known in Colombia until 1906 when seeds were inadvertently included in packets of seed of *jaraguá*, another African invader, that were being sent from Brazil by the Colombian Minister to that country, General Rafael Uribe (Parsons, 1968, p. 133). The true jaraguá took hold slowly and unimpressively in Antioquia, where the seeds were first sown, and since two grasses resulted from the packets sent by General Uribe, the public gave the name yaraguá (jaraguá) to that which prospered better, the unsuspected *Melinis*. As a result it became known, quite erroneously, as yaraguá or yaraguá uribe. The confusion in terminology resulting from this circumstance still persists, not only in Colombia but in neighboring Venezuela and in Puerto Rico, to which the species apparently was carried from Colombia.

The spread of molasses grass outward from the point of its initial introduction in Colombia was remarkably rapid. Only three years after it had first been planted in the Amalfi district of Antioquia a hacienda there had demands for more than 4,000 kilograms of seed coming from all parts of the republic and from Ecuador in response to some articles in a Bogotá newspaper. It was heralded as "the salvation of Antioquia," a province with particularly steep slopes and much thin, eroded soil. At first it was carefully seeded in beds of ashes with the first maize crop in new forest clearings, but it quickly became a volunteer, invading abandoned *caretales*, road cuts, railway embankments and even pastures dominated by native grasses. Continuing forest destruction, together with man-set dry-season fires and assiduous roguing of weedy woody growth is encouraging its expansion. A recent study of the Colombian llanos (Blydenstein, 1967) identifies a "*Melinuis minutiflora* association" on the higher terraces and foothills at the eastern base of the Andes.

In one generation molasses grass has largely taken over the temperate uplands of tropical America. During the 1920s it spread southward into Peru and Bolivia and northward through Central America and Mexico. Henri Pittier had observed it in Venezuela in 1913, but restricted only to the immediate vicinity of Caracas. Twenty-three years later, he found it to be "completely naturalized and reproducing spontaneously, as well as being cultivated on a large scale as a forage crop of recognized excellence" (Pittier, 1937). It is first mentioned in Costa Rica in 1908; 20 years later it was described as "completely naturalized" there in some areas. Hitchcock and Chase (1917) do not mention it in their "*Grasses of the West Indies*." By 1920, however, it was being distributed by a Cuban experiment station, from whence it was introduced into Mexico (Tabasco) 4 years later (Martinez, 1959). In Mexico, however, it has never become very well established. It was present in Puerto Rico by 1923, but it was only after a second and well-publicized introduction from Colombia 3 years later that it began to take hold vigorously (Chardon, 1930). A study of the Puerto Rico grasslands includes a *Melinis minutiflora* disclimax as one of the principal plant associations in the central highlands (García-Molinari, 1952). In Jamaica's Blue Mountains it has become widespread on "ruinate" lands above 2,500 feet elevation. There is it known as

Wynne grass and its characteristic spicy fragrance is even mentioned as an attraction in the tourist literature.

Jaraguá

Jaraguá (*Hyparrhenia rufa*) is a member of one of the two most common and widespread genera of grasses in tropical and subtropical Africa. It is dispersed by seed with uncommon ease and it seems reasonable to assume repeated accidental introduction on slave ships. It was certainly in Brazil early, and like the other grasses previously mentioned has frequently been considered to be part of the native flora. It was first identified taxonomically in 1829 (originally *Trachypogon rufus* Nees) on the basis of a specimen collected by Martius in Piauí in the northeast of Brazil (Chase and Níles, 1962). Throughout Latin America, it is known by the Tupi name jaraguá ("yaraguá," faragua") meaning roughly "master of the field." In Brazil, it is also known as *capim vermelho*, because the tips of the leaves redden conspicuously on maturing.

Remarkably, jaraguá seems not to have spread beyond Brazil to any other part of Latin America prior to General Uribe's introduction of seeds into Colombia in 1906. He himself presumed it to be a native of Goiás, observing that it was spreading rapidly there, often driving out molasses grass (Uribe Uribe, 1955, p. 330-333). "If it doesn't deserve the title 'Queen of the grasses,'" the General wrote with reference to Brazil, "it is only because of the incomparable guinea grass." Cheese made in Minas Gerais from dairy cows fattened on jaraguá he pronounced the most exquisite he had ever eaten and he hoped that Colombians might one day enjoy a comparable product. Once established in Colombia, he accurately predicted, it would be only a matter of time before it would take over the country, at least below the 1,500-meter contour.

Colombia seems to have served as the staging base from which the red-tipped jaraguá, like molasses grass, spread to the rest of tropical Spanish America. It is in the decade of the 1920s that it is first reported in the Central Andes, in Central America and in the West Indies. Especially in the drier areas, where the dry season lasts 5 months or more, it has held a strong competitive advantage. Outside of Brazil, it has perhaps reached its maximum development in the drier western side of Central America, especially in Guanacaste and in Nicaragua where it is recognized as the base of a substantial livestock industry. It was surprisingly slow in reaching Mexico. It is first recorded for the Vera Cruz coast in 1924 and the following year was introduced into Tabasco where today it supports an important livestock industry around Palenque. Jaraguá is also prominent in Cuba where it was first sown on marginal lands in Oriente province as early as 1920. Six years later it was reported by Hitchcock as "becoming naturalized" near Camaguey. By 1950, it was found throughout the island, "no pasture grass having ever spread so rapidly" (Alonso Olivé, 1953). In Puerto Rico, in contrast, it seems to have established itself much more slowly. In Venezuela, too, its establishment initially must have been slow. As late as 1936 Pittier could write that he had not yet encountered it there, although he suspected that it had been introduced (Pittier, 1937). Thirty years later it was one of the most widespread and conspicuous exotic grasses in that country.

Jaraguá's remarkable aggressiveness and its self-seeding ability is demonstrated by its capacity to compete with native savanna grasses. Clumps of jaraguá, well established and vigorously spreading, can be seen at the Llanos Experimental Station at Calabozo, Venezuela, far removed from any possible seed source and in the midst of a coarse *Trachypogon* savanna scattered with gnarled, fire-resistant *Curatella* and *Byrsonima* trees. Within a generation, parts of the open Venezuelan llanos may well be dominated by this aggressive African invader. Even more than the other exotic grasses in the New World tropics jaraguá appears to be aided by fire. After a number of years it may tend to weaken and eventually be invaded by other species unless regularly burned. Stockmen, who know this well, fire jaraguá ranges each year in the dry season and graze it rather closely during the rainy period to avoid its becoming rank and fibrous, with progressively lower nutritive value.

Kikuyu Grass

In contrast to other African immigrants previously discussed, Kikuyu grass (*Pennisetum clandestinum*) belongs chiefly to the *tierras frías*. In the last 20 years, it has spread explosively throughout the higher elevations wherever there is no severe drought period. It shows very vigorous vegetative development of runners and stolons, but its reproductive organs tend to be reduced and stunted. This concentration on vegetative matter probably enhances its value as pasture. In Ecuador and Colombia it prospers best above 6,000 feet coming down progressively lower as it moves away from the equator. In Mexico city, where it was introduced as a lawn grass perhaps as late as 1950, it has invaded vacant lots as a weed and is a common grass in Chapultepec Park. But there it needs watering for good growth. In La Paz it crowds out other lawn grasses and grows aggressively in cracks in the pavement. It is a weed along the temperate coasts of California, at least as far north as the San

Francisco Bay area, where it is employed sparingly as a lawn grass. Originally from the slopes of Kilamanjaro and the Kenya-Uganda lake country, this mat-forming, stoloniferous species seems to have first reached the Americas in the early 1920s, probably through agricultural experiment station activity. The first references that I have found to it are from 1923, and at three widely separated places--Brazil, Guatemala, and Peru. Characteristically, it has escaped from trial plots to overrun adjacent areas. At first considered an ineradicable weed, it is today recognized as a valuable pasture grass in lower latitudes. In a period of about 40 years since its introduction onto the Sabana de Bogotá it has almost completely overrun every open field and roadside, choking out all competition. Similarly it has invaded the Quito basin and the upper *yungas* of Peru and Bolivia. It mantels the terraces of the famous ruins of Machu Pichu in Peru. On the slopes of Costa Rica's Irazú volcano, where it was introduced about 1928, it was long considered a pest which tended to dominate the so-called noble grasses such as orchard, rye and fescue in the zone from 6,000 to 9,000 feet. Following the 1964-65 eruptions of Irazú, when all other grasses were killed off, Kikuyu came back early and strong, apparently invigorated by the ash. Dairymen who once scorned it now describe Kikuyu as their strongest, most resistant and resilient pasture, supporting one head per acre throughout the year.

Pangola Grass

The most recent African invader is Pangola grass (*Digitaria decumbens*), apparently a very unimportant species in its home on the Pangola River in South Africa. It was introduced into a Florida experiment station in 1935 and from there was taken to the West Indies and the mainland of Central and South America. Like Kukuyu, it is propagated exclusively by stolons or stem cuttings, being a sterile triploid that does not produce seed. Currently it enjoys great popularity in tropical America, although in some areas it is subject to a destructive virus disease. When healthy, its low, thick sward tends to crowd out all competition.

Pangola grass was introduced into Puerto Rico in 1946 and the same year into Costa Rica. For most other countries the date of its introduction is some time in the fifties. It has a wide range of adaptability and has been found doing well to elevations as high as 5,000 feet in Costa Rica and even higher in Colombia. In Jamaica it has been used extensively for rehabilitation of mined out bauxite areas. Its susceptibility to disease is currently resulting in its displacement on newly cleared lands in Mato Grosso, where it has enjoyed recent popularity, by an even newer African introduction, signal grass or *Brachiara brizantha*, also considered to have great promise.

There are other grasses, including several from the more temperate parts of the African continent, that are contributing to the "Africanization" of the tropical American grasslands. Among these are the ubiquitous Bermuda grass (*Cynodon dactylon* L.), Johnson grass (*Sorghum halepensis* L.), Rhodes grass (*Chloris gayana* Kunth), elephant grass (*Pennisetum purpureum* Schumach) and Natal grass (*Tricholaena rosea* Nees). Although some of these are aggressive colonizers, none has assumed the importance within the American tropics of the species reviewed.

This African invasion is reminiscent of the replacement of the California bunch grass by Mediterranean annuals, but in the tropical example human agency plays a larger role. The movement has been almost all one way, from Africa to the Americas, as is also the case with the Mediterranean grasses. The African grasses stand up better to grazing and have higher nutritive values than native American species. In this respect the invasions can be considered advantageous, although botanists may mourn the disappearance of native members of the flora that it may cause. A somewhat similar, but less spectacular, spread of African grasses into the Southeast Asian tropics may also be documented (e.g., Burkhill, 1935; Bor, 1960; Whyte, 1968) but the secondary role of stock-raising there, together with the existence of aggressive, indigenous species such as *Imperata cylindrica* and *Saccharum spontaneum*, makes this invasion of a lesser order of consequence.

Good grazing grasses appear to develop under grazing pressure. Few cultivated grasses are indigenous to the New World. We have to go to the Great Plains, with its buffalo and grama grasses, to find anything remotely equivalent to the Old World grasses in terms of grazing value. From the American tropics come Bahia grass (*paspalum notatum* Fluegge), Carpet grass (*Axonopus compressue* Beauv.), and Imperial (*Axonopus scoparius* L.). But none of these are of major importance. It is instead the largely unnoticed but massive invasions of the vigorous African species that are at the base of the new hope for the development of a viable commercial livestock industry in the low latitudes of the New World tropics.

Literature Cited

Alonso Olivé, R.F. 1953. Pastos y forrajes, una vista panorámica de su historia en Cuba. *Revista de Agricultura*, Habana. 36:89-108.

Anon. 1922. Efwatakala grass--Melinis minutiflora, Beauv. *Kew Bull.* 10:305-316.

Blydenstein, J. 1967. Tropical savanna vegetation of the llanos of Colombia. *Ecology.* 48:1-15.

Bor, N.L. 1960. *The grasses of Burma, Ceylon, India and Pakistan, excluding Bambuseae.* Pergamon Press, Oxford, London, New York, Paris, 767 p.

Burkill, I.H. 1935. *Dictionary of the economic plants of the Malay Peninsula.* Crown Agents for Colonies, London, 2 vols.

Chardón, C. 1930. *Reconocimiento agro-pecuario del Valle del Cauca.* Misión agrícola al Valle del Cauca, San Juan, Puerto Rico, 342 p.

Chase, A. 1944. Grasses of Brazil and Venezuela. *Agr. in the Amer.* 4:123-126.

Cooper, J.P. 1965. The evolution of forage grasses and legumes. In: Sir Joseph Hutchinson, ed., *Essays in crop plant evolution.* Cambridge Univ. Press, Cambridge, pp. 142-164.

Edwards, B. 1801. *The history, civil and commercial, of the British colonies in the West Indies.* J. Stockdale, London, 3 vols.

Esponda, J.M. 1888. *Manual práctica del nuevo ganadero mexicana.* Secretaría de Fomento, México, 132 p.

García-Molinari, O. 1952. Grasslands and grasses of Puerto Rico. Univ. Puerto Rico., *Agr. Exp. Sta. Bull.* 102, Río Piedras, Puerto Rico, 167 p.

Gardner, G. 1846. *Travels in the interior of Brazil.* Reeve, London, 562 p.

Harris, D.R. 1965. *Plants, animals and man in the outer Leeward Islands.* Univ. Calif. Publ. Geogr., 18, Univ. of Calif. Press, Berkeley and Los Angeles, 184 p.

Hartley, W., and R.J. Williams. 1956. Centres of distribution of cultivated pasture grasses and their significance for plant production. In: *Proceedings*, 7th Int. Grassland Congr., Palmerston North. Wellington, N.Z., pp. 190-200.

Hitchcock, A.S., and A. Chase. 1917. *Grasses of the West Indies.* Contrib. U.S. National Herb. Vol. 18, pt. 7, pp. 261-471. Government Printing Office, Washington.

Martinez, M. 1959. *Plantas útiles de la flora mexicana.* Ediciones Botas, México, 621 p.

Official Correspondence Relating to Para Grass. 1949. *Royal Hortic. Soc.*, 4:44-49.

Ospina Vásquez, L. 1955. *Industria y protección en Colombia, 1810-1930.* Editorial Santafe, Medellín, 531 p.

Parsons, J.J. 1968. *Antioqueño colonization in western Colombia.* Revised. Univ. of Calif. Press, Berkeley and Los Angeles, 233 p.

Pittier, H. 1937. Lista provisional de las Gramineas señaladas en Venezuela hasta 1936. Min. Agr. y Cria, *Bóletin Técnica 1*, Caracas, p. 77.

Pittier, H. 1957. *Ensayo sobre plantas usuales de costa Rica.* 2d ed. Editorial Universitaria, San José, Costa Rica, 264 p.

Rattray, J.M. 1960. *The grass cover of Africa.* FAO Agricultural Study No. 49, Rome, 168 p. with accompanying map.

Restrepo, J.M. 1952-1963. *Historia de la Nueva Granada.* Editorial Cromos, Bogotá, 2 vols.

Rivas, M. 1946. *Los trabajadores de tierra caliente.* Ministerio de Educación, Bogotá, 364 p.

Sloane, H. 1707-1725. *A voyage to Madera.* . . . Printed by B.M. (British Museum) for the author, London, 2 vols.

311

Sternberg, H. O'R. 1968. Man and environmental change in South America. In: E.J. Fittkau et al. (eds.), *Biogeography and ecology in South America*, 1:413-445. W. Junk, The Hague.

Torres, A. Di P. 1954. Agressividade de algunas gramíneas forrageiras na regio de Piracicaba. *Anais de Escola Superior de Agricultura* (Luis de Queiroz) Brazil, 11:93-114.

Uribe Uribe, R. 1955. *Por la América del Sur.* Editorial Kelly, Bogotá, 2 vols.

Weintraub, F. 1953. *Grasses introduced into the United States.* U.S. Dep. Agr. Handbook 58, 79 p.

Whyte, R.O. 1968. *Grasslands of the monsoon.* Frederick A. Praeger, New York, Washington, 325 p.

21

The Changing Nature of New World Tropical Forests Since European Colonization*

Broadleafed, multi-stored, evergreen or semi-deciduous forest, typically comprised of tall, straight-boled trees with a closed canopy, and supporting a diverse understory of palms, climbers, epiphytes and ferns, is the natural vegetative cover of the humid tropics. This life zone, with optimal conditions for vegetative growth and a soil and forest microclimate that is continuously moist, includes most lowland areas of low latitudes where warmth is uninterrupted (average annual temperatures above 24°C) and where annual rainfall values are usually in excess of 1,500 millimeters, although with a dry season of variable length. The New World has the largest terrestrial block of such climate on earth, including almost the entire Amazon basin, the Guiana highlands and coasts, the foothills and lower slopes of the eastern Colombian and the adjacent Venezuelan Andes, and the southern half of the Lake Maracaibo depression. It includes a significant part of the lower Magdalena valley, as well as the Sinú and Atrato valleys and the entire Pacific coast of Colombia, reaching southward to Esmeraldas, Ecuador. It encompasses most of the east coast of Central America, the Yucatán peninsula and northward along the lower flanks of the Mexican highlands to beyond Vera Cruz. Finally, it also includes several localized high rainfall pockets on the west coast of Central America and Mexico (e.g. the Osa peninsula, Costa Rica, and the inner Western foothills of the Guatemala volcanic range) as well as most of the islands of the Caribbean.

---

*Reprinted from *The Use of Ecological Guidelines for Development in the American Humid Tropics*, International Union for Conservation of Nature and Natural Resources Publications New Series, No. 31, Morges, pp. 28-38 (1975).

313

Where forest is absent in this vast area, it seems always attributable either to edaphic conditions (impeded drainage, shallow or sandy soils) or to the actions of man, including his fires and his livestock. Natural lightning fires and wind blow-downs may play a temporary but not yet well understood role in opening up the forest cover and altering it to more xeric conditions, but given sufficient time without further disturbance there seems to be few if any areas that would not eventually be re-colonized by tropical forest.

The relative role of natural and human factors in the origin of non-forested tracts within this broad climate zone, especially the llanos of the Orinoco, the enclaves of grassland (*campos*) within the Amazonian rain forest, the brush woodlands (*cerrado*) of north-central Brazil and the pine savannas of eastern Nicaragua, Honduras and some of the West Indian islands, is a major and unresolved ecological question (Blydenstein, 1968). If these are in part man-made, as appears certain (Budowski, 1956, 1966), their origins nevertheless probably would take us back to the beginnings of the human presence in the Americas, even to a time when climate may have been significantly different from that which we know today.

Aboriginal Population Densities

The extent and state of the tropical forest at the time of the first European contact would have been dependent in large measure on the numbers of aboriginal peoples present in the warmer and wetter parts of the American lowlands. In a continent then apparently free from the debilitating influences of malaria, measles, smallpox and yellow fever, they now appear to have been very much larger than was originally believed (Borah, 1966, 1970). Indeed, it is quite possible that as many people occupied the American humid tropics in 1492 as live there today, especially if the large, modern, urban concentrations are excluded. Colonists clearing "new land" from Ecuador to Costa Rica still uncover indications of former occupation in extraordinary abundance. Along with pottery and habitation sites are encountered elaborate burials with accumulations of gold of sufficient value to make *guaquería* (grave robbing) a highly profitable profession. The recent and spectacular Olmec discoveries in the Mexican lowland rain forest, like the surprisingly abundant and extensive black earth (*tierra preta*) habitation sites on the upland surfaces of Amazonian, attest to very considerable aboriginal population densities. This is especially true along coasts and rivers where a rich variety of protein-rich aquatic resources such as fish, shellfish, turtles, iguanas, rodents and birds were available to supplement a predominantly carbohydrate diet dominated by root crops (Denevan, 1966). In Colombia, Ecuador, Venezuela, Surinam and in the Llanos de Mojos of Bolivia extensive agricultural fields, elaborately ridged to improve drainage, have been exposed in recent years by *colonos* clearing the forested lowland surfaces, yet another indicator of at least locally numerous and sophisticated populations (Parsons and Denevan, 1967).

Recent estimates have suggested a pre-Columbian population of at least 15 million for lowland South America alone (Denevan, 1970) of whom perhaps a third might be attributed to the tropical interior (greater Amazonian). For Mexico and Central America another 8-10 million may reasonably be added plus an equal number for the Caribbean islands. Everywhere the decline of aboriginal populations was extraordinarily abrupt, the natives seeming often "to die at the breath of the Spaniards." Cook and Borah (1971) estimate a 90 to 95 percent decrease from an original New World population of perhaps 100 million within a century. For the *tierra caliente* of Mexico, with the singular exception of Yucatán, the depopulation was almost complete. So was it in the West Indies where most islands were virtually swept clean of natives within half a century despite large scale importation of enslaved Indians from the mainland. In this decline social disruption probably played a role at least comparable to European diseases, for which the natives lacked all resistance (Sauer, 1966). The nadir in aboriginal numbers in the New World seems to have occurred in most areas between 1570 and 1650, perhaps substantially later in remoter parts of Amazonian, after which there was a slow recovery.

The tropical lowlands of both Mexico and South America are currently being postulated as major centers for the innovation and diffusion of ideas on which much of Andean and Meso-American high culture came to be based. If these areas were significant cultural hearths, they almost certainly supported fairly dense populations of agriculturalists who would of necessity have had a significant impact on the original vegetation. On alluvial or coastal plain soils where fertility was naturally higher, they would have created open landscapes of manioc and maize fields that may in some cases have been in the process of being taken over by intractable sod-forming grasses at the time of European contact (Morley, 1956). Where shifting cultivation was practiced they must have left a mosaic of clearings and second growth as plots were rotated to maintain yields and to flee from encroaching insects and noxious weeds. As man set up and maintained ecologic disturbance, driving the primary forest back, he would have effectively encouraged forest margin brush and herbs of a productive edge habitat. Towards the drier margins of the humid tropics, where a dry season of several months duration would have made clearing with fire easier, such impact would have been greatest (Sauer, 1958).

The Openness of the Land at Contact

Testimony as to the openness of the vegetation on tropical coasts at the time of the first European contact with the natives comes from many sources. Thus, Columbus describes the island of Santo Domingo as a vast and well peopled garden, "as fully cultivated as the countryside around Cordoba." It may have supported as many as 8 million persons (Cook and Borah, 1971), a figure only recently again approached. What is today the near-empty rain forest of Darien was an open landscape of corn and manioc fields (Sauer, 1966), as was the Sinú country of Colombia (Gordon, 1957) and the Caribbean coast of Costa Rica. Earliest descriptions of the coasts of Brazil, too, refer to numerous native populations and open, garden-like landscapes. Likewise, the early Amazon travellers, especially Carvajal and Orellana, were emphatic regarding the density of settlement along the great river. The numerous large villages and elaborate ceramics from large archaeologic sites, as well as historical documentation of their organizational and material accomplishments, suggest locally dense populations with economic surpluses and social stratification (Denevan, 1970). The distinctive flood plain (*varzea*), annually enriched by silt deposition, doubtless provided the principal support of these large sedentary populations, combining hunting and fishing for aquatic resources with root crop farming. The much larger part of the Amazon basin, the 98 percent comprised of older, leached upland surfaces (*terra firme*) with soils of low productivity, supported only small, mobile, widely dispersed groups perhaps as dependent on game as on farming. Yet even here in some areas, especially where basalt outcrops produced a kind of *terra roxa* soil, relatively dense populations are indicated by the profusion of ceramics mixed with the black, nitrogen-rich kitchen middens (Sternberg, 1968). On balance, however, the impact of the pre-Columbian Indians on this great interior mass of rain forest was minimal (Richard, 1968; Sioli, 1973).

Reestablishment of the Forest

The virtual elimination of man from the more accessible and more productive coastal lowlands was followed by rapid replacement of abandoned fields by woody growth. This has been well documented in such areas as the Sinú (Gordon, 1957) and Panama (Bennett, 1968; Sauer, 1966). Elsewhere, as on the island of Santo

Domingo and on the Gulf Coast of New Spain, semi-wild Spanish cattle in effect occupied the niche left by the Indians (Simpson, 1952; Sauer, 1966), effectively exploiting the grasses and secondary browse of the abandoned fields. Intensive grazing often facilitated the spread of selected species of brush and trees, such as guava (*Psidium guajava*), *Guazuma ulmifolia*, the *Acrocomia* palm and *Brosimum* spp., which reproduce after being eaten and excreted by cattle (Budowski, n.d.).

The speed of repossession by trees was sometimes startling. Portobelo, Panama, was so overgrown when the buccaneer Dampier was there in 1684 that there was no sign left of the town that Drake had plundered only 80 years earlier (Dampier, 1906). The degraded secondary forest succession that followed land abandonment would have included such weedy sun-loving species as *Cecropia*, *Ochroma* (balsa) and other soft woods, creeping vines, herbs and grasses, at times in near solid stands. In turn would come the secondary tree species (e.g., *Cordia*, *Swietenia*), usually deciduous, somewhat drought resistant species native to slightly drier habitats. Eventually, perhaps in 100 years, something approaching a true rain forest would have been reconstituted. Where burning was frequent, on the other hand, things equally resistant to fire would have been encouraged, especially grass but including palms and such spongy-barked genera as *Curatella* and *Brysonima*.

Once these are established and the original forest microclimate is destroyed, susceptibility to fire would be further increased. Such fires have vastly expanded and perhaps produced savanna at the expense of forest, especially where species not well adapted to resist burning have been involved (Budowski, 1956). In Northern Central America and parts of Mexico pines have played an important part in such fire successions.

Some of the largest trees in the tropical forest may often be secondary species that have remained in the area for a long time but do not regenerate, e.g., *Bombacopsis sepium*, *Ceiba pentandra*, *Cavanillesia platanifolia*, *Swietenia macrophylla*, *Cedrela mexicana* (Budowski, 1963). Some of these, such as mahogany, Spanish cedar and laurel, have in our day offered some of the most attractive species for commercial exploitation for lumber. Others, like *Achras sapote* (chicle), *Brosinum*, and such fruit-producing palms as *Orbignya* and *Acrocomia*, represent useful plants that were apparently encouraged and protected by earlier peoples. Some are persistent things that have merely hung on.

Extractive Forest Industries

Extractive forest industries, based on distant export markets, have affected the composition of the tropical forest, especially in more accessible areas, since colonial times. Thus Brazil (*Caesalpinea* spp.) and other dye woods were largely removed from the more accessible areas of coastal South America, as was logwood (*Haematoxylon* spp.) from the swampy coasts of Campeche and Central America. Later there was heavy pressure on cinchona from the montane forests of the Andes and especially on Brazilian rubber (*Hevea brasilensis*) and other latex-producing species that were often felled rather than tapped to maximize yields.

Chicle, bixa, Brazil nuts, rosewood (for oil), tagua nuts, copaiba and Tolú balsams, guaraná, hearts-of-palm, sarsaparilla and ipecacuana are but a few of the other wild products that have been subject to heavy exploitation, sometimes to the detriment of the tropical forest ecosystem. The wholesale slaughter of forest game for meat, skins, hides and plumage must also be recorded, as well as the heavy demands of the pet trade and laboratories on such tropical forest denizens as the spotted cats, alligators, monkeys and parrots.

Commercial lumbering has been largely confined to the high-value cabinet woods except in the few cases where single species stands occur, e.g., *Cordia* (laurel) in Central America; *Cariniana* (abarco) in Colombia; and *Mora* and *Ocotea* (greenheart) in the Guianas. High value hardwoods, especially mahogany and tropical cedar, have been largely removed despite the distance between individual trees and the corresponding difficulty of discovery and access. Their logging has required extensive road building and destruction of much adjacent woodland. Only the best specimens are taken, and there is seldom another of the same species to take the place of that removed. Recently new demands for plywood have created a strong market for such woods as *Prioria* (cativo), and *Virola*, but there has been no significant use of tropical American species for paper pulp. Indeed, a mill at Tingo Maria, Peru, designed to reduce tropical forest trees to wood pulp, has been largely supplied by eucalyptus logs trucked down from the Andean altiplano. In the lower Amazon, plantations of *Pinus caribaea* and various fast-growing African broad-leaved species are seen to offer more hope than the heterogeneous native forest as the basis for a woodpulp industry.

The demand for fuel wood in the past has had a substantial impact on many areas of tropical forest. The requirements of the sugar mills of Pernambuco early left the *Zona de Mata* of that coast a forest in name only (Sternberg, 1968). Similarly the West Indian sugar islands were early stripped of wood for boiling sugar. Steamboats on the Amazon and Magdalena rivers consumed enormous quantities of wood in their boilers from the mid-1850s onward which was gathered indiscriminately along the rivers' banks. Removal of tropical non-coniferous species for fuel wood is still several times more important by volume than removals for lumber, plywood and pulp combined in most countries of tropical America. Local markets absorb significant amounts for charcoal production. Most lumber, too, is locally consumed. Belize, the Guiana coast, the Urabá area of Colombia, north coastal Ecuador, and the Brazilian state of Pará are the principal exporting areas for logs and sawn wood.

The Modern Onslaught on the Tropical Forest

For most of the past 400 years man-induced modifications of the tropical forest have been restricted to its drier margins, where clearing with the aid of fire was relatively easy and yielded maximum returns. In recent decades this partial equilibrium between man and forest has broken down, and we are witnessing an unprecedented onslaught on the forests of the rainier tropical lowlands that some observers believe may eventually threaten the very survival of the rain forest as a viable ecosystem. The frenzied drive to replace the forest by cropland and grassland is gaining momentum on uncounted fronts. In every country there are government-supported colonization schemes, not infrequently under military auspices, often involving a crusade that seems aimed at eliminating all vestiges of woodland. The forest is conceived not as a friendly and productive environment, as was the usual Indian attitude, but rather as a foe to be subjugated (Sandner, 1964).

La marcha against the remaining selva is fed by the rising tide of nationalism which demands the incorporation of sparsely settled areas into the political and economic life of the country, sometimes for presumed reasons of defense. It is increasingly held that "to govern is to people." Any aboriginal populations that may stand in the way of such colonization activities are generally either eliminated or driven deeper into the forest. In conflicts between the Indian and the colono the latter always wins. Grandiose schemes for la conquista de la selva, however disruptive ecologically they may be, are likely to be seen as providing a unifying cause, a common purpose or rallying point to which all factions may subscribe, or perhaps as a distraction from more intractable internal social or political issues.

It is the Brazilian government's headlong plunge into an all-out campaign to people the vast Amazon basin that has alerted world attention to the acceleration of destruction of the Neotropical forest ecosystem. The 2,000-kilometer Belem-Brazilia highway, completed in 1960, proved beyond doubt the revolutionary nature of roads as a tool for opening the country's interior. In a decade it is said to have attracted some 2 million settlers and produced a cleared zone some 20 kilometers wide along its route. By 1974 it is scheduled to be asphalted! Now Brazil is embarked on a much more ambitious scheme which would grid the Amazon basin with a network of long, straight highway corridors. The 6,000-kilometer Trans-Amazonica, running east-west from the Atlantic coast to the Peruvian border, with major branches to Santarém and to Cuiabá, is nearing completion. Some 30,000 men are reported to be doing nothing but cutting down trees along this route, either for highway construction or in land preparation (Anderson, 1972).

Other Amazonian countries are nervously considering the consequences if they, too, do not follow suit. Bolivia, Peru, Colombia, Venezuela and Guiana are all contemplating the advisability of linking up with the Brazilian system. The projected 5,600-kilometer Carretera Marginal de la Selva, proposed by a former president of Peru and enthusiastically embraced by neighboring countries, would run north-south through the Andean foothills from Venezuela to Bolivia, linking up some 30 existing or planned penetration roads that reach down from the Andes into the *Oriente* (Snyder, 1967). In the northwestern corner of the continent work is being initiated on closing the 385-kilometer "Darien gap" in the Interamerican Highway, thus opening the hyper-humid selva of northwest Colombia and adjacent Panama for the first time. There is a mystique and urgency typically associated with such projects that leaves little room for rational assessment and balancing of social and economic costs against ecological consequences, or even for route surveys that would assure that soil areas of optimal potential to benefit from modern agricultural technology would be served.

This accelerating attack on the tropical forest is in part a response to rising population pressures in long settled areas and to a land hunger of landless peasants in a continent wracked with an archaic land system dominated by latifundia. The need to increase food production to feed rapidly growing numbers of mouths makes the opening of "new lands" an appealing and politically attractive program. It has been enormously facilitated by the revolution in public health that has virtually eliminated malaria and other "tropical diseases" which for four centuries served as an effective barrier to the colonization of the more humid low-lands of most of the American tropics. At the same time road construction and land clearing costs have been radically reduced, and new lines of international development credit have been made available that have encouraged investments in costly projects that the individual governments would seldom have been able to afford.

The New Technology for Land Clearing

Tropical land clearing (*desmonte*) has always been slow and costly, with land development under government auspices costing perhaps $450 (U.S.) per hectare even where the land itself is free. Now we are witnessing a revolutionary development in such activities that threatens to pose an even more serious ecologic threat to the rain forest in the future. Land clearing no longer is dependent on dry season fires and the colonists' machete and axe. First has come the portable chainsaw, the tractor and the bulldozer, and now a whole array of specialized land clearing machinery that is rapidly replacing the *quema y tala* technique and vastly accelerating rates of forest clearing. The heavy equipment companies are developing machinery of Gulliver-like proportions for this task--a giant caterpillar tractor mounted with cable winch and a blade that cuts trees at the base like a razor; or with a "tree stinger" (*aguijón*), a kind of ram which hits the trunks of the most resistant specimens to weaken them and facilitate their felling; or a "tree puller," a long arm which permits application at greater heights of the power of the tractor; or "tree crushers" which can push over and render to trash even the largest forest giant in a matter of minutes. In Costa Rica the government colonization institute (ITCO) has used such techniques to clear a half hectare an hour at the cost of $127.50 (U.S.) per hectare. Large trash piles are left for burning and smaller trash is broken up to decay in place, the land itself being left ready for planting with rice or bananas (Anon., 1967). Even where the use of specialized land clearing machinery is more costly than traditional clearing techniques, it is infinitely faster, a critical advantage in areas where labor shortages may be a limiting factor in development schemes and where it is very difficult to mobilize a large gang of laborers for any length of time.

There is a fascination with machinery of such power and potential for altering the landscape that reminds us of primitive man's fascination with fire, so often an agent of landscape change and forest destruction. The potential for forest clearing is increasing almost logarithmically as new inputs of technology and capital are applied to the problem. In Central America perhaps two-thirds of the original tropical forest is gone, mostly replaced by pasture grasses. In Colombia forest destruction may approach a million hectares a year; in Brazil it is several times that. One estimate is that at least 5 percent of the non-riverine original Amazon forest may have been cleared in the last 20-30 years, chiefly along the Andean foothill zone (Denevan, 1973). Now, with the new Brazilian transcontinental highway projects, the rate is sharply higher.

Penetration Roads

Penetration roads probe the margins of the rain forest at 100 points from Vera Cruz to Mato Grosso. Some of these new routes initially have been designed to serve new oil and gas fields, as is the case with the recently developed Putumayo-Aguarico area along the Colombia-Ecuador frontier, or earlier in the Magdalena Valley (Barrancabermeja), in the southern Maracaibo depression (Catatumbo), or in the natural gas fields of Tabasco, Mexico. Others provide access to new mining developments, as the Bonanza-Siuna district of eastern Nicaragua, the Cerro Bolivar iron deposits in Venezuela, and the bauxite deposits of Surinam and Guyana. Commercial lumbering operations have led to the opening of much of the Sinú valley, the Tabasco coast, and parts of the east coast of Central America. Plantation agriculture, chiefly bananas, has been the stimulus behind the opening of such more accessible coastal areas as Urabá (Colombia), Esmeraldas-Quevedo (Ecuador) and the Central American banana districts of Guatemala, Honduras and Costa Rica. The United Fruit Company, with some 360,000 hectares in Central America alone, has led the way in opening up many of these tropical lowlands of high rainfall, providing not only the agricultural technology but the infrastructure of roads, schools, hospitals and housing. Along the Guiana littoral the new land has gone into rice and sugar, in Colombia into cotton and pasture grasses, in the Andean montaña into cinchona, in the Brazilian Amazon into black pepper, jute and pasture. The tropical forest fringe along the Brazilian coast was largely cleared in the century between 1850 and 1950 for cacao, sugar and for charcoal-making. Where it survives, as in parts of the Serra do Mar, it owes its existence largely to the steepness of the mountain slopes.

Whatever its original purpose, every road into the forest attracts spontaneous colonists whose slash-burn agriculture gradually creates a mosaic of fields and secondary vegetation. Maize and manioc, planted initially in the ash of the burned forest trees, are generally replaced by grass or degraded shrub in a relatively few years as soil fertility wanes. Crops tend to serve only as an intermediate stage in the transition between forest and pasture. But these grasses, whether natural or introduced African species, will almost certainly require fertilizing, machine discing and frequent clearing of invading shrubs if they are to be maintained. Retrogression to secondary scrub is a constant threat. There nevertheless seems to be an inexorable trend towards the conversion of the tropical forest into one great cattle ranch. The "grass revolution," however short-sighted and however unsound ecologically, finds its basis in cheap land, improved breeds, improved grasses, and an insatiable demand for red meat protein. It is not likely to be easily stayed.

And there may be no turning back from this juggernaut course of forest clearing. Primary tree species from the tropical forest are probably incapable of recolonizing large blocks of land opened to agriculture or to pasture. The clear-cutting that these entail must often result in the elimination of seeds and seedlings of species that would permit the eventual rehabilitation of the forest in normal successional evolution, as occurs with shifting cultivation (Gómez-Pompa, 1972).

The Role of the Multi-National Corporation

Large multi-national corporations are playing an increasingly important role in such developments. They have been welcomed by governments anxious to see their forest lands converted to cropland or pasture and to facilitate the rapid transfer of modern technology to lagging frontier areas. The lumber, banana and oil companies of an earlier day recently have been joined by others more specifically concerned with land clearing for agricultural development. The first major attempt at forest farming, other than by the banana companies, was Henry Ford's rubber plantation at Fordlandia near Santarém, Brazil, in the 1930s. It ended in disaster. Of quite different motivation was the 1954 entry of Le Tourneau del Peru into the Peruvian Oriente, near Pucallpa. Here a millionaire American manufacturer combined a comprehensive colonization scheme with the testing of giant earth-moving and tree-clearing equipment manufactured by his company in Texas. The project's recent demise suggests the uncertainties associated with such massive programs to convert natural forest to agricultural uses in the absence of adequate fertility-maintenance practices. Now others, such as the King Ranch and the Daniel Ludwig interests, have moved in on the Brazilian selva, as have numbers of absentee European investors, attracted by government incentives, tax write-off opportunities and generous land concessions (Sternberg, 1968). American lumber interests have recently stripped the West Indian island of Granada almost clean of commercial timber in a controversial cut-out-and-get-out operation much as cedar and mahogany operators earlier did in Mexico, Honduras and Colombia. Such operations have usually left behind them a net of logging roads and forest clearings that have been readily expanded by colonists. These have often been workers originally attracted to the area by high wages, who have been left unemployed with the cessation of activities when the commercially valuable species have been cut out.

Satellite Monitoring of Forest Clearing

The extent and pattern of this continuing attack on the neo-tropical forest has badly needed monitoring. Now satellite (ERTS) imagery, available for the entire earth, offers the prospect of accurately doing so. Where persistent cloud cover may interfere, as within the Intertropical Convergence Zone, radar imagery may be similarly used, as is occurring with Brazil's RADAM project in Amazonia. Such a "watch" on the pioneer fringes of the selva should have high and immediate priority.

A fundamental conflict in values, as well as an inexcusable deficiency in facts, is involved here. In much of the developing world the elimination of the selva tends to be seen as inevitable and even desirable, one more step towards man's mastery of nature, while ecologists and scientists generally view its probable ecologic consequences with unrestrained alarm. What to one group is "progress," to others is "wanton destruction." If this vigorous yet fragile ecosystem is indeed endangered, we must know what is happening to it and where, before any rational program of planning can be undertaken. We must know the processes at work and consider carefully and critically the consequences as well as the alternatives to it that may exist.

References

Anderson, A. 1972. Farming the Amazon: the devastation technique. *Saturday Review.* 40:60-64.

Anonymous. 1967. Habilitación económica de tierras. *Progreso: Revista de Desarrollo Latinoamericana* (New York). Sept.-Oct. pp. 36ff.

Bennett, C.F. 1968. Human influences on the zoogeography of Panama. *Ibero-Americana* 51. Berkeley and Los Angeles: University of California Press.

Blydenstein, J. 1968. Burning and tropical American savannas. *Proceedings, 8th Tall Timbers Fire Ecology Conference.* Tallahassee, pp. 1-4.

Borah, W. 1966. The historical demography of aboriginal and colonial Latin America: an attempt at perspective. *Actas del XXVII Congreso Internacional de Americanistas* (Argentina 1966).

_____ 1970. The historical demography of Latin America: sources, techniques, controversies, yields. In *Population and Economics*, P. Deprez, ed., Winnipeg: University of Manitoba Press, pp. 173-205.

Budowski, G. 1956. Tropical savannas, a sequence of forest felling and repeated burnings. *Turrialba:* Interamerican Institute of Tropical Agriculture. 6:23-33.

_____ 1964. Distribution of tropical American rain forest species in the light of successional processes. *Turrialba*: Interamerican Institute of Tropical Agriculture (mimeo.).

_____ 1966. Fire in tropical American lowlands. *Proceedings, 5th Tall Timbers Fire Ecology Conference*, Tallahassee, pp. 5-22.

_____ n.d. Distribution studies of tropical American trees, a review. *Turrialba*: Interamerican Institute of Tropical Agriculture (mimeo.).

Cook, S. and Borah, W. 1971. *Essays in Population History: Mexico and the Caribbean.* Berkeley and Los Angeles: University of California Press.

Dampier, W. 1906. *Dampier's Voyages.* Edinburgh: J. Masefield. Vol. 1.

Denevan, W. 1966. A cultural-ecological view of the former aboriginal settlement of the Amazon basin. *Professional Geographer.* 18:346-351.

_____ 1970. The aboriginal population of tropical America: problems and methods of estimation. In *Population and Economics*, P. Deprez, ed., Winnipeg: University of Manitoba Press, 251-269.

_____ 1973. Development and the imminent demise of the Amazon rain forest. *Professional Geographer.* 25:130-135.

Gómez-Pompa, A. et al. 1972. The tropical rain forest: a non-renewable resource. *Science.* 177:762-765.

Gordon, B.L. 1957. Human geography and ecology in the Sinú country of Colombia. *Ibero-Americana* 39. Berkeley and Los Angeles: University of California Press.

Morley, S.G. 1956. *The Ancient Maya.* 3rd ed., rev. Palo Alto: Stanford University Press.

Parsons, J.J. 1971. Ecological problems and approaches in Latin American geography. *Geographic Research on Latin America: Benchmark 1970.* B. Lentnek et al., eds. Muncie, Ind.: Ball State University.

_____ and Denevan, W. 1967. Pre-Columbian ridged fields. *Scientific American.* 217:93-100.

Richards, P.W. 1957. *The Tropical Rain Forest: an Ecological Study.* Cambridge: Cambridge University Press.

_____ 1968. *Proceedings, 9th Pac. Sci. Congr.,* Vol. 20, pp. 104-110.

Sandner, G. 1964. Die Erschliessung der Karibischen Waldregion im Südlichen Zentralamerika. *Die Erde.* 94:111-131.

Sauer, C.O. 1966. *The Early Spanish Main.* Berkeley and Los Angeles: University of California Press.

_____ 1968. Man in the ecology of tropical America. *Proceedings, 9th Pac. Sci. Congr.,* Vol. 20, pp. 104-110.

Simpson, L.B. 1952. Exploitation of land in Central Mexico in the sixteenth century. *Ibero-Americana* 36. Berkeley and Los Angeles: University of California Press.

Sioli, H. 1973. Recent human activities in the Brazilian Amazon and their ecological effects. In *Tropical Forest Ecosystems in Africa and South America: A Comparative Review.* B.J.

Meggers, F.S. Ayensu and W.D. Duckworth, eds., Washington: Smithsonian Institution Press, pp. 63-88.

Snyder, D.F. 1967. The "Carretera Marginal de la Selva": a geographic review and appraisal. *Revista Geogr.* (Rio de Janeiro) 67:87-100.

Sternberg, H. O'R. 1968. Man and environmental change in South America. In *Biogeography and Ecology in South America.* F.J. Fittkau et al., eds., The Hague: N.V. Junk. Vol. 1, pp. 413-445.

22

The History of the Hawksbill Trade on the Caribbean Coast of Central America*

The shoal waters of the Caribbean coast of Central America, from Cape Gracias á Dios to the Gulf of Urabá, has long supported the principal hawksbill turtle population of the Caribbean Sea. Its exploitation for the mottled, translucent shell known commercially as tortoise shell (*caret*, *carey*) was long dominated by the Miskito Indians of Nicaragua, who traded it to English merchants for guns, cloth and alcohol. Later, men of English stock from the Cayman islands entered the trade in connection with their pursuit of the more abundant and highly valued green or soup turtle, which feeds on the submarine pastures around the Miskito Cays. Yankee traders out of New York and Boston also came for the shell, as did others from the Colombian islands of San Andrés and Providencia. Today, with a vastly expanded market for turtle products and a declining hawksbill population, the industry is largely in the hands of Central American nationals.

The hawksbill fishery has always been intermingled with that for the green turtle, which has traditionally been the more prized of the two species, valued chiefly for its succulent flesh and calipee. Although hawksbill feed on the Miskito Shore and occasionally nest there, they are much less numerous than the greens. Indian, and later Caymanian, turtlers seeking the major congregations of hawksbills have traditionally sought them to the southward. El Cocal beach, Nicaragua, a few miles north of Greytown, and Chiriquí beach, Panama, some 40 miles beyond Bocas del Toro, are apparently the principal hawksbill nesting beaches in the Caribbean. Con-

---

*English version of "Historia del comercio del carey en la Costa Caribe de Centro América," in *Memorias de Arrecife Tortuga: Historia Natural y Económica de las Tortugas en el Caribe de América Central*, Bernard Nietschmann, editor, Serie Geografía y Naturaleza No. 2, pp. 78-83, Banco de América, Managua (1977).

siderable numbers also come ashore to nest, along with the vastly more numerous greens, at Costa Rica's great Tortuguero rookery. But massed nesting at localized beaches is not generally characteristic of the species and randomly scattered strays may come ashore almost anywhere. Although some female hawksbills have always been turned on beaches for commercial purposes, and their nests often robbed of eggs, substantially larger numbers have been taken in nets or with harpoons from adjacent waters. The shell, removed by the application of heat, has been purchased by traders at such places as Bluefields, Barro Colorado, Limón, Bocas del Toro and Colón, important markets in the past which still today handle substantial quantities of tortoise shell.

English interest in the exploitation of sea turtles on the Nicaraguan coast begins with the Puritan colonists of Providence Island (Providencia) who traded with the Indians at Cape Gracias á Dios and the Miskito Cays for tortoise shell and such exotic products as parrots, monkeys, animal and bird skin, sarsaparilla, lignum vitae, wild flax (*Pita floja*) and mahogany. The records of the Puritan Company, which occupied Providence from 1629 to 1641, contain frequent references to tortoise shell obtained from the Miskito Indians along this coast.[1]

From the beginning English relations with the Indians of the Nicaragua coast were especially cordial. "You are to endear yourself with the Indians and their commanders," said the instructions of the Company directors to the settlers, "and we conjure you to be friendly and to cause no jealousy." The Indians were not to be provided with gunpowder. On the one occasion of a fight with the natives near Cape Gracias a severe reprimand was meted out from London. The alliance between the English and the Indians of this coast was perhaps the most remarkable and lasting that has existed anywhere between the English and a native people.

The Miskito were superior boatmen and fishermen and their skills were soon put to use by the English, who goaded them again and again into raiding the rival Spaniards' establishments along the coast from Yucatán to Darien. For more than a century the harassed Spanish colonies of Central America schemed and plotted to eliminate this "zambo and Miskito scourge" and their English prompters, but an all-out effort was never made. In the shallow waters of this exposed coast it was clear that the Spaniards' lumbering galleons would be no match for the fleet Miskito *canoas*, each manned by

---

[1]James J. Parsons, *San Andrés and Providencia: English-Speaking Islands in the Western Caribbean*. University of California Publications in Geography, 12(1):1-84, Berkeley (1956).

from 12 to 20 men. A favored objective was the cacao groves of Matina in Costa Rica. Much of the time raiding and tortoise shell collection went hand in hand.

The English settlers and traders along this inside coast of Central America gradually came under the jurisdiction of Jamaica after that island had been occupied by the British in 1655. By 1739 about 100 Englishmen were living on the Miskito Shore, and the Governor of Jamaica proposed bringing them together in a single settlement, hopeful that with the help of friendly Indians a general revolt against Spain might be induced. Accordingly Captain Robert Hodgson of Jamaica was appointed to the post of 'Superintendent of the Shore' and shortly thereafter a formal cession of their lands to England was obtained from the Miskito chiefs. Black River, Honduras, became the principal settlement, but there were others at Cape Gracias á Dios, Bragmann's Bluff (Puerto Cabezas), Bluefields, Corn Island, and the Bay Islands of Honduras. Tortoise shell, along with sarsaparilla and mahogany, was a principal item of export. In 1757 the Shore was reported to have produced 6,000 pounds of shell worth 10 shillings a pound. Twelve years later Bryan Edwards placed the output at 10,000 pounds, but still valued at less than the sarsaparilla. For the Indians it was said that "getting tortoise shell is their grand employment," some 15-20 *piraguas* of 12 or more men each going out each season. They harpooned them at sea and they turned them on the beaches. The Escudo de Veragua, a small high island off the Costa de Coclé was one of their favorite rendezvous points. So too, in later years, was Bocas del Toro on Almirante Bay. The shell taken was exchanged with English agents on the coast for cloth, muskets and rum. Exports to Europe averaged 6-10,000 pounds of shell annually in the mid-eighteenth century. Later it increasingly went to Yankee traders out of New York and Boston. A 1776 *interrogatorio* in the Sevilla archives[2] tells how one Colville Cairns, an English settler at Bocas, employed a band of Miskito Indians from Nicaragua for 6 months each year to take *caret* on this coast. This was with the agreement of the Spanish Crown, which asked their people not to molest the Indians. In return the Indians were not to harass Spanish subjects between Bocas and Portobello.

In a convention signed in 1786, a modification of the Treaty of Versailles, the English agreed to evacuate the Miskito Shore (Nicaragua) and adjacent islands. But they continued the trade out of San Andrés Island, going seasonally to Bocas to fish for *caret* "of

---

[2]Archivo de Indias, Sevilla. "Auto año del 1776 sobre las diligencias acuadas por el Sr. Don Pedro Carbonello y Pinto, Coronel," Guatemala, Sección 5, Legajo 665.

which they are enamoured." Cuna Indians from the San Blas Archipelago to the south and east also brought shell here to exchange for English trade goods and firewater. When Bocas del Toro was formally established as a Colombian town in 1826 by men from San Andrés it was described as little more than a camp for tortoise shell traders.

There is no way to tell how much tortoise shell was taken from this coast in the eighteenth and nineteenth centuries. It appears that Nicaraguan Indians dominated the turtlery, but that the larger share of the shell was taken from south of the mouth of the Río Grande del Norte, in Costa Rican and Panamanian waters. The first documentation of turtlers from the Cayman islands working off the Miskito Shore is in 1837, a year after the Cayman colony was established on Roatán in the Bay Islands. The Caymanians apparently took such hawksbills as may have come up in their nets, slaughtering them on the keys for their shell, which was removed by boiling in water, and drying the flesh in the sun for salting. The greens, on the other hand, were commonly shipped as "live" deck cargo to Key West or Tampa or transshipped to London markets from "crawls" at Grand Cayman.

It was the men from tiny Cayman Brac, a raised coral reef some 40 miles east of Grand Cayman Island, that came to specialize in the hawksbill trade, while those from Grand Cayman sought chiefly the greens. The Caymanians roamed southward to Bocas and beyond, and also frequently visited Roncador and other uninhabited reefs lying between Providence Island and Jamaica where they found an abundance of hawksbills. Roncador seems to have been a major nesting beach for hawksbills, perhaps including some of those that in earlier times pastured off the Miskito Cays. Jamaicans who had resettled Providence in the eighteenth century joined the Caymanians in exploiting the hawksbill turtles at Roncador. E. G. Squier, U.S. Minister to Nicaragua, shipwrecked on Roncador in 1855, was rescued by a crew of Providence men taking hawksbill there.[3] The shell was warehoused at Providence, where it was picked up by vessels from Kingston that had come for locally-grown Providence cotton or, in the nineteenth century, by U.S. trading vessels returning from the Costa del Indio (Central America). The Colombian government, which claimed the coast north to Cape Gracias á Dios, required that they stop at San Andrés or Providence for a trading license, costing $1.50 per registered ton, in lieu of duty and other charges. Some 12 U.S. vessels were reported in the trade in the

[3]E. George Squier, *Waikna: Adventures on the Mosquito Shore*, New York, pp. 39-48 (1835).

1820s. Tortoise shell was often the most valuable cargo laden on trading vessels bound to New York from San Andrés or the Central American coast. Thus, the U.S. schooner *Mosquito*, captured by Spanish corsairs en route to New York in 1823, carried 1,313 pounds of tortoise shell valued at $10,300.[4] A substantial part of it had apparently been picked up at Bocas del Toro, where three English brothers named Shepard collected *carey* and sarsaparilla and cut cedar for sale to Yankee traders and others from San Andrés and Jamaica. The "Miskito Kings," with the support of their British allies, at times collected tribute for turtle and tortoise shell taken on the coast as far south as Bocas del Toro and even to the San Blas Archipeligo. Even with the decline in prices in the latter part of the nineteenth century good West Indian shell was still bringing 30-50 shillings a pound, while the best brought up to 80 shillings.

After 1900 the trade seems increasingly to have fallen into the hands of other nationalities, including Germans and Poles, with the Caymanians also maintaining an active role in the commerce. In the summer of 1905 a Bluefields newspaper reported 23 Cayman turtle boats at the Miskito Cays, probably chiefly after green turtles. At the time the Nicaraguan government objected to the violation of the 3-mile limit. A monopoly on turtling granted to a company called Pesquería de la Costa does not seem to have offered effective controls on poachers. Finally, in 1916, a treaty between Nicaragua and the United Kingdom spelled out the fees Cayman turtlers would pay in return for fishing rights along this coast, including a head tax on each turtle taken. These rights were finally terminated in 1968, but by this time virtually all the Cayman boats had retired from the trade.

Production of tortoise shell from the Caribbean coast of Central America (Nicaragua-Costa Rica-Panama) in the early decades of the present century seems to have approximated that of the eighteenth century fishery, ranging from 5-10,000 pounds annually. The market for the shell weakened in the Great Depression of the 1930s and large stocks of shell accumulated at places like Bluefields, Limón, Bocas, Colón, Providence and Cayman Brac. More recently the demand has reached new peaks, but now it is from Japan as well as for the supply of the burgeoning curio shop trade in the new tourist centers around the Caribbean. In addition there is a new demand for skins, calipee and meat, so that total returns from a

---

[4]National Archives, Washington, D.C. "Case of the Schooner 'Mosquito', Thomas Tefft, Master, San Juan del Puerco Rico, 12 Nov., 1823," Records of Boundry and Claims Commissions and Arbitrations, Claims vs. Spain, Convention of 1834, Envelope 20.

good-sized hawksbill may be greater than ever. But now, with most of the Providence and Cayman men out of the trade, attracted by better paying and safer employment (many lost their vessels in hurricanes in the 1930s), the industry is chiefly in the hands of Nicaraguan, Costa Rican, and Panamanian nationals, including Miskito, Guaymí and San Blas Indians.

It has been said that tortoise shell is produced commercially, for export, in more countries than any other product. Central America continues to be one of the more significant suppliers of the world market. El Cocal beach, north of Greytown, is still a significant hawksbill nesting beach between May and September, but the turtle-turners and egg collectors are placing it under extremely heavy pressure. Hawks are also netted and harpooned off Greytown Rocks by boats from both Nicaragua and Costa Rica. The shell is sold to the dealers at Barro Colorado and Bluefields. A buyer at the latter port is reported to have sold 1,500 pounds to Japan at $6.50 a pound in 1968, shipping through Corinto. Recently prices for *carey* have moved up sharply. With the value of skin, flesh and calipee added to that of the shell a single hawksbill may bring a $15-20 (1977) return to a lucky fisherman. At this rate, and unless effective controls are soon instituted, the stock will certainly soon be eliminated from these Caribbean waters.

23

The Future of the Edible Green Turtle in an Expanding World*

The highly localized feeding and nesting grounds of the green turtle, its clumsiness in matter to do with procreation, and its sheer size have made it an easy target for man. It first attracted attention as an antiscorbutic to supplement the monotonous shipboard fare of the buccaneers. Later it became a staple, either fresh or salted, of the slaves and persons of the lower classes in the tropical colonies. Eventually it reached the tables of the rich and of royalty, until green-turtle flesh and green-turtle soup became a symbol of status, particularly in England. The prestige thus attached to it, coupled with the growing food requirements of the tropical world, has helped sustain the market demand for *Chelonia mydas* until today the green turtle is in trouble. In Archie Carr's words "the people are expanding too fast for the turtle," and growing populations, faster ships, and better refrigeration will pose grave threats to its survival in the near future in many areas. It has long since been swept from the Bermudas, the Bahamas, Florida, the Dry Tortugas, and the Cayman Islands in the New World, and from the islands of the Indian Ocean along the sailing routes to Bengal and Malacca. One can scarcely imagine a more clear-cut example of how man, in his folly and ignorance, has found it within his power permanently to impair a highly prized and desirable resource that, wisely managed, might contribute significantly to his own welfare.

The recognition of the vulnerability of the green turtle to man dates at least as far back as 1620, when the Bermuda legislature passed a conservation law in its behalf. Nearly 200 years ago

---

*Reprinted from *The Green Turtle and Man*, University of Florida Press, Gainesville, pp. 94-96, 109-110 (1962).

Oliver Goldsmith (1825:676) wrote that "at present, from the great appetite that man has discovered for this animal, they are not only thinned in their numbers, but are grown more shy." In discussing the green turtle the *Nouveau dictionnaire d'histoire naturelle* (1904:248) observed that in view of the avid demand for both the meat and the eggs, it was not surprising that the animals were becoming scarce in the very places that they had originally been most abundant. This situation, it observed, had led the philanthropist Martin Moncamps to propose the establishment in the Seychelles, under the authority of the French government, of some turtle reserves (*parcs à tortues*) "where both males and females might be protected for better reproduction." These reserves, it was emphasized, would contrast with the turtle "crawls" of Jamaica and elsewhere, "which only hasten the depopulation of the turtle by making them more readily available to the luxury trade of London." But there is no evidence that anything ever came of this enlightened proposal.

In later years most of those who have been concerned with the green turtle have warned of the dire consequences to be expected from the animal's continued uncontrolled exploitation. Yet the pace has slackened but little. It was being proposed in a London journal only 90 years ago that tinned turtle meat, long the cherished luxury of the rich, might provide an almost unlimited source of low-cost meat for the workers of industrial Europe "were the business but properly organized" (Cochrane, 1872:289).

Until the past 5 or 10 years there has been a notable lack of protective legislation covering the green turtle in the face of the almost universal belief that the population of the species is rather rapidly diminishing. Almost simultaneously in the Caribbean, in the Seychelles, in Queensland, and in the Pacific Islands there has been an awakening to the fact that rapid action may be necessary to salvage the green-turtle resource. In Sarawak thousands of turtle eggs are now being put down in special hatcheries so that the young may be put into the sea in such a condition that they may better resist the attacks of sharks and other predators that normally take the majority of them in the first few minutes of their lives. Similar experiments are being made in the Pacific Trust Territory, in the Seychelles, and in Costa Rica. Tagging programs have been proposed elsewhere so that the mysteries of the green turtle's migrations and life history may be better understood. Archie Carr, who is spearheading the turtle conservation program in the Caribbean, has expressed the situation succinctly but with optimism: "It is not often that we are offered a set of circumstances so promising; a one-item feeder with its pastures undamaged, vast in extent and used by no other animal; a species attuned to building and thriving in dense populations and yet flexible enough to proliferate and scatter in dilute colonies; above all, a depleted species, the cause of whose depletion is clear and surely possible to remedy. There is a skeletal breeding stock and the best of remaining nesting shores are the least cluttered by man. Group action by governments concerned would surely save Chelonia and build unity and strength in the Caribbean by raising the yield of the sea to the people around it. In the field of live-resource management it is not often that you can hope for so much" (Carr, 1954:19).

The green-turtle problem has been attracting much attention during the last few years and steps are beginning to be taken in several areas to save this fabled creature, so beloved of epicures and gourmets, from going the way of the passenger pigeon, the heath hen, and the great auk. A case in point is the Brotherhood of the Green Turtle, an informal layman's organization that was founded in New York City in the spring of 1959, inspired by Professor Carr's delightfully readable book of Caribbean wanderings and turtle lore, *The Windward Road* (1956). The club, sparkplugged by a New York publisher's representative named Joshua B. Powers, has established a non-profit subsidiary known as the Caribbean Conservation Corporation, of which Carr is the technical director, supported by a small field staff comprised mostly of graduate students in biology. Its first project is the provision of free stock from a hatchery at Tortuguero, Costa Rica, to any agency able to ensure protection for any beach formerly used for nesting green turtles and since abandoned. In the summer of 1960 some 20,000 baby greens were hatched. About one-fourth of these were released off Tortuguero, the remainder shipped by air express to Florida, Puerto Rico, the Cayman Islands, and other Caribbean points just like day-old chicks. The hatchlings are released at dark, in small groups, a few hundred yards offshore to circumvent predator loss insofar as possible. It is hoped that survivors will be imprinted by the conditions of their first immersion in the sea and go back to the site of introduction at nesting time, as some fish do. But even if their genes send them back to Tortuguero to nest, Professor Carr notes, the protection will have been achieved and there will be a net gain for the green turtle (Bowen, 1960).

There is some evidence that the green turtle has best held its own against man in those areas where the eating of turtle flesh is held repugnant and the eggs alone are prized, as in the Malay world and much of Buddhist Southeast Asia. Hendrickson (1958:525-29) has recently argued, in his study of the breeding populations of Malaya and Sarawak, that the key to the rational management of the species lies in the fact that the exploitation for eggs has a much less adverse effect than the slaughter of adult green turtles. He points out that the species is adapted to sustain enormous losses in the first part of its life and that this loss might be represented instead by a 95-per-cent egg harvest if the turtles hatched from the remaining 5 percent could be reasonably sure of surviving the first few days of life. A hatchery program is proposed much as has been initiated in Costa Rica, involving the transportation of egg clutches to protected spots, the removal of predators, wire enclosures to prevent newly hatched turtles from wandering into the sea, and tanks in which the young turtles may live for perhaps a week or until the yolk supply which they carry with them from the egg is exhausted.

It is argued that the average mature green turtle yields about 150 pounds of edible meat and that this is about the weight of the lifetime egg production of a female, assuming 600 eggs for each of three egg-laying seasons (the number may well be twice this). But as most of the eggs could be utilized without removing the producing unit, there seems no doubt that exploitation for eggs would yield the larger nutritional product. Hendrickson suggests that no luxury demand should be allowed to produce a net nutritional loss in the protein-poor areas of the tropics, particularly when past history indicates that the form of exploitation necessary to supply the luxury obliterates the industry concerned after a time. If green-turtle soup is to continue to be made available to the epicures, he argues, its price must go up and a significant share of the higher profits obtained from its sale must be plowed back into intensive management programs for the remaining turtle populations. In an egg-oriented turtle industry, he suggested, the biologically exhausted females might be called upon to provide at least a minimal supply of flesh and fat.

Convincing and logical as this argument is, it nevertheless seems improbable that it will govern the green-turtle economy of the future any more than it has in the past. The extraordinary role which cultural attitudes and preferences have played in the exploitation of the species has been demonstrated. All men do not like turtle meat and many even find it repugnant on religious or esthetic grounds. Others find the gritty, soft-shelled eggs equally unattractive; they are the size and shape of ping-pong balls and have an albumen that does not coagulate but remains watery after cooking. A rational, conservative system of harvesting the sea will have to consider cultural attitudes along with biological facts. In the case of *Chelonia mydas*, a species peculiarly vulnerable to man's activities, the lesson of history is already quite large. Now amateur "skindivers" must be added to its list of enemies. Should present exploitation practices and human population trends prevail, its days as an economically significant source of protein food for the tropics are undoubtedly numbered. Yet the very persistence of this giant reptile to date in the face of such tremendous odds is in itself something of a tribute to the vigor of the species, the vastness of the Seven Seas, and the importance of cultural differentiation among men.

Bibliography

Bowen, J. David. 1960. "To Save the Green Turtle," *Américas*, Vol. 12, pp. 14-17.

Carr, Archie. 1954. "The Passing of the Fleet," *Bulletin of the American Institue of Biological Science*, Vol. 4, pp. 17-19.

Carr, Archie. 1956. *The Windward Road*, Knopf: New York.

Cochrane, William. 1872. "Turtle," *The Food Journal*, Vol. 3, pp. 255-258, 286-290.

Goldsmith, Oliver. 1825 [ca. 1770]. *A History of the Earth and Animated Nature*, London.

Hendrickson, John. 1958. "The Green Sea Turtle, *Chelonia mydas* (Linn.), in Malaya and Sarawak," *Proceedings of the Zoological Society of London*, Vol. 130 (Ser. A), pp. 445-535.

Nouveau dictionnaire d'histoire naturelle. 1904. Paris, Vol. 22, pp. 242-271.

PART SIX

Spain and the Canaries

24

The Moorish Imprint on the Iberian Peninsula*

The surge and ebb of the tide of Moorish rule across the Iberian Peninsula between the eighth century and the fifteenth left enduring marks on its cultural landscape and economic life. These Muslim legacies are chiefly the reason for the extra-European character of much of present-day Spain and Portugal and give rise to the popular remark, "Africa begins at the Pyrenees." The extent of these influences is not easily assessed and has probably been greatly exaggerated, for many features of peninsular life and land popularly attributed to Islam have pre-Roman, Roman, and Gothic antecedents.

Hermann Lautensach, who has devoted much of his full and productive life as a geographer to studies of the Iberian Peninsula, has recently examined this Moorish imprint on the landscape and culture (Maurische Züge im geographischen Bild der Iberischen Halbinsel, *Bonner Geogr. Abhandl. No. 28*, 1960). His personal observations, extending over more than 30 years, are supplemented by an extraordinarily rich and diverse bibliography (244 works), including numerous contributions in the scholarly review *Al-Andalus*, translations of the Arab geographers, and the erudite studies of such Arabists and Hispanists as E. Lévi-Provençal, L. Torres Balbás, M. Gómez-Moreno, C.E. Dubler, and Wilhelm Giese. The literature on the subject is impressive in its abundance, range, and quality, and Professor Lautensach's familiarity with it, whether in art history, ethnology, or linguistics, lends his survey much authority.

---

*Reprinted from *The Geographical Review*, Vol. 52, pp. 120-122 (1962).

In nothing else are the marks of the Moorish occupation so evident as in the architecture and urban forms, especially in the Algarve and Andalusia, and in the Levant. The horseshoe arch, paired and grilled windows, fortifications with pointed spires and turrets, the mosques (many of them converted into Christian churches or cathedrals, as at Córdoba), the flat roof (*azotea*), the planlessness and narrow, shaded streets of the inner town, are among the inheritances from the Muslim past. The patio, of similar peripheral southern distribution, probably has another origin, as does "whitewashing." There are flat-roofed "Arabic villages" (for example, Mojácar in Almería, pictured on the cover of *Landscape*, Vol. 10, No. 3, 1961) that are not whitewashed, and there are others, beyond the range of primary Arab influence, that are. In parts of southern Portugal, as in Lisbon, pinks and greens may be preferred to white. Lautensach gives special attention to the distribution of the flat-roofed house, so characteristic of that last stronghold of Moorish culture in Spain, the mountainous Alpujarras. But the mapping of this, as of other Moorish elements in the landscape, produces no simple picture; for the distributions are discontinuous and disjunct, a reflection of the varying intensity of Islamic influences between regions and between city and country.

No less important were the Moorish contributions to the economic geography of the peninsula. Among the numerous economic plants introduced by the Arabs the most important--rice, sugar cane, pomegranate, carob, cotton, apricot, bitter orange--are at home only in the subtropical coastal regions of the south and east. Saffron (*azafrán*) seems to be the sole significant contribution of the Arabs to the agricultural complex of the interior Meseta, though there is a question regarding buckwheat, which likewise has an Arabic name (*alforfón*) in modern Spanish. The Moors also developed and adopted plant resources already present, as in the artificial pollination of dates, the caprification of figs, and the drying of raisins. Olive culture, well developed in Roman times, was intensified and extended under the Arabs. This is true, too, of irrigation, which was much elaborated by the Moors on the basis of the Roman inheritance. Many words in modern Spanish relating to irrigation are of Arabic origin (*acequia, noria, aljibe, alberca*), and it is in areas where irrigation is most intensively developed today that place names of Arabic origin are most numerous. The hydraulic, or Persian, water wheel and the mule-driven vertical water lift (*noria*) were Arab introductions, and, from the evidence of recent discoveries south of Madrid, so was the underground lateral canal (foggara, qanat) for tapping ground waters. Among other Moorish introductions and influences examined by Lautensach are the merino sheep, silk raising, pack transport by mule and donkey, paper manufacture, coastal-fishing techniques, and clothing.   It is suggested, but not proved, that the slash-and-burn system of hillside farming found, for example, in the Algarve and the Montes de Toledo may have been brought with the Berbers from North Africa.   The farther south one goes on the Iberian Peninsula, the longer was the period of Moorish occupation and the greater the evidence of it in the landscape.   The correlation of these clearly Moorish culture elements with the drier, warmer climate is partial and incomplete but suggestive.   A detailed examination of the Córdoba agricultural calendar of 961 makes it appear that the seasons of planting and harvesting were as much as 4 weeks earlier than they are today, which suggests that the warming of Central Europe in the Middle Ages may have extended to Gibraltar and beyond.

Just as a study of Hispanicized Arabic words affords insight into which areas of human activity were the ones where Moorish influences were strongest, so the distribution of modern place names of Arabic and Berber origin reflects the impact of the occupation. Lautensach's introductory chapter, originally published substantially in *Die Erde* (Über die topographischen Namen arbischen Ursprungs in Spanien und Portugal, Vol. 6, 1954, pp. 219-243), is a study of the distribution of 2,343 place names in Spain, and 564 place names in Portugal, that are of Arabic origin.   The principal source for these, a dictionary of Arabic toponyms in Spain prepared by the eminent Arabist Miguel Asín Palacios, has also been employed by David E. Sopher in a brief but critical geographical analysis (Arabic Place Names in Spain, *Names*, Vol. 3, 1955, pp. 5-13).   As expected, the maps suggest a relationship between the length of the Arab domination and the frequency of Arabic place names.   Yet the correlation is uneven.   Arabic place names are distinctly more common in the northern half of the peninsula than most of the other culture elements commonly associated with Islam.

The areas of origin of the bearers of the Muslim culture traits that persist today in Iberia are imperfectly known.   The first contingent to cross the Strait of Gibraltar in 711 and 712 comprised only a few thousand Arabs.   The mass of the invaders were of Berber stock and were assimilated into Islam, not without internal conflicts, only during the first century of their occupance of Andalusia. Berbers continued to be an important element in the "Moorish" population, and the so-called "Arabic" imprints on the culture and landscape are often as much Riffian Moroccan as Arabic.   The Berbers were the farmers and stockmen, the Arabs the administrators and city dwellers.   In the first centuries the Arab rulers and urban-dwelling bureaucrats had come largely from Syria, Yemen, and other parts of the Eastern world. Later, ties with North Africa, especially Morocco, became dominant.

Despite its title, the recent study by the distinguished French economic historian Henri Lepeyre, "Géographie de l'Espagne morisque" (École Pratique des Hautes Études, VIe Section, S.E.V.P.E.N., Paris, 1959) has only marginal relevance to this theme. Lepeyre's rigorously documented study, one of an extraordinary series on economic history and historical demography (of which the contributions of Huguette and Pierre Chaunu, Frédérico Mauro, and Fernand Braudel, should especially attract the attention of geographers), is in reality less a geography of Moorish Spain than an attempt to establish the numbers and distribution of the Muslims remaining in the country at the time of the final expulsion in 1609-1614, together with their ports of embarkation and destinations. On the basis of new documentation, especially from the archives of Valencia and Simancas, they are shown to have been perhaps 300,000 in all, of whom 135,000 were in Valencia, out of a total population of 8 to 9 million. The evacuation, almost without precedent, was carried out with stunning technical efficiency.

More pertinent are the recent works of two anthropologists. Julio Caro Baroja (Los moriscos del reino de Granada [Instituto de Estudios Políticos, Madrid, 1957]) has made a detailed analysis of Moorish life in the province of Granada in the fifteenth century, and George M. Foster (Culture and Conquest: America's Spanish Heritage, *Viking Fund Publs. in Anthropol., No. 27*, New York, 1960) has described with much insight the "conquest culture" of sixteenth-century Spain, including the Moorish contributions to it, as the base line from which the acculturation of much of aboriginal America may be viewed. Both these analyses, like Lautensach's more explicitly geographical volume, suggest the opportunities that await the student concerned with origins, distributions, and the functional significance of culture elements and culture complexes in the Iberian Peninsula--the only extensive area on earth that, once won by Islam, has ever been wrested away.

25

The Acorn-Hog Economy of the Oak Woodlands of Southwestern Spain*

The image of southwestern Spain as a barren, eroded skeleton largely bereft of its vegetation cover is much distorted. The visitor from other lands of summer drought and winter rain, such as California, with its much shorter history of intensive human use, is as likely to be impressed by the durability of the Iberian hill soils as by their misuse, by the extent and density of the woodland as by its paucity.

Over most of the rest of the Iberian Peninsula, but most conspicuously on the Meseta, the formerly extensive oak forests (*monte alto*) have been destroyed or degraded to worthless scrub (*matorral*) as a result of man's long-continued use and abuse of the land. But on the uplands of Andalucía and Extremadura, where shallow soils have discouraged the plow, and the mild marine climate promotes abundant and reliable crops of sweet acorns, the expert hand of the countryman has created and preserved extensive tracts of open oak parklands. These neatly groomed, evergreen oak parks support a singular and remarkably persistent mixed farming and herding economy in which the mast fattening of hogs (*montanera*) plays a conspicuous role (Fig. 25.1). Within this woodland association it is the dusty green ilex, or holm oak (*Quercus ilex*), the encina of the Spaniards (Portuguese, *azinheira*), that gives special character to the landscape and is the area's principal economic wealth. The western Sierra Morena, the lower-lying Paleozoic hill lands of the provinces

*Reprinted from *The Geographical Review*, Vol. 52, pp. 211-235 (1962). Nine months of field work were undertaken in Spain and Portugal in 1959-1960 on a fellowship from the John Simon Guggenheim Memorial Foundation.

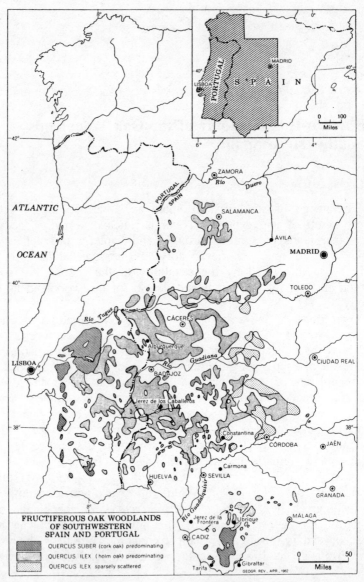

Figure 25.1 The Fructiferous Oak Woodlands of Southwestern Spain and Portugal. Sources: for Spain, Servicio de Plagas Forestales, Madrid; for Portugal, H. Gaussen: Le milieu physique et la forêt au Portugal, *Rev. Géogr. des Pyrénées et du Sud-Ouest*, Vol. 11, pp. 219-267.

of Badajoz, Cáceres, and Salamanca and of western Toledo, and the adjoining Alentejo region of Portugal probably support the most extensive stands of these heavy-fruiting live oaks in the world. They perhaps reach their optimum development in southern Badajoz, in the vicinity of the towns of Jerez de los Caballeros and Fregenal de la Sierra for example, but there are equally fine stands elsewhere, as in the Tagus Valley north of Trujillo and in Beja and Evora Districts in Portugal. Smaller but similarly productive ilex forests exist on the flanks of the rugged and higher Cordillera Bética, between the Guadalquivir depression and the Mediterranean. The trees are not large and give more the aspect of an orchard than a forest, in part because of the systematic and periodic pruning they receive.

On sandy soils the cork oak, alcornoque (*Quercus suber*), tends to occur, either in pure stands or codominant with the ilex. Wherever the two species intermingle, a hybrid form, known as *mesto*, may appear. The cork forests are best developed near the coasts; for example, on the Pilocene sands southeast of Lisboa and on the rocky hills that rise behind Gibraltar. In the Gibraltar area the semideciduous *quejigo* oak (*Q. lusitanica*) is likewise of some importance, as is *Q. pyrenaica* in parts of Salamanca. The acorns of both the cork oak and the quejigo are valued as mast, but the trees tend to bear in alternate years and less abundantly than the ilex. On at least four-fifths of the forested areas of Andalucía and Extremadura the ilex is the dominant species.

Extent and Utility of the Forests

These beautiful open oak groves, or *dehesas*[1] (Portuguese, *montados*), with their abundant sweet acorns and winter pasturage, represent an unstable forest formation maintained only by the continuing intervention of man, who has long exploited them for food, fodder, fuel, and construction material. Calculations of their geographical extent must be approximate; for over wide tracts, especially in the old mining districts of the Sierra Morena and on the thin limestone soils of the mountains of Cádiz and Málaga, the oak forest fades almost imperceptibly into low scrub forms (*chaparro*), includ-

---

[1]*Dehesa* is a regional term for a wooded country property; where the name persists in agricultural areas that are now treeless, it can be taken as evidence of the former presence of oak trees. It derives from *defensa*, meaning a property protected (defended) against outsiders. The original land grants made by the town councils of Extremadura in the thirteenth century were termed *adehesamientos*. See, for example, Antonio Floriano: *Estudios de historia de Cáceres: El fuero y la vida medieval, siglo XIII*, (Oviedo, 1959), pp. 236-237.

ing the dwarf kermes oak (*Quercus coccifera*), or into a Cistus matorral with only scattered individual oaks. Of the one and three-quarters million hectares of oak forest in the eight southern and western provinces from Málaga to Salamanca, 84 per cent are classified by the Spanish Forest Service as predominantly ilex, 15 per cent as cork oak, and 1 per cent as quejigo.[2] These oak woodlands cover some 15 per cent of the total area of the eight provinces, or perhaps one-third of their total area of thin, primary upland soils. In earlier times the forests doubtless were much more extensive; attrition has been most intense on the deeper soils attractive to the plow and on lands close to the mines and urban centers, where charcoal has been in greatest demand.

This oak forest, with its grass and matorral understory, remains the principal resource of the people of the sierra. For generations it has supplied a premium-grade charcoal to the urban centers of much of the peninsula. From its hard, tough woods have been wrought the traditional tools and implements of home, farm, and mine. Tanbark, especially from the cork oak, was so intensively exploited during the nineteenth century that in some areas the forest was threatened with extinction.[3] Today these cork forests, stripped of their outer bark every 9 years, are contributing another, and potentially self-perpetuating, source of income to their owners; for this part of the Iberian Peninsula is the source of nearly three-fourths of the world's production of commercial cork. In many sections the land beneath and between the oak trees is commonly plowed and planted to grain, broad beans, chick-peas (*garbanzos*), or lupines every fifth or sixth year. During the winter and spring, sheep may

---

[2]*Estadística Forestal de España*, 1957, Ministerio de Agricultura, Dirección General de Montes, Madrid, 1959, p. 74. Large-scale, detailed vegetation maps exist only for the provinces of Málaga and Cádiz. They accompany Luís Ceballos and M. Martín Bolaños: *Estudio sobre la vegetación forestal de la provincia de Cádiz* (Instituto Forestal de Investigaciones y Experiencias, Madrid, 1930); and L. Ceballos and C. Viciosa: *Estudio sobre la vegetación y la flora forestal de la provincia de Málaga* (Instituto Forestal. . . , 1933).

[3]In Cádiz alone more than 1.3 million cork trees are said to have been felled for tanbark during a twenty-year period in the middle of the nineteenth century (Salvador Cerón: Industria forestal agrícola [Cádiz, 1879]). The tanning industry, once so important in Andalucía and Extremadura (for example, Cordoban leather), has all but disappeared there today. However, the tanneries of the picturesque mountain village of Ubrique (Cádiz), renowned for its leatherworking industry, still use some 350,000 kilograms of tanbark from the cork oak each year. These tanneries produce only sole leather. The fine leather for Ubrique's craft industry comes from modern commercial tanneries in Barcelona and Valencia, which use chemical tanning agents almost exclusively.

be grazed on the volunteer grass or stubble, and goats may be brought in to help contain the matorral.

But more important is the plentiful annual crop of sweet acorns, or *bellotas* (Portuguese, *bolotas*). Strabo (III.3.7) tells us that they were an important human food in the more mountainous parts of the peninsula, the country people living on acorn bread for much of the year. In Moorish times the district of Los Pedroches (al-Bitrūdjī) in the Sierra Morena northeast of Sevilla was called "the plain of acorns" (Fahs al-Ballūt). The Arab chronicler al-Himyarī described the acorns from its oak forests as surpassing all others in quality. The inhabitants, he noted, took the trouble to spare the trees and to tend them. According to al-'Awām the ilex was sometimes even planted in gardens, irrigated and fertilized with cow dung.[4] Don Quixote waxed eloquent on the joys and innocence of the simple pastoral life, in which acorns served as the staff of life. Acorn bread and acorn gruel are still eaten by the poorer country folk, especially in times of scarcity, but today the acorns are sold in the village markets and on the streets, along with chestnuts and pine nuts, more as a confection than as a staple. It is as mast, however, that they attain their principal importance when, from October through January, large numbers of rangy red or black Iberian swine are driven through the forests *en montanera* to fatten on the fallen fruit. At least 40 per cent of Spain's 9 million swine are believed to be of the Iberian race, and of these perhaps two-thirds are fattened on acorns for slaughter. Thus nearly one-third of the pork produced in Spain can be said to be acorn-finished, and pork represents nearly one-half of the country's meat consumption. For Portugal the proportions are roughly similar.[5]

The Greek and Roman chroniclers had much to say about the utility of these forests for the winter fattening of swine, but under the Muslims, with their restrictions against pork, the oak woodlands seem to have been of greatly reduced importance. Probably the *Reconquista* would have been much more difficult had not the sierra, with its easily exploited pannage and pasturage, been so attractive to the Christian pig raisers moving back down from the north onto these *encomienda* lands of the military orders.

---

[4]Quoted in Hermann Lautensach: Maurische Züge im geographischen Bild der Iberischen Halbinsel, *Bonner Geogr. Abhandl. No. 28*, 1960, pp. 66.

[5]It must be noted, however, that the per capita consumption of fish in Spain today considerably exceeds that of red meat, despite the country's traditional orientation toward stock raising. Lower prices, coupled with improved refrigeration and transport facilities, have played an important role in this development.

By the early sixteenth century at least, the fame of the Sierra Morena hams had become well established, and they frequently appeared on the manifests of ships leaving from Sevilla for the Americas. In 1554 from 80,000 to 100,000 hogs were reported as being fattened annually in the oak forests of the jurisdiction of Jerez de los Caballeros,[6] which is close to the total swine population of the modern *partido judicial* of the same name today. Here and to the north there were early conflicts between the village swineherds and the shepherds of the *Mesta*, come down from the Meseta with their great flocks of merinos to exploit the rich winter pasturage of Extremadura. As the swineherds gained the upper hand and hogs replaced sheep, the area of *encinares* may well have expanded at the expense of the open range. There is at least a suggestion of this in the testimony presented at the Mesta trials in the latter part of the eighteenth century, in which much emphasis is given to the past destruction of trees by the intentionally set fires of the sheepmen.[7] Today fires are relatively infrequent in this area, and damage to the vegetation by burning is of curiously little account.

The Montanera Season

Although extensive tracts of oaks exist in other parts of Spain, it is only in the west and south, from Salamanca southward along the Portuguese frontier to the shores of the Atlantic and the Mediterranean, that the acorns are sufficiently sweet, and the harvest sufficiently abundant and reliable, to make their exploitation profitable. This is the zone of the densest stands of oaks and highest acorn yields, where the spring climate is mild and the days with frost number fewer than 20 a year. Freezing weather in late March and April, when the female flowers of the ilex are formed, means failure of the fall acorn crop, but this rarely happens within the areas mapped in Figure 25.1.

The ilex bears with considerable regularity, but the cork oak tends to be highly erratic. Although the swine find the acorns of the cork oak less palatable, its longer bearing period, from mid-September through the first weeks of February, permits an extension of the montanera. The early-fruiting habit of the quejigo offers the

---

[6]Matías Martínez y Martínez: *El libro de Jerez de Caballeros* (Sevilla, 1892), p. 192.

[7]"Memorial adjustado . . . entre Don Vicente Parno y Hurtado como diputado de las ciudades de . . . toda la provincia de Extremadura y el Honrado Consejo de la Mesta. . . ." (Madrid, 1771[?], pp. 16, 107, and 287 for example.

same advantage. Moreover, the blossoming period of both these species is longer than that of the ilex, so that the chance of failure of the acorn crop caused by an unseasonal spring cold snap is lessened.

On a much reduced scale the nuts of the beech, chestnut, and various deciduous oaks are still exploited for swine and cattle feed in the more humid Cantabrian and Pyrenees mountains of northern Spain. There, however, single-species stands are less common, and this fact, coupled with both the excessive parcelization of property and the widespread existence of common pasturage rights, has made the exploitation of forest pannage en montanera more difficult. Much of the mast so used is harvested by hand, for in the north stall-feeding is traditional.

In the Spanish forest economy acorns loom surprisingly large. In 1957 they were valued in Forest Service estimates at almost one billion pesetas ($1.7 million), or .one-sixth of the value of the total product of all forest lands, including returns from lumber, pulpwood, fuel wood, cork, and cultivation and pasturage rights.[8] Badajoz alone accounted for 60 per cent of all "forest fruits," and its acorn crop of 685,000 metric tons made it the first province in Spain in value of forest products. Badajoz is also the leading center or charcoal production. Cáceres was the second-ranking province in "forest fruits," followed by Córdoba, Salamanca, Cádiz, and Huelva (Table 25.1).

Livestock Fairs and the Mast Harvest

The traditional date for taking the hogs into the oak woods varies from village to village in southwestern Spain, but most commonly it falls somewhere in middle or late October. Some animals are born and reared in the sierra, others come to their acorn orgy lean and hungry from the lowlands. In either case they have usually spent most of the first 18 months of their lives foraging skimpily on dry pasture and stubble, without supplementary feed.

There is a great movement of such ready-to-be-fattened swine at the traditional fall stock fairs, especially in Extremadura and in the neighboring Alentejo of Portugal (Fig. 25.2). Since the fifteenth century the great San Miguel fair at Zafra (October 3-7) has been

---

[8]The product of Spain's forests in 1958, in millions of pesetas, was officially estimated as follows: lumber, 3145; pasturage, 1270; acorns and other forest fruits en montanera, 875; nuts collected by hand, 180; firewood, 400; resin, 181; cork, 149; esparto grass, 66 (*Memoria . . . , 1958*, Dirección General de Montes, Madrid, 1959).

Table 25.1 - Area of Fructiferous Oaks and Acorn Production, southwestern Spain, 1957

Province	Area (thousands of hectares)			Acorn Production[a]	
	Encina (Quercus ilex)	Cork (Q. Suber)	Quejigo (Q. Insitanica)	Volume (hectoliters[b])	Value (million ptas.)
Badajoz	334.2	26.9	---	9,520,000	628
Cáceres	289.6	29.7	---	2,128,000	140
Córdoba	356.5	9.1	---	793,000	52
Salamanca	146.0	0.3	---	705,000	47
Cádiz	23.7	80.6	19.6	409,000	27
Huelva	86.2	38.4	---	308,000	20
Málaga	13.1	20.9	7.0	268,000	18
Sevilla	76.6	30.6	---	100,000	7

Source: *Estadística Forestal de España, 1957*, Ministerio do Agricultura, Dirección General de Montes, Madrid, 1959, pp. 74, 112, and 129.

[a]Figures for acorn production (*frutos forestales*) include pine nuts from public forest lands as follows: Huelva, 57,050 hectoliters; Cádiz, 4400; Sevilla, 1130. Also included are 1250 hectoliters of chestnuts from the public forests of Cáceres and 2200 from Málaga.

[b]Of 72 kilograms.

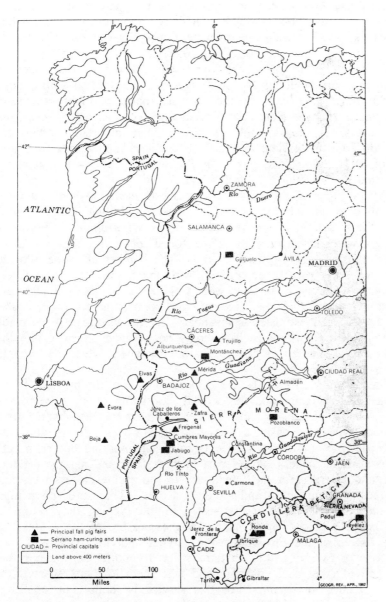

Figure 25.2 Orientation Map, Showing Location of the Principal Pig Fairs and of the Ham-curing and Sausage-making Centers.

pre-eminent. This sleepy Badajoz village, its huge medieval castle brooding over it, lies strategically at the margin of the oak woodlands of the Sierra Morena and the fertile Tierra de Barros plain of the Guadiana Valley, at a convergency of transport routes and on a site with abundant spring water. There is reference to the Zafra fair as early as 1489, when the town petitioned the Catholic Crown for exemption from the law prohibiting free fairs,,and again in 1510, when the rights to the Zafra fair were granted to the Duke of Mediniceli. Although all types of livestock are sold at Zafra, hogs are the most important. In the past as many as eighty thousand swine have changed hands here in a week, but in recent years the number has been considerably reduced. Other important markets are those of Trujillo, Mérida, Fregenal de la Sierra, and Ronda in Spain, and of Beja, Elvas, and Evora in Portugal, but there is scarcely a town that does not have its fall livestock fair.

At the close of the fairs the pigs are formed into herds of forty to a hundred animals by their new owners, and each herd is placed under the direction of one or two swineherds (*porqueros*). Formerly the pigs were driven on foot to the forest, but today they are more commonly delivered by truck or rail. The number of swine allowed on a dehesa is usually determined with the advice of expert forest assessors, who walk through the woodlands in late August and September estimating the size of the coming acorn crop. The accuracy of their estimates is legendary. A flat charge may be made for montanera rights, or each pig may be weighed on entry into the forest and again on departure 3 months later, when the weight gained determines the fee.

Frequently the animals are divided into two troops, one to be fattened for slaughter and the second, consisting of animals from 6 to 12 months of age, to clean up the acorns overlooked by the first. A good swineherd makes a true art of his work, judging with care the capacity of his charges. He begins each morning on the roughest part of the dehesa or the part farthest from the nightly bedding place and reserves for the late afternoon hours the closest trees and the trees with the ripest and sweetest acorns. These are active pigs, and their pace is often a fast trot. In the evening they return to their bedding place, "made happy by the pleasure of the acorns," as Vergil wrote of the Etruscan swine. When individual villagers own only one or two pigs, it is customary for a youthful herder to gather them all together each morning and take them to their repast if the forest is not too distant. For this service he collects a small fee from each owner. In the evening the grunted, acorn-sated porkers return to the village "at a full gallop, like a legion possessed with devils, in a handicap for home, into which each single pig turns, never making a mistake."[9]   It was such an onrushing troop that caught up and nearly carried away Don Quixote, horse and all, as it well may a modern visitor.

Sometimes the swineherd beats down the ripening acorns with a long pole to which a cord with a short stick on the end has been attached.   This practice, however, is considered detrimental to the trees, especially the more tender cork oaks, and it is commonly forbidden by landowners.

The carbohydrate-rich acorn diet is conveniently supplemented by the green grass brought forth by early fall and winter rains, or by worms rooted from the moist earth.   Indeed, the quality and quantity of the pasturage may be as important as the size of the acorn crop in evaluation of the montanera season.   Thus the 1959-1960 season was generally rated a good one in the Sierra Morena more because of the excellent grass than because of the acorns, which were of only average size and abundance.

An 18-month-old Iberian hog will more than double its weight in the 3 months of montanera, say from 60 kilograms to 140-150. Occasionally animals may be permitted to reach 170 kilograms or more, especially if they are destined for home slaughter.   Under the most favorable conditions the average daily weight gain may be about one kilogram; it is greatest in the older animals and during the first weeks of the fattening period.

Acorn Yields

A good Sierra Morena *encinar* will, on the average, produce about 600-700 kilograms of acorn per hectare,[10] with production per tree running from 12 to 18 kilograms. Exceptional trees may exceed this figure many times.   One holm oak near Fuenteovejuna (Córdoba) is said to have yielded 600 kilograms of acorn in 1 year, and a tree in Portugal 400 kilograms.   Every countryman recognizes that some trees are heavy acorn producers and others are almost sterile. In view of this, it is remarkable that the selection of superior-yielding stock for seeding or grafting has received almost no attention.[11]

---

[9][Richard Ford:] *Gatherings from Spain* (London, 1846), p. 127.

[10]Compare average yields of dry-farmed wheat and barley in Andalucía of about 1,000 kilograms per hectare.

[11]See Manual Medina Blanco: *Contribución al estudio del área de la encina en la provincia de Córdoba y sus posibilidades alimentícias para el ganado* (Departamento de Zootecnia, Córdoba, 1956); J. Nosti: la selección de la encina para

Under a rational dehesa improvement program yields of as much as 2,500 kilograms of acorns per hectare might conceivably be attained. At a ten to one conversion ratio this would represent a weight gain of as much as 250 kilograms of meat per hectare, almost five times the present rate. In cork forests the potential is much lower, both because of smaller acorn yields and because of the less complete exploitation that results from the lower palatability of the fruit.

Yields of acorns per hectare of mature *Quercus ilex* are probably as large in southwestern Spain and Portugal as in any other part of the world where oak forests occur, but comparative data are scarce.[12] Large yields, the sweetness of the fruit, and the conservatism of the peasantry have permitted these tended oak "forests" to continue to support a type of economy that has disappeared from most of Europe and North America, though it was once widespread.

Perhaps the greatest threat to the success of a montanera season is caterpillars, for a bad caterpillar year can play havoc with the acorn crop. The most destructive of these leaf-eating Lepidoptera is *Tortrix viridana*, an oak-moth caterpillar endemic in the Iberian Peninsula, whose incursions appear to have become epidemic in the present century. In some years when *Tortrix* has been quiescent, there have been serious invasions of another caterpillar, *Lymantria dispar*, particularly in the colder areas in the north. These pests destroy the tender new spring shoots that bear the female flowers, and, thus, the future acorns. Treatment of infected areas with 10 per cent DDT was initiated in 1952 by the Forest Pest Control Service, using either hand rigs or low-flying aircraft. Success has been spectacular, and today some 900,000 hectares, more than two-thirds of all Spanish encinares exploited for their acorns, are under treatment by public or private agencies. The Service estimates, probably with some exaggeration, that before the initiation of this treatment the encinares of Spain produced about 26 million kilograms of pork annually, and that within 6 years the figure had risen to 64 million

---

montanera, *Agricultura*, Vol. 25, Madrid, 1956, pp. 506-507; Adolfo Rúperez Cuéllar: La encina y sus tratamientos (Madrid, 1957); Luis Romero Candau: La montanera extremeña, *Montes*, Vol. 15, Madrid, 1959, pp. 375-383.

[12]See J. Russell Smith: *Tree Crops: A Permanent Agriculture* (New York, 1950), especially pp. 156-186; also Earl B. Shaw: Geography of Mast Feeding, *Econ. Geogr.*, Vol. 16, 1940, pp. 233-249, and Carl B. Wolf: *California Wild Tree Crops* (Rancho Santa Ana Botanic Garden, 1945), pp. 19-54. In Domesday England and in Carolingian Germany forests were commonly evaluated in terms of their carrying capacity for swine, but this varied widely according to local conditions.

kilograms, largely as a result of the spraying program.[13] There is no doubt that acorn production has been sharply increased, but the secondary effects on the biota of this chemical treatment are still uncertain and are the subject of much controversy. A similar campaign, employing techniques developed in Spain, is also under way in the oak woodlands of southern Portugal.

The Management of the Forest

A critical element in the management of an oak forest in this montanera zone is the spring pruning, which with *Quercus ilex* is directed toward maximizing acorn yields.[14] However, the abusively severe pruning, stimulated especially by high charcoal demand in Spain during recent periods of war and civil unrest, has left many dehesas deplorably run-down. To this may be linked the reported increase in the virulence and frequency of caterpillar invasions, which trees with reduced crowns seem less well able to resist. Although some among the peasantry say that "wounded trees tend to set more acorns," the intensity of pruning appears to have been closely associated with the price of charcoal. As the use of kerosene has spread in recent years and the charcoal market has weakened, the wood obtained from pruning has become a by-product, which little more than pays for the labor necessary. As the temptation to "get rich quick" by severe and frequent pruning for firewood and charcoal making fades away, the oak dehesas may recover some of their former lushness.

Proper pruning, usually done by itinerant crews of experts, is designed to promote the horizontal growth of a few main boughs from a common crotch and thus to open the inner foliage to light and maximize the number and growth of the new vertical shoots on which the acorns set. More light is also admitted to the ground below for any grain planted there. The initial, formative pruning in a tree's sixth to eighth year is especially critical. In well-managed encinares the pruning is usually done every 6 years thereafter; in cork forests, every 3 to 4 years. It is, of course, the bark of the

[13]José Torrent: La nueva técnica de tratamiento contra las plagas del encinar y su importancia económica, *Bol. Servicio de Plagas Forestales*, Vol. 2, Madrid, 195, pp. 11-35; see also *idem:* Aviation in Spain and Its Part in the Control of Pests in Forestry, *Agricultural Aviation*, Vol. 2, The Hague, 1960, pp. 14-20.

[14]Rúperez Cuéllar, *op cit.* [see footnote 11 above], pp. 72-91; and Eduardo Teixeira Pinto: *A azinheira, contribuição para o estudo da sua cultura no Baixo Alentejo: Relatório final* (Universidade Técnica de Lisboa, Instituto Superior de Agronomia, Lisboa, 1957).

cork oak, not the acorns, that brings the greatest returns, especially with the high cork prices of recent years.

The spacing of trees also affects the production of acorns, as it does the yield of grain or pasturage from the land beneath. Normally at least fifteen meters is left between the trunks, so that no more than half of the land surface, and usually much less, is shaded by the tree canopy. In a well-kept dehesa there is little brush. The removal of matorral and the maintenance of a grassy sward under the trees are made easier by the fact that the principal species of invading woody growth, though heavy seeders, do not sprout and can be readily removed by chopping, pulling or plowing, to be piled and burned at the beginning of spring.

A good encinar may have the same carefully manicured appearance as a French vineyard or a California peach or apricot orchard. In Portugal the higher price of charcoal and the larger percentage of the oak woodland under cultivation seem to promote more careful and more severe pruning than in Spain. The contrast is immediately evident to the observant traveler crossing the border from Extremadura into the Alentejo. The striking flat-topped appearance of most Portuguese *azinhais* tends to emphasize their man-made nature. A similar system of pruning is characteristic in Salamanca, where wood and charcoal become more important because of colder winters and less reliable acorn crops. Where acorns have been even more subordinate to wood, as in the drier and colder parts of Spain and in North Africa, abusive exploitation by wood-cutters has more commonly led either to the complete destruction of *Quercus* stands or to their degeneration into a scrub formation without value except as browse for goats.

Both cork and ilex forests in Spain have almost always been regenerated by natural means, but clearing of the brush and plowing make regeneration difficult unless care is taken to protect new seedlings and sprouts. In Portugal, on the other hand, cork plantations are numerous, and ilex plantations not uncommon. For centuries in Spain trees yielding bitter acorns, and those with a tendency toward setting male flowers and few fruits, have been suppressed. The present oak dehesas are thus the product of a long history of selection and must be considered a human artifact quite as much as the swine that are fattened within them.

The fabric of laws and customs associated with the utilization of these oak woodlands, unrivaled in its complexity, dated from the Reconquista. In the provinces of Cádiz and Málaga extensive tracts of forest are owned by the towns and cities. The cork strip and the rights to montanera, to wood-cutting, to cultivation, and to the gathering of leaves of the dwarf palm (*Chamaerops humilis*) and of aromatic plants are periodically auctioned off to the highest bidder. The *término* of Jerez de la Frontera, for example, still owns 6,800 hectares of cork, ilex, and quijigo forest, from which it derives an annual income of some four million pesetas ($67,000). Tarifa, on the Strait of Gibraltar, receives enough from the auction of its cork strip alone to pay in some years for all of the town's expenditures. In Badajoz and Cáceres Provinces there are many common woodlands of medieval origin in which the trees are the common property of the villagers, their usufruct subject to sale or to "turns" by the citizens, while the land beneath is held by private owners. In other places the trees may be privately owned while the land is held in common. At least one Extremadura community, Albuquerque (Badajoz), until recently held title to two common woodlands jointly with a town across the border in Portugal, and the residents of the two places utilized the woodlands for pasturage in alternate years. Proximity to Portugal also has had an influence on land inheritance systems; for in three Badajoa *partidos judiciales the fuero de bailío* remains in effect. This legal principal, of Portuguese origin, provides for equal division of all property between husband and wife (community property) and is thus in contrast with the established Spanish code.

Iberian Swine and the Lard Problem

The Spanish swine industry may be divided into two geographical sections of almost equal extent, one based on the traditional red or black Iberian hogs, for the most part driven in herds to feed in pasture, stubble, and oak forest, the other on white Celtic or improved North European crossbred stock given intensive stall or dooryard feeding. A line drawn diagonally across the map of Spain from the northern border of Portugal southeastward to Valencia and passing slightly south of Madrid separates the two. The black swine of Mallorca (*mallorquinas*), which are often fattened on carob beans and acorns, belong with the southern group. Enclaves of improved "crossbreds" occur in the zone of extensive herding, as on the plain of Granada and the irrigated lands of Murcia and Valencia.

In former times the black Iberian hog was dominant throughout most of the southern part of the peninsula, but the russet variety, somewhat less prone to fatness, has gradually replaced the black, especially in Andalucía and southern Badajoz, until today it is numerically dominant almost everywhere south of the Río Guadiana. In the Guadalquivir Basin and in the Cordillera Bética the blacks have almost entirely disappeared. These red or black Iberian swine, with long heads and legs, drooping ears, and sparse bristles (the more primitive forms tending to have short, shallow bodies with convex backs), are closely akin to the feral razorbacks of the southern United States, which are almost certainly descended from them.[15] Disease resistance is high, except for hog cholera, and for this vaccination is general. The sows occasionally cross with the wild boar (*jabalí*) that abounds in certain parts of the Cordillera Bética and in the mountains of Córdoba, but breeding is generally controlled. Litters tend to be small, and the pigs develop slowly, but the rusticity of this small-boned, rangy Iberian hog makes it ideally suited for foraging in the oak forests. Whereas a modern inbred meat hog such as the Danish Landrace will gain 1 kilogram of weight for each 3 kilograms of feed, an Iberian *en montanera* requires 10 kilograms of acorns to put on 1 kilogram of meat. However, perhaps one-quarter of the calories consumed by the Iberian hog must be used simply in getting about, for a hog questing for acorns may cover as much as six kilometers in a day. Neither the white Celtic races of northern Spain nor crosses of Iberians with them or with the lighter-colored North European breeds such as the Large White or Danish Landrace are adapted to this alfresco dining under the bright autumn sun of Andalucía or Extremadura.

In North America and in most of Europe modern inbred meat hogs finished on grain and concentrates are normally slaughtered at 5 to 8 months of age and at weights of 80 to 100 kilograms. Mast-fattened Spanish hogs, on the other hand, are slaughtered at 20 to 24 months and at much greater weights--as much as 160 kilograms or more. This reflects the seasonal availability of acorns and the fact that the protein-deficient diet of the oak groves can be properly assimilated only by hogs that have completed their structural development.

This structural development is very slow. Most Iberian hogs manage on minimum rations, gained with a maximum of exertion, during precisely those months of most rapid bodily development when the protein content of their diet should be highest. Pigs farrowed in January and weaned in March find green grass until

---

[15]Swine were brought to Florida from Cuba by the De Soto expedition in 1539 and were driven with them in their wanderings through the southeastern states. The swine increased rapidly. There are numerous reports of thefts of hogs by Indians; others escaped into the forest. These and later Spanish introductions were almost certainly the base from which the feral southern "woods hog," or razorback, evolved. There is some evidence that red Iberian swine imported into Virginia and Kentucky in the nineteenth century provided the foundation stock for the modern Duroc-Jersey, a breed noted for its rusticity (Charles W. Towne and Edward N. Wendtorth: *Pigs from Cave to Corn Belt* [Norman, Okla., 1950], pp. 73-74 and 173).

mid-May. Then comes a hungry time when the grain has been harvested in late June or early July, when they enter the stubble for the gleanings. But today the leavings are less abundant than formerly, as a result of the gradual extension of mechanized harvesting equipment, especially in the wheat and barley fields of the plain. In August and September there is a more prolonged food shortage, alleviated only occasionally by niggardly rations of pulses, grain, or olive press cake, until the first acorns begin to drop in the sierra, in late September or early October. But because of their deficient diet the animals have not yet completed their bodily development and are not able to gain any worth-while benefit from an acorn diet of almost pure carbohydrate. For this they must wait a second year, unless they should be sent to Valencia or Barcelona for earlier stall-fattening and sale on those more demanding markets.

Spain's increasing demand for animal proteins, the shift in public taste toward leaner meats, and the increasing availability and consumption of vegetable oils, especially olive and soya oil, have disrupted traditional livestock marketing patterns in recent years. The heavy lard-type hog of the past is no longer in demand. The finishing of 8-month-old animals on low-cost acorns has been shown to be feasible when supplementary rations of high-protein, vitamin-enriched food are provided during their early development.[16] Under these conditions they may enter montanera at 50-60 kilograms and come out, ready for slaughter, as meat hogs of 90-100 kilograms at ages of 11 to 12 months. Although tradition is a powerful retarder of change, and the cost of feed concentrates is high (in Spain the price of maize, for example, is almost twice what it is in America), The shortening of the hog cycle by this means appears an attainable goal. Market demand, stronger each day, for lighter-weight, bacon-type hogs will be an important influence. Excessively fat animals, often scarcely able to waddle up to the slaughtering block under their own power, are already becoming rare. Selective breeding of Iberian Swine has begun, aimed at increased litter size and precocity, straighter backs, and better development of shoulder and front hams.

---

[16]See, for example, the following publications of the Departamento de Zootecnia Córdoba: Gumersindo Aparicio Sánchez: Capacidad evolutiva del cerdo de tipo ibérico (1956); Amalio De Juana Sardón: El cerdo de tipo ibérico en la provincia de Badajoz (1954); Manuel Pérez Cuesta: Experiencia de alimentación intensiva para la ceba precoz de cerdos de raza colorada (1954).

364

Hams and Sausages

Almost every family in rural Andalucía and Extremadura keeps a pig or two for fattening, as often on household refuse or garden surplus as on acorns, and the family slaughter is a traditional and festive occasion.[17] Probably one-third of the hogs fattened annually in Andalucía and Extremadura are sacrificed in this manner. The conjunction of cold weather and a superabundance of feed at year end has provided the basis for a household pork-products industry here dating from the remote past. The long, thin hams are trimmed of skin and fat, rubbed with salt, and hung raw to cure for 9 or 10 months before they are ready to be eaten. The commercial production of these *jamones serranos*, an outgrowth of the traditional household activity, has expanded greatly since the beginning of the century. It is localized today in some half a dozen mountain towns, long famed for their home-cured meats, where numerous small slaughtering firms specialize in these fine hams and in a variety of highly spiced, semidehydrated sausages colored with red pimiento, of superior keeping qualities. Among the most important of these towns are Jabugo, Cortegana, and Cumbres Mayores in the western Sierra Morena; between them they process some sixty thousand acorn-fattened red hogs each winter (Fig. 25.2). Montánchez (Cáceres) and Guijuelo (Salamanca) are similarly famed for their hams and sausages, as are, to a smaller extent, some of the higher towns of the Cordillera Bética in the vicinity of Ronda (Benaoján, Montejaque). The high village of Trevélez (Granada) in the Alpujarras cures its renowned sweet hams, which are only lightly salted, in the snows of the Sierra Nevada.

The distinctive flavor of the raw hams from these towns is popularly attributed to the "climate," which in the sierra is not only cooler in summer than in the lowlands but also, because of the absence of radiation fogs, much drier in winter. Even the big commercial packing house at Mérida, which slaughtered some fifty thousand hogs in the 1959-1960 season, sends it larger hams to cure in the mysteriously beneficent air of the mountain villages of Extremadura. These mold-coated, strong-flavored country hams, which hang from the rafters of almost every rural house in the sierra and in almost every food store and bar in Spain, and whose preparation requires only salt and open air, brought 120-140 pesetas ($2.00-$2.35) a kilogram in the winter of 1959-1960--about 650 pesetas

---

[17]Julian A. Pitt-Rivers (*The People of the Sierra* [London, 1954], p. 85) describes a household hog slaughtering in a village in the Cordillera Bética. See also Huldine V. Beamish: *The Hills of Alentejo* (London, 1958), pp. 61-68.

($11.00) for an average five-kilogram ham. At such prices it becomes a real luxury. Middle- and upper-class Spaniards of the cities are tending to eat more and more "York style" cooked hams, which most commonly come from the meat-type white Celtic hogs of the north. The sierran ham is becoming increasingly a specialty food, a confection to be taken in razor-thin slices at the wine bars or in larger portions at traditional celebrations and fiestas. In the mountain villages, however, the home-cured raw ham and spiced red sausage from acorn-fattened hogs remain important.

The municipal slaughterhouses that daily supply the city markets with their fresh meat are not happy with the lardy, acorn-fattened hogs that come to them from the sierra dehesas. A rising standard of living has brought a shift in consumer habits and tastes in Spain as elsewhere, and olive and soya oil and lean meats have gradually replaced lard and bacon fat in the kitchen and on the table. Soft pork is no longer in favor. The industrial slaughterers have an outlet of sorts for most of their fat meat and lard in sausages and in bulk sales to the baking industry, but there is little demand for them in the meat stalls of the urban markets. Yet these acorn-fattened swine dress out at 55-60 per cent fat content, and the figure is not easily reduced.[18] Although grain-fed animals bring a premium of four to six pesetas a kilogram, more than 80 per cent of the twenty thousand hogs slaughtered each winter at the Sevilla slaughterhouse, for example, are acorn-fattened Iberians. The proportion should not be much different for Málaga, Cádiz, Córdoba, Huelva, or Salamanca. The large commercial packers at Mérida (Badajoz) and Carmona (Sevilla), which put up a diversified line of canned meats, including York-style cooked hams, slaughter acorn-fattened and grain-fattened hogs in about equal proportions. In the more discriminating Madrid and Barcelona markets meat-type hogs have largely driven out the lardy Iberians in recent years. This appears to be less true in Lisboa, where the acorn-fattened Alentejana swine continue to supply the greater part of the receipts of the municipal slaughterhouse.

Notwithstanding the growing consumer preference for leaner meat, no significant shift away from the traditional system of mast fattening seems in prospect. What can be expected is the increased feeding of protein supplements to young pigs during the spring and

---

[18]De Juana (*op. cit.* [see footnote 16 above], pp.192-193) found an average back-fat thickness of 6.0-6.3 centimeters in sixty Iberian-type hogs slaughtered at Mérida. This is twice the average figure for a modern Iowa or Denmark bacon hog. He cites a figure of 8.7 centimeters for Portuguese hogs from the Alentejo.

summer hungry time, with a consequent shortening of the cycle.[19] Hand gathering of acorns forestal-feeding, either along with or mixed with other feeds, is generally uneconomic, even in low-wage Spain, though some modern feed mills include acorn flour in their commercial concentrates. With acorns bringing two pesetas a kilogram, a fattening hog may eat 25 pesatas' worth of acorns a day, or close to the daily wage of a swineherd. Artificial drying of the acorns, so that they can be stored for several months before the feeding, is being experimentally tried, but the cost of gathering seems certain to be prohibitive in the long run.

The Mediterranean Tree-Crop Complex

The carefully tended oak groves form an integral part of the Mediterranean tree-crop complex, which J. Russell Smith[20] has suggested might well be copied in other parts of a world harried by the specter of soil erosion and soil exhaustion. "If I wanted to be comfortably and permanently rich," Smith wrote in 1916 in the lead article of the first issue of the *Geographical Review*,[21] "I could ask for few more secure bases for it in the line of agricultural lands than the undisturbed possession of a few hundred acres of Portuguese land with a good stand of cork-oak trees (*Quercus suber*) and evergreen-oak trees (*Quercus ilex*)...[with] its crop of cork and pork." Smith thought the Iberian Oak-woodland economy he had observed in the Alentejo unsurpassed as a rational, conservative form of land

---

[19]The very quality of the celebrated Spanish *serrano* hams, which Richard Ford (*op. cit.* [see footnote 9 above], p. 130) a century ago recommended to his readers as "fit to set before an emperor," may be compromised by any major shift toward lean-bacon animals fed on strictly controlled rations. In the slower-maturing, acorn-fattened hog the quality and size of the muscle improve with age, and one may presume the flavor. The resulting quantity of lean meat, trimmed of its surplus fat at the factory, may well be more cheaply produced on a price per pound basis, especially if the processor exploits to the full the versatility of the pig in the factory by converting the extra fat into marketable products.

Although advocates of the lean-bacon animal, tailored on the farm to meet the requirements of either the bacon curer or the butcher, have been in the ascendancy in America and in Northwestern Europe, at least one packing company in Britain has recently come out in favor of the "heavy hog," generously fed on cheap carbohydrate rations, holding that the quality of the product is such as to bring a premium price over competitive Danish imports.

[20]*Op. cit.* [see footnote 12 above], pp. 21-35.

[21]"The Oak Tree and Man's Environment," Vol. 1, 1916, pp. 3-19; quotation on pp. 7-8.

use, and one that might well be employed on the thinner hill soils of many other lands.

There is striking similarity between the management practices employed in the oak woodlands and those used with olives, almonds, chestnuts, carobs, and even the nut-producing stone pine (*Pinus pinea*). Rural life in southwestern Spain and Portugal is remarkably oriented toward the maximum utilization of both wild and cultivated trees, and the distinction between the two often becomes blurred. Wild olive (*acebuche*), wild chestnut (*castaño*), and wild carob (*algarroba*) seedlings are frequently left in cleared fields, as are the oaks, sometimes to be grafted to better-yielding strains. The grafting of high-yielding holm oaks, with its interesting possibilities, is more frequent in Portugal and Mallorca than in southern Spain, where absentee ownership has long tended to discourage agricultural innovation and improvement.

The oak woodlands are, of course, under continuing pressure from farmer, charcoal burner, and goat alike. The reduced demand for charcoal and the tendency to concentrate agriculture on the better lands have somewhat ameliorated what seemed a few years ago to be a catastrophic situation. Now the face of Spain, north and south, is rapidly being altered by a massive reforestation campaign in which fast-growing eucalyptuses, pines, and poplars are being planted on vast areas that were once the domain of evergreen oaks or matorral. In the province of Huelva, for example, the total area of eucalyptus now approaches that of the oak groves, and 4,000 additional hectares are being planted each year. In these impatient days there has been a tendency to forget the slow-growing oaks, and their numbers have been gradually decreasing in many areas. A government irrigation project (*Plan Badajoz*) in the Guadiana Valley alone has taken more than 50,000 hectares of oak forests in the past decade and will convert the valley into a grain-surplus area where grain-fattening of livestock, including pigs, may become the major importance. Already one modern pig farm on the Portuguese border near the city of Badajoz is shipping 4500 stall-fattened crossbred swine a year to Barcelona and Madrid markets at ages of 8 or 9 months. On the margins of the Guadalquivir plain, too, and in all the smaller valleys of the south, the better soils are in demand for more intensive farming. But through much of the hill country of Andalucía and Extremadura the oak woodlands continue to play their homely role as providers of mast much as they did in Domesday England, in medieval Central and Southern Europe, and in Daniel Boone's Kentucky. Richard Ford's century-old characterization of Extremadura as "the *Ham*pshire of the Peninsula," where the villages "more correctly may be termed coalitions of pigsties,"[22] still has some validity.

The Future of the Oak Woodlands

Large landholding and absentee ownership have had a conservative influence on land use in southern Spain. The great hacienda houses, nestled in the oak-covered sierras, serve as retreats from the turmoil of the city and symbolize a set of values in which the prestige of landownership looms large. The traditional addiction to the hunt, whether of doves, partridges, deer, or wild boars, often gives these wildlands a value above and beyond the traditional norm.

Foresters and stockmen alike are becoming increasingly aware of the importance of the oak woodlands as producers of meat. It is recognized that the destruction of the forest is the initial step in an inexorable cycle of degradation that has often led to disaster.[23] That it has been avoided in so much of southwestern Spain and adjacent Portugal is in significant measure attributable to the economic value which man since early times has placed on the sweet acorn of *Quercus ilex* and, more recently, on the bark of the cork oak. A hectare of oaks in these hills may yield a better income than a hectare of grain, and with intelligent management permanent productivity of the soil is at the same time assured.

Whereas cattle raising and sheep raising have historically encouraged the destruction of the forests of Spain, hog raising has favored their perpetuation and improvement. Here, where summer drought sharply reduces the number of alternative uses of the land, the traditional extensive form of land use that includes the forest herding and fattening of swine--once widespread in the more humid latitudes to the north and east--probably constitutes as rational a type of exploitation as can be found. Its survival, despite its obvious inconveniences, reflects both the strong cultural conservatism of southern Spain and Portugal and an exceptionally favorable set of environmental conditions that have been gradually and subtly modified, both by accident and by design, at the hands of man.

---

[22]Ford, *op. cit.* [see footnote 9 above], pp. 126-127. For a more detailed early account of this mast-fattening economy see Johannes Rein: Die Steineiche (Quercus ilex L.) und die spanische Schweinezucht, in his "Geographische und naturwissenschaftliche Abhandlungen," Vol. 1 (Leipzig, 1892), pp. 158-168. The system also survives today, on a reduced scale, in the Balkans.

[23]Manuel Marten Bolaños: Consideraciones sobre los encinares de España, *Inst. Forestal de Investigationes y Experiencias Bol. No. 27*, Madrid, 1943.

26

Starlings for Seville*

One of the more fascinating examples of Spain's inexhaustible cultural diversity and the persistence of its folkways is the large-scale capture and consumption of *pajaritos*, or small wild birds. In Andalucía the species principally involved is the common English starling or *estornino* (*Sturnus vulgaris*), come south from Central Europe to spend the winter in a milder climate and to feed on ripe olives and the fruits and berries of the *monte bajo* of the Iberian wildlands. The visitor to the public markets of Seville during the winter months is struck by the abundance of these tiny birds offered for sale in the meat and poultry sections. Weighing little more than three ounces, innards and all, they are piled high on the vendors' counter and, at two to three pesetas (3 to 5 cents) apiece, business is lively.

To supply the Seville demand they are netted in amazing numbers on dark winter nights at half-a-dozen widely separated points in Andalucía, Extremadura, and, recently, in Aragon (Fig. 26.1). It is estimated that anywhere from one million to two-and-a-half million of them may be consumed in Seville alone in a season, both as a substitute for more expensive forms of poultry and as traditional snacks that are served in the city's unnumbered wine bars and cafés, where chalkboards proclaim, "*Hay Pajaritos.*"

In Seville everyone eats *estorninos* from November to February, when they are in season, yet nowhere else in Spain or perhaps the world are they a significant human food. Even at nearby Cádiz,

---

*Reprinted from *Landscape*, Vol. 10, No. 2, pp. 28-31 (Winter 1960-61). Copyright (c) 1960 by J. B. Jackson.

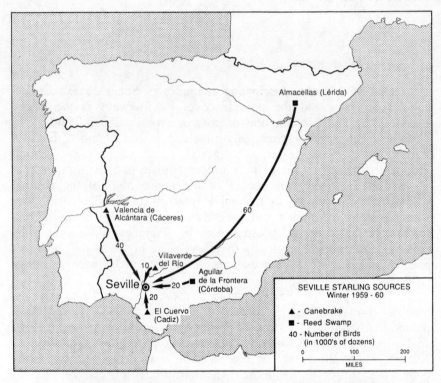

Figure 26.1   Source Areas of Seville Starlings, Winter 1959-1960.

Córdoba, Jerez and Huelva these birds are seldom seen in the market place. When they are, they are likely to be outnumbered by the sparrows, larks, thrushes, woodpeckers and partridges, all usually taken individually, either for pets or to be marketed as food alone. Tradition ties the eating of starlings to *Sevillanos* alone, but after centuries of such intensive exploitation the wonder is that the birds continue to arrive each winter in apparently undiminished numbers.

The Case Against Them

If such a mass slaughter of wild things tends to rouse our indignation, it is tempered by the realization that these little birds provide a cheap and needed protein food. In the cold logic of the Spanish countryman the starling is deserving of no more sympathy than a White Leghorn or an acorn-fattened pig. In any case sympathy for wildlife is not one of the stronger Spanish character traits. The starling is not a much loved bird at best, and on balance it must be considered a detriment to agriculture, for a large flock may quickly and completely ruin a crop. From a practical point of view it seems reasonable enough to make an economic resource of such an interloper.

The netting of starlings is the traditional activity of the men of the white-washed village of Villaverde del Río, on the right bank of the Guadalquivir river, some thirty miles above Seville. During the present century the activity has been extended from Villaverde to several distant canebrakes and reed swamps, but personnel and techniques are from Villaverde, the traditional town of the *pajareros*, or "birdmen."

In the first months of 1624, Don Gabriel de Santana, traveling through Andalucía, visited Villaverde and described the taking of starlings there in words that would apply almost as well today.

"At this place," he wrote, "the Count of Cantillana owns a piece of property which he rents for 500 ducats a year for the taking of starlings. These birds are taken with nets on the dark nights of November, December and January in a canebreak on the banks of the Guadalquivir, one-quarter league from the town, which has the length and breadth of a musket shot. The fewest taken in a night are 100 dozen, but the night before the pre-Lenten carnival they ordinarily kill a thousand dozen and there have been nights when they have taken 2,500 dozen. They carry them to Seville where they are sold for 1 *reales* a dozen, a single buyer taking all of them."

Villaverde still has its canebrakes where starlings are taken in nets for a single Seville buyer, and there are others at nearby Cantil-

372

lana, but since the turn of the century the starlings have been flocking here at night in considerably reduced numbers. Still, in a good year, these canebrakes may still supply more than 10,000 dozen birds for export, while many more are consumed within the two villages. Local opinion attributes the decline in numbers of the Villaverde starlings more to the clearing of the *monte bajo* of the adjacent Sierra Morena foothills, where the birds fed, than to any overdraft by the nocturnal netting parties (*cazerías*) of the past. In any event there are starlings in abundance elsewhere.

Plumage and Meat

Although the starling is today valued only for its meat, as it apparently was three centuries ago, there was a time in the last years of the nineteenth century, and the first years of the present one, when its plumage was in high demand as ornamentation for women's hats. French buyers came to Andalucía in search of bird skins for the Paris market. It is said that the meat left from the birds caught for their skins was offered on the Seville market at very low prices and that it is from this time that the custom of eating starlings, and the taste for them, became firmly established among the city's population. As the heavy draft on the Villaverde canebrakes could not meet the demand, the residents of that town turned their attention to other areas where starlings were known to be abundant during the winter months.

It was then that the present eleven-hectare canebrake at El Cuervo, fifty miles south of Seville and just inside the Province of Cadiz, was first planted, on rolling hill land watered by two springs where *junco*, or rushes, had originally grown and to which bands of starlings had nightly come to roost in season. The property is still known as the Huerta del Juncal. Men and nets were from Villaverde. Somewhat later, *cazerías* were begun in a stand of Phragcites, or *carrizo*, at Aguilar de la Frontera, Córdoba, and also near Valencia de Alcántara, Cáceres, where the present canebrake was planted by a citizen of Villaverde in 1928.

A wild stand of *Phragmites* in the Ebro valley of the far northeast of Spain, near Almacellas, Lérida, where clouds of starlings come each winter night to sleep, began to be exploited in the 1958-59 season for the first time, again by Villaverde men working on shares. As at Aguilar, the standing water makes the work more arduous than in the drier canebrakes, but the product of this new *cazería* has been extraordinary. In early January, 1960, a record 5,700 dozen birds were taken in the net in a single night, to be trucked south to Seville in a 24-hour, non-stop run. The yields from

Almacellas may be explained by the newness of the *cazería*, but the establishment of a second *cazería* near Zaragoza is being contemplated in view of the singular success of this venture. In the markets of Catalonia and Aragon, however, starlings are unmarketable.

The common cane in which the starlings roost is a commercial crop in Andalucía. Planted along irrigation ditches and in other moist places, it is used as a building material, for fences, broom handles, basket-making, and in many other ways. The cane from El Cuervo and Villaverde, cut annually at the end of the starling season, has been sold to the Canary Islands in recent years for staking the early tomatoes that, along with bananas, are the islands' principal export. New stands of cane are sometimes planted to attract roosting starlings in areas where the birds are known to be plentiful. In early 1960 I heard of such plantings at Castilblanco (Sevilla), Coto Doñana (Huelva) and Torrejón del Rubio (Cáceres), none of which had as yet attracted sufficient quantities of birds to be worth exploiting. All of the canebrakes now being worked have been planted with the specific aim of developing a starling *cazería*. It would appear to be a profitable business. A cane stand such as that at El Cuervo or Valencia de Alcántara may yield an income of perhaps 600,000 pesetas ($10,000 U.S.) annually from starlings alone. And if the birds do not come there is still the cane to be harvested and sold.

The net or *maquina* used for taking starlings was developed in Villaverde. It was patented in its present form by Señor Manuel Benitez Fernández about twenty years ago, so that wherever starlings are taken in Spain today it is with such a net. Of cotton and linen, it is generally about 100 feet on a side. It can be used only on moonless nights or after the moon has set, for the birds scare easily. In the first days of 1960, for example, a net was unfurled at El Cuervo at 3:00 A.M. on January 7, and at 5:00 A.M. two days later, each time within minutes after the disappearance of the moon below the horizon. One or two hours of total darkness seem to be as satisfactory as twelve. Cloudy or rainy nights are especially favored. During the day preceding a *cazería* the net is placed in position, rolled up at the foot of six poles, each about twenty feet high, placed in a line along a trail cut through the cane or reed. Long ropes are stretched taut from each of the six posts to six similar posts on the far side of the tract be covered. On signal, with the setting of the moon, the net is hoisted and unfurled by a system of ropes. The net, once in place, clears the top of the cane or reed, where the birds are roosting, by two or three feet. It also has sides, perhaps fifteen feet high, reaching to the ground along trails cut in the dense growth. When the net is being opened out, many birds are disturbed and escape. Hence, after it is in place one side is left open, and into this birds from adjacent roosts are slowly driven by the workers, who rustle the cane and whistle in the darkness to move them along. Then the fourth side flap is brought down and the crew retreats to the warmth of an inside fireplace to await the dawn.

Some ten minutes before sunrise the loud whistling chorus of the awakening birds is suddenly stilled and a cloud of starlings arises from the cane, circles, and is off for distant feeding grounds. All except the fortunate ones, seldom ten percent of the total population present that night, find themselves surrounded by the net. As they flutter desperately about, some become entangled in the webbing by a leg or a wing, but most remain in the cane tops. Now a giant net sleeve, some thirty feet long and the same height as the net, is sewn into one corner of the *maquina* with the fibers of the dwarf fan palm, and is supported at its extremity by a tall pole with a short crossbar at the tops. Once the sleeve is in place, the workers enter the came and from the far corner of the net begin to drive the hapless birds toward it. When the sleeve is sufficiently full-- perhaps 600 dozen were in it on the first round when I witnessed the operation at El Cuervo--it is collapsed and the birds, now piled twenty or thirty deep, are quietly and systematically dispatched, one at a time, by squeezing their heads between the index finger and thumb. Considerable force is needed and for most workers the task requires two hands. When all have been killed, they are sacked and removed from the sleeve to be spread out on a shaded concrete floor for three hours to cool before being crated for trucking to the refrigeration units in Seville. This operation may be repeated two or three times, or until all of the starlings have been removed from the net. For this work a team of twelve or fourteen men is generally employed most of the day.

A single dealer, Manuel Gallegas Aguilar, holds a monopoly of the wholesale starling market in Seville. As did his father before him, Gallegas owns and operates the El Cuervo canebrake and has purchase contracts with each of the other *cazería*. From his stall in the wholesale market the birds are distributed in crates to retail outlets. Demand generally reaches its peak during the Christmas-Epiphany season, for *pajaritos* are traditionally a fiesta food among Sevillanos. Although the netting of starlings after the first week of February without special government consent is forbidden, as a measure to insure their reproduction, they generally are available in the markets until early March. Under refrigeration the unplucked, undressed birds may be kept thirty days or more.

Their Habits

Perhaps because their principal foods are the ripe fruits of the cultivated olive and the small wild olive, along with the bitter berries of the lentisco, the dark meat of the wintering starling is rather strongly flavored and not particularly attractive to those not accustomed to it; but at least it contains no buckshot. The average bird weighs some three and one-fourth ounces as caught, reaching to three-and-a-half ounces at the end of the season. It takes at least three of them, fried in olive oil, to make a respectable plate. More commonly, perhaps, they are stewed with rice and pimiento as *arroz con pajarito*, a traditional wintertime dish in Seville homes. In this the birds go into the pot head and all.

The daily flight range of the wintering starlings from their habitual roosts is believed by local observers to exceed forty or fifty miles. Their extraordinary navigational ability, which permits them to return to the same stand of cane or reed night after night, cannot but evoke awe in anyone observing the great clouds of birds that descend on these resting places at sunset each night, in rain, fog, wind or fair weather. It is widely but erroneously held that the birds return nightly to their roosts with an olive in each claw and another in the mouth and that in the morning half-eaten fruit and their pits lie thick on the ground at the base of the cane or reed.

On rare occasions a white starling may be taken in the net. When this occurs the bird is always set free, as these are popularly thought to be the guides that bring the flock back at night. Although most of the birds have black feathers specked with white or buff and with green and purple iridescence on the male's breast, some are jet black all over. The latter, known as *tordos* in Andalucía, belong to another species, *Sturnus unicolor*, which is in permanent residence, breeding in these southern latitudes. Indeed, the Benítez patent on the net described it as for taking "*tordos ó estorninos.*" In Lérida the term *tordo* is often used synonymously with *zorbal* (lark).

European starlings have two main wintering areas, the western Mediterranean and the British Isles. From recoveries of marked birds it is possible to draw a line east-west across the North German Plain dividing the populations with a WSW standard direction, wintering in the British Isles (the northern and western populations) and those with a SW standard direction, wintering in the Mediterranean basin, especially Iberia (the central and eastern European populations). According to Robert Spencer of the Bird-Ringing Committee of the British Trust for Ornithology, no starling ringed in Britain has ever been recovered in Spain or Portugal. However, birds ringed at Helgoland are occasionally taken, indicating the presence of at least some north European representatives in the migrants to the western Mediterranean.

Their Origin

That the Spanish starlings are immigrants from Central Europe is abundantly proven by the numerous bands that are taken in every netting operation. Germany is the country best represented by these bands, followed by Poland, the U.S.S.R., Austria, Czechoslovakia, Switzerland, and, more rarely, France and Hungary. There is no systematic collection and return of the metal bands, however, and only a small part of those taken find their way back to their point of origin. Although probably more starlings have been ringed in Europe than any other species, there has been almost no interest in such activities in Spain. I was told, however, that the director of a prominent wine house in Jerez de la Frontera planned to purchase some of the live birds taken in the last *cazería* of the 1959-60 season at El Cuervo for banding and release, thus initiating marking activities at the southern end of the migration route. No comprehensive study of the seasonal migrations of starlings to Spain seems to exist, although the *cazerías* described above would provide abundant and easily accessible materials for such an investigation. It is widely believed that the birds return to the same roosting place not only every night during the season but year after year, perhaps until caught. Yet, there are years of few starlings and years of many; and there are numerous unexploited starling roosts at various points throughout the peninsula. It would be worth knowing whether years of abundance and of scarcity in other winter areas, such as Italy, southern France, and North Africa, correlate with those of Spain and Portugal.

Starlings do considerable damage in Spain, especially to olives and to newly sown grain fields, and any reduction in their numbers would probably be welcome by the rural population. Yet despite the heavy and continuing drain imposed by the *cazerías*, the 1959-60 season was described by the Andalucía *pajareros* as the "best" within memory. Learning that starlings had become a nuisance in parts of eastern North America, where they were introduced in 1890, the owner of the Villaverde *maquina* patent recently offered his services to the United States government. Instead of taking only a small part of the pesteriferous birds from their communal resting places he would take them all. The well-known preference of many American starlings for city halls and office buildings as roosts is but one of several and considerable complications to such a scheme of extermination, but he would like to try.

Their Future

It is their geographical localization that makes both the starling *cazerías* and the starling market of Spain unique. Is there anywhere else on earth where 60,000 wild birds may be taken at one fell swoop in a single net? We are reminded of the netting of migrating pigeons and other birds in the passes of the Pyrenees and the Alps, but the techniques are rather different and the numbers involved certainly fewer. However, *The New York Times*, under the headline, "Bird Slaughter Stirs Italy Again," recently stated that 800,000 hunters and 60,000 netters were expected to kill 100 million birds during the year, some legally, others not. Professor Erhard Rostlund, in calling my attention to this, observes that the breeding power of these little birds must be terrific and points out that this netting and killing has been going on at least since Roman times. They still provide an inexpensive and not insignificant seasonal source of protein to the expanding, meat-hungry population of southern Europe, but one wonders how much additional pressure they can withstand. If starlings were as popular a culinary item elsewhere as they are in Sevilla their story, at least, would be a quite different one.

27

Sand-Bed Agriculture: A Remarkable System for Early Truck Crop Production on the Arid Southeast Coast of Spain*

During recent years parts of the semi-arid southeast coast of Spain have been transformed into some of the most prosperous agricultural lands of Europe through a unique system of sand-bed or sand mulch agriculture (*arenado*) for the production of extra-early tomatoes, vegetables, and melons. Between 8,000 and 9,000 hectares of irrigated truck crops, for the most part broken up into family-farm parcels of one hectare or less (*huertos enarenados*), have been brought under this remarkable production system in Almería and Granada provinces and extending along the Mediterranean coasts as far west as Torrox (Malaga), (Fig. 27.1). Extraordinarily high yields of premium early crops are being obtained, often from land and irrigation water that had previously been considered too saline for agricultural use (Mendizabal and Verdejo, 1961; Bosque Maurel, 1964).

The sand-bed is nothing more than a mantle of clean beach sand 10-12 centimeters (4-5 inches) thick that is spread over the natural soil, graded or terraced to receive ditch irrigation water (Rueda Cassinello, 1965). On steeper alluvial fans the small plots or "bancales" are enclosed by concrete retaining walls. The underlying soil serves as the growing medium into which the seeds or transplant sets are placed, but the cultivator works only the sand layer, taking special care not to mix the sand with the earth below. A 4-centimeter (1.7 inches) layer of farmyard manure, laid down before the sand is applied, separates the latter from the soil and must be replaced every three years or so by a laborious process involving the

---

*Reprinted from *Proceedings, Association of American Geographers*, Vol. 5, pp. 216-220 (1973).

380

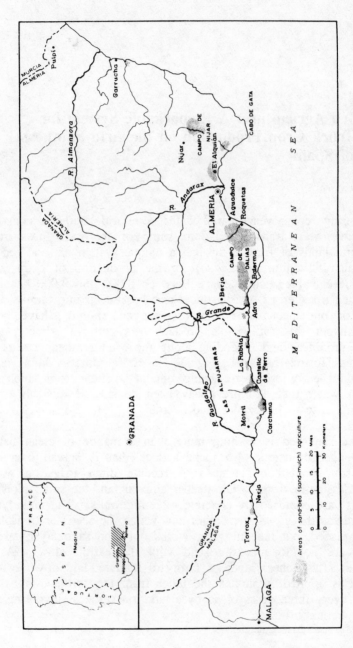

Figure 27.1 Map Showing Areas of Sand-Bed (Sand-Mulch) Agriculture in Southern Spain, 1972.

removal and replacement of the sand ("retranqueo"). A well prepared sand-bed may last 10-12 years, with periodic renewal of the manure layer, if care is taken to keep it clean and free of soil and organic matter, but eventually it must be either replaced by new sand or piled and washed clean of foreign matter. In some cases soil itself may be brought in and spread over the natural surface to a depth of 30 centimeters (12 inches), with the manure layer and the sand top-dressing placed over it.

The distinctive visual aspect of the new landscape of sand-bed farms derives from the wind screens (*bardas*) woven of common cane (*Arunda donax*) or, alternatively, of cloth bunting dyed a bright green, which enclose individual plots and protect the crops against the strong westerly winds that characterize much of this coastal zone. Occasionally casuarina, eucalyptus and cypress trees are also used as windbreaks. Frequently additional, shorter inclined structures of cane may be introduced behind each row of plants, so oriented as to absorb and reflect the rays of the low winter sun and thus to promote earlier maturing dates. Air drainage is generally good in most areas and temperatures as low as 0°C are a rarity.

The principal acreage is in early tomatoes, but green beans, pimientas, cucumbers, melons, and egg plants are also important crops, usually interplanted. Virtually all of the produce moves by truck, either to Madrid, Barcelona, and Bilbao, or to export markets in northwestern Europe. Principal emphasis is on the more profitable spring harvest, but almost all of the sand beds are double cropped, with a fall planting that brings a second harvest peak towards the end of the year. Summer cropping is relatively rare, due to the intense heat, and where practiced usually is confined to maize. Although truck crops are the dominant beneficiaries of sand mulch, the technique has also been extended to trellised table grapes and citrus, reducing water requirements and bringing new plantings more rapidly into production. At El Alquián, west of the Almería airport, a tract of 350 hectares of government-planted henequen, now abandoned, is on sanded land. Along the Granada coast spectacular stair-case terraces, with semi-abandoned almond and olive trees, have been brought back into production as *huertos enarenados* wherever water could be delivered to them.

Each hectare sanded requires about 1,000 cubic meters of sand, equivalent to 1,750-2,000 tons, together with some 60-70 tons of manure. The demand for beach sand has brought agriculture directly into conflict with the burgeoning Spanish tourist industry, for which the sun and sand have become the principal attractions. Permits to take sand must be purchased by *contratistas* from the Intendencia de Marina. A fairly coarse, rice-sized grain (*arrocero*)

3-5 millimeter diameter, is preferred because it warms faster than finer textured material. The cleanest and most uniform sand usually comes from behind breakwaters where it has been naturally sorted. Occasionally sand from dry washes (*ramblas*) is employed, but the cost of screening and cleaning it is generally prohibitive. While sand shortages are likely to occur in the immediate future, increased license fees and increased haulage distances have already led to substantial cost rises in some areas.

The advantages of sand-bed agriculture are so numerous and obvious that it seems something of a wonder that its general adoption has been so long delayed. They include the following.

1) Earlier harvest, with consequent premium prices, especially during the spring. Because of its low specific heat the sand warms up much more rapidly during the sunny spring days than does the natural soil with its high clay content, increasing daytime temperatures below the surface as much as 5°C. The temperature of the air around the plants may also be raised several degrees due to the solar radiation reflected from the sand. The manure layer, further, functions as an accumulator, receiving heat from the sand above during the hours of sunshine and transmitting it to the soil below. Thus, tomatoes which would normally ripen about May 1 may be ready for harvest April 10 when grown in sand beds. Other crops are similarly precocious.

2) Reduction of water requirements by as much as two thirds. The sand mantle has a moisture-holding capacity up to 50 percent greater than the normal soil. It permits the precious well-water to infiltrate better with consequent reduced evaporation loss. At the same time the sand and manure layers break up the capillary of the soil, eliminating the capillary rise and the soil moisture loss normally associated with it. Any water loss is believed to be more than made up for by the night time condensation of atmospheric humidity of the sand particles, resulting from their rapid cooling.

3) Increased tolerance of soil salinity. The sand mulch, by breaking the capillarity and eliminating the capillary rise, precludes the accumulation of salts in the surface layer of the soil. Soils with excess salt content are common on this coast. If the soil is permeable and drainage is good desalination may be complete after a few years. Where this is not the case there may be a concentration of salts at a depth of about one meter, but, in the early years at least, this is likely to be beyond the root zone of most plants. At Roquetas land formerly occupied by solar salt evaporation ponds is said to have been successfully converted to *cultivos enarenados*.

4) Increased tolerance of salinity in irrigation water. Again, because of the one-way movement of water downward through the

soil, together with the low retention rate of sand particles for salt, water from wells with a fairly high salt content (to 3 parts per million chlorine) can be used without impairment of yields.

5) Elimination of the need for plowing or otherwise disturbing the soil in the root zone of plants.

6) Cleaner produce because of the absence of dust or dirt.

7) Elimination of soil erosion and reduction of weed problems.

8) Spread of labor requirements relatively evenly through the year, favored by multiple cropping and intensive cultural practices.

9) Increased yields, from 15 to 50 percent, of superior quality produce.

Against these impressive advantages the high capital investment required for sand-bed agriculture stands as the principal deterrent. Yet complete amortization, under multiple-cropping practices, usually requires no more than three years, and credit is readily accessible. Weed control may at times be difficult, especially for those weeds resistant to herbicides, because plowing or discing is not practical, while the high soil temperature and humidity may invite soil fungus diseases that would not otherwise be present.

On balance the high yields and high unit value of the produce makes the economics of sand-bed farming compelling. There are many stories of campesinos who, by virtue of hard work and good luck, have become capitalists within a decade. Virgin land, leveled into walled *bancales*, with wells and irrigation ditches, in 1972 was bringing up to 700,000 pesetas ($11,000) a hectare in the Campo de Dalías. Another 250,000 pesetas ($4,000) was required for land preparation, including sanding, manuring, and windbreak construction. The farmer and his family provided the bulk of the labor for planting, cultivation, fertilization, and harvesting so that with annual returns per hectare ranging from 300,000 to 600,000 pesetas ($5,000-$10,000) early amortization of investment was insured.

However, further expansion of the areas of sand-bed agriculture on the Granada and Almería coast seems likely to be limited by available water supply unless irrigated land presently in table grapes, citrus, or sugar cane is converted to truck crops or the practice is extended to dry-land (*secano*) farming. Recently capitalists from Valencia have introduced fairly large-scale sand-bed operations in eastern Almería, betwen Garrcha and Pupí. At least half of the area in sand beds is land newly developed for irrigation by the Instituto Nacional de Colonización (INC) in the Campo de Dalías, Campo de Nijar and Campo de Carchuna (Calahonda) districts where, in most cases, the original interest in this system of production came from a search for ways to use high salinity well water and excessively saline soils.

These remarkable sand beds represent an enormous expenditure of human energy, made practical in part by prevailing wages that are still relatively low (200 pesetas or about $3 a day) in Andalucía. One hectare requires 1,000-1,200 cubic meters of sand, the equivalent of between 1,750-2,000 tons, or perhaps 500 truckloads (substantial amounts are actually moved by pack animals). Assuming 8,000 hectares under sand, this would represent the equivalent of more than 4 *million* truckloads or some 14-16 million tons of sand removed from Mediterranean beaches to fields along the coast, and the process is continuing.

The origin of this intriguing system of forcing-bed agriculture has been much discussed in Spain. A early as 1880 a few innovative peasants near the fishing village of La Rábita on the rugged coast of Granada province are said to have been piling sand around individual plants (Mendizaal and Verdejo, 1961). About 1920 some of them seem to have begun spreading sand as a uniform blanket over small plots of soil, perhaps with a layer of manure at the base. The system evolved slowly, by observation and intuition, beign confined to the environs of La Rábita and the *vega* of Casteldeferro some 20 kilometers to the west. After World War II, with the enormous expansion of the European market for early vegetables, some La Rábita farmers migrated westward to the Llano de Carchuna and eastward towards Adra and Balerma on the boundary of Almería province. In 1957, in connection with new irrigation developments on the Campo de Dalías, and Carchuna. In all of these areas *colonos* from La Rábita are said to have played a significant role.

The Almería-Granada sand-bed farming system bears a striking similarity to the technique used on the desert island of Lanzarote in the Canary archipelago (Jensen, 1934; Matznetter, 1955). There a black volcanic cinder (*picón* or lapilli) has been spread over more than 2,000 hectares of land. Seen from the air the aspect is one of squared off asphalt parking lots. The principal crops are green beans, garbanzos, lentils, and melons. On Lanzarote there is no irrigation water available. Crops are dependent solely on the sparse rainfall (125-150 millimeters or 5-6 inches) and such night time moisture as may condense on the picón. The Lanzarote system of picón farming, recently spread to nearby Fuerteventura and to Tenerife, seems also to have originated some time late in the last century but it is not possible to say whether reciprocal influences with the mainland have been involved.

The revolutionary impact of irrigation with sand-bedding, converting worthless steppe and desert into highly productive farmland, has been compounded since about 1968 by the rapid expansion of low-cost unheated plastic greenhouses (*veranaderos*) (Mendizabal, Garcia, and Torres, 1971). In a period of four years more than 800 hectares of sanded land has gone under transparent polyethylene in eastern Andalucía (close to 600 hectares at Campo de Dalías). The first structures were low, simple ones designed only to provide protection against the wind. Now they are built higher and on permanent metal frames, being recognized as an extraordinarily effective device to alter the microclimate by increasing the air temperature and humidity, thus further hastening the maturing of crops. On sunny spring days the temperature under plastic is 10-15°C higher than ambient temperatures, while most of the moisture transpired by the crops is retained in the system. The result is not only a further shortening of the crop cycle but an additional substantial increase in yields. Gross returns per hectare may be as high as 1 million pesetas ($25,000), so that amortization of the cost of installation in the first year is almost assured. The inexpensive plastic, subject to shredding by the wind, must normally be replaced every two or three years, but the framing is permanent. In addition to the plastic *veranaderos*, so conspicuous in the landscape of the Campo de Dalías, there is a growing use of transparent plastic mulching, especially with melons and strawberries, as well as smaller polyethylene "forcing tunnels."

This coast has an average of more than 3,100 hours of sunshine a year and an annual precipitation of between 150-225 millimeters (6-9 inches), confined almost wholly to the winter months. It is precisely in such desert or near-desert areas that agricultural innovations such as sand mulching and the use of plastics, designed to maximize the concentration of solar energy and to minimize water use (and water quality requirements), offer the greatest potential. In this case the result has been nothing less than the complete re-evaluation of extensive areas formerly considered all but useless.

Almost overnight a healthy, if highly commercialized, family-farm economy has arisen on the Almería-Granada coast which in turn supports a small army of truckers, middlemen, auctioneers, warehousemen, farm-supply salesmen, and government agents. Per capita incomes in the affected *municípios* are three times or more the provincial averages (Puyol Antolín, 1971). The cultivator, often coming directly out of the regime of peasantry, is able to move from the status of share-cropper to proprietor in four or five years as a result of the very high returns the system offers. From the social point of view we have here a most unusual situation--an immensely prosperous and rapidly growing rural economy of small-holders that is a strong magnet to immigration rather than the continuing exodus from the countrysides that is so characteristic of most of Spain.

386

Thus, the combined population of the *municípios* of Roquetas and Vicar (Campo de Dalías) rose from 7,769 in 1960 to 16,798 in the 1970 census. The new prosperity of this scenic and sun-drenched coast has been bolstered further by the burgeoning of tourist hotels and high-rise condominiums which provide supplementary employment especially in the summer months when agricultural activities are at a low ebb. These remarkable developments have brought new vitality and renewed hope to what only a few years ago was one of the most traditional, backward and impoverished parts of eastern Andalucía, the driest and sunniest corner of the European continent (Reparaz, 1933). There may well be lessons here for other areas of similar environmental endowments and limitations.

References Cited

Bosque Maurel, J. "El cultivo en huertos 'enarenados' en la Costa Mediterranea entre Almería y Málaga (España)," *Aportación Española al XX Congreso Geogr. Int., Reino Unido*, Inst. J. S. Elcano, CSIC, Zaragoza, 1964, 219-226.

Jensen, S. "Agricultural methods of the Canaries, Fuerteventura and Lanzarote," *Economic Geography*, Vol. 10 (1934), 99-108.

Matznetter, J. "Das Trockenfeldbau auf den Kanarischen Inseln," *Mitt.* Geogr. Gess. Wien, Vol. 97 (1955), 79-97.

Mendizabal, M., F. Garcia and M. Torres. "Une nouvelle technique de la plasticulture: la culture sur sable à Almería," *Compte Rendu du 4e Congrès International des Plastiques en Agriculture*, Paris, Juin 1970, Paris, 1971, 311-315.

Mendizabal, M., and G. Verdejo. "Conservation de l'humidité et utilisation des sols salins par la culture sous sable ("arenado"), *UNESCO Arid Zone Research XVI, Plant-Water Relationships in Arid and Semi-Arid Conditions*--Proceedings of the Madrid Symposium, Paris, 1961, 323-316.

Puyol Antolín, R. "Estudio geoecónomico de la Provincia de Almería," memoria presentada para la obtención del grado de Doctor bajo la dirección del Cat. J. M. Casas Torres, 2 tomos, Univ. Complutense de Madrid, Fac. Fil. y Letras, Madrid, 1971 (MS).

387

Reparaz, G. "La zona più arid d'Europa (Spagne de SE)," *Boll. Real Soc. Geogr. Italiana*, Vol. 6 (1933), 157-162.

Rueda Cassinello, F. and J. M. *Cultivos enarenados de hortalizas extratempranas* (Madrid, 1965).

Vila Valentí, J. "La lucha contra la sequía en el Sureste de España," *Estudios Geográficos*, Vol. 22 (1961), 25-47.

28

The Migration of Canary Islanders to the Americas: An Unbroken Current Since Columbus[*]

The Canary archipelago lies off the coast of Africa at 29° N latitude, some 700 nautical miles south of Gibraltar. Its conquest and occupation, including the subjection of the native Guanche population, represented Spain's first overseas venture, a blueprint and precedent for the colonization of America. For nearly a century prior to Columbus the Spanish Crown found here a laboratory and testing ground for colonial administration, including relations with an aboriginal population that offered an irresistible attraction for enslavement and evangelization.[1] The philosophical justification and legitimization of conquest was first faced in the Canaries as a new colonial bureaucracy sought to adapt and refine the medieval, European institutions of government to the new situation. Authority to appoint officials and to distribute land and natives in service was delegated to local governors while exhaustively detailed ordinances formulated by appointed councils (*cabildos*) regulated every phase of life through a complex structure of regulations, fines and taxes.[2]

---

[*]Reprinted from *The Americas*, Vol. 39, pp. 447-481 (1983).

[1]See, *e.g.*, Alonso García Gallo, "Las sistemas de colonización de Canarias y América en los siglos XV y XVI, in *Coloquio de Historia Canario-Americana* I (1976), (Las Palmas: Cabildo Insular de Gran Canaria, 1977), 424-442; Leopoldo de la Rosa, *Evolución del régimen local en las islas Canarias* (Madrid: Instituto de Estudios de Administración Local, 1946); Silvo Zavala, "Las Conquistas de Canarias y Americas," *Tierra Firme*, 1(4):81-112 and 2(1):89-115 (1935-1936).

[2]José Peraza de Ayala, *Las ordenanzas de Tenerife* (Madrid: Aula de Cultura de Tenerife, 2nd ed., 1976); Leopoldo de la Rosa, Catálogo del Archivo Municipal de La Laguna (Sucesor del antiguo cabildo de Tenerife), *Revista de Historia* (Uni-

The model was in place and operative by the time there was need to organize the first Spanish government in the Antilles.

Possession of the Canary archipelago gave Spain the strategic key to the Atlantic world, ideally situated as a way station to the Indies. The 11,000-foot high peak of Tenerife (Pico de Teide) conveniently marked the route, serving as a reassuring reference point where caravels turned west to pick up the full force of the friendly trades. From the beginning the islands were an obligatory stop, "a great caravansary on the road to America" in Humboldt's words, where water, wood and supplies were obtainable and where rosters might be filled out and experienced pilots sought for the journey ahead.[3]

Effective colonization, with the accompanying mestization and eventual elimination of the native Guanches, had begun in 1402. The less populous peripheral islands of Lanzarote, Fuerteventura, Gomera and Hierro were awarded as donatories by the Crown, a projection of the medieval principles of governance that had evolved on the peninsula. Gran Canaria had been occupied in 1483, but Tenerife and La Palma were still *tierra brava* when Christopher Columbus stopped off at Gomera for repairs and provisions on the First Voyage.

It was from the Canaries that such tropical crops as sugar-cane, bananas and yams were introduced to the New World, along with a plantation system based on irrigation and slavery employing either Africans or Guanches. The technology of sugar-making, with its distinctive terminology, was transferred almost intact to the Antilles from Tenerife, La Palma and Gran Canaria, as it was to be

---

versidad de La Laguna), various issues, 1944-1960; *Acuerdos de Cabildo de Tenerife, Fontes Rerum Canarium IV*: 1497-1507, 1949; V:1508-1513, 1052; XI:1514-1518, 1956; XVI:1518-1525, 1970 (edited by Elias Serra Rafols and Leopoldo de la Rosa; La Laguna: Instituto de Estudios Canarias); Francisco Morales Padrón, *Ordenanzas del Consejo de Gran Canaria, 1531* (Sevilla: Cabildo Insular de Gran Canaria, 1974); *Libro Rojo de Gran Canaria* (edited by Pedro Cullén del Castillo; Las Palmas: Tipografía Alzola, 1947); and Leopoldo de la Rosa, *Evolución del régimen local....*, especially 76-90, 154-156.

[3]Alexander de Humboldt and Aimé Bonpland, *Personal Narrative of Travels to the Equinoctial Regions of the New Continent during the Years 1799-1804* (1818; reprinted ed., New York: AMS Press, 1966). The frigate on which Humboldt sailed to the Americas stopped at Tenerife for six days, providing for the great naturalist a good look at the island, including an ascent to the summit of Teide. He wrote to his brother of his enchantment with the island, even indicating that he would one day like to live there. Alejandro Cioranescu, *Alejandro de Humboldt en Tenerife* (Santa Cruz de Tenerife: Aula de Cultura, 1978)

somewhat later from Madeira and São Tomé to Brazil.[4] Slaves from the African mainland with experiences in the Canary sugar industry were especially prized in the West Indian markets. As late as 1615 a description of Canary Island sugar-making practices provided a guide to sugar mills then in operation in Mexico. The *colono* system that was to develop in Cuba traces its origins in part to the archipelago.

At the same time a constellation of culture traits, the rich residue of the rural folkways of fifteenth century Andalucia, with Portuguese and Genoese leavening, was passed on to the Americas from the islands, beginning with the earliest days. Most studied have been the peculiarities of *canario* language and speech, especially the provincialisms and archaic expressions that have their roots in the south of Spain and the Atlantic islands.[5] Distinctive Canario family names, toponyms, nautical terms and words for plants and agricultural activities are readily identifiable today in those areas of America that at times in the past have received substantial influxes of islanders. So, too, in matters relating to peasant dress, dancing, music, domestic architecture, popular medicine, cooking and dietary preference (especially for *gofio*, a finely ground corn meal eaten as a gruel), the Canario influence persists.[6] Among the most distinctive transfers has been that of the cult of the Virgin of Candelaria, *patrona* of the archipelago, who miraculously appeared out of the

---

[4]Noel Deerr, *The History of Sugar* (London: Chapman and Hall, 1949) 115-116. Sugar dominated the economy after 1520 and substantial fortunes were made in the business in only a few years. Deerr quotes Sir Francis Bacon on how "being the first in an invention does sometimes cause a wonderful overgrowth of riches, as it was with the first sugarmen in the Canaries." See also J. H. Galloway, "The Mediterannean Sugar Industry," *Geographical Review* 67 (1977), 177-194; Mervin Ratekin, "The Early Sugar Industry of Española," *Hispanic American Historical Review* 34 (1954), 1-19; Guillermo Camacho y Pérez Galdos, "El cultivo de caño de azúcar y la industria azucarero en Gran Canaria, 1510-1535," *Anuario de Estudios Atlánticos* 7 (1960), 11-60; Paulino Castañeda Delgado, "Pleitos sobre diezmos del azúcar en Santo Domingo y en Canarias," *Coloquio do Historia Canario-Americana* II (1977) (Las Palmas: Cabildo Insular, 1979), 2: 249-272; Fernando Ortiz, *Cuban Counterpoint: Tobacco and Sugar*; translated by Harriet Onis (New York: Knopf, 1947), especially 255, 275.

[5]Canario speech is not a dialect but rather a variant of that of Andalucia but with significant Portuguese influence. See Manuel Alvar, *Atlas lingüístico y etnográfico de las islas Canarias,* 3 vols. (Las Palmas: Cabildo Insular, 1975-1978).

[6]José Pérez Vidal, "Aportacion de Canarias a la población de América, su influencia en la lengua y en la poesía tradicional," *Anuario de Estudios Atlánticos* 1(1955), 91-197; Daniel Vidart and Renzo Pi Hugarte, "El llegado de los inmigrantes II," *Nuestra Tierra* (Montevideo) 39 (1969).

sea in the fifteenth century onto the rocky volcanic coast of Tenerife.[7] Wherever "Candelaria" appears in Latin America today, usually in the name of a plaza, cathedral, church or hermitage, there is reason to believe that settlers from the Canaries may have played a significant role in the establishment.

The almost unbroken current of migration from the archipelago to the New World from the time of Columbus, favored by proximity and favorable winds, has been further encouraged by the persistent rural poverty and high birth rates that have characterized the islands during most of the last four centuries. Inevitably the continuous procession of ships stopping off took on passengers as well as supplies, but because the traffic was controlled through the Casa de Contratacíon in Sevilla records of such boardings are generally lacking.[8] As many as half a million persons from the Canaries (the figure is a wild guess) may have passed to the Americas since Columbus set off into the unknown from gomera in 1492, reassured by talk of the legendary San Borondón and other lands that might lie to the west.

Initially many of those joining *la carrera a las Indias* would have been transplanted Andalusians who had participated in the conquest of the Canaries. Others, lacking the required documentation, came from the peninsula seeking clandestine passage to America. But island-born *criollos*, along with those of mixed Spanish-Guanche blood, soon dominated the migratory current. They were

---

[7]Fray Alonso de Espinosa, *Historia de Nuestra Señora de Candelaria* (1594; Santa Cruz de Tenerife: Goya Ediciones, 1952); English version, translated and edited by Sir Clements Markham, *The Guanches of Tenerife, the Holy Image of Our Lady of Candelaria, and the Spanish Conquest and Settlement* (London: The Hakluyt Society, 1907, series II, vol. 21).

[8]Pérez Vidal, "Aportacíon...." 10-14. The contribution of the Canary Islands to the early settlement of the New World has been vastly underestimated because of the tendency of scholars to accept the *Lista de Pasajeros a las Indias,* the authorized departures from Sevilla in the 16th century, as representative of the geographic origin of the participants in Spain's "Great Enterprise." Only a handful of Canarios are included among the many thousands thus inscribed, for those embarking from the islands were completely beyond the reach of the peninsular authorities. Thus Peter Boyd-Bowman, *Indice geo-biográfico de 40,000 pobladores españoles de América en el siglo XVI,* vol. 1, 1493-1519 (Bogotá: Instituto Caro y Cuervo, 1964), and vol. 2, 1520-1539 (México: Editorial Jus, 1968) list only 39 Canary Islanders as having departed for the New World for the period 1493-1539! Later periods show no significant increase. Boyd-Bowman, "Patterns of Spanish Emigration to the Indies, 1579-1600," *The Americas* 33 (1976), 78-95. Juan Friede, "The *Catálogo de pasajeros* and Spanish Emigration to America in 1550," *Hispanic American Historical Review* 31 (1951), 333-348, shows that less than one-third even of those embarking from Sevilla were recorded in the registry.

identified not as Spaniards but as *isleños*, a term still current in those parts of the Americas where they remain a conspicuous cultural force. There were Guanches, too, both free men and slaves, in the earliest trans-Atlantic movements, including the sailor who is celebrated for having captured a fleet Carib on the island of Guadeloupe after a footchase that drew the admiration of Columbus and his crew as recorded in the diary of the Second Voyage.

The archipelago has been a kind of cultural museum of late medieval Andalusian folkways, the "conquest culture" of George Foster,[9] but with its own distinctiveness and peculiarities. It remains so in more remote areas to the present. An important part of that culture has been the close identification with America, seen by the islanders since earliest times as a kind of El Dorado or "land of promise." The Indies have been part of the islanders' "living space" where friends and relatives were to be found. For the young "going to America to improve one's fortune" has been the norm, made easier by trade links and family ties.[10] Many who emigrated have returned after longer or shorter terms of residence in the New World, often bringing with them accumulated savings that have been invested in the archipelago. At every turn one encounters *indianos*, those who have been to America, in the Canaries of today, and virtually every *campesino* has relatives or friends "allá."[11]

The Canario contribution of the peopling of Spanish America appears especially disproportionate when considered in relation to the

---

[9]Foster, *Culture and Conquest: America's Spanish Heritage* (New York: Wenner-Gren Foundation, Viking Fund Publications in Anthropology 27, 1960).

[10]Analola Borges, "Aproximación al estudio de la emigracíon canaria a America en el siglo XVI," *Anuario de Estudios Atlánticos* 23 (1977), 239-262; Borges, *El archipelago Canario y las Indias Occidentales* (Madrid: Editorial Cultura Hispánica, 1969).

[11]There is considerable literature on the Canario migration, but it is written almost exclusively from an island vantage point and from island sources--the archives and libraries of La Laguna and Las Palmas--and published in local journals of restricted circulation or, more recently, in the proceedings of a series of colloquia on Canario-American relations sponsored by the Casa de Colón of Las Palmas and the Cabildo Insular of Gran Canaria. The prime mover in these, and the most influential contributor to the literature, has been Francisco Morales Padrón, professor of American history at the Universidad de Sevilla and himself an islander. E.g., "Colonos Canarios en Indias," *Anuario de Estudios Americanos,* 8 (1951), 399-441; *El comercio canario-americano, siglos XVI, XVII y XVIII* (Sevilla: Escuela de Estudios Hispano-Americanos, 1955); *Sevilla, Canarias y América* (Las Palmas: Cabildo Insular, 1970); "Las Canarias y la política emigratoria a Indias," *Coloquia de Historia Canario-Americana* I (1976), 210-293. The fifth of these colloquia was held in Las Palmas in October 1982.

population of the archipelago. The islands accounted for only one half of one percent of the population of Spain in the sixteenth century (pop. in 158 of 738,700) compared to nearly four percent of the population of contemporary Spain, of which the archipelago, comprising the provinces of Santa Cruz de Tenerife and Las Palmas, is an integral part. But they were long considered as a separate entity, almost as much a part of America as of Europe. Some early chroniclers referred to them as *las Canarias indianas.* Simón Bolivar, in his famous manifesto to the people of Venezuela in 1813, addressed his audience as *"peninsulares y canarios."* An independent Canary Islands may have been a part of the Liberator's grand design for a family of Latin American republics.[12]

This continuing migratory flow from the Canaries to America, the subject of this paper, has not been random. It has been geographically focused (Fig. 28.1), at first by government design and later as a result of geopolitical considerations, the networks of families and friends, and the hospitality that these offered to new arrivals. The Canario implantations have been primarily in the Greater Antilles and in Venezuela, with a secondary and later concentration in the Plata estuary lands, especially in Uruguay where the capital city was founded by Canario colonists.[13] Isleños have tended to be sparsely represented in Mexico, Central America, Colombia and the west coast of South America.[14] A review of the literature suggests that these areas, constituting some two-thirds of the population of Spanish America today, may not have received more than three or four percent of the total Canario migration to the New World.

Poor countryfolk, illiterate peasants, have numerically dominated the Canario migrations from the beginning, although merchants, bureaucrats and adventurers have also been represented. Many gained their passage in the past by signing on as militiamen or sailors. The islanders, widely reputed as reliable, hard-working

---

[12]This is suggested by Eduardo Barrenechea, *Objectivo: Canarias* (Barcelona: Dopesa, 1978).

[13]In Brazil a native of Tenerife, Father José de Anchieta, was one of several priests and brothers who established the primitive Jesuit mission in 1554 at what was to become the city of São Paula. Anchieta, to gain fame as the "Apostle to the Indians," has been proposed for canonization. Several Spanish sources credit him with being the founder of São Paulo. E.g., Borges, El archipelago Canario..., 20-27.

[14]But see Guillermo Lohmann Villena, "Notas para un estudio sobre recuerdos canarios en el Perú," *Coloquio de Historia Canario-Americana II* (1977), I., 165-189.

Figure 28.1 Map of 18th and 19th Century Isleño Migration

folk and ideal colonists, were often recruited to settle frontier areas where their presence might serve as a "human barrier" against the threat of Dutch, French, English and finally United States interests. In Texas, as in the Venezuelan Guyana and perhaps on the Miskito Coast, they were assigned a support role to programs of missionization of native peoples.

The Sixteenth Century Expeditions

The Canary Islanders' participation in Spain's "Great Adventure" was most widely dispersed during the first year of the Conquest. There was scarcely an expedition that did not stop at the Canaries and almost all took on sailors and soldiers to flesh out their forces, with artisans, sugar technicians, priests and families of colonists often filling any leftover space. Virtually all of the "great captains" had Canarios at their side according to the chronicler Juan de Castellanos.[15] To him they were valiant fighters, reliable and experienced guides (*baquianos*), "buenos isleños." Between 1492-1506 at least twelve major expeditions stopped off either at Gomera (the favored base in those years) or Santa Cruz de Tenerife en route to the New World to fill out their complement with islanders searching for something better or at least for something new.[16] Among them were to be found many of the major names of the Conquest: Columbus, Ojeda, Vespucci, Pedrarias, La Cosa, Yañez, Ovando. Many who went remained in America or lost their lives there but others returned, caught up in the web of coming and going across the Atlantic. Most had left home illegally, or at least without record. Sevilla had no effective means of controlling the movement. A royal order of 1511 simply dictated that those departing should sign on with the ship's captain.[17] Direct trade between the Canaries and the Indies had been authorized in 1509 so that ships might be fitted out on the islands as well as at peninsular ports.

---

[15]Pérez Vidal, "Aportación...," 128-129.

[16]Analola Borges, "Notas para un estudio sobre la proyección de Canarios en la Conquistade América, "*Anuario de Estudios Atlánticos* 20 (1975), 145-265, details the participation of Canarios in the Conquest and town-founding in the New World.

[17]Apparently the isleños had a considerable reputation for their boisterous ways. A *visitador* advised in 1547 that they should be permitted to depart only with special authorization.

With the new and tantalizing opportunities in Mexico and Peru usurped in good measure by *peninsulares*, Canarios continued to be an important component of most of the expeditions of exploration and conquest directed elsewhere. Pedro de Mendoza, en route to the La Plata estuary and the first founding of Buenos Aires, took on three companies of soldiers at Tenerife in 1535; the next year Pedro de Lugo, son of the first *adelantado* of that island, led an expedition of 1,500 men, half of them isleños, to New Granada. Reinforced by others, they played a significant role in the *entrada* of Jiménez de Quesada up the Magdalena river and to the *sabana* of Bogotá. Pedro de Heredia in the Sinú, Diego de Ordáz at París, Jorge Spiva at Coro, Francisco de Montejo in Yucatán and Hernán de Soto in Florida (financed in part by the Count of Gomera) all filled out their companies in the islands, sometimes clandestinely. Analola Borges has documented more than 10,000 islanders as having crossed over in the course of the sixteenth century, including no small number from the upper echelons of society.[18]

The first reference to organized settlement by Canarios seems to be from 1533, when Pedro de Bolaños was authorized to establish a *villa* at Monte Cristi in the *espoblado* of the dry northwest coast of Hispaniola with a company of 70 *labradores* from both the peninsula and the Canaries.[19] The fate of this foundation is in doubt for in 1545 another agreement, recorded in Madrid between the Crown and one Francisco de Mesa, a Canario, again called for the founding of a settlement at Monte Cristi, this time with "30 Canario families." As governor of the new settlement de Mesa was to be granted authority to appoint officials and to distribute land. Should additional persons, especially Portuguese residents in the Canaries, choose to participate they were to be encouraged, but for all land titles would only be confirmed after eight years of residence.

There were other early mentions of families of Canario settlers (*familias pobladores*). In 1534 officials of the island of La Palma petitioned the Crown that the many residents of Portugal and Castile who were "desirous of going to live in the Indies" should be

---

[18]Borges, "Aproximación....," 261.

[19]Santo Domingo en los manuscritos de Juan Bautista Muñoz (Santo Domingo: Fundación "García Arévalo," 1980), 1, 366 *Colección de documentos inéditos relativos al descurbrimiento, conquista y organización de las antiguas posesiones españoles...*, 1st ser., 23 (Madrid 1875), 110-117; 2d ser., 17 (Madrid 1925), 289; *Péréz Vidal, "Aportacíon...,"* 112. An inscription in a park in the modern pueblo of Montecristi reads "Montecristi fue fundado el 30 de Mayo del año 1533 por Juan de Bolaños y 60 familias procedentes de las islas Canarias."

granted licenses to embark and to receive grants of land on arrival.[20] Three years later a royal cedula ordered that no impediments should be placed in the way of any potential Canario colonists who might be desirous of crossing over to the Antilles. This was repeated in 1555, but freedom to emigrate was coupled with a minimum residence requirement. It was especially the northern part of Hispaniola, left open to incursions by French and Dutch buccaneers as a result of the mass flight of Spaniards to Peru and Mexico, to which these early settlers were directed.

Colonization and Trade

The en masse migration of families of colonists, chiefly to the Greater Antilles, came in the second half of the century. It required a relaxation of the barriers to direct trade between the Canaries and the Indies, with the consequent loosening of Sevilla's dominance of the traffic.[21]

Sufficient numbers went that it was feared that the Canaries would be left depopulated and defenseless against "the Lutheran and other enemies."[22] A 1574 decree, later reaffirmed, that no one could go from the Canaries to remain permanently in America seems to have been ineffective. Pierre Chaunu's data suggests that as many as twenty vessels a year passed from the Canaries to the Indies between 1550-1627.[23] Canary-based merchant vessels, sailing independently of the fleet and often without authorization, were much appreciated, especially in the Antilles, for the lower priced wine and contraband merchandise that they brought. Restrictive measures later forced them to join the flotilla from the peninsula as it passed the islands and to return via Sevilla after an obligatory stop at Havana.

---

[20]Morales Padrón, "Las Canarias y la politíca emigratoria," 212.

[21]Pierre Chaunu, *Seville et l'Atlantique, (1404-1650)*, tome VIII (1), *Les estructures géographiques* (Paris: S.E.V.P.E.N., 1959), 377-441.

[22]Morales Padrón, Colonos Canarios en las Indias," 406.

[23]Chaunu, *Seville et l'Atlantique,* VIII (1), 388-391. He terms the data on the Canaries traffic, along with that of the slave trade, "the weakest point in our statistical elaboration." Their strategic location made the islands a favorite base for contraband trade and as such they were a continuous source of annoyance to Spanish authorities. Prohibitions or restrictions on Canarias traffic, designed to protect Seville interests, were generally shortlived and ineffective.

From the beginning ties were exceptionally close between the Canaries and Santo Domingo, both through trade and by blood. A small Canario merchant colony prospered there and Santo Domingo copper coins circulated widely in the archipelago, where money always was in short supply. In some years nearly as much of the westbound traffic emanated from the island of La Palma as from Tenerife. The Venezuelan ports were served in this period largely from Santo Domingo although occasional vessels went there directly from the Canaries.[24]

There were also Canarios in numbers in Puerto Rico from an early date. The island's governor between 1464-1568 was an isleño. As sugar replaced gold as the foundation of the Puerto Rican economy the call went out in 1569 for Gran Canario sugar-masters to man the island's *ingenios*. It was specified that they must agree to remain at least six years.[25] The Atlantic crossing increasingly became a commonplace among the islanders, especially the younger men with families. As the drain continued there were periodic decrees seeking to restrict emigration from the islands but they seem to have had little effect.

Havana replaced Santo Domingo as the principal destination of shipping to the Antilles in the latter part of the sixteenth century. The inability of the Sevilla monopoly to supply the Caribbean islands obliged the Casa de Contratación to open trade from the Canaries, though on a limited basis. The traffic in wine was particularly active. *Vino de las islas* is frequently mentioned in the documents but seldom that from Castille.[26] Canario wine merchants established in Havana were the founders of some of Cuba's leading families.[27] There were also a few agriculturalists and wage laborers among the arrivals. In 1611 the administrator of the copper mines at Santiago del Prado suggested that 50 *familias canarias* be sent at Crown expense to grow food for the slaves working there. When

---

[24]Eduardo Arcila Farías, *Economía colonial de Venezuela* (México: Fondo de Cultura Ecónomica, 1946), 64.

[25]Morales Padrón, *Sevilla, Canarias y América,* 326.

[26]Levi Marrero, *Cuba: economía y sociedad* (Madrid: Editorial Playor, 1974-1978), II:184-185. This extraordinary study, when completed, will total 14 volumes and carry Cuban economic history through to the arrival of the socialist society in 1960.

[27]*Ibid.,* IV:97. One of these was the Diaz Pimienta family. Francisco Diaz Pimienta, born to Canario parents in Havana in 1596, became supreme commander of the Royal Navy.

the mines were finally exhausted, he noted, there would be an established population to develop the sugar and tobacco production as well as to help defend the nearby *villa* of Santiago de Cuba.[28] Authorization was granted, but for only 20 families.

Levi Marrero, whose monumental work on the evolution of the Cuban economy and society is opening so many doors, infers that the number of Canarios who passed to Cuba in the first eight decades of the seventeenth century was "proportionately very high." Concrete data, however, is largely lacking.[29] The cabildo of Santiago made special reference to the "surplus" population of the archipelago (*de las muchas que sobran en las islas*) in justifying their requests for Canario settlers.[30] Expansion of the tobacco production was of special concern to the authorities and Canarios were sought specifically for this activity, from the beginning largely a preserve of white colonos.

The Antillean Settlements

The new migrations were "family" oriented, with substantial Crown subsidies to those who volunteered. A royal cedula issued in 1681 was to be a landmark in Canario-American relations. It directed that ship owners departing from the Canaries for the Indies take five families of emigrants for each 100 tons of cargo carried.[31] There were normally to be five persons in each family and there was an exemption from customs duties (*alcabalas*) for ten years. This "tribute in blood" was modified in 1697 to apply only to Santo Domingo-bound traffic. Following the hiatus caused by the War of the Spanish Succession (1702-1718) it was reaffirmed.[32]

The first families had arrived in Santo Domingo in 1684 with the expectation that they would not only help reinforce Spain's geo-

---

[28] *Ibid.*, III:18, 263, 270.

[29] *Ibid.*, III:18-19.

[30] E.G., in 1659 Jamaica sent a representative to Madrid to request colonos *de trabajo y provecho como lo esde las Canarias.* Pérez Vidal, "Aportación..." 115.

[31] Morales Padrón, *El Comercio Canario-Americano,* 195-196; Pérez Vidal, "Aportación...", 117-118.

[32] A Royal Order of 1718 allocated the Canaries 1,000 tons of cargo annually to certain American ports: Havana 300, Campeche 300, Caracas 200, Cumaná, Trinidad, Puerto Rico and Santo Domingo 50 each. There was included an obligation to deliver 50 families of five annually to Santo Domingo.

political claims but also promote tobacco cultivation.[33] There seems to have been little difficulty in finding recruits among the illiterate peasantry although there were occasional complaints about "worthless vagabonds and wastrels" among those signed on. In the first sixteen years some 386 Canario families were established on the island, mostly in the interior and the north coast. The settlement of San Carlos, founded in this era in what eventually was to become a suburb of the capital city, was to remain identifiable as a Canario community, whiter than the norm, until at least the end of the last century.[34]

Compliance with the 1697 order was slow in forthcoming, in part because of intervening wars. For a time Puerto Rico was a principal recipient of colonists.[35] But between 1735 and 1739 some 439 persons disembarked at Santo Domingo under this program.[36] Free passage was to be offered as well as substantial subsidies in the form of seeds, livestock, tools, food, housing, and an initial small cash advance. The island government complained of the financial burden and in 1741 the Crown ordered that the Viceroy of Mexico should henceforth remit to the officials on Santo Domingo 16,000 pesos annually to cover these costs.[37] War again intervened, but in all but two years between 1749 and 1764 at least one ship a year carried Canario immigrants to Santo Domingo, although never

---

[33]Frank Moya Pons, *Historia coloial de Santo Domingo* (Santiago: Universidad Católica 'Madre y Maestra,' 1974), 217 ff.

[34]H. Hoetink, *The Dominican people, 1850-1900* (Baltimore and London: Johns Hopkins University Press, 1982), 26-27. Some of the original residents of San Carlos early moved to Cuba. José Peraza de Ayala, *El régimen comercial de Canarias....*89n.

[35]Peasants were not the only ones involved in this migration. Thus, in 1729 the cabildo of Tenerife proposed that "persons of nobility or distinction" among settlers in America should be awarded twice the amount of land given to others. *Ibid.,* 135.

[36]Francisco Marales Padrón, "El desplazaminento a las Indias desde Canarias," *Revista Museo Canario* 30-35 (1950), 1-25, lists departures of emirant ships between 1720 and 1764. In addition to those persons going to Santo Domingo in this period others went to Puerto Rico (786), Florida (707), Venezuela (439), Texas (162), Campeche and Bacalar (149), Montevideo (97) and Trinidad (13). For another 100 persons no destination is indicated. Apparently all were subsidized by the Crown, but at various levels.

[37]Maria Rosario Sevilla Soler, *Santo Domingo: tierra de frontera (1750-1800)*, (Sevilla: Escuela de Estudios Hispano-Americano, 1980), 52.

in the numbers called for by the Crown. In that period a total of some 1,640 persons (323 families) departed from the archipelago as against the 4,000 called for under the annual quota. In the latter year Mexico ceased underwriting the expenses of the colonists, arguing that the funds involved had been much in excess of the amount needed to support the modest number of immigrants. Santo Domingo officials immediately asked the Council of Indies to cease the recruitment of Canario colonists, the island itself being unable to finance the project. Moreover, the need was no longer urgent.

Although the Canario immigration never reached the goal set, it nevertheless led to the founding of seven new towns on sparsely settled Santo Domingo and the reestablishment of three others (Puerto Plata 1736, Monte Cristi 1751, and San Juan de la Maguana 1757) that had been abandoned in the previous century.[38]

Puerto Rico, too, sought settlers. Especially in the late years of the seventeenth century there were several pleas from the island's authorities for colonists "from the Canaries or elsewhere," but few ships sailed directly from the archipelago to San Juan. In 1695 twenty families from Tenerife were at Hato Sabana Larga near Río Piedras. There undoubtedly were other isleño colonies. Direct traffic from the Canaries to Puerto Rico was periodically authorized, then denied. Already in 1731 there was a fiesta of Candelaria in San Juan. More than half of the twenty-eight town foundations on the island prior to 1800, mostly on the north and west coasts, have been attributed to Canarios, suggesting an active movement.[39] Between 1720-28 six shiploads of families are recorded as having embarked for San Juan but there is little later documentation.[40] Immigrants were dropped off from vessels en route to Santo Domingo or Havana, sometimes without authority. On at least two dif-

---

[38]*Ibid.*, 57-63; Moya y Pons, *Historia colonial...*, 286-290. These places survive today as significant regional trade centers (e.g., San Juan de La Maguana, Neiba, Dajabón, Samaná, Sabana la Mar, Bani). Bani, in the southern part of the country, founded in 1764, had such a perdominance of isleños that it could be called by Eugenio María de Hostos "the Dominican Canaria, maintaining the purest lineage to the point that until only a few years ago there were scarcely any colored people there...a veritable ethnological parenthesis." Quoted in Hoetink, The Dominican people..., 27. Even today its people have a special reputation as superior businessmen. The city has produced an unusual number of politicians and intellectuals. Earlier Canaria establishments included Banica and Hinche.

[39]Manuel Alvarez Nazaro, *La herencia Lingüística de Canarias en Puerto Rico* (San Juan: Instituto de Cultura Puertoriqueña, 1972), 47.

[40]Morales Padrón, "El Desplazamiento...," 18.

ferent occasions Canarios who jumped ship off Aguadas on the northwest coast encountered isleños already established where they went ashore. An 1803 cédula forbid natives of the Canaries to disembark in Puerto Rico without a passport and ordered those already there to apply for one.

Cuba was a continuing attraction to emigrants and island authorities actively sought Canarios, in part as a leaven to the rapidly increasing number of African slaves. Twenty isleño families are recorded as having gone to Cuba under the "obligatory" quotas in the 1680s and there were probably others.[41] By 1693 more than 800 families of Canarios are said to have been settled on the *estancias* and *haciendas* around Havana. In that year a group of 37 families from the archipelago had founded the city of Matanzas on an ample bay on the north coast, the first planned urban nucleus in Cuba established in accordance with the *ordenanzas de población* of Felipe II (1573).[42] In addition to free passage and exemption from taxes each family had received a cash subsidy of 50 pesos. Town lots and land for cultivation (*estancias*) were distributed by public drawing (*sorteo*). Soldiers at the garrison were to assist the colonists whenever their other duties permitted.

Cuban immigration throughout the eighteenth century, except for slaves, seems to have been largely of Canario origin. Tobacco cultivation on the red clay soils close to Havana attracted many of the migrants, "*veguero*" and "isleño" becoming interchangeable terms.[43] It is impossible to put numbers on this migration but it left a strong imprint on the colony. The isleños were generally considered to be superior agriculturists. In 1738, for example, the governor proposed that another 80-100 *familias canarias* be brought in to grow food to support the rehabilitation of the Santiago del Prado copper mine. One Canario nucleus, at Sacalohondo (later Wajay), was founded by *colonos* who ostensibly were en route to San Bernardo (Espíritu Santo Bay), Texas. They had been ordered

---

[41]Pérez Vidal, "Aportación...", 27.

[42]Marrera, *Cuba...*, *III*: 73-74. More than one-third of all registered vessels departing from the Canaries for America during the seventeenth century listed Havana as their destination. *Angel López Cantos, "El tráfico comercial entre Canarias y América durante el siglo XVII," Coloquio de Historia Canaro-Americana II, I:*303-372, reference 313.

[43]Marrero, *Cuba...*, VI:6-7.

not to proceed further by the Viceroy of New Spain during the group's stop in Havana.[44]

Florida, Texas and Louisiana

On the adjacent North American mainland both the English and French threats loomed menacingly. In 1681 the Spanish governor of Florida had suggested that Canarios, specifically, might be brought in as colonists to support the garrison there.[45] Nothing seems to have come of this proposal. But the conditions under which the Havana Company (*Real Compañía de Comercio de Habana*) was set up in 1740 included an obligation to establish fifty Canario families annually for ten years at St. Augustine, outfitting them with the necessary supplies and equipment.[46] War intervened and the period was extended but finally in the last years before the British accession of Florida in 1763 there was a flurry of colonizing activity. Eight ships carrying 707 passengers are documented as having departed from Tenerife for Florida between 1757-1761.[47] But at the time of the evacuation of St. Augustine in 1763 only 246

---

[44]Of vessels out of the Canaries in the Indies trade, 1708-1776, 87 out of 208 were destined to Havana with most of the rest going either to Venezuela (62) or Campeche (52). Javier Ortiz de la Tabla y Ducasse, "Comercio colonial canario, siglo XVIII: nuevo índice para su cuantificación, la contabilidad del Colegio de San Telm, 1708-1776" *Coloquio de Historia Canario-Americana II*, II:7-17. In contrast none of the passenger-carrying vessels on the 1718-1765 list (Morales Padrón, "El desplazamiento..." 18-22) were bound for Cuba, presumably because immigration to that island was not under a mandatory quota.

[45]Kathryn Abbey Hanna, *Florida: Land of Change* (Chapel Hill: University of North Carolina Press, 1948), 60. It was proposed that the colonists be brought first to Havana to learn something of cotton and indigo cultivation, then transferred to Apalache (Florida).

[46]Morales Padrón, "El desplazamiento...," 15-17.

[47]*Ibid.*, 21. Better than five percent of the 1,101 males whose names were recorded in the marriage records of St. Augustine parish, 1658-1756, were listed as natives of the Canary Islands. There were 27 in the 1692-1732 period, 15 from 1733-1756. Theodore G. Corbett, "Migration to a Spanish Imperial Frontier: St. Augustine," *Hispanic American Historical Review* 54 (1974), 414-430. I have found no other evidence of Canarios in Florida prior to 1756.

Canarios, including 49 men and 56 women, were present in the colony.[48]

When the Spaniards returned to Florida twenty years later (1783-1821) another and much smaller group of isleño colonists was recruited to bolster the St. Augustine garrison and to provide it with provisions. These came by way of Pensacola in West Florida perhaps remnants of the earlier settlement. But the governor was not pleased, describing them one year after their arrival as "shiftless vagabonds" who were "a useless charge on the Royal Treasury."[49]

Spain, in compensation for the loss of Florida under the Treaty of 1763, had acquired New Orleans and all of Louisiana west of the Mississippi River from France, but it was not until the United States' Declaration of Independence thirteen years later that the Spanish Crown moved to establish colonists there. Again it was the Canarios to whom it turned, the settlers coming through Havana, the transfer and organizing point for the colonizing expeditions. The goal was set at 700 isleño recruits and their families, the men to be between the ages of 17 and 36 years of age. It was a period of depression in the islands, the wine trade having fallen on hard times, and enlistments were heavily oversubscribed. Due to fiscal difficulties the plans to employ the newly arrived Canarios in the military were scrapped and they were assigned instead to agricultural colonies south, west and north of New Orleans. Free passage, land, shelter, tools, food for the first year and a small cash subsidy were supplied by the Crown. Between 1779-1783 from 1,700 to 2,000 Canary Islanders as well as other Spaniards from the peninsula were established in Louisiana. Family groups predominated. Of the Canario adults 54 percent were male, 46 percent female, with the majority coming from Tenerife.[50]

The largest colony was established on Bayou Terre aux Boefs in what is now St. Bernard Parish, a few miles southeast of New Orleans. Its population was early augmented by others driven by

---

[48]Pablo Ternero Tinajero, "Emigración canaria a América: la expedición cívico-militar a Luisiana de 1777-1779," *Coloquio de Historia Canario-Americana I*, 345-354.

[49]Joseph B.Lockey, "The St. Augustine Census of 1786," *Florida Historical Society Quarterly* 26 (1945), 325-344.

[50]Antonio Acosta Rodríguez, *La población de Luisiana expañola, 1763-1803* (Madrid: Ministerio de Asuntos Exteriores, 1979), 145. Those departing for Florida numbered 2,373 (Ternero Tinajero, "Emigración canaria...") but some perished en route and othes defected in Cuba. Disease further reduced their numbers once established in Louisiana.

406

floods from another settlement at Barataria some 20 miles to the west and across the Mississippi. Other colonies were established at Valenzuela (near modern Donaldsonville, Ascension Parish), on Bayou la Fourche (264 persons), and at Galveztown on Bayou Manchac south of Baton Rouge (404 persons, of whom almost half perished from malaria and smallpox within the first year).[51] From 1783 until the termination of Spanish rule in 1800 there seems to have been no further augmentation of the Canario presence in the prosperous Louisiana colony, perhaps a reaction to complaints from the archipelago on the debilitating effect of the high emigration rate on the islands' economy. In one five-year period the Louisiana migration had taken two percent of the population of Tenerife and Gran Canaria.[52]

In 1818, 300 of the isleño families in Louisiana were evacuated to Nuevitas, Cuba, but others remained behind. Their descendants retain their cultural identity to the present. Canario Spanish, still spoken almost within sight of downtown New Orleans, has been the subject of considerable scholarly study.[53] It is still the common speech of the towns of Delacroix, Reggio and Ycloskey and also persists in Shell Beach. The majority of the residents are perfectly bi-lingual in Spanish and English. A few also speak Louisiana French. The men trap muskrats during the winter and fish in the summer months.

A half century before the Louisiana emplacement another group of Canarios had been recruited to provide support to the frontier garrison at what was to become the city of San Antonio in Texas.[54] Orders had gone out in 1723 and again in 1729 for the

---

[51]Acosta Rodríguez, *La población...*, 140-145; Charles Gayarré, *History of Louisiana* (3 vols.; New York: W. J. Middleton, 1866), vol. 3, "The Spanish Domination."

[52]Terneroo Tinajero, "Emigración canaria...," 353.

[53]E.G., Raymond MacCurdy, *The Spanish Dialect in St. Bernard Parish, Louisiana* (Albuquerque: University of New Mexico Publications in Language and Literature No. 6, 1950); "Spanish Folklore from St. Bernard Parish, Louisiana," *Southern Folklore Quarterly*, 13 (1940), 180-191.

[54]In proposing the settlement the Marques de Aguayo had written the King that "one permanent family would do more to hold the province than 100 soldiers." He urged the sending of 200 Canarios and another 200 Tlaxcalans, who had been successful settlers in Saltillo and Parras on the northern frontier of New Spain. Charles Ramsdell, *San Antonio: a Historical and Pictorial Guide* (Austin: University of Texas Press, 1976).

settlement of certain localities in that province in the face of growing concerns about French encroachment. In 1730, after a number of plans had aborted, a small company of 56 men, women and children (15 families) set sail from Tenerife for Vera Cruz, from where they were to move overland to the presidio of San Antonio de Bexar. Arriving on March 9, 1731, they immediately set up a civilian government following the Crown's instructions, the first such in Texas. Although they were soon outnumbered by other arrivals from Mexico and the United States, by terms of their charter cabildo offices all went to Canarios, who had life-time appointments as *regidores*[55].

The founding Canarios left a significant mark on the land and society of Texas. This has been traced in unusual detail by Thomas Glick in his study of the irrigation system of San Antonio with its distinctive arrangements of water rights and water distributions as well as water-related terminology.[56] Municipal control of water, public sale of irrigation "turns" (*dulas*) and the setting aside (*secuestro*) of the proceeds from every fifth turn to meet expenses of the system, were essential elements of the operating procedure. These and other idiosyncratic institutions set the Canary Islands irrigation usage apart even today from antecedent ones on the peninsula.[57]

The mainland of Mexico and Central America were but lightly touched by Canario migrations. In 1681 28 families from the islands along with a detachment of soldiers were established at Cam-

---

[55]The seven missions along the San Antonio river hemmed in the Canario settlers and there were numerous law suits over land titles, water rights and grazing privileges. In 1745 a viceregal auditor reported that "the 14 families of Canary Islanders complain against the reverend fathers of the missions, against the Indians that reside therein, against the captain of the presidio and against the other 49 families settled there so that it seems they desire to be left alone in undisputed possession. Perhaps even then they may not find enough room in the vast area of the province." *Ibid.*; see also Samuel M. Buck, *Yanaguana's Successors: the Story of the Canary Islanders' Immigration into Texas in the 18th Century* (San Antonia: Naylor, 1949.

[56]Thomas Glick, *The Old World Background of the Irrigation System of San Antonio, Texas* (El Paso: Texas Western Press, 1972), Southwestern Studies monograph 35.

[57]Although there seem to have been no later additions to the colony, Canario family names still survive in San Antonio and there is an active Canary Island Descendants Association, recently split by a factional dispute. "Solution Eyed to End Canary Islander Feud," *San Antonio Express,* May 9, 1982. Las Palmas de Gran Canaria and San Antonio are "Sister Cities."

peche.[58] Nearly 50 years later the governor requested more of them. Between 1733-1735 a contingent of 149 islanders set sail for Villa de Bacalar on the lower Yucatan peninsula, probably to better establish Spanish claims against the British to this logwood and mahogany coast.[59] One presumes that there must have been other Canario groups established in Campeche, especially, in the seventeenth and eighteenth century, for that port followed after only Havana and the Venezuela coast as the preferred destination of registered vessels departing for the Indies from the Canaries.

Towards the end of the century, in 1789, a group of 306 Canary Islanders were established at Trujillo and Black River on the Miskito Coast of Honduras along with other settlers from Galacia and Asturias. The Canarios comprised the principal Spanish element in that area when the Black Caribs and refugee negroes from Hispaniola arrived in the 1790s. Some, at least, were still in Trujillo in 1803. Soon after they were overrun and ousted by sambos and Miskito Indians responding to British encouragement.[60]

Canarios in Colonial Venezuela

The largest numbers of Canarios going to the mainland of the New World were to establish themselves on the coast of Venezuela and, later, the La Plata estuary on the east coast of South America.

The coast of Venezuela, usually the first *tierra firme* landfall for sailing vessels from the Canary Islands, had early attracted the attention of Spaniards for its pearls, dyewoods, salt and the numerous Indian populations. The last were always in demand in the Antillean slave markets. This northern shoulder of South America was a natural landfall for vessels crossing from the Canaries and there had been a disproportionate number of isleños involved in the early conquest and exploration of the area. More than elsewhere, they seem to have become active in public life and commerce, as well as in the slave traffic and in the profitable cacao business.[61]

---

[58]Morales Padrón, "El desplazamiento...," 7.

[59]*Ibid.,* 20; Peter Gerhard, *The Southeast Frontier of New Spain* (Princeton: Princeton University Press, 1979), 73.

[60]Troy S. Floyd, *The Anglo-Spanish Struggle for Mosquitia* (Albuquerque: University of New Mexico Press, 1967), 168-171.

[61]Robert J. Ferry, "Encomienda, African Slavery and Agriculture in Seventeenth Century Caracas," *Hispanic American Historical Review* 61 (1981), 609-635.

Such surnames as Ponte, Betancour, Perdomo and Melián are still recognizable today in Venezuela as distinctively Canario.

Alejandro Blanco Ponte, for example, was a wealthy cacao grower, a Canary Islander who had left Tenerife sometime after 1627, the year when the *Casa de la Contratación* formally prohibited direct trade between the Canaries and the Indies.[62] With his brother, who had been in Caracas since at least 1619, he participated directly in the African slave trade. As buyers their credit was respected from Lisbon to Luanda to Cartagena. Like many other successful merchants Alejandro had married well. Soon after his marriage he obtained an encomienda on the basis of the station and merits of his Caracas-born wife's family. It was the access to large numbers of African slaves that assured them of a continuing return on their investment in cacao production for the export market.

In Venezuela, too, Canarios were considered to be highly desirable immigrants. In 1686 the governor specifically requested that 30 families be sent from the islands for Cumaná. Four years later the Council of the Indies was inquiring of Tenerife whether an additional 200 families might be available for that place.[63] Although the conditions proposed were unacceptable the island officials observed that such emigration, far from being prejudicial to the archipelago, "would bring relief to large numbers of poor."[64]

A study of marriages recorded in the Caracas cathedral shows a sharp increase in the number of Canary-born participants in the late seventeenth century. Between 1684-1750 a total of 713 men and women registered in the Book of Matrimony were natives of the Canaries. This was nearly 17 percent of all those inscribed and a full 70 percent of those born outside Venezuela.

---

[62]*Ibid.*, 619.

[63]One official noted in 1720 that bringing families from the Canaries to Venezuela as colonists had been "a superb idea in principal but in practice of little benefit because they have not been allocated good land or enough of it but rather the worst...their misery eventually forcing them into other activities, often the contraband trade." He urged that knowledgeable persons be named to select land for such settlements and that advice be given on the best crops to grow and the market for them. Arcila Farías, Economía colonia..., 172.

[64]Leopoldo de la Rosa, "La emigración a Venezuelaen los siglos XVII y XVIII," *Anuario de Estudios Atlánticos* 22 (1976) 617-631, reference p. 626.

Nearly three times as many of the latter were from the islands as were from peninsular Spain.[65]

Venezuela's ties with the Canaries were closer than with the peninsula through the seventeenth and eighteenth centuries. As much as half of the white population of the colony was described as being Canarios or descendants of Canarios, an impressive contribution from so small a population pool as the archipelago represented. They were widely dispersed, although San Carlos de Austria on the llanos margins and the *partido* of Panaquire in the Río Tuy valley southeast of Caracas had special reputations as Canario centers of settlement. They were conspicuous as merchants, as churchmen and in government, three isleños having served as governors of the province between 1698-1721.[66] The revolt against the monopoly Caracas Company (*Compañía Guipuzcoana de Caracas*) in 1749 was headed by the well-to-do Canario, Juan Francisco de León. It seems to have been in part a protest against the displacement of islanders from key government posts by Basques, in part against the company's hindrance of the contraband trade, in which many isleños were active.[67] In a report to the Crown by Jacobo Bervegal,[68] sent in 1749 to investigate the controversy, he said:

> [Isleños are] not only those born in the Canaries who have moved to Caracas, but also the sons, grandsons, and later generations of people who arrived many years ago...Their number is impossible to even roughly estimate. I understand that there may be some thousand families, but in this figure I may be greatly in error. Very few of them have

---

[65]*Ibid.*, 623-624. Until 1751 the Cathedral held the only records of marriage for Caracas. Thereafter other parishes, probably in modest *barrios*, drew off many couples with a consequent sharp decline in the percentage of Canarios. Of the Canary Islanders identified in the Book of Matrimony during the 65-year period referred to better than 80 percent were from the island of Tenerife.

[66]Analola Borges, "Presencia de 'Isleños' en el cargo de Gobernador y Capitán General de Venezuela, 1699-1721," *Anuario de Estudios Atlánticos* 7 (1961), 215-237.

[67]Donald D. Hussey, *The Caracas Company, 1728-1784: a Study in the History of Spanish Monopolistic Trade* (Cambridge: Harvard University Press, 1934), especially 122 ff. In the same year as the revolt against the Caracas Company a 20-year monopoly privilege for settling and trading with the island of Trinidad had been proposed unsuccessfully by a Tenerife group. Peraza de Ayala, *El régimen comercial...*, 165.

[68]Quoted in Hussey, *The Caracas Company...*, 120-121.

connection or kinship with those of the country since they are accustomed to marry among themselves...Among them there might be some 150 vagabonds at present. This number increases or decreases in proportion to the profit found in illicit trade...[to which] many are devoted...[These, and the other] Canarians who do not attend crops,...are prejudicial to the quiet and tranquility of the province through the scandals, deaths and harms that such a caste of abandoned men occasion. They defraud the Royal Treasury of large amounts and are generally...rebellious and insubordinate, as may be seen in the disturbances they have caused in their [own] islands and in Havana. For this reason His Majesty his ordered that the only Isleñs that go in the annual ship between the Canaries and the province shall be merchants and members of the crew. But this is not observed... From the great love that they have for illicit trade proceeds, to my understanding, the general hatred that they feel for the Royal Guipuzcoan Company as the result of its restriction of that trade...

The Montevideo Settlement

When, in the 1720s the establishment of a Spanish presence on the Banda Oriental of the La Plata estuary became an objective of the Crown, the Council of the Indies again had turned to the Canary Islands. Twenty isleño families arrived at the site Montevideo in 1726, the Gallegan contingent that was to lend additional support to the venture having failed to materialize. Three additional shiploads from the Canaries later joined the group as well as other Spaniards from the Buenos Aires side of the estuary.[69] The city was officially established on December 20, 1729, without opposition from the Portuguese who had held nominal control of this shore. Men from the Canaries occupied all of the principal offices. In return for their services Felipe II had agreed to permit free trade between the islands and the new settlement under the familiar condition that ships bound from Montevideo should carry five families of immigrants for each 100 tons. Although this was annulled shortly thereafter the immigrants carried in the interval, together with a handful

---

[69]David W. Fernández, "José Fernández Romero y la fundación de Montevideo," *Revista Histórica* (Museo Nacional de Uruguay, 29 (1959), 201-204; Pérez Vidal, "Aportación...," 158-161, citing especially Enrique Azarola Gil, *Los Origenes de Montevideo, 1607-1749*, (Buenos Aires, 1933). All but one of the original 20 families was from Tenerife.

of settlers from Argentina, constituted the base of the population of the new capital, as shown in the *Actas del Cabildo* of Montevideo, which specify in detail the point of origin and quality of the families involved. No further movements from the islands to the La Plata region are documented until the following century, when the isleño colony there was substantially augmented.

The current of migration to America had been episodic throughout the eighteenth century fluctuating according to Crown policy, European Wars and the state of the archipelago's export trade. The 'boom and bust' that epitomizes the history of the islands' economy, from sugar to wine to barilla to cochineal and recently to bananas, tomatoes and an aggravated form of international tourism, dictated the longer term swings while wars, epidemics, famine and natural disasters brought short term fluctuations in the migration current.[70] Their documentation is hindered not only by the variable character and incompleteness of the official registries of arrivals and departures, but also by the existence of an extensive clandestine traffic, a traffic that has continued even to the present.[71]

There have been suggestions that 2,000 Canarios a year migrated to the New World between 1770-1808, which could have represented a drain of approximately 1.3 percent of the archipelago's population every twelve months.[72] This flow was fed by an extraordinary rate of natural increase, perhaps in excess of three percent annually. Records are piecemeal and incomplete. Detailed studies in

---

[70]Recurrent famines on drought-prone Lanzarote and Fuerteventura led to frequent surges of outmigration from these drier eastern islands that intensified pressures on Gran Canaria and Tenerife. *E.g.*, James J. Parsons, "Drought and Hunger on Fuerteventura," *Geographical Review* 65 (1975), 110-113; Roberto Roldán, *El hambre en Fuerteventura, 1600-1800* (Santa Cruz de Tenerife: Aula de Cultura, 1968).

[71]Levies by both the army and the navy took thousands of additional island youths, many of whom doubtless ended up in America. Peraza de Ayala, *El régimen comercial....*, 135, documents 2,500 such enlistments of Canarios, 1721-1758.

[72]*E.g., Ibid.*, 161 n; Antonio de Bethancourt Messieu, "Aproximación a la economía de las islas Canarias, 1770-1808," *Estudios de Historia Moderna y Contemporánea* (Madrid) 27 (1978), 185-202, reference 193.

   Humboldt, on Tenerife in 1799, observed that "emigration would be diminished if uncultivated demesne lands were distributed among private persons, if those which are annexed to the *majorats* of the great families were sold, and feudal rights were gradually abolished." He judged that "the misery of the people has considerably diminished since the cultivation of the potato has been introduced and since they have begun to sow maize more than wheat or barley." There were, he suspected, more isleños on the new continent than in their own country. *Personal Narrative...*, I:289-292.

progress in local island archives and those on the mainland should provide a much closer approximation to the facts than is now available.

Cuba and Puerto Rico in the Nineteenth Century

The Wars of Independence and their aftermath substantially altered the character of the Canario migration to the Americas. Cuba and Puerto Rico, as the only units remaining under the Spanish flag, now became the most favored destinations. For the most part the isleños had royalist sympathies. Substantial numbers of them, especially from Venezuela, found refuge in the Antilles during and after the conflict.[73] Some of the leading figures on the side of the Crown were Canarios, including Domingo Monteverde, who led the Spanish troops on the assault against Caracas, and Field Marshall Tomás Morales. It was the capitulation of the latter in 1822 at Maracaibo that marked the end of serious resistance by royalist forces.

The establishment of formal diplomatic relations between Spain and the newly independent republics came slowly so that movement to the mainland, such as it was, had to be largely clandestine. On the other hand migration to Cuba, especially, was much facilitated and that island, in the throes of a new prosperity, became the 'land of promise' for a new generation of Canarios under the spell of 'the magic of America.' With the termination of the slave trade and the expansion of sugar and tobacco production the demand for labor there increased sharply. Canarios and Gallegos provided it.

Recruitment activities were intense throughout most of the nineteenth century as the central government as well as private immigration societies and individual *hacenderos* sought to channel migration, especially of isleños, towards Cuba and Puerto Rico and away from the mainland republics. The plethora of schemes came at an opportune time, for the cochineal market had collapsed in the 1830s. At the same time there was a series of drought years in the archipelago. In 1836 for example, some 528 men were brought from Gran Canaria by the Junta de Fomento y Agricultura in Havana to

---

[73]Many of the isleños who chose the losing side in the wars were left destitute. The shock waves brought on by the carving out of most of the Americas from the Spanish empire has been termed one of the principal causes of the "ruin and general poverty" of the archipelago to which many returned. Francisco María de León, *Apuntes para la historia de las islas Canarias, 1776-1868.* (Santa Cruz de Tenerife: Aula de Cultura, 1966) 219.

work on the Havana-Güines railway project.[74] The Junta put up the money for their passage, to be paid off by a monthly levy of one-third of the immigrants' wages. Food and housing were provided and the remittance of a part of what was left of their pay was made automatic. Between 1835-1850 some 16,300 Canarios (an average of about one thousand a year) arrived in Cuba, a large proportion of them to stay.[75] A study in 1846 ordered by the island's governor reported that there were 27,251 peninsulares in the province and 19,795 Canarios.

To go to Cuba to improve one's economic condition (*'con fin de mejorar de suerte'* or *'de salir de pobreza'*) was the ambition of virtually every Canario youth. To obtain a *comendaticia* or license to leave it was necessary to establish, through the testimony of a witness, that one was sober and free of debt and without military obligations. In some cases it seems to have been necessary to be single and not in love (*'no es enamorado'*). The ratio of males to females in some years approached nine to one.[76] Women and children left behind often crossed over later on receipt of the famous *cartas de llamadas* with the head of family's announcement *'ya no piensa volver.'* In other cases the men went home at the termination of their work contracts. A French visitor to the Canaries in the 1860s described how the return of a ship from Cuba had formerly been a major event, great crowds being attracted to witness the arrival of the *indianos*, as the high-stepping, *puro*-smoking returnees were called, in their Panama hats, white cloth cassocks and other finery:[77]

> "It was to Havana, especially, that the isleños went. It was their El Dorado. About five percent came back rich; another twenty percent gained a little money and then, a prey to

---

[74]María Cristina Albelo Martín, "La emigración Canarias-América (1826-1853)," *Aguayro (Boletín Informativo de la Caja Insular de Ahorras de Gran Canaria)* 132:5-9;133: 10-13 (1981).

[75]Julio Hernández García, "La planificación de la emigración canaria a Cuba y Puerto Rico, siglo XIX," *Coloquio de Historia Canario-Americana* II, I: 201-238, reference 221-222.

[76]Juan Francisco Martín Ruiz, *El N.W. de Gran Canaria: un estudio de demografía histórica, 1485-1860* (Las Palmas: Mancomunidad de Cabildos de Las Palmas, 1978).

[77]E. Pegot-Ogier, *The Fortunate Isles: the Archipelago of the Canaries*; translated by Frances Locock (2 vols., London: Richard Bentley, 1871), I: 246.

nostalgia, returned to their beloved islands. But very shortly they went back (to America), regretting what they had left behind....In Havana they were considered honest, active and intelligent....finding employment as soon as they landed."

He noted that once they had accumulated some capital, they tended to devote themselves to speculative commercial activities. The island of La Palma furnished a disproportionate number of immigrants, "going to Cuba being a kind of tradition" among its inhabitants. Migrants from there had an advantage over the others because, on arrival, they could rely on the support of friends and relations until becoming established. He thought the process had been a selective one, the most self-reliant, active and energetic being attracted from the islands "where the general tendency is to ease and idleness."

Migration to Cuba reached a high point in the 'fifties. In the four years 1857-61, for which there is data on the movement from each municipio in the archipelago, 10,335 emigrants left for America or 4.4 percent of the entire population.[78] The overwhelming majority went to Cuba. There were numerous royal orders and decrees encouraging and facilitating such movements. Most of them applied specifically to Canarios. They provided for free passage and other subsidies as well as guarantees against contract abuses whether by ship owners or by the employers in Cuba.[79] Much of the promotion

---

[78]Pedro de Olive, *Diccionario estadístico-administrativo de las islas Canarias* (Barcelona, 1865). A much discussed proposal for a regular steamship service between Tenerife and Havana was to carry 400 passengers a month. The fare was to be 17 dollars steerage. The round trip was to require one month, with stops at both Gran Canaria and La Palma. The promoters estimated that one-fifth of those who went would return. At the time some twenty sailing vessels were reportedly in the business, all making a profit. With the more comfortable facilities to be offered by the new service the migration current was expected to be substantially augmented. The plan does not seem to have been put into effect. *Recopilación de los diferentes artículos publicados en pro y en contra del proyecto de una línea de de vapores entre las islas Canarias y ésta* (Habana: Barcina, 1855).

[79]Hernández García, "La planificación...." "cites nearly a dozen such schemes. A Tenerife agent for a wealthy Cuban hacendero is quoted as saying in 1878, "In spite of the distance [Cuba] is not so much an American island as the richest of our own archipelago which provides most of the money in circulation here." 233. A review of the petitions to emigrate filed at La Laguna (Tenerife) 1848-1885 but broken 1867-1872 shows that in this period 1,420 such requests were filed. Most were in family groups but 216 individuals were included. Of the total, 936 petitioned to go to *la isla de Cuba*; Venezuela, with 86 was a distant second. Others included Puerto Rico 56, Argentina 24 and Uruguay 14. The Cuban requests tailed off in the late years while those for the La Plata countries in-

had not-so-subtle racial overtones, such as that originating with the Real Junta de Fomento in Havana which, from its establishment in 1831, had as its main objective "the promotion of immigration of the white race to Cuba, especially Canarios." The substitution of Negro slavery by salaried labor fundamentally was made with whites from the Canaries.

Puerto Rico, much smaller than Cuba, was always an attraction of substantially lesser magnitude. During and after the Wares of Independence in South America, Canario refugees from Cumaná, Puerto Cabello and La Guaira flooded into Ponce on the southern coast. Many later returned to Venezuela. Others came directly from across the Atlantic. An account of the arrival of one brig with 80 men from the island of La Palma in 1814 *(labradoes todos)* explains how the captain had made arrangements on a previous voyage for a part of the group but that the rest would go on to Cuba if they did not find appropriate opportunities a *probar sus fortunas*.[80] In 1835 the governor of Puerto Rico sent an emissary to Madrid seeking Canario colonists forthe island. The declining availability of slaves conflicted with the expansion of sugar production, and the need for more workers was urgent. The decade of the 'fifties may have accounted for as much as one-third of all immigration from Spain to Puerto Rico during the nineteenth century but Canarios constituted not more than twelve percent of the total.[81] This mid-century wave of arrivals was seen as filling vacancies left by the cholera epidemic of 1855-56 that had left some 26,000 dead on the island.

Relations With the New American Republics

Spain's slowness in establishing diplomatic relations with the new American republics did not stop the flow of emigrants from the poverty-stricken Canaries. But with Spanish ships requiring special permission from the Council of State to visit countries that had separated from the Crown, the traffic was largely diverted to illicit foreign vessels. These found the poorly patrolled Canaries especially

---

creased. The additional 219 that listed "America" would have been going to either of the two remaining Spanish possessions, Cuba or Puerto Rico. Julio Hernández García, "La emigración de La Laguna en la segunda mitad del siglo XIX (1848-1895)," *Revista de Historia Canaria* 25 (1976), 91-124.

[80]"Inmigración de Canarias," *Boletín de Historia de Puerto Rico* 7 (1920), 53-54.

[81]Estela Cifre de Loubriel, "Los inmigrantes del siglo XIX: sus contribuciones a la formación del pueblo puerrtorriqueño," *Revista del Instituto de Cultura Puertorriqueña* 3 (1960).

attractive recruiting grounds. Captains of United States schooners were among those who sought to play a part in this traffic. The American consul in Tenerife noted in 1836 that "American vessels are prohibited from carrying passengers from these islands under the pretext that they might convey them to the separated colonies." Ships flying the Spanish flag, however, were doing so with impunity. "This extraordinary abuse of power," he writes, "deprives American flags from employment; those that call in here, frequently depart without deriving any benefit."[82]

Even during the Wars of Independence and immediately after as many as 1,500 persons were said to be leaving annually for Uruguay alone on foreign-owned vessels operating illegally from Canary ports. Because the fighting did not last long there nor acquire much intensity the La Plata lands had had a special attraction in this period.[83] By 1838 officials in the archipelago were complaining that the intensity of the clandestine movements from island ports on French, Tuscan, Sicilian and especially English vessels was such that the islands were being left without hands for their defense.[84]

Legal or illegal, the conditions encountered by the emigrants on the small, grossly overloaded foreign vessels carrying them, usually to Montevideo or to Venezuela, became a preoccupation of authorities. On arrival the poor immigrants, often lured under false pretenses or even "highjacked," were forced by *empresarios* to enter abusive contracts for their labor simply to pay off the cost of passage. Some, after submitting to up to eight years of virtual slavery without obtaining their freedom, managed to slip away to Cuba or Puerto Rico. The majority fell into the hands of the police and were

---

[82]National Archives, Washington, D.C., Consular Despatches, Tenerife, "Joseph Cullen to the U.S. Minister, Madrid, April 20, 1836." Two years later the difficulties seemed to have been resolved but on April 20, 1839, it was again complained that "obstructions and all manner of impositions" were being placed in the way of American vessels that sought to embark with passengers to La Guaira and to Havana.

[83]Enrique Guerrero Balfagar, "La emigración de los naturales de las islas Canarias a las repúblicas del Río de la Plata en la primera mitad del siglo XIX," *Anuario de Estudios Atlánticos* 6 (1960), 493-517; Santos Fernández Arlaud, "La emigración española a América durante el reinado de Isabel II," *Cuadernos de Historia* (Madrid) 4 (1973), 419-455.

[84]For Spanish vessels going to Cuba or Puerto Rico clearance from the *Juez de Arribada* in the Canaries was all that was required. Individuals seeking permits to go to one of the "rebelling countries" had to go to the Council of the Indies; but as the "red-tape" generally discouraged them they usually joined the illicit traffic.

returned to their "owners" to pay off their debts, including fines imposed on them for "attempting to escape."

The Río de la Plata ports were opened to immigration in 1833. In that year a *goleta* carrying the Spanish flag landed 180 Canarios at Maldonado on the Banda Oriental, the first colonists to arrive following independence. The new Uruguay government, concerned about the shortage of labor, sent an emissary to Madrid to facilitate further migration, "Canarios being especially desired because most of the Motevideo families are of this origin." But diplomatic relations between Spain and the republics deteriorated and from 1838 to 1853 there was an outright prohibition against emigration other than to Cuba, Puerto Rico or the Philippines. The Crown, however, made little effort to enforce it in the case of the Canaries. Officials openly expressed their concern for the islanders' "rights to seek a livelihood elsewhere if their overcrowded homeland could not provide it."

The carrying of immigrants across the Atlantic to the beckoning Americas became a well organized and lucrative business as the nineteenth century progressed.[85] Vessels ostensibly bound for San Juan and Havana often changed their destinations en route to end up at Montevideo or La Guaira, or even Brazil, especially when their captains knew that labor contractors were waiting there and ready to make it profitable for them.[86] In Uruguay the new arrivals repeatedly found themselves caught up in the recurrent civil wars as well as in conflicts with Argentina and with France. Government decrees ordered them to take up arms, as in defense of the city of Montevideo. The protests of the Spanish Crown had little success in lifting these obligations.

By 1853 Spain finally had established diplomatic representation with both Uruguay and Venezuela so that all of the traditional

---

[85]The history of one such *contratista de colonos* has been documented by Nelson Martínez Ruiz, "La emigración Canaria en Uruguay durante la primera mitad del siglo XIX; una sociedad para el transporte de colonos." *Revista de Indias* 38 (1978), 349-402. Capitalizing on the government's interest, a prominent Uruguayan business man and ship-owner, Juan María Pérez, had obtained a license in 1835 to bring 3,000 Canario families to Montevideo. The society he founded for this purpose, with influential agents in Madrid and in the islands, had little difficulty in circumventing Spanish government restrictions on the traffic.

[86]Martínez Ruiz, "La emigración Canaria en Uruguay...," Guerrero Balfagar, "La emigración de las naturales...." and Fernández Arlaud, "La emigración española..." all describe in detail the exploitation of the Canario migrants to the La Plata region. Similar conditions prevailed in connection with the Venezuela traffic, and somewhat later that to Cuba.

impediments to emigration to those countries were removed. Spanish consular agents were instructed to look after the interests of any new arrivals and to insure their liberty of work and the fair administration of the contracts. The Royal Orders relating to such matters make specific reference to Canarios as an exploited group requiring special protection. Migration was also successfully encouraged from the densely peopled and depressed north of Spain.[87] Those who before would have gone to Cuba or Puerto Rico now had a wider choice. But through most of the nineteenth century the Canaries contributed more immigrants to the New World than any other Spanish province.

Uruguay and Venezuela rivalled Cuba as the preferred destination of isleño immigrants. Argentina, too, became of some significance, especially after the fall of the Dictator Rosas brought the beginnings of peace to the area and security for Spanish vessels calling there. Official statistics show that more than 3,000 Canarios arrived in Argentina in the 11-year period 1885-1895, but this represented only two percent of total Spanish immigration to that country in those years.[88]

Venezuela, with a long and close association with the Canary Islands and influenced by Bolivar's conviction that immigration would be critical to the future of the American republics, had been the first of the new mainland countries to make overtures toward the mother country for the establishment of normal diplomatic relations. Projects to encourage foreigners to come to Gran Colombia (1819-1830) had had few positive results,[89] but with its break-up that changed. In 1831 the new Venezuelan congress authorized the country's chief executive to actively promote immigration from Europe. It was decreed that

> residents of the Canary Islands should be [especially] encouraged to come to this country and to this end they should be provided with the necessary facilities because their religion, speech and customs are the same as ours and because, with their known frugality and work habits, they are certain to prosper, as already has been demonstrated.

---

[87]Fernández Arlaud, "La emigración española...," 443.

[88]Vicente Vásquez Presedo, *Estadísticas históricas argentinas, 1875-1914* (Buenos Aires: Ediciones Macchi, 1941), 46.

[89]Fernández Arlaud, "La emigración español...," 443.

Subsidies to support such migration were voted three years later. Only in 1837 were they extended to peninsulares and to other Europeans. Emissaries were sent to Madrid to facilitate recruitment and the issuance of proper authorizations to embark.[90] Between 1831 and 1845 some 12,000 Canarios are recorded as having arrived in Venezuela. The traffic was apparently a profitable one from the numerous complaints about the maltreatment of passengers and their exploitation by labor contractors on arrival at La Guaira. Most of this movement was apparently of spontaneous nature, without benefit of government assistance.[91] The relations between the islands and Venezuela became increasingly close as the nineteenth century progressed, but the documentation of the migrations that followed has not been found.

Santo Domingo (later the Dominican Republic) chaotically independent and living under the shadow of Haitian invasion threats, offered little to attract immigration during most of the nineteenth century. Isleño colonies previously established there did, however, retain their identity as white enclaves within an increasingly mulatto society. The Baní district on the south coast, in particular, remains known today as a Canario center.

There was, in the 1880s, at least one effort to revive immigration to the Dominican Republic from the archipelago, with subsidies from the Public Treasury of 1500 pesos being offered for each person. At least one contingent of isleños contracted for by a Dominican entrepreneur, arrived and settled on land given to them adjacent to the sugar plantation where they were employed.[92]

---

[90]In connection with government efforts to promote emigration from the Canaries the Junta de Comercio de Canarias observed in 1841 that Cuba was the preferred country for islanders and that those who went to Venezuela or other overseas destinations did so because of the attraction of subsidized passages. It took a dim view of emigration on ships of foreign flags. Peraza de Ayala, *El régimen comercial...* 234n.

[91]Immigration directly contracted for by the Venezuelan government involved less than 500 persons in the 19th century; later it became more significant. But most of the 29,000 Canarios who are said to have arrived between 1904-1935 came independently of government-supported schemes. Prior to World War II the Basque provinces rather than the Canaries provided the majority of the Spanish immigrants to Venezuela. *Memoria del Instituto Técnico de Inmigración y Colonización* (Caracas, 1940).

[92]H. Hoetink, *The Dominican people...*, 27-28.

Canarios in Post-1898 Cuba

The migratory current from the Canaries to Cuba in the later years of the 19th century fluctuated with changing economic and political conditions. With the restoration of order in the newly independent Cuba in 1898 it intensified. While the majority of migrants were young men seeking work in the sugar or tobacco industries, many others went to avoid the military service that was obligatory in the Canary Islands. The United States Consul on Tenerife wrote that "they leave with the intention of remaining a year or so in Cuba, obtaining 'papers' showing them to be Cuban 'subjects,' and then returning here." His office was beseiged, he said, by islanders coming back from America who asked to be registered in the consulate as 'Cubans' and as such to be afforded U.S. protection.[93] For the moment Washington, not Madrid or Havana, was presumed to be the source of ultimate authority.

In these transition years the U.S. Consul in the Canaries played an active role as intermediary in the migration to Cuba. On May 29, 1900, he wrote to his superiors in Washington that he was doing all in his power "to encourage emigration (and) to prevent embarcation of undesirable persons, an object I can best accomplish by (personally) examining each emigrant."[94] He was not especially sympathetic to those who wanted to emigrate simply to avoid military conscription or, in the case of young women, those "whose object is solely prostitution." The notion was abroad in the archipelago, he wrote, that people wanting to emigrate "have only to communicate with me to ensure their being sent to Cuba." He had been at some trouble to ascertain where this "erroneous" idea might have originated. He complained of the increasing amount of time required to prepare the necessary documents for emigrants, who had to meet the requirements of U.S. health and immigration authorities in Havana. His office often was required to hire additional clerks, for

[93]National Archives, Washington, D.C., Consular Despatches, Tenerife, "Solomon Berliner to Daniel J. Hill, Assistant Secretary of State, October 9, 1902."

[94]*Ibid.*, May 29, 1900, March 2, 1900 and December 4, 1899. Emigrants leaving for either Cuba or Puerto Rico for a time were required to have their visas stamped by U.S. Consular officials and to obtain public health clearances before embarking. A fee of one dollar (later two dollars) imposed by consular agents at Las Palmas and Santa Cruz de Tenerife was later lifted in the face of strenuous protests from the two companies carrying immigrants, Cía. Transatlántico and Pinillos.

422

the emigrant steamers, which had "the disturbing habit of arriving on weekends," did not remain long in port.[95]

Fragmentary data suggests the intensity of the traffic. In the last three months of 1900, according to the U.S. Consul in the Canaries, 1,615 emigrants had left for Cuba and 16 for Puerto Rico. In the following year Las Palmas de Gran Canaria alone had embarked 1,233 persons for Cuba and Puerto Rico.[96] Others would have left from Tenerife and La Palma. Substantial numbers were seasonal migrants (*golondrinas*) who returned at the end of the sugar harvest. Others waited a few years until they had accumulated a small 'nest egg.' "Once home," the Consul wrote, "these generally devote their money and energy to the cultivation of fruit (bananas) in which a large and increasing business is transacted with the English markets."[97] As workers in Cuba the islanders earned the equivalent of about 22 U.S. cents a day, the women a trifle less. On this they managed to rear and sustain their families "in comparative decency." Their food, supplied by their employers, was of the simplest, consisting mainly of *gofio* cake and salt fish.

When the pace of emigration temporarily slackened the Consul thought it due chiefly to reports of crop failures and a general economic malaise in the Cuban economy. Immigration subsidies offered by Brazil apparently had lured away some groups. "If free

---

[95]U.S. quarantine officers at San Juan and Havana complained to the Surgeon General in Washington about conditions on emigrant ships from the Canaries and the peninsula. They urged that U.S. consular officials in those ports should not sanction the departure of such vessels unless they provided adequate accommodations and had enforced vaccination and disinfection requirements. The steamship companies were blamed for the violations. Some of the ships in service were described as "tramp vessels, filthy beyond description" and very overcrowded. Few if any of them provided the 12 cubic feet of space per passenger suggested as an acceptable minimum. *Ibid.*, Official Correspondence 22 "U.S. Consul General, Barcelona, to Solomon Berliner, Consul General, Tenerife, the Surgeon General, U.S. Marine Hospital Service, Washington, D.C., December 27, 1900.

[96]*Ibid.*, Official Correspondence 22, "Annual Report on Commerce, Trade and Navigation for the Canary Islands for the Year 1901," February 26, 1902. Emigration was said to have fallen off significantly from the previous year. The table giving the breakdown of emigration from all of the islands for 1901 and 1902, referred to as an annex to this report, is missing.

[97]*Ibid.*, "Report on Emigration," March 2, 1900. Not more than eight percent of male emigrants were being accompanied by wives and families at this time.

passage were offered," he wrote in his annual report for 1901,[98] "it would induce all (sic) migrants to go to Cuba and in the long run would be of great benefit to both Cuba and Puerto Rico...I can only reiterate that there are no better laborers to be found for plantation work than those of the Canary Islands. They are hard workers, industrious and honest."

The majority continued to go under contract, the money for passage advanced in the Canaries to be deducted later from wages earned in America. During 1905 emigration was especially active, amounting to about 10,000. Most went to Cuba, with Venezuela the next country of preference.[99] While lauding their contribution to the agricultural work force ("their equals are hardly to be found") the Consul questioned their desirability "for settling or building up the country...as fully 90 percent return to these islands as soon as they have accrued sufficient money to be able to buy a small piece of land." By 1906 the Consul in Tenerife observed that "affairs in Cuba have become so unsettled that the emigration from here has entirely stopped and I am informed that as many people have returned from, as have left for Cuba during the year."[100]

The Cuban migration waxed and waned in the following years, but its intensity and direction is largely undocumented. By the early 1930s the *gran movimiento* was over, victim of economic depression, the Spanish Civil War (1936-1939) and World War II (1939-1945). A resident of the archipelago who was invited by La Asociación Canaria de Cuba to visit isleño social clubs in Havana and the provinces in 1914-15 had written that he was engulfed everywhere in "*un delirio de canarismo.*" He estimated that there were more than 100,000 of his compatriots living and working in the island. Those who took up permanent residence tended to become rapidly "Cubanized" but they retained close ties with their homeland. The sense of community impressed him. He remarked especially on the concentration of his compatriots in Matanzas and Santa Clara provinces and in the cities of Cabaiguán, Camajuaní and Zaza del Medio, which had been founded and peopled by Canarios.

---

[98]*Ibid.*, "Annual Report on the Canary Islands for 1901." Free passage or fare refunds were, in fact, later provided by the Cuban government.

[99]*Ibid.*, Department of State Copy Book 3, "Report on Trade and Commerce for the Canary Islands for 1905," 50.

[100]*Ibid.*, "Report on Trade and Commerce for the Canary Islands for 1906," 181.

424

Many of them had been active earlier in the movement for a "Free Cuba" that had culminated in independence.[101]

Canarios in Modern Venezuela

In the Río de La Plata republics the Canario immigrants were increasingly submerged in the early years of this century by the masses of Italians and peninsular Spaniards who dominated the migratory flow. Cuba had lost some of its attraction now that it was independent. Increasingly, Venezuela became the preferred goal of isleños seeking a new start in the New World. This was especially so after the death of the Dictator Gómez in 1935 when an open immigration policy was adopted that was to last for more than 20 years.

Modern Venezuela has the largest, most active and most easily identified Canario colony in the Americas. Prior to 1958, government efforts to recruit agricultural colonists were usually pointed specifically at Canarios. Recent development planning has led to a more selective immigration policy in which preference is given to skilled professionals. The Canario peasant is no longer seen in the positive light of earlier years, although the close family and business ties between the archipelago and Venezuela continue to facilitate trans-Atlantic movement.

There is a *Hogar Canario* or *Casa de Canarias* in almost every Venezuelan provincial capital and in many smaller towns. Caracas a few years ago had five of them. Social clubs, bars, restaurants and soccer teams carry names suggesting the closeness of island ties. Venezuelan politicians find it advantageous to include the islands in their electioneering itinerary. Charter tours and religious peregrinations to the archipelago, as from the islands to Venezuela, are frequently advertised. Of the distinctive Canario

---

[101]Francisco González Diaz, *Un Canario en Cuba* (Havana: Imprenta "La Prueba," 1916). He described the seasonal migration of illiterate peasants who came for the sugar harvest, travelling steerage under almost inhuman conditions. On arrival they traditionally congregated at the Hotel Triscornia in Havana to await friends or employers. The "voice of the colony" at the time was *Islas Canarias,* a periodical edited by Francisco Bethancourt Apolinario. I have been unable to locate its file nor that of any of the numerous other Canario periodicals of the era published in America. David W. Fernández, "*Los periódicos de las islas Canarias* (Madrid,1905) lists some 20 such journals from the 1880s onward, the majority of them from Cuba. *El Guanche,* published in Caracas in 1897 by a refugee Cuban war veteran, is said to have been the first newspaper to publicly support independence for the Canary Islands themselves. In 1980 graffiti along Venezuela highways proclaimed "Canarias Libre" and "Somos Guanches Siempre," apparently the work of a minor splinter group of politicized isleños.

surnames that of Betancourt (with variant spellings) is particularly prominent in Venezuela.[102] A late distinguished president was Rómulo Bethancourt; another (Belisario) was elected president of neighboring Colombia in 1982.

Periodicals designed specifically for the Canario community in Venezuela, or for the former residents of that country in the Canary Islands, still prosper. As recently as 1973 one of the former, *Canarias Gráficas* of Caracas, claimed 20,000 readers of whom 95 percent were said to be "of the upper social class." This may have been a generous estimate. In Caracas the isleños are still best known as taxi drivers, market gardeners and dealers in fresh fruits and vegetables. Much of the trade in the city's central market is said to be still in Canario hands. While their considerable success in moving up the economic ladder is undeniable, it still makes headlines in Tenerife that the chauffeur of the president of Venezuela (Luis Herrera Campíns) is an isleño!

In the archipelago the *Casa de Venezuela* on Tenerife is the island's most elegant country club. The Venezuelan consulates there and on Gran Canaria are inordinately busy. The leading newspaper of Tenerife maintains a Caracas correspondent and carries a *'Balcón de Venezuela'* supplement in the Sunday edition.[103] Remittances from isleños in Venezuela or investments by those returning home from there have contributed substantially to the development of the export-oriented banana and tomato growing industries in recent years, especially the reclamation of sloping land through the construction of costly agricultural terraces.

In the past twenty years there has been a net reverse flow of Canarios back to the home archipelago. Gone are the subsidized passes and prior labor contracts of the past. Restrictive measures on immigration to Venezuela, coupled with the investment and employment attractions of the islands' highly capitalized agriculture and the new mass tourism, with the unparalleled speculative fever for land that it has induced, has reversed the historic westward flow. But the cultural identification of the isleño community, especially in Venezuela, remains strong. The political geography of the home islands,

---

[102]Leopoldo de la Rosa, "Los Bethancourt de las islas Canarias y en América," *Anuario do Estudios Atlánticos* 2 (1956), 111-164.

[103]The same periodical carried an advertisement of a St. Augustine, Florida, industrial park although it has been nearly 200 years since Canarios were active in that community! The Cabildo Insular was urging investment on Tenerife while travel agencies in Caracas urged readers to visit the Canaries "por ser continuación de Venezuela." A charter flight was offered to La Palma for the traditional *bajada de la Virgen* in July.

an integral part of Spain and soon of the European Economic Community, lying less than two hours flight south of the Iberian peninsula and almost within sight of the African coast, has emphasized the uniqueness of the island heritage and reinforced the sense of community both of the immigrants and their descendants.

Conclusion

Canario migration to the New World, in large measure a response to an extraordinarily high rate of natural increase in the island, has been surpassed numerically in this century by the migration of Gallegans from the green north of the peninsula. Between 1946-57 official statistics indicate that total Spanish emigration to the Americas averaged approximately 43,000 persons per year, with a peak of 55,000 being reached in 1955.[104] The province of Santa Cruz de Tenerife (chiefly Tenerife and La Palma) contributed 10.58 percent of the total emigration in these years of 54,938 individuals of whom 9 out of 10 went to Venezuela. The comparable figure for Las Palmas (Gran Canaria) province is not available but the archipelago could well have been responsible for 18-20 percent of all Spanish emigration to the Americas in this period, or approximately 8,000 persons per year. Galicia, with a population base several times as large, contributed 45.8 percent of the migrants.

There has been an almost unbroken current of Canary Islanders that has crossed the Atlantic to new homes in the New World in the nearly five centuries since Columbus.[105] They probably have been the most distinctive and most localized geographically of

---

[104]"La emigración en la provincia de Santa Cruz de Tenerife," *Estudios Geográficos* (Madrid) 75 (1959), 284-290.

[105]Significant as it has been, estimates of the Canario migration to America in this century may have tended to be exaggerated. Decennial censuses of Spain, begun in 1857, show a steady increase in the population of the islands from 233,784 in the first one to 1,170,224 in 1970. The archipelago's growth rate consistently has been higher than that of the peninsula. At the beginning of the present century the Canaries represented 1.9 percent of the total national population compared to 3.4 percent in 1970. Adjusting for recorded births and deaths (reliability unknown) the islands show a positive net migration of 60,040 individuals in the seventy year period. Immigration from the mainland and returnees from America appear, then, to have more than compensated statistically for the outmigration. Barranechea, *Objetivo: Canarias...*, 49-50.

The 1970 Census of Spain lists as *'ausente'* (absent) 32,000 individuals from Santa Cruz de Tenerife province and 10,000 from Las Palmas. Most of these may be presumed to have been in America but to have retained Spanish citizenship.

the Spanish immigrant groups in the Americas. The persistence of their migration and their concentration at different times in different places--the Greater Antilles, Venezuela, Uruguay, the frontier outposts of Spain in Florida, Louisiana, Texas and Campeche--provide a striking but little recognized example of the persistence and the clustering tendency of different cultural groups within the wide reaches of Hispanic America.

29

Drought and Hunger on Fuerteventura*

The persistence of agricultural settlement in the face of recurrent adversity is commonplace in marginal lands where the attachment of people to place is strong. Few peoples have endured longer than the farmers of Fuerteventura, second largest and most starkly barren of the Canary Islands. This tawny volcanic land, which stretches for some 85 kilometers along the desert coast of West Africa, is too low to intercept significant precipitation from the trade winds or the occasional incipient frontal systems that pass over the archipelago. Despite the stratus cloud deck that prevails through most of the year, persistent winds make evaporation rates fairly high. Approximately one year in every three or four the rains fail, with resultant widespread crop failure. Over the centuries the uplands have been largely bared of vegetation by browsing goats and camels as well as by peasant wood gatherers seeking fuel for lime kilns. The stately Canary Island palm, of which a few are left standing in alluvial valleys, is the only large tree.

To counter the low and unreliable precipitation a specialized system of dry farming was early developed in which storm runoff is diverted from the usually dry arroyos into a series of almost level fields (*gavias de bebederos*) bounded by earthen dikes and arranged in step-like order on outwash fans. One storm may flood a properly constructed gavia to a depth of several inches. A gavia is said to have "drunk" when the water in the catchment has been absorbed, leaving the soil ready for planting. One such flooding will support a crop of wheat or barley. Violent rains, on the other hand, may completely wash out the system.

---

*Reprinted from *The Geographical Review*, Vol. 65, pp. 110-113 (1975).

By the mid-sixteenth century Fuerteventura, with nearby Lanzarote, had become known as the granary of the Canaries. In good years it exported surplus wheat and some goat cheese to the more populous Gran Canaria, Tenerife, La Palma, and even Madeira. One year of crop failure could be survived by dipping into reserves stored in the straw silos which still give character to the Fuerteventura landscape, but two successive drought years generally led to famine and mass exodus to well-watered Gran Canaria and Tenerife. Yet invariably, with better times, the settlers would return and in a few years Fuerteventura, never rich, would regain its former aspect.

The resolution of the island's governing council (*cabildo*) in the seventeenth and eighteenth centuries graphically recount that body's continuing concern to ameliorate the impact of the violent fluctuations in cereal production in this "dry and bitter land" where hunger was endemic (Roberto Roldán: Acuerdos del cabildo de Fuerteventura [3 vols.; La Laguna, Tenerife, 1966-1970]). Death from malnutrition was widespread, and at least a dozen major famines occurred. Each led to a temporary emigration, often of more than half of the island's population, which in normal years seems to have been stabilized at about 10,000 (Roberto Roldán: El hambre en Fuerteventura (1600-1800) [Encyclopedia Canaria, Aula de Cultura de Tenerife, Tenerife, 1968]).

An almost complete dependence on wheat as the money crop magnified the effect of Fuerteventura's aridity and isolation. Barley, although extensively planted on poorer lands, was normally kept at home for domestic consumption. In bad years it too might fail. Occupance was confined to the interior valleys, the coasts being avoided in fear of raids by English freebooters or by Berbers from the African mainland. The fish resource of the adjacent seas was largely neglected. The rights to develop solar saltworks were held by a marquis who chose not to exploit them. There was some gathering of orchilla, the lichen used as a dyestuff, but the rights to it belonged to the feudal lord. Only after the latter's hold was broken in the late eighteenth century did Fuerteventura find a significant alternative source of income to supplement its unpredictable grain harvest.

In the 1790s cultivation of a wild barilla (*Mesembryanthemum spp.*) was initiated. The plant, a succulent, was burned to produce a carbonate of soda for export to European glassmakers. When the church pressed for the right to tax barilla the cabildo objected that it was a substitute crop, replacing barley on the poorer, steeper soils. Shortly thereafter, with the introduction of nopal cactus, cochineal, another dyestuff, was added to the export list. With these new sources of cash there were funds to purchase emergency grain in drought years, thus easing the pressures for emigration. But these products were soon displaced by cheaper synthetics and substitutes. By the 1840s the market for barilla had largely disappeared, and by the 1870s that for cochineal was on the decline.

Pascual Madoz (Diccionario geográfico-estadístico-histórico de España y sus posesiones de Ultramar [16 vols.; Madrid, 1845-1850], Vol. 8, pp. 254-255) thought that the Fuerteventura settlers were wasting time scratching their unproductive land after five years without rains and suggested that they would be much better off to abandon their beloved island and emigrate to America. Some did so in the general wave of nineteenth-century Canario migration to the New World, but Fuerteventura continued to support about the same population. Only at the end of the period did the establishment of the first coastal fishing community offer new hope for diversification of the economy. On Lanzarote a much more intensive agriculture, based on vines and, later, on truck crops, had evolved following the devastating volcanic eruptions of the 1730s. A major fishing and fish processing industry further contributed, as it still does, to the Lanzarote economy. Ten years ago the contrast between the culture and the economy of the two islands, of such similar physical endowments, was still striking (H. Homer Aschmann: Divergent Trends in Agricultural Productivity on Two Dry Islands: Lanzarote and Fuerteventura [unpublished paper presented at the Twentieth International Geographical Congress, London, 1964]).

Today, however, Fuerteventura's long sleep in the African sun has suddenly ended. A frenzy of land speculation, supported by massive advertising campaigns in the capitals of Europe, has made Fuerteventura a household word from Stuttgart and Stockholm to Liverpool. Luxury hotels, condominiums, and cabanas, dependent on their own seawater desalinization plants, are springing up at many places along the island's beaches. The 1970 census gave the island 18,192 persons, up from 13,506 in 1950, and growth since then has sharply accelerated. Fuerteventura still lags well behind the more prosperous and diversified Lanzarote (population 41,912 in 1970, up from 29,388 in 1950), but it has a much more extensive beach frontage and thus, in the idiom of the times, greater "potential for growth." In 1972 more than 100,000 visitors were received at the island's new airport, and the first of the charter "jumbo jets" were arriving loaded with package-tour groups and potential "investors" from West Germany and other European countries.

With a real estate and construction boom fueled by outside capital, the peasants of this most traditional of the Canary Islands face a future of continuing and unpredictable change Apathy and resignation are being replaced by cautious optimism. Employment opportunities abound. Moreover, the island's agriculture has undergone significant changes. A dam has been built across its only noteworthy stream course, the Río Cabras, but the reservoir behind it is fast silting. Some six hundred working windmills, many of them new, are lifting brackish water to irrigate more than a thousand hectares, chiefly in alfalfa and in tomatoes for export. Salinization forces land abandonment after a few years, but additional fertile desert soil is abundant. The limited groundwater supply, however, is clearly being depleted. Black cinder has been spread on some areas at the northern end of Fuerteventura, following the example of Lanzarote, to reduce soil-moisture losses. On such lands garbanzos, lentils, and maize, as well as wheat and barley, are successfully grown, but the government henequen plantation has proved uneconomical. Production of the island's distinctive goat cheese is expanding. The recurrent hunger that gripped the island in the past has largely been forgotten.

After centuries of dependence on precarious and uncertain rainfall Fuerteventura now finds itself abruptly facing a new future as an integral part of the world tourist economy that, for better or worse, is reshaping life and land in so many of the more remote and physically attractive corners of the tropical and subtropical world (John Mercer: Canary Islands: Fuerteventura [David and Charles, Newton Abbot, England, 1973]). The pressures for development are largely of external origin, but they are real. On neighboring Lanzarote, where the process is more advanced, an impressive 37 percent of those interviewed in a recent study thought that the development of tourism had not been and would not be beneficial to their interests ("Lanzarote" [Centro de Investigaciones Económico y Social de la Caja Insular de Ahorros, Las Palmas de Gran Canaria 1971]). A new materialism is eroding the traditional values that tied men closely to their local environment. But for the peasant societies of this world, whether on Fuerteventura or elsewhere, there appears to be little possibility of stemming these inexorable tides of change.

30

Human Influences on the Pine and Laurel Forests of the Canary Islands*

The effect of human activities on the vegetation mantle of the earth historically has tended to be especially severe on island eco-systems. The Canary Islands, which originally supported substantial stands of both coniferous and broadleaf evergreen forests, offer an instructive, but little-known example of this continuing interaction between man and environment. Located some 100 kilometers off the North African coast at 28°N, the Canary archipelago, structurally an extension of the Atlas Mountains, has been an isolated ecologic system since the Tertiary period. The extravagantly broken volcanic topography has created a remarkable diversity of niches, from sea level to the snow-capped summit of Tenerife (Pico de Teide, elevation 3,715 meters) and from the dripping cloud forests of exposed trade-wind slopes to the desertic lee sides where annual precipitation may be less than 100 millimeters.[1] Tenerife and Gran Canaria, the largest of the seven islands, have been termed with some reason "continents in miniature." The Canary Islands lie on the subsiding eastern side of the semipermanent Azores anticyclone. This subsidence produces a warm, dry atmosphere aloft that is separated at an average height of 1,500 to 1,800 meters from a lower layer of moist, southward-streaming air.[2] From the high parts of Tenerife in

---

*Reprinted from *The Geographical Review*, Vol. 71, pp. 253-271 (1981).

[1]Telesforo Bravo, *Geografía general de las islas Canarias* (Santa Cruz de Tenerife: Goya Ediciones, 1954), Vol. 1, pp. 206-225.

[2]Luis Ceballos and Francisco Ortuño, *Vegetación y flora forestal de las Canarias occidentales* (Madrid: Instituto Forestal de Investigaciones y Experiencias, 1951). A revised second edition of this work with superb color illustrations was published by the Cabildo Insular, Santa Cruz de Tenerife, 1976, reference on pp. 65-94. See

the good visibility of the clean, dry air, it is usually possible to see the small cumulus-cloud layer that marks the upper part of this inversion extending to the horizon.

When these clouds rise against the northern slopes of the islands with high elevations, the result is the light showers that may account for more than half of the annual rainfall of approximately 800 millimeters. Elsewhere almost all precipitation occurs during short periods of disturbed weather in the winter half of the year, associated with the close approach of the polar front or with the development of small cyclones off the African coast. Thus the precipitation regime is suggestive of the Mediterranean region with nearly rainless summers, but milder temperatures due to latitude.

The high degree of endemism that characterizes the plant life of the Canary Islands is a product of both environmental diversity and isolation.[3] Of the almost 2,000 species recorded from the archipelago, approximately 30 percent are known only in these islands. Xerophytic shrubs dominate the low, dry eastern islands of Lanzarote and Fuerteventura where the stately Canary Island palm, *Phoenix canariensis*, is locally conspicuous as the only naturally growing tree. Similar semidesert plant associations with numerous *Euphorbiaceae* cover the low slopes where the Atlantic influence is strongest. The windward slopes on the western islands between approximately 500 and 1,200 meters elevation originally supported a diverse broadleaf evergreen forest (*monte verde*) dominated by the Canary laural (*Laurus* sp.) and its relatives to which European plant ecologists applied the term *laurisilva*. This dense canopied assemblage has been largely destroyed on Gran Canaria and much depleted elsewhere to make way for terraced cropland and to provide firewood and lumber. The verdant and luxuriant laurel woodland was extravagantly described by early visitors. Today remnants of this broadleaf forest are of interest, especially to students of plant evolution. On Gran Canaria this forest survives only in two steep-

---

also P.R. García-Prieto, F.H. Ludlam, and P.M. Saunders, The Possibility of Artificially Increasing Rainfall on Tenerife, *Weather*, Vol. 15, 1960, pp. 39-51.

[3]David Bramwell, The Endemic Flora of the Canary Islands, in *Biogeography and Ecology of the Canary Islands* (edited by Gunther Kunkel; The Hague: Dr. W. Junk, 1976), pp. 207-240; A. Machado, Introduction to the Study of the Canary Islands' Laurisilva with Special Reference to Ground Beetles, in *Biogeography and Ecology of the Canary Islands*, this footnote, pp. 347-412, especially 342-356; Per Sunding, The Vegetation of Gran Canaria. *University of Oslo, Natural History Series 29*, Oslo, 1972; and J.V. Malato-Beliz, Conservación de la naturaleza y recursos genéticos, *Botánica Macaronésica*, Vol. 1, 1976, pp. 67-82.

walled barrancas. Less than 6,000 hectares, perhaps 10 percent of its original extent, remain in the other western islands.[4]

The life zones of the high-elevation islands are popularly defined in terms of altitude as "below," "in," and "above" the clouds, especially on the northern and eastern exposures. Upslope from the monte verde and reaching through the persistent clouds into the trade-wind inversion is the pine forest (*pinar*). These pine stands have been under heavy pressure from woodcutters since the earliest European settlement and, before then, from the fires and the domestic animals of the aboriginal Guanches. The pine forests have been reestablished in recent years over most of their original extent through a massive government reforestation program. Pine forests, in varying conditions and density, today cover some 70,000 hectares in the archipelago (Fig. 30.1). Nearly a third of these is on lands that have been reforested during the last 35 years.

On Tenerife pines form a continuous belt around the island between 1,200 and 1,800 meters, although scattered stands may occur down to sea level and upward to 2,200 meters. Above the 2,000-meter contour, pines are generally replaced by xerophytic leguminous shrubs, especially *retama* (*Cytocytisis* sp.) and *codeso* (*Adenocarpus* sp.). The steep cinder flanks of the conical Pico de Teide are devoid of plant life except for a pansy-like endemic, *Viola cheiranthifolia*.

On the island of Hierro (elevation 1,520 meters) and more especially on the better-watered La Palma (elevation 2,423 meters), there are still impressive stands of old-growth pines, but on Gran Canaria (elevation 1,980 meters), larger and drier than Hierro or La Palma, with its tangled interior topography, such stands are sparse and scattered except where they have been recently replanted. Only on Gomera (elevation 1,484 meters) and on the eastern desert islands were pine forests originally absent.

The Canary Island Pine Forest

The Canary Island pine, *Pinus canariensis*, is a familiar ornamental in Mediterranean and California gardens. Its closest relative, *Pinus roxburghii*, is found in the Himalayas, not in Europe or North Africa.[5] The Canary Island pine has one of the most restricted distributions of any of the more than 100 species of the

---

[4]Francisco Ortuño and Andres Ceballos, *Spanish Woodlands* (Madrid-Sevilla: INCAFO, 1967), p. 224.

[5]Nicolas T. Mirov, *The Genus Pinus* (New York: Ronald Press, 1967), p. 74.

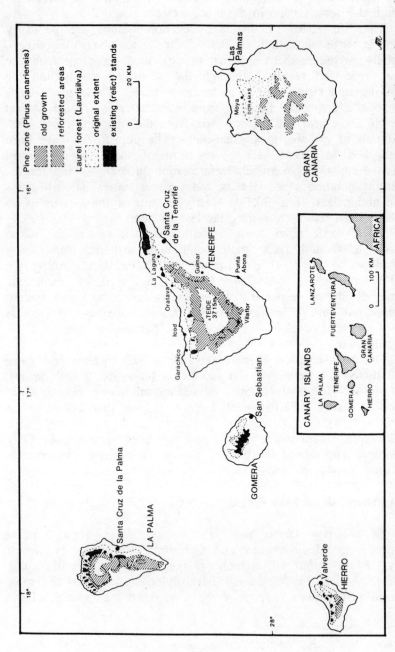

Figure 30.1 The Forest Lands of the Canary Islands. Sources: Personal observations of the author, and adaptations from Ceballos and Ortuño (fn 2), Machado (fn3), and Sunding (fn 3).

genus *Pinus*. Mature, straight-boled trees normally reach a height of 20 to 30 meters. Much influenced by human activities, stand densities vary greatly, but a light, open forest with sparse undergrowth is most characteristic, especially on drier sites. Open or disturbed areas are usually invaded by shrubs such as heather, myrtle, broom, and rockrose, although a tradition of using this growth for agricultural mulch has tended to hold them in check. The long, grayish-green needles, in fascicles of three and bunched in slightly drooping fashion near the ends of the branches, give the tree a distinctive appearance. On the ground the needles decompose slowly, emitting a pleasant fragrance in the afternoon warmth. The rough, reddish bark is fire-resistant and light enough to be used as buoys on fishermen's nets. The species is unique among the pines in its ability to sprout from the base and the trunk after fire or frost damage. The species is well adapted to shallow, rocky soils with small amounts of humus. In its growth habit and tolerance for drought conditions, it somewhat resembles the yellow pine, *Pinus ponderosa*, of the American West or some of the Mexican pines. Growth rates are rapid, especially when the trees are young. The largest specimens have a girth probably exceeding that of any European member of the genus, and in some cases take on almost sequoia-like proportions.

Individual pines of exceptional size have long been the object of special attention and veneration in the archipelago.[6] Shrines or hermitages often have been built alongside them, for example, the *Pino de la Virgen* near El Paso (La Palma), the *Pino de Buen Paso* near Icod (Tenerife), and the *Virgen de Los Angeles* at Victoria de Acentejo (Tenerife). For festivals, pine boughs are traditionally brought from the mountains to festoon the paths of processions and to decorate streets and churches. *Nuestra Señora del Pino* at Teror on Gran Canaria is the *patrona* of that island and the subject of fervent devotion, although the tree in which the Madonna is asserted to have miraculously appeared in 1484 fell three centuries ago.

The Cultural History of the Archipelago

There is uncertainty as to when the first Gaunche peoples reached the Canary Islands from North Africa with goats, sheep, and

---

[6]Leoncio Rodriguez, *Los arboles históricos y tradicionales de Canarias* (2 vols.; Santa Cruz de Tenerife: La Prensa, 1946); and Ceballos and Ortuño, footnote 2 above, 2nd ed., p. 166n.

pigs, but their arrival was definitely well before the time of Christ.[7] The Guanche were of Berber stock and full neolithic culture and apparently were isolated on the islands from other influences until the first arrival of Europeans in the fourteenth century. Livestock constituted the principal wealth of those cave-dwelling pastoralists, who also cultivated wheat and barley and gathered edible wild plants and shellfish. Remarkably, by the time of the European conquest they seem to have all but abandoned the art of boat building and interisland travel so that the groups on each island were isolated and lacked communication with their neighbors.

The European presence in the archipelago dates from the activities of Catalan and Mallorcan missionaries on Gran Canaria between 1352 and 1391 associated with the sparsely documented bishopric of Telde.[8] The presence intensified in 1402-1403 with the conquest of Lanzarote, an early target of Andalusian slaving expeditions, by the Breton Jean de Bethencourt under the auspices of Henry III of Castile. By 1409 Fuerteventura and distant Hierro were occupied, as was Gomera, an important source of slaves, in 1447. These five islands were awarded as seignores by the Spanish Crown, but they offered little opportunity for economic gain other than from slaves and orchilla. They served as springboards for the conquest of Gran Canaria, Tenerife, and La Palma where the Guanche defenders were numerous and formidable. These three islands offered the promise of great wealth from the cultivation of sugar cane by irrigation and were proclaimed crown lands in 1477.

The Canary enterprise was in the hands of a small aristocracy until the conquest of Gran Canaria (1477-1484). The conquistador and first governor of that island, Pedro de Vera, was authorized by the Crown to distribute land and water rights to deserving noblemen, soldiers, and sailors according to their merits. So was the Adelantado Alonso de Lugo a few years later on Tenerife and La Palma. Persons who would build sugar mills and plant sugar cane, intro-

---

[7]Luis Diego Cuscoy, Los Guanches: vida y cultura del primitivo habitante de Tenerife, *Museo Arqueológico de Tenerife, Publicación No. 7*, Santa Cruz de Tenerife, 1968; Luis Diego Cuscoy, El Conjunto ceremonial de Guargacho, *Museo Arqueológico de Tenerife, Publicación No. 11*, Santa Cruz de Tenerife, 1979; and Ilse Schwidetsky, The Prehispanic Population of the Canary Islands, in *Biogeography and Ecology of the Canary Islands*, footnote 3 above, pp. 15-36.

[8]Antonio Rumeu de Armas, *El obispado de Telde, misioneros mallorquins y catalanes en el Atlántico* (Madrid-Las Palmas: Biblioteca Atlántica, 1960); and Augustín Millares Torres, *Historia general de las Islas Canarias* (10 vols.; Las Palmas de Gran Canaria: Edirca, S.L., 2nd ed., 1977 [originally published 1873-1895]), Vol. 3, p. 31.

duced from the Iberian Peninsula or from Madeira, were to be given the largest and best tracts. Genovese merchants, who had the necessary capital for such ventures, played a major role in establishing the activity. The technology for sugar making was brought by Portuguese from madeira, already a "sugar island." To assure that the best lands and the water rights would not be monopolized, the sale of either land grants or sugar mills was forbidden.

With the completion of the conquest, councils were appointed to govern each of the crown-land islands. The councils were also authorized to make additional grants of unoccupied land. Much of it was forested or in the rough or drier parts of the islands. Some tracts close to settlements were set aside as commons for the use of local residents, especially for grazing and woodcutting. With the passage of time, most of these commons were distributed in allotments for cultivation.[9]

During much of the past 450 years, island society has been polarized between a subsistence agricultural-pastoral sector dependent on maize, potatoes, and domestic animals and a commercial export sector, long controlled by foreigners, that has gone through recurrent cycles of prosperity and depression. Orchilla dyestuff, sugar, wine, *barilla* (*Mesembryanthemum*, an ice plant that was a source of soda ash), and now tomatoes and bananas have been the base of the export economy.[10] tobacco and winter vegetables have made less contributions to it. Since 1950 a sun-and-sand-oriented mass tourism has engulfed the archipelago, which has brought both unprecedented prosperity and serious social and environmental ruptures.

The Canary Islands, with a population of 1.4 million, are an integral part of Spain and since 1929 have constituted the two provinces of Las Palmas (Gran Canaria, Lanzarote, Fuerteventura) and Santa Cruz de Tenerife (Tenerife, La Palma, Gomera, Hierro). The two provinces are almost equal in population, as are the provincial capitals of Las Palmas and Santa Cruz de Tenerife. The proposed entry of Spain into the European Economic Community and

---

[9]A.M. Macías Hernández, La transformación de la propiedad agraria consejil en el paso del antiguo régimen al nuevo régimen, *Revista de Historia Canaria*, Anexo 1, 1978, pp. 44-47; and Germán Hernandez Rodriguez, Los montes de la Gomera y su conflictividad, *Aguayro* (Casa Insular de Ahorros de Gran Canaria), No. 84, 1977, pp. 31-34.

[10]Josef Matznetter, *Die Kanarischen Inseln, Wirtschaftgeschichte und Agrargeographie* (Gotha: Hermann Haack, 1958). On the "export" of people as a component of the commercial relations of the islands, see *Coloquio de Historia Canario-Americano I*, 1976 (edited by Francisco Morales Padrón; Las Palmas-Sevilla: Cabildo Insular de Gran Canaria, 1977).

possibly into the North Atlantic Treaty Organization recently intensified concern for the always uneasy economic and political equilibrium of the archipelago.

Forests and Water

Water is the overriding problem in the Canary Islands today. "Mined" for more than a century from pervious lenses in the complex volcanic rocks that make up the islands and used mostly for irrigation, water is now in perilously short supply. These haphazardly distributed underground veins of water have been tapped since the nineteenth century by an extraordinary system of horizontal perforations (*galerías*), some as much as 5 kilometers long, on the middle and high slopes.[11] They are owned by public stock companies that sell water to banana and tomato farms below at increasingly higher prices. Shares in these speculative ventures are bought and sold through a "water exchange" (*Bolsa de Aguas*) in Santa Cruz de Tenerife. Extraction rates from underground reserves substantially exceed replenishment, and the galerías are drying up. There were 913 of them on Tenerife and 154 on La Palma in 1977. Many of these were abandoned, but new ones continue to be drilled in the hope of finding additional productive lenses of water. On Gran Canaria, where the more impermeable lavas make wells and small reservoirs feasible, galerías are less common than on the other islands. But on this dry island water shortages are especially acute. Seawater distillation, weather modification, and additional reservoir construction have all been resorted to, but the survival of commercial-irrigated agriculture depends primarily on a sharp reduction of water use. Mulching with either volcanic ash or organic matter and the new technique of drip irrigation provide partial answers.

The forests of the Canary Islands are dripping wet environments when shrouded in clouds. Moisture added to the soil beneath by "fog drip" often substantially exceeds that reaching the ground as rain. The legendary *garoé* or "rain tree" of the island of Hierro, probably a *til* (*Ocotea foetens*), is said to have condensed cloud droplets sufficient to support two permanent pools of water at its base until felled by a storm in 1612. This "horizontal precipitation" tends to be greatest where air movement is strongest and is especial-

---

[11]Hans Hausen, On the Ground Water Conditions in the Canary Islands and their Irrigation Cultures, *Acta Geográfica* (Helsinki), Vol. 12, No. 2, 1951.

ly pronounced in the pine forests.[12]   In one extreme case, 5,090 millimeters were recorded during twelve months in one Tenerife pine forest, while only 650 millimeters fell on a nearby clearing.   Because the seasonal distribution of fog precipitation is similar to that of normal precipitation, the character of the winter-rain climate is not changed by this additional source of moisture.   Tolerance of seasonal dryness is more decisive than fog interception to the distribution of pines, although the additional water added to the soil may range from 300 to 2,500 millimeters annually.

Horizontal precipitation, still little studied, is clearly a significant factor in the water economy of the archipelago.   However, the same trees that induce this precipitation also transpire substantial amounts of moisture.   Although they significantly reduce runoff rates, trees probably take more water out of the ground than they add to it under most circumstances.   In mid-latitude forests transpiration rates have been shown to be substantially higher for pines than for mature broadleaf stands.[13]   Data on this are still unavailable for the Canary Islands.   In the popular mind there remains a conviction that there is a close relationship between declining availability of ground water and the destruction of the tree cover on the islands. This unsubstantiated belief has been the basis of the widespread support for forest conservation and replanting programs in recent years.

Early Exploitation of the Woodlands

From the Spanish establishment on the better-watered western islands, beginning with Gran Canaria in 1477, the woodlands were the object of intense exploitation.   They supplied wood for fuel and construction, as well as pitch and livestock forage in an environment largely dominated by aridity.   The woodlands were the object of insistent concern by the island councils that viewed them as both a source of income and a fragile resource demanding close supervision and control.

---

[12]Luis Ceballos and Francisco Ortuño, El bosque y el agua en Canarias, *Montes* (Madrid), Vol. 8, 1952, pp. 418-423; Luis Ceballos, Consideraciones sobre la flora y la vegetación forestal de las islas atlánticas, *Anuario de Estudios Atlánticos*, Vol. 2, 1956, pp. 9-44; and Franco Kämmer, Klima und Vegetation auf Tenerife besonders im Hinblick auf den Nebelniederschlag, *Scripta Botánica* 7, Göttingen, 1974.

[13]W.T. Shank and J.E. Douglas, *Science*, Vol. 185, 1974, pp. 857-859.

This preoccupation is evident from the minutes of early council meetings and from the numerous protective ordinances that were adopted.[14] Detailed restrictions on the use of the forests were enforced by a guard system with severe fines for violations. Every form of exploitation required a license, and the fee schedule was a topic of continued discussion. The export of lumber and firewood was closely controlled and at times prohibited, although there was always an active clandestine trade. Lanzarote and Fuerteventura, destitute of wood, imported it from the western islands. This trade was generally frowned on by local authorities, concerned about the threatened depletion of their own forest resources.

Restrictions on the use of the forest were specific. The cutting of trees near springs was prohibited; none that were large enough for use in construction were to be taken for fuel wood; for each pine removed, ten new trees were to be planted; livestock were prohibited from entering the forest; fires in it were outlawed; night hunting in the dry season was illegal. There were explicit prohibitions on the taking of certain species such as *aceviño* (*Ilex canariensis*). The monte verde of the Montaña Doramas of Gran Canaria was the object of particularly detailed restrictions that dated from the first years of the sixteenth century. The insular archives contain many volumes of litigation on the illegal activities in the forests. The excesses of the woodcutters and charcoal makers, the destructive fires, the incursions of livestock, and the perpetual shortage of reliable forest guards all contributed to what was early seen as an ecological disaster in the making.

Sugar manufacturing made the heaviest levies on the forests in the early years.[15] Tenerife and Gran Canaria each had twelve sugar

---

[14]José Peraza de Ayala, *Las ordenanzas de Tenerife* (Madrid: Aula de Cultura de Tenerife, 2nd ed., 1976); Leopoldo de la Rosa, Catálogo del Archivo Municipal de La Laguna (Sucesor del antiguo cabildo de Tenerife), *Revista de Historia* (Universidad de La Laguna), various issues, 1944-1960; Acuerdos de Cabildo de Tenerife, *Fontes Rerum Canarium* IV: 1497-1507, 1949; V: 1508-1513, 1952; XI: 1514-1518, 1965; XVI: 1518-1525, 1970 (edited by Elias Serra Rafols and Leopoldo de la Rosa; La Laguna: Instituto de Estudios Canarias); Francisco Morales Padrón, *Ordenanzas del Consejo de Gran Canaria*, 1531 (Sevilla: Cabildo Insular de Gran Canaria, 1974); *Libro Rojo de Gran Canaria* (edited by Pedro Cullén del Castillo; Las Palmas: Tipografía Alzola, 1947); and Leopoldo de la Rosa, *Evolución del régimen local en las Islas Canarias* (Madrid: Instituto de Estudios de Administración Local, 1946).

[15]Miguel Angel Ladero Quesada, La economía de las Islas Canarias a comienzo del siglo XVI, *Anuario de Estudios Americanos*, Vol. 31, 1974, pp. 725-749; Guillermo Camacho y Pérez Galdos, El cultivo de caña de azúcar y la industria azucarero en Gran Canaria, 1510-1535, *Anuario de Estudios Atlánticos*, Vol. 7,

mills in the 1560s, while La Palma had four and Gomera one.[16] Other evidence suggests as many as 22 for Gran Canaria somewhat earlier. The typical mill operated for 6 months of the year, with eight copper cauldrons continuously boiling cane juice. Substantial fortunes were made in the business in only a few years. Sir Francis Bacon wrote of how "being the first in an invention does sometimes cause a wonderful overgrowth of riches, as it was with the first sugarmen in the Canaries."[17] At 500 *maravedis* for one *arroba* (10 kilograms) of sugar, the capital investment in a sugar mill with a capacity of between 8,000 and 9,000 arrobas might be paid off in 3 years. The mills ground not only their own cane but also the production of smallholders on a shared basis. Each mill thus had 15 to 20 independent suppliers. This practice was later to become the basis of the *colono* system of sugar production in Cuba. By the end of the sixteenth century, with new competition from the Americas and the North African coast, where *Canarios* were generally the sugar masters, sugar production was in sharp decline and wine was in the ascendancy. As sugar disappeared from the Canary Island economy, the drain on the deteriorating woodlands slowed but did not stop.

The gradual increase in the rural population, augmented by refugees from Lanzarote and Fuerteventura during drought periods, brought further pressures on the forest lands as subsistence agriculture pressed upward to the wooded mid-slopes of Gran Canaria, Tenerife, and La Palma. Additional titles granted on crown lands, together with clandestine occupations, led to widespread clearing, while livestock made increasingly destructive incursions into the remaining forests.[18]

George Glas, an English visitor, wrote in 1764 that on the high slopes above Oratava, Tenerife, where the clouds remained most of the day, "there was formerly a great abundance of stately pine trees; but being easy to come at they were almost all cut down by the inhabitants of the adjacent villages so that few now

---

1960, pp. 11-60; and Maria Luisa Fabrellas, La producción de azúcar en Tenerife, *Revista de Historia* (La Laguna), Vol. 18, 1952, pp. 455-480.

[16]Thomas Nichols, *A Pleasant Description of the Fortunate Islands Called Islands of Canaria (London*: Thomas East, 1583).

[17]Quoted in Noel Deerr, *The History of Sugar* (London: Chapman and Hall, 1949), p. 155n.

[18]Antonio Manual Macías Hernández, El motín de 1777 en Gran Canaria, *Anuario de Estudios Atlánticos*, Vol. 23, 1977, pp. 263-345.

remain...but in other places of the island at the same altitude, and which are distant from any habitations, there are great numbers of them."[19] The effect of the fuel-hungry sugar mills would have been particularly heavy in those forests immediately above the best-watered and most productive lowlands where the cane plantings were concentrated. Accounts of visitors, including Alexander von Humboldt in 1799, who climbed the Pico de Teide, make no mention of a pine forest but instead describe a few named landmark conifers that stood as solitary guideposts along the route.

On the island of La Palma, Glas reported that rabbits had been the cause of the destruction of the high pine forests. Although the trees on the summits had been destroyed, they remained abundant in the cloud zone so that from a distance of 2 leagues "it appeared as a solid forest." Pines here were all enough to serve as spars for large ships, but the timbers were heavy, and the broken terrain made the cost of transporting them to the coast almost prohibitive. The captain of an American sloop with a broken mast paid 25 pounds sterling to transport one tree to the harbor. "Nevertheless," Glas noted, "much wood is exported from here to the rest of the islands."[20]

The Destruction of Montaña Doramas

The history of the monte verde of Montaña Doramas on Gran Canaria exemplifies the continued pressures on the forests of the islands. Early travelers and poets wrote of its Arcadian verdure and its sparkling streams.[21] An observer in 1634 termed Montaña Doramas "one of the most grandiose possessions of Spain." For the historian José Viera y Clavijo, it appeared to be "a work of art, appreciated the more because it is not."[22] Glas thought that the

---

[19]George Glas, Descripción de las islas Canarias, 1764, *Fontes Rerum Canarium XX* (La Laguna: Instituto de Estudios Canarias, 1976), pp. 79-80.

[20]Glas, footnote 19 above, p. 96.

[21]Alfredo Herrera Piqué, La destrucción de los bosques de Gran Canaria a comienzos del siglo XVI, *Aguayro* (Casa Insular de Ahorros de Gran Canaria), No. 92, 1977, pp. 7-10; and Mariano Nougues Secall, *Cartas histórico-filosófico-administrativo sobre las Islas Canarias* (Santa Cruz de Tenerife: Salvador Vidal, 1858), p. 380.

[22]José Viera y Clavijo, *Noticias de la historia general de las Islas Canarias* [1782-83] (edited by Alejandro Ciorenescu; Santa Cruz de Tenerife: Ediciones Goya, 1971).

forest made "a charming scene," the lofty boughs of its fragrant trees "so thickly interwoven as to exclude the rays of the sun." The rills that watered those shady groves, the whispering of the breeze among the trees, and the melody of the birds formed for him "a most delightful concert." A person in that "enchanting solitude," he reflected, was inevitably reminded of the descriptions of the Fortunate Islands by the ancients.[23]

The Montaña Doramas, named for a renowned Guanche chieftain, lay directly above the best sugar lands on the island. From the first years of Spanish control the forest was under heavy pressure. Many ordinances were passed by the council aimed at the conservation and the regeneration of the forest, but apparently to little avail.[24] There were prohibitions against the grazing of stock, the making of charcoal, and the setting of fires of any sort, the last under penalty of lashes, banishment, and even death. In 1533 when the forest was closed to any further exploitation for 10 years, the sugar mills were directed to seek their firewood requirements elsewhere, chiefly in the less accessible pine lands. However, complaints caused the order to be rescinded. Soon thereafter the Crown ordered that during future council deliberations on matters related to forests, the members who owned sugar mills should be excluded from the sessions. The linkage of economic and political power was already evident.

The assault by settlers and woodcutters continued unabated, even as the sugar era neared its end. Already in the 1560s Thomas Nichols could write of Gran Canaria that "wood is the thing that is most wanted."[25] Increasingly wood was sought from the other islands as land clearing for agriculture impinged more and more on the remaining forests. A late eighteenth-century report referred to Montaña Doramas as "a picture of desolation." In 1802 fire further reduced by half what was left. Browsing livestock effectively prohibited regeneration. Already much of the area was in private hands and under cultivation. The remainder was a constant source of conflict among neighboring towns. With the proclamation of the constitutional system in 1820, influential citizens of the *ayuntamiento* of Moya requested distribution of the remaining Montaña Doramas as private property, on the argument that this was the only way to eliminate clandestine cutting and grazing. But the adjacent com-

---

[23]Glas, footnote 19 above, p. 65.

[24]*Libro Rojo*, footnote 14 above, p. lxiii.

[25]Nichols, footnote 16 above.

munities opposed such concessions and threatened armed intervention, if necessary, to prevent them.[26]

In 1831, as payment for salary arrears and for services rendered to the country, Fernando VII granted most of the remaining Doramas forest, some 1,000 hectares, to General Francisco Tomás Morales, celebrated field marshal of the defeated Spanish forces in the Americas.[27] Returning to his native islands in 1827, he was named governor of the archipelago. Deposed seven years later after a political dispute, he retired to develop his new property, which he named Hacienda San Fernando. An enigmatic figure, his name is still associated with the destruction of the legendary Montaña Doramas, although by his time it was only a caricature of what it had been in the past. He publicly proclaimed his innocence and good intentions with the assertion that he assigned guards to keep poachers and livestock from the remaining woodland and set severe penalties for sharecroppers who cut trees unnecessarily. Pascual Madoz wrote in his "Diccionario" that the forest of Doramas, "once the pride of the Canarios, has been reduced to some groups of trees which the proprietor condescendingly preserves but that are slowly disappearing."[28]

The Early Naval Stores Industry

There had been incursions into the pine forests of Tenerife for lumber and naval stores even before the Spanish conquest. By 1498, 2 years after the end of Guanche resistance, a tax of five maravedis per quintal (100 kilograms) of pitch (*pez*) was levied by the council. Later the sum was doubled. Licenses to take pitch were offered at public auction. The product was in demand not only for shipbuilding and repairs but also for caulking the wooden aqueducts that carried water across often considerable distances to the cane fields. An early prohibition on the export of pitch was soon relaxed. In an economy short of money, pitch was occasionally used as a medium of exchange, as were sugar and wheat. In the first years of the sixteenth century pitch was valued at 100 to 150

---

[26]Pascual Madoz, *Diccionario geográfica-estadística-histórica de España y sus posesiones de ultramar* (16 vols.; Madrid: P. Madoz, 1845-1850), Vol. 7, p. 308.

[27]Francisco Morales Padron, Francisco Tomás Morales, último Capitán General de Venezuela, *Anuario de Estudios Americanos*, Vol. 33, 1976, pp. 641-712.

[28]Gunther Kunkel, Die Lordbeerwaldrelikte auf Gran Canaria, *Schriften des Geographischen Instituts der Universität Kiel*, Vol. 30, Kiel, 1973, pp. 121-129.

maravedis dockside. Twenty quintals might buy a cask of wine, 120 a healthy African slave.[29]

The authorities expressed continuing concern for the lifestyle of the pitch makers, many of whom were Portuguese. An ordinance in 1500 required that pitch makers must have a permanent residence and have "planted and fenced at least 800 vines" before they could be granted licenses. Later it was specified that they should be married. The council worried that the men who worked away from the towns for extended periods would not hear Mass, but no remedy for that situation was forthcoming.[30]

Pitch works were concentrated in the best stands of mature pines, above Icod on the northwestern coast and on the drier lee side of Tenerife. As early as 1500, it was explicitly forbidden to cut pines to make pitch in the Taora district (Oratava), "because they are for the sugar ingenios." There was less production of pitch on Gran Canaria, La Palma, and Hierro. The Tenerife archives at La Laguna contain an almost continuous record of council income from the pitch works of Icod and of Agache, between present-day Güimar and Abona, prior to 1651, when the record terminated.[31] Production peaked in 1593. In the nineteenth century, with the progressive destruction of the old-growth pines, references to pitch making were rare.

To obtain the resin-rich, red heartwood characteristic of old-growth Canary pines, it was the practice to fell the tree. The resinous wood was then cut into chunks and slowly cooked for 24 hours in three-chambered brick ovens. A charge of 1,600 kilograms was said to yield 200 to 240 kilograms of the black, lustrous pitch.[32] Because the works were in isolated locations, the remaining white sapwood was without value and was left to rot. The wastefulness of this primitive method of exploitation troubled Tenerife authorities.

---

[29]Emma Gonzalez Yañez, Importación y exportación en Tenerife durante los primeros años de la conquista, 1497-1503, Revista de Historia de Canarias, Vol. 29, 1953, pp. 71-91, reference on p. 78; and Emma Gonzalez Yañez and Manuela Marrero Rodriguez, Protocolos del escribano Hernán García, La Laguna, 1508-1510, Fontes Rerum Canarium VIII (La Laguna: Instituto de Estudios Canarios, 1958).

[30]Gonzalez Yañez, footnote 29 above, pp. 79-80; and Acuerdos de Cabildo de Tenerife, 1508-1513, footnote 14 above, June 16, 1511.

[31]de la Rosa, Catálogo, footnote 14 above.

[32]Gaspar Frutuosa, Las Islas Canarias de "Saudades da Terra," 1590 (translated from the Portuguese; La Laguna: Instituto de Estudios Canarios, 1964).

They made the cutting of trees to obtain pitch illegal in some areas. For the most part, such restrictions were unenforceable. Alternatively the heartwood might be hollowed from the lower part of a standing tree with an axe. This technique might yield one or two loads of the resin. Scattered old pines in the forest still bear evidence of the practices--their charred basal scars at least twice the height of a person. Ignited, these resin-saturated lesions, which also supplied torchwood for night fishing, might burn for 3 or 4 days.

Heartwood of Pine--A Prized Construction Material

The same resinous heartwood that produced the pitch of commerce was also prized as a building material. Valued for its rich, natural beauty and for its resistance to weathering and insect damage, the heartwood was considered "incorruptible." A memorial on the state of the carpentry trade on Tenerife in 1778 observed that the growing shortage of *tea*, as this wood was known, was having a damaging effect on the construction industry.[33] Builders, accustomed to using this material, found its cost prohibitive. They blamed the scarcity on the sorry state of the pine forests. The short supply of *viñatigo* (*Persea indica*), a wood favored by furniture makers, was also noted. The alternatives were either to bring in West Indian cedar or mahogany at much increased cost or to use inferior materials.

A distinctive "Canary style" of architecture, featuring half-timbering, exposed beams, and handsomely carved exterior balconies of natural wood evolved in the archipelago in response to the availability of this unique material.[34] So did a sophisticated furniture industry. Church interiors as well as the doors and the balconies of old townhouses or public buildings that have been exposed to the elements continuously for 300 or more years show no signs of deterioration. Today *tea* is rarely available on the market, and the demand for the wood has made the dismantling of old structures a profitable business. Buildings featuring the use of this dense, slightly translucent wood have become tourist attractions. A reviving nostalgia for the past, fueled in part by the new mass tourism, has further promoted public interest in the diversity of architectural uses to which *tea* has been put.

---

[33] Memoria sobre el estado actual del oficio de carpinteros de esta ciudad, 12 Diciembre, 1778, Archivo Municipal de La Laguna, *Industrias*, tomo 3.

[34] Fernando Martín Rodriguez, *Arquitectura doméstica canaria* (Santa Cruz de Tenerife: Aula de Cultura, 1978).

The Sociedades Económicas

The deteriorated state of the vegetative cover of the islands was a central concern of the *sociedades económicas de los amigos del pais* after their establishment in the late eighteenth century on Gran Canaria, Tenerife, and La Palma. In their publications and in the minutes of their meetings, these active, civic-improvement groups, so typical of the Spanish Enlightenment, reflected a preoccupation with the progressive destruction of the forests.[35] It was noted that the woodlands supplied construction materials, fuel wood, and naval stores, that they reduced runoff and erosion, and that "by attracting moisture from the atmosphere [they] assured the flow of the springs on which agriculture depends."

The first session of the Gran Canaria branch of the society at Las Palmas in 1777 discussed the condition of the pine forests, unable to reproduce because of livestock depredations and fires set maliciously by stockmen to encourage new grass. It was lamented that the government had no control over privately owned forest lands where cutting, burning, and goat damage were also increasing. Five years later a report described "the sad spectacle of our once dense pinar" in which the actions of man and his livestock left no opportunity for the pines to regenerate.

Representations to the Supreme Council of Castile in 1788 brought the closing of a part of Montaña Doramas and the nearby Montaña Lentiscal, but bribery and intimidation of guards by "insolent woodcutters" only intensified. A committee returning from an inspection tour predicted that the useful forests of the island would be gone in a short time. The committee proposed, among other measures, that a reforestation program be initiated, "if necessary at the society's own expense."

Two inspectors, sent to the pine lands of the interior in 1836, returned to describe "a scene of mutilation" there. A few months later a "horrendous fire" had brought further extensive destruction. It was the goats, however, that were seen as the principal culprits. Gran Canaria, the inspectors reported, was being converted "from an island oasis crowned with perpetual green to an ugly skeleton floating in the sea." The rains were believed to have diminished

[35]Sociedad Económica de Amigos del Pais, Las Palmas, *Boletín*, No. 7-10, 1862, and Nos. 72-73, 1868; Sociedad Económica de Amigos del Pais, Las Palmas, Annales, 1872, pp. 44-45, and 1879, pp. 7-23; and Enrique Roméu Palazuelos, *La Económica a través de sus actas, años 1776 a 1800* (La Laguna: Real Sociedad Económica de Amigos del Pais de Tenerife, 1970).

450

and become less regular, and there was "more sickness at all seasons and an increase in rabid dogs." It was notorious that licensees were taking twice the authorized quantities of wood. The guards were irresponsible and completely ineffective in enforcing existent ordinances. There were not enough guards, and they easily fell under the influence of the exploiters. "We must tear the masks from these spurious sons of the island," the inspectors concluded, "to whom the care of our forest has been confided." On Tenerife and La Palma the situation was no different.

A report to the Gran Canaria branch of the society in 1878 stated that of the original 40,000 hectares of pines on the island only a few tracts remained, leaving the once forested land as "sad and ugly *páramos* supporting only rachitic stands of heather." At least eight different pine forests were described as having been destroyed during previous years. The society went to the highest authorities in Madrid but encountered only indifference. Royal orders that excluded livestock from state forests and authorized the replanting of the pine lands were ignored. The society was especially forceful in urging that state-owned forests should not be sold under the disentailment legislation (*desamortización*) of 1855 because of the special conditions in the archipelago. Instead such land continued to be sold, usually at a fraction of its true value.[36] On Gran Canaria the Crown had retained title to unalienated lands, in contrast with Tenerife and La Palma where most of the untitled woodlands had been ceded to the local governments in the 1830s.

The La Laguna branch of the Sociedad Económica heard its first account of the condition of forests on Tenerife and proposals for their restoration in 1778. Six years later the branch announced a prize of 200 *reales* or a medal for the best report "on the present state of the forests, the causes of their ruin, and possible means for their restoration." Neither these reports nor a study commissioned in 1794 on the same theme has been found in the society's archives.

There was repeated mention of the promise of reforestation of the pine belt. In 1813 and again in 1841 royal orders specified that such activities were the responsibility of local authorities. But, with few exceptions, there was little interest from the municipal officials who now controlled the woodlands of Tenerife. Those officials complained about the difficulties of obtaining supplies of planting stock and about the impossibility of keeping goats, sheep, and even camels from the forest during the dry season when the animals voraciously sought out the grayish-green pine seedlings. An observ-

[36]Juan José Ojeda Quintana, La desamortización en Canarias (1836 y 1855) *Cuadernos Canarias de Ciencias Sociales* (Las Palmas), No. 3, 1977.

er wrote in 1858 that "if no remedies are taken these islands will soon be denuded and converted to unproductive crags...it is not enough to preserve the forest, it is necessary to replant it."[37] Because some of the original vegetation remained, he thought that "it would not take long to reclaim what has been lost if administrators would pay closer attention." The wealth of seedlings on the floor of the pine forest would reproduce if given protection. But this they did not receive.

On La Palma the records of the society are sketchier than those of the Tenerife and Gran Canaria branches, but the concerns were comparable to those of the other chapters. An 1859 classification showed 37,000 hectares of pines in the public forests of the island, an estimated 20 percent of the total for the archipelago.[38] They were in much better condition than those on the larger islands, although most were said to need "cleaning and thinning." On Hierro, 1,000 hectares of pine lands had been donated to the council by their owner, the count of Adeje.

Pine Needles as a Resource

The peculiar economy of the Canary Islands inverts the traditional scale of values of forest products. The minor items, not the logs or the lumber, provide the principal income.[39] And this pattern continues even today when charcoal and firewood are no longer of much significance. Pine needles (*pinocha*), sometimes mixed with heather, broom, and bracken fern, provide the most important source of income from the forests of the islands. The peasant custom of collecting the fallen needles from the forest floor was recorded as early as the middle of the nineteenth century. Thus an 1858 account suggested that the forest administrators for Tenerife should prohibit the extraction of the dry needles for use as fertilizer or mulch "because it removes the precious humus cap as well as many ungerminated seeds and young shoots on which the future of

---

[37]Nougues Secall, footnote 21 above, pp. 380 and 386.

[38]Miguel Bosch, Rapid ojeada sobre el estado de los montes de Canarias, Puerto Rico, Cuba y Filipinas, *Revista Forestal, Económica y Agrícola* (Madrid), Vol. 1, 1868, pp. 169-188, reference on p. 183.

[39]Francisco Ortuño, Aprovechamientos forestales en los montes de Canarias, *Montes* (Madrid), Vol. 16, 1960, pp. 271-275.

the forest depends."[40] By the end of the nineteenth century the dry needles also were being used as a packing material for bananas that was called "grass" by British importers.

Luis Ceballos and Francisco Ortuño wrote in 1951 that the extraction of pine needles, done with increased intensity during and immediately after World War II, had all but exhausted the existent supplies.[41] As silviculturists, Ceballos and Ortuño advised termination of "this continuing drain on the only fertilizer materials available to the forest soil, which could have disastrous long term effects on the forest." But they recognized the potential social consequences of such a move. "It is difficult to imagine," they write, "the number of persons who presently support themselves by these forest products. In our travels through the pinares we encounter many persons each day, with loads on their heads, descending from the heights (cumbres) on the rocky trails. They are mostly women and children contributing their bit to the family's subsistence." The meager remuneration of five to ten pesetas that the gatherers received from their one daily load emphasized the extent of their need. The dislocations of the war years were blamed for this unecological exploitation, and conditions were improving. But Ceballos and Ortuño warned that the forest could not wait. They urged a division of the pine forests in administrative districts so that some forest areas could be rested and the soil continue to receive "the substances necessary for its maintenance." In the next years, this suggestion was implemented by a system of auctions instituted under the supervision of the Forest Service, and later the Instituto Nacional para la Conservación de la Naturaleza (ICONA). The system continues.

In recent years auctions of pine needles produced two or three times the monetary returns received from all other forest products, including lumber. On Tenerife in 1977 rights to collect 270,000 metric tons of pine needles and other organic materials from the forest floor brought 7.9 million pesetas (1.1 million U.S. dollars) at public auctions in 23 municipios.[42] In comparison, rights to take 4,933 trees brought only 3.1 million pesetas, while grape and tomato stakes yielded another 1.3 million pesetas.

---

[40]Nougues Secall, footnote 21 above, p. 390.

[41]Ceballos and Ortuño, footnote 2 above, 1st ed.

[42]Information from the files of the Instituto para la Conservación de la Naturaleza (ICONA), Santa Cruz de Tenerife, courtesy of Ing. Enrique Mira.

During the late 1960s, when bananas began to be boxed, demand softened, but with the recent expansion of banana terraces (12,500 hectares in 1977), the market for organic mulch from the forest floor has been strong. In 1978 ICONA supervised the auction of rights to collect more than 2 million tons of pine needles at $1.50 US to $4.50 US a ton on Tenerife and La Palma. Many contractors doubtlessly took more than was authorized. Trucks loaded with pine needles, often mixed with heather or bracken fern, are a common sight on the country roads, while in the pine forests great stacks of the long, reddish-brown needles, awaiting collection, stand along the roads. In addition, subsistence farmers living on the forest edges still collect pine needles to use as bedding for their animals and manure on their potato fields.

The effect of the periodic removal of needles from the forest floor continues to be debated. *Pinus canariensis* thrives on shallow mineral soils, even on fresh lava and cinder. Yet in the long run, removal of this organic matter must reduce water-infiltration rates and must encourage runoff and sheet erosion with a consequent decline of soil nitrogen, carbon, and humus substances that regulate soil structure. The slow rate of decomposition of the needles has led to speculation that fire may be required to recycle completely their minerals into the soils of more arid habitats.

The collection of pine needles is sometimes justified by the reduced fire hazard resulting from removal of these combustible materials. After a recent destructive burn on La Palma, a correspondent to the local press criticized ICONA for the restrictiveness of its auction policy, which was said to have made more favorable conditions for fire.

A local custom on La Palma is to leave scattered pines in the midst of fields of potatoes and cultivated forage plants, principally *tedera* (*Psorlea bituminosa*) and *tagasaste* (a cultigen of *Cytisis proliferus*). The branches of these trees are pruned every 3 or 4 years. After drying on the ground, the pruned branches and any available crop residue are burned, the ashes being used to fertilize the fields in preparation for the next planting. Although the trunks sprout freely after such treatment, the branches never attain their normal horizontal spread because of the repeated pruning. Like stark skeletons with a tuft of greenery at the top, these trees suggest something "created by the genius of El Greco."

454

Reforestation

After four centuries of continued abuse, the pine forests of the Canary Islands have been reestablished through most of their former extent under a vigorous and well-managed reforestation program administered initially by the Patrimonio Forestal of the Spanish Forest Service and now by ICONA.[43] Almost 25,000 hectares have been planted, principally with *Pinus canariensis*, but this total includes approximately 3,400 hectares of *Pinus radiata* from California and a small area of *Pinus halepensis*. Most of this reforestation has been accomplished through partnership or *consorcio* agreements with local governments and less commonly with private landowners. On Gran Canaria, however, the Crown has retained control of most publicly held land, although the Cabildo Insular, an intermediate jurisdiction unique to the archipelago, purchased approximately 4,100 hectares for replanting with conifers under agreements with ICONA. Under the partnership agreements, the government conducts and pays for the planting, the protection, and the maintenance of the reforested tracts and supervises their exploitation. Proceeds from auctions, permits, and licenses are shared between ICONA and the landowners until the investment by the former has been recovered.

In the first years of the reforestation program there was much to be learned. Direct seeding of *Pinus canariensis* proved impractical, and there were problems with seedling transplants caused by the unusually long taproot of the tree. A unique system of transplanting from nurseries that used open-ended plastic sleeves was eventually developed. To promote the development of a secondary root system, the radical was pruned when it emerged from the bottom of the sleeve. Drought brought extensive early losses, but by 1950 some 4,200 hectares were reforested, mostly on the once well-wooded northern slopes of Tenerife.

Planting continued at an accelerated pace and extended to Gran Canaria, La Palma and Hierro. Piles of rocks placed around each seedling protected it from rabbits and other animals as well as from severe storms. Stand densities were high, averaging approximately 2,500 trees per hectare. By the end of 1978, total plantings had reached 18,972 hectares in the province of Santa Cruz de Tenerife (13,000 hectares on Tenerife, 3,000 hectares on La Palma,

---

[43]Ceballos and Ortuño, footnote 2 above, 1st ed., pp. 187-188.

455

and approximately 1,500 hectares each on Hierro and Gomera). Gran Canaria accounted for another 8,867 hectares.[44]

The tradition and the infrastructure for a lumber or wood-products industry are lacking on the islands. Most necessities are imported, the trade being facilitated by the free-port status of the archipelago. The small-scale logging operations in old-growth *Pinus radiata* was being harvested for box wood in 1979 as part of a program to reestablish the endemic monte verde that had originally covered the high slopes of the island. As kerosene has replaced charcoal and firewood for domestic use, as fire-prevention programs have become effective, and as livestock numbers have declined, conditions in the forests have greatly improved. A prolific seeder, the native pine is naturally reestablishing itself with aggressiveness in many situations, especially on bare mineral surfaces.

The program for the reforestation of the Canary Islands was a part of the grand design for the *repoblación forestal* of Spain in-itiated in the first years of the Franco regime. It was at a military encampment in the pine forest of La Esperanza on Tenerife that the Caudillo had first raised the cry of rebellion against the republican government in 1936. With the final victory of the Falange 3 years later, reforestation was given the highest priority. On the peninsula, devastated by civil war, it appears to have been strongly supported by Keynesian considerations--the creation of jobs and the stimulation of investment in depressed rural areas. In the Canary Islands, which represented only a minor part of the program, the maximizing of horizontal precipitation and water yield was the important guiding rationale. Recently aesthetic and recreational values have been given comparable emphasis.

The gradual decline of the rural population of subsistence farmers and graziers on the Canary Islands, coupled with an ambi-tious reforestation program, largely has checked the destructive land use patterns of the past. Today the sunny coasts, with their water-demanding export agriculture and their swarmings of visitors on "package tours," are especially under siege. In reaction to past excesses there is currently a substantial opinion among islanders against almost all types of forest exploitation. For professional foresters this disinclination to "harvest" the standing timber of the pine lands, in particular, is seen as "clearly exaggerated," though based on the best of intentions.[45] The monte verde in most areas is

---

[44]ICONA *Memoria 1978* (Madrid: Instituto para la Conservación de la Naturaleza, 1979).

[45]Ceballos and Ortuño, footnote 2 above, 1st ed., p. 182.

only a memory, long since converted to cropland or secondary scrub. But extensive tracts on the Canary Islands today support a vigorously growing forest of endemic pines of perhaps greater density and luxuriance than has been known at any time since the arrival of Europeans five centuries ago. The rehabilitation of these upland forests stands as an example of the positive potential of human intervention in ecologically sensitive island ecosystems.

POSTSCRIPT

Toward a More Humane Geography[*]

We hear around us frequent and insistent pleas for a heightened "relevance" in our teaching and research. Relevant, we may well ask, to whom, when, for what? Is a utility-oriented, operational geography all that society really wants and expects from us? Is this where our own deepest personal satisfactions, and those of our students, are likely to be found? The generation we are teaching, bright and volatile, gives increasing indication of being more concerned with esthetics, human values, and something they call "life style" than with social "laws" or mechanistic analyses of make-believe or model worlds. The promise of predictability, the test and crown of intellectual detachment (i.e., science), is proving increasingly illusory in human affairs. Research results are seldom commensurate with the sophistication of the techniques used. The most respected authorities often do little better than the star-gazers. Man, it turns out, does not always behave rationally; moreover, changes and reversals of trends, of values, of goals are rarely foreseeable.

Such organizations as the Audubon Society, the Sierra Club, and California Tomorrow (its aim "to keep the state beautiful and productive") represent a gathering social force that increasingly influences our lives and the face of the earth that we live on. Their recent successes underscore a tremendous resurgence of interest in the environment. Not everyone is as sensitized to esthetic values in the landscape, nor as concerned with their preservation, as the conservationists, but sizable and growing numbers are, and they cry out to be shown an intellectually satisfying way. When Darwin, long before Kenneth Boulding, called it "that grandest of all subjects" he was hardly thinking of geography in terms of its immediate and practical utility. The simple pleasure and satisfaction to be derived from getting to know a piece of real country, the phenomena that give it character and their arrangement, is still its sufficient and crowning justification for many, perhaps for most, of us. Competent use of direct field observations, as opposed to impersonal data

---

[*]Reprinted from *Economic Geography* (Guest Editorial), Vol. 45, p. 188 (1969).

gathered from the census office and the printed page, often give special credence and legitimacy to our findings. We cheat ourselves and geography to the extent that we turn our backs on field work--and we miss much of the fun.

Academia has not been immune to fads. For a time after World War II, it was "scientism," reflected in the concern with precision and measurement that seemed to engulf us and mark our way. Economics has gone farthest in this, developing a rigorous framework for analysis that all but eliminates subjective human or moral values. Geography at times has seemed headed down the same path, taking distance and direction as its units of measure. Some have worried that we might be permitting ourselves to be knocked off balance and our subject permanently askewed by excessive subservience to spatial analysis, the search for optimal solutions, and the concept of geography as a system of logic. But attitudes are changing. There is an increasing hunger for involvement, for enduring values to live for and by, for beauty in both the natural and the man-made landscape--a beauty stemming as much from diversity as from order and regularity. Thoreau, who observed that "some things are more to be admired than used," has become a minor prophet. The maintenance of the fragile man-land system in some sort of ecological equilibrium is more and more recognized as our principal challenge and responsibility. Aldo Leopold called it "the land ethic." Each day more and more Americans seem to be marching to the tune of this other drummer. The slide rule and the computer may well be losing ground to the heart. Something of this new set of attitudes may even be seen in the so-called "flower children" and in the student rebels' demands for "liberation" from the computer and from all that is materialistic, planned, or stemming from authority.

The humanistic approach to learning may prove more congenial to the coming generation than any other viewpoint. Geography as landscape appreciation faces previously undreamed-of new horizons and opportunities. It would appear to be in an excellent position to capture, channel, and nurture a growing share of this expanding consciousness of man. From the scientists aboard Apollo-8 we heard for the first time of "the beauty of Earth." Geographers, at closer range, are in a much better position to analyze, to know the endless diversity and intricacy of its natural and humanized landscapes. Can there be a higher or more satisfying calling than the appreciation, preservation, and enhancement of this earthly environment?

459

There is room for all kinds and conditions of men in such a human geography. An impatient but favorably predisposed audience awaits.

Publications by James J. Parsons

Books and Monographs

1949. *Antioqueño Colonization in Western Colombia*, Ibero-Americana, Vol. 32, University of California Press, Berkeley. Second edition, revised, 1968. Spanish edition, translation by Emilio Robledo, Medellín, 1950; Second Spanish edition, revised, Banco de la Republica, Bogotá, 1961; Third Spanish edition, revised, Carlos Valencia, Bogotá, 1979.

1956. *San Andrés and Providencia: English-Speaking Islands in the Western Caribbean*, University of California Publications in Geography, Vol. 12, No. 1, pp. 1-84. Spanish edition, translation by Marco Archbold Britton, Banco de la Republica, Bogotá, 1957; second edition, revised, El Ancora, Bogotá, 1985.

1957. *San Francisco*, Nelson Doubleday Inc., Garden City (Know Your America Series). Revised edition, 1967.

1962. *The Green Turtle and Man*, University of Florida Press, Gainesville.

1967. *Natural Resources: Quality and Quantity* (co-editor with S.V. Ciriacy-Wantrup), University of California Press, Berkeley.

1967. *Antioquia's Corridor to the Sea: An Historical Geography of the Settlement of Urabá*, Ibero-Americana, Vol. 49, University of California Press, Berkeley. Spanish edition, translation by Carolina Evans de Villa, Instituto de Integración Cultural, Medellín, 1979.

1980. *Historical Geography of Latin America: Papers in Honor of Robert C. West* (co-editor with William V. Davidson), Geoscience and Man, Vol. 21, School of Geoscience, Louisiana State University, Baton Rouge.

Articles, Notes, etc.

1940. "Hops in Early California Agriculture," *Agricultural History*, Vol. 14, pp. 110-116.

1941. "The Topia Road: A Trans-Sierran Trail of Colonial Mexico" (with Robert C. West), *Geographical Review*, Vol. 31, pp. 406-413.

1945. "Coffee and Settlement in New Caledonia," *Geographical Review*, Vol. 35, pp. 12-21.

1949. "California Manufacturing," *Geographical Review,* Vol. 39, pp. 229-241.

1949. Note: "Changes in the Geographic-Economic Structure of the United States," *Geographical Review*, Vol. 39, pp. 491-492.

1950. "Recent Industrial Development in the Gulf South," *Geographical Review*, Vol. 40, pp. 67-83. Reprinted in *Readings in the Geography of North America*, pp. 429-445, American Geographical Society, New York, 1952.

1950. "La Nueva Era Industrial Antioqueña," *Universidad de Antioquia* (Medellín), No. 96, pp. 391-399. (Extract from *Antioqueño Colonization in Western Colombia*, 1949, et seq.).

1950. "Antioquia Vista por un Yanki," *Dominical* (Bogotá), June 4, pp. 1, 26. (Extract from *Antioqueño Colonization in Western Colombia*, 1949, *et seq.*).

1950. "El Pueblo Antioqueño," *Universidad de Antioquia* (Medellín), No. 100, pp. 525-531.

1950. "The Geography of Natural Gas in the United States," *Economic Geography*, Vol. 26, pp. 162-178.

1951. "Notes on the Geography of the Sinú Valley, Colombia." Prepared for the Caja de Crédito Agrícola of the Government of Colombia, Bogotá, 90 pp. (processed).

1951. Note: "Potentialities of Tropical Soils," *Geographical Review*, Vol. 41, pp. 503-505.

1951. "Natural Gas," *Scientific American*, Vol. 185, No. 5, pp. 17-21.

1952. "The Settlement of the Sinú Valley of Colombia," *Geographical Review*, Vol. 42, pp. 67-86.

1952. "Davis to San Francisco, California," *Transcontinental Excursion Guidebook*, XVII International Geographical Congress, International Geographical Union, Washington, D.C., pp. 168-179.

1953. "Die Amerikanische Golf-Küste: Ein Neuer Industrieller Schwerpunkt," *Die Erde*, Vol. 5, pp. 83-94.

1953. "Note: "Manufacturing and Agricultural Self-Sufficiency in Cuba," *Geographical Review*, Vol. 43, pp. 412-414.

1954. "English Speaking Settlement of the Western Caribbean," *Yearbook of the Association of Pacific Coast Geographers*, Vol. 16, p. 3-16.

1954. "Solar Radiation, Tides, and Winds," *California Development Problems*, University of California, Berkeley, pp. 111-121 (processed).

1955. "The Miskito Pine Savanna of Nicaragua and Honduras," *Annals of the Association of American Geographers*, Vol. 45, pp. 36-63.

1955. "The Uniqueness of California," *American Quarterly*, Vol. 7, pp. 45-55. Reprinted in *California Controversies*, Leonard Pitt, editor, pp. 12-19, Scott, Foresman, and Co., Glenview, 1969. Reprinted in *California: Its People, Its Problems, Its Prospects*, Robert Durrenberger, editor, pp. 5-15, National Books, Palo Alto, 1969. Japanese translation in *Americana*, Vol. 3, pp. 77-87, U.S.I.S., Tokyo, 1957.

464

1955. "Gold Mining in the Nicaragua Rain Forest," *Yearbook of the Association of Pacific Coast Geographers*, Vol. 17, pp. 49-55.

1955. Note: "The San Francisco-Oakland Metropolitan Area," *Geographical Review*, Vol. 45, pp. 264-265.

1956. "The Home-Building and Furniture Industries," in *California and the Southwest*, Clifford M. Zierer, editor, pp. 262-271, John Wiley and Sons, New York.

1956. Note: "Economic Development in the Northern Andes," *Geographical Review*, Vol. 46, pp. 411-413.

1956. "San Andrés and Providencia," *Caribbean Society and Culture* (Trinidad), Vol. 1, No. 2, pp. 1-5.

1957. "Bananas in Ecuador: A New Chapter in the History of Tropical Agriculture," *Economic Geography*, Vol. 33, pp. 201-216.

1957. Note: "Irrigation Civilizations," *Geographical Review*, Vol. 47, pp. 136-137.

1957. "Colombia," *Focus* (American Geographical Society), Vol. 7, No. 7, pp. 1-6. Revised edition, *Focus*, Vol. 20, No. 1, pp. 1-11, 1969.

1958. "The Natural Gas Supply of California," *Land Economics*, Vol. 34, pp. 19-36.

1958. Note: "The Brazilian Territory of Amapá," *Geographical Review*, Vol. 48, pp. 429-431.

1959. Forward to: *Estructura Económica de Colombia*, by Julio Hincapie Santa María, Universidad de Antioquia, Medellín, pp. i-viii.

1959. Letter: "Strontium-90 Levels and Wheat," *Science*, Vol. 130, p. 733.

1960. "Fog Drip from Summer Stratus with Special Reference to California," *Weather* (London), Vol. 15, pp. 58-62.

1960. "Starlings for Seville," *Landscape*, Vol. 10, No. 2, pp. 28-31. Reprinted in *The Cultural Landscape*, C.L. Salter, editor, pp. 105-109, Duxbury Press, Belmont, 1971. Spanish translation, revised, in *Adreola: Revista Ibérica de Ornitología*, Vol. 6, pp. 235-241, 1960.

1960. Note: "Santa María la Antigua del Darién," *Geographical Review*, Vol. 50, pp. 274-276.

1962. "The Acorn-Hog Economy of the Oak Woodlands of Southwestern Spain," *Geographical Review*, Vol. 52, pp. 211-235. Spanish translation by José Ortega Valcarcel, *Estudios Geográficos* (Madrid), Vol. 27, pp. 309-329, 1966; German translation in *Beiträge zur Geographie der Wald-und Forstwirtschaft*, H.W. Windhorst, editor, pp. 147-175, Darmstadt, 1978.

1962. "The Cork Oak Forests and the Evolution of the Cork Industry in Southern Spain," *Economic Geography*, Vol. 38, pp. 195-214.

1962. "John Ernest Kesseli: An Appreciation" (with H.H. Aschmann and F.L. Kramer), *California Geographer*, Vol. 3, pp. 64-67.

1962. Note: "The Moorish Imprint on the Iberian Peninsula," *Geographical Review*, Vol. 52, pp. 120-122.

1963. Note: "Agricultural Colonization in Costa Rica," *Geographical Review*, Vol. 53, pp. 451-454. Spanish translation in *Informe Semestral*, Instituto Geográfico de Costa Rica, Enero a Junio, pp. 97-107, 1963.

1963. "Discurso del Dr. Parsons a la Entrega del Doctorado Honoris Causa," *Revista Universidad de Antioquia* (Medellín), No. 158, pp. 679-682.

1964. "The Contribution of Geography to Latin American Studies," in *Social Science Research on Latin America*, Charles Wagley, editor, pp. 33-85, Columbia University Press, New York.

1965. Note: "British West Indian Export Crops," *Geographical Review*, Vol. 55, pp. 110-112.

1965. "Cotton and Cattle in the Pacific Lowlands of Central America," *Journal of Inter-American Studies*, Vol. 7, pp. 149-159.

1965. Various articles, including "Amazon" (co-author), Vol. 1, pp. 709-715, and "Colombia," Vol. 6, pp. 72-76, *Encyclopaedia Britannica*, Encyclopaedia Britannica, Inc., Chicago. Reprinted in subsequent editions; "Colombia" also in 1962 edition.

1965. "Vegetation, Soils and Man on the Caribbean Coast of Central America and Colombia," *Comptes Rendus du XVIII Congrés International de Géographie*, Rio de Janeiro, 1956, Vol. 3, pp. 90-97.

1966. "Ancient Ridged Fields of the San Jorge River Floodplain, Colombia" (with William A. Bowen), *Geographical Review*, Vol. 56, pp. 317-343. Reissued as Reprint No. 253, Center for Latin American Studies, University of California, Berkeley. Spanish translation in *El Tiempo* (Bogotá), Lecturas Dominical, August 14, p. 8, and August 21, p. 3, 1966.

1966. "Los Campos de Cultivos Pre-Hispánicos del Bajo San Jorge," *Revista de la Academia Colombiana de Ciencias Exactas, Físicas y Naturales*, Vol. 12, No. 48, pp. 449-458.

1966. "La Marcha hacia el Mar en Antioquia: La Colonización Bananera de la Zona de Urabá," *Conferencia Regional Latinoamericana*, Unión Geográfica Internacional, México, Vol. 1, pp. 259-266.

1967. "Geography" (departmental history), *The Centennial Record of the University of California*, pp. 86-87, University of California Press, Berkeley.

1967. "Pre-Columbian Ridged Fields" (with William M. Denevan), *Scientific American*, Vol. 217, No. 1, pp. 92-100. Reprinted in *The Indian Historian*, Vol. 1, pp. 27-32, 1967. Reprinted in *New World Archaeology: Theoretical and Cultural Transformations*, E.B. Zubrow, *et al.*, editors, pp. 240-248, W.H. Freeman, San Francisco, 1974. Reprinted in *Pre-Columbian Archaeology*, G.R. Willey and J.A. Sabloff, editors, pp. 197-205, W.H. Freeman, San Francisco, 1980.

1968. "Carl Sauer," *International Encyclopedia of the Social Sciences*, Vol. 14, pp. 17-19, Crowell, Collier, and Macmillan, New York.

1969. "Ridged Fields in the Río Guayas Valley, Ecuador," *American Antiquity*, Vol. 34, pp. 76-80. Spanish translation in *Cuadernos de História y Arqueología* (Guayaquil), Año 23, No. 40, pp. 185-201, 1973.

1969. "Toward a More Humane Geography" (Guest Editorial), *Economic Geography*, Vol. 45, p. 188.

1970. "The 'Africanization' of the New World Tropical Grasslands," *Tübinger Geographische Studien*, Vol. 34, pp. 141-153 (Festschrift für Herbert Wilhelmy).

1971. "Realejo: A Forgotten Colonial Port and Shipbuilding Center in Nicaragua" (with David R. Radell), *Hispanic American Historical Review*, Vol. 51, pp. 295-312.

1971. "Ecological Problems and Approaches in Latin American Geography," *Proceedings of the Conference of Latin Americanist Geographers*, Vol. 1, pp. 13-32. Reissued as Reprint No. 420, Center for Latin American Studies, University of California, Berkeley.

1972. "El Cultivo del Café," *Economía Colombiana* (Bogotá), No. 95, pp. 37-46. (Extract from *Antioqueño Colonization in Western Colombia*, 1949, *et. seq.*).

1972. "The Hawksbill Turtle and the Tortoise Shell Trade," in *Etudes de Géographie Tropicale Offertes à Pierre Gourou*, pp. 45-60, Mouton, Paris.

1972. Note: "The California Gold Country," *Geographical Review*, Vol. 62, pp. 269-271.

1972. "Spread of African Pasture Grasses to the American Tropics," *Journal of Range Management*, Vol. 25, pp. 12-17.

1972. "Slicing Up the Open Space: Subdivisions without Homes in Northern California," *Erdkunde*, Vol. 26, pp. 1-8.

468

1973. *50 Years of Berkeley Geography*, 1923-1973 (editor), Department of Geography, University of California, Berkeley (processed).

1973. "Man's Impact on the Vegetation of Southern Spain," *Year Book of the American Philosophical Society*, pp. 338-340.

1973. "Colombia," in *Focus on South America*, Alice Taylor, editor, pp. 112-126, New York, Praeger.

1973. "Sand-Bed Agriculture: A Remarkable System for Early Truck Crop Production on the Arid Southeast Coast of Spain," *Proceedings, Association of American Geographers*, Vol. 5, pp. 216-220.

1973. "Southward to the Sun: The Impact of Mass Tourism on the Coast of Spain," *Yearbook of the Association of Pacific Coast Geographers*, Vol. 35, pp. 129-146.

1973. "Latin America," in *Geographers Abroad: Essays on the Problems and Prospects of Research in Foreign Areas*, Marvin Mikesell, editor, pp. 16-46, University of Chicago, Department of Geography Research Paper No. 152.

1975. "The Changing Nature of New World Tropical Forests Since European Colonization," in *The Use of Ecological Guidelines for Development in the American Humid Tropics*, pp. 28-38, International Union for Conservation of Nature and Natural Resources, Morges. Reprinted in *The Social Dynamics of Deforestation in Latin America and its Alternatives*, Susanna Hecht and James Nations, editors, Cornell University Press, Ithaca, in press.

1975. Note: "Drought and Hunger on Fuerteventura," *Geographical Review*, Vol. 65, pp. 110-113.

1975. "The Historical Preconditions of Industrialization--Medellín Reconsidered," *Proceedings of the Conference of Latin Americanist Geographers*, Vol. 5, pp. 119-124.

1975. "Carl Ortwin Sauer (1889-1975)," *Year Book of the American Philosophical Society*, pp. 163-167. Reprinted in *CoEvolution Quarterly*, No. 10, pp. 45-47, 1976.

1975. Comments on Ridged Fields, in *Manual of Remote Sensing*, R.G. Reeves, editor, Vol. 2, pp. 2004-2008, American Society of Photogrammetry, Falls Church.

1975. Abstract: "Putting 'Life' into Geography: Biogeographical Reflections on Plants, Animals, and Environmental Quality (The President's Program), *Proceedings of the Association of American Geographers*, Vol. 7, p. 306.

1976. "Carl Ortwin Sauer, 1889-1975," *Geographical Review*, Vol. 66, pp. 83-89.

1976. "Forest to Pasture: Development or Destruction," *Revista de Biología Tropical*, Vol. 24 (Suppl. 1), pp. 121-138.

1977. Note: "Corporate Farming in California," *Geographical Review*, Vol. 67, pp. 354-357.

1977. "Geography as Exploration and Discovery," *Annals of the Association of American Geographers*, Vol. 67, pp. 1-16. Spanish translation in *Trimestre Geográfico* (Bogotá), Vol. 1, pp. 1-25, 1980.

1977. Abstract: "Late Quaternary Cyclic Sedimentation, San Jorge River Floodplain, Colombia" (with Roy J. Schlemon), *Abstracts*, X[th] International Quaternary Association Congress, p. 419, Birmingham, England.

1977. "Una Clase de Alimento tan Delicioso," pp. 66-70; "Historia de la Pesca de la Tortuga en el Caribe Occidental," pp. 71-77; "Historia del Comercio del Carey en la Costa Caribe de Centro América," pp. 78-83; "Conducidas Cada Año a sus Propias Manos," pp. 89-92, in *Memorias de Arrecife Tortuga: História Natural y Económica de las Tortugas en el Caribe de América Central*, Bernard Nietschmann, editor, Banco de América, Serie Geografía y Naturaleza No. 2, Managua.

1977. "Carl Ortwin Sauer, 1889-1975" (with J. Leighly, W. Borah, and L.B. Simpson), *In Memorium*, University of California, Berkeley, pp. 205-206.

1978. "More on Pre-Columbian Raised Fields (Camellones) in the Bajo San Jorge and Bajo Cauca, Colombia," *Proceedings of the Conference of Latin Americanist Geographers*, Vol. 7, pp. 117-124.

1979. "Footloose and Fancy Free: Residential Choices of SFO- and LAX-Based Airline Pilots," *Yearbook of the Association of Pacific Coast Geographers*, Vol. 41, pp. 81-92.

1979. "The Later Sauer Years," *Annals of the Association of American Geographers*, Vol. 69 (75th Anniversary edition), pp. 9-15.

1980. "Europeanization of the Savanna Lands of Northern South America," in *Human Ecology of Savanna Environments*, David R. Harris, editor, pp. 267-289, Academic Press, London.

1980. "Robert C. West, Geographer" (with William V. Davidson), *Historical Geography of Latin America*, Geoscience and Man, Vol. 21, pp. 1-8, School of Geoscience, Louisiana State University, Baton Rouge.

1981. "The Ecological Dimension: Ten Years Later," *Proceedings of the Conference of Latin Americanist Geographers*, Vol. 8, pp. 23-33.

1981. "Human Influences on the Pine and Laurel Forests of the Canary Islands," *Geographical Review*, Vol. 71, pp. 253-271. Spanish translation in *Documents d'Anàlisi Geogràfica* (Barcelona), Vol. 7, pp. 149-173, 1985.

1982. "The Northern Andean Environment," *Mountain Research and Development*, Vol. 2, pp. 253-262. Spanish translation in *Informe sobre los conocimientos Actuales de los Ecosistemas Andinos*, Vol. 3, Dennis V. Johnson, editor, pp. 15-34, Man and the Biosphere Program, UNESCO, Montevideo, 1985.

1982. "Nuevo Informe sobre los Campos Elevados Prehistoricos de la Cuenca del Guayas, Ecuador" (with Roy Shlemon), *Miscelánea Antropológica Ecuatoriana*, Vol. 2, pp. 31-37. English version in *British Archaeological Reports*, International Series, No. 359 (Oxford), pp. 207-216, 1987.

471

1983. "Beef Cattle," in *Costa Rican Natural History*, Dan Janzen, editor, pp. 77-79, University of Chicago Press, Chicago.

1983. "The Migration of Canary Islanders to the Americas: An Unbroken Current Since Columbus," *The Americas*, Vol. 39, pp. 447-481.

1983. *60 Years of Berkeley Geography, 1923-1983* (co-editor with Natalia Vonnegut), Department of Geography, University of California, Berkeley (processed).

1984. "Algunas Observaciones sobre la Isla Mona, un Emporio de Pan de Casabe en el Caribe durante el Siglo XVI," *Yearbook of the Conference of Latin Americanist Geographers*, Vol. 10, pp. 10-18.

1985. "On 'Bioregionalism' and' Watershed Consciousness'," *Professional Geographer*, Vol. 37, pp.1-6.

1985. "The Canary Islands Search for Stability," *Focus* (American Geographical Society), Vol. 35, No. 2, pp. 22-29.

1985. "Raised Field Farmers as Pre-Columbian Landscape Engineers: Looking North from the San Jorge, Colombia," *Prehistoric Intensive Agriculture in the Tropics*, Ian Farrington, editor, *British Archaeological Reports*, International Series, No. 232 (Oxford), pp. 149-165.

1986. "A Geographer Looks at the San Joaquin Valley," *Geographical Review*, Vol. 76, pp. 371-389.

1987. "Now this Matter of Cultural Geography: Notes from Carl Sauer's Last Seminar at Berkeley" (editor), in *Carl O. Sauer: A Tribute*, Martin Kenzer, editor, pp. 153-163, Oregon State University Press, Corvallis.

1987. "John Leighly, 1895-1986" (with D. Hooson, T. Oberlander, and D. Stanislawski), *In Memorium*, pp. 174-177, University of California, Berkeley.

1987. "The Origin and Dispersal of the Domesticated Canary," *Journal of Cultural Geography*, Vol. 7, No. 2, pp. 19-33.

472

1988.   "Hillside Letters in the Western Landscape," *Landscape*, Vol. 30, No. 1, pp. 15-23.

1988.   "The Scourge of Cows," *Whole Earth Review*, No. 58, pp. 40-47.

1988.   "The San Joaquin Valley, Cornucopia" (with Paul F. Starrs), *Focus*, Vol. 38, No. 1, pp. 7-11.

n.d.   John Leighly, 1895-1986," *Geographers: Biobibliographical Studies*, T.W. Freeman, editor, Mansell Pub. Ltd., London, in press.

n.d.   "Geography," in *Latin America and Caribbean Studies: A Critical Guide to Research Resources*, Paula Covington, editor, Seminar on the Acquisition of Latin American Library Materials, Greenwood Press, New York, in press.

n.d.   "Reminiscencias de La Colonización Antioqueña," *Seminario sobre Colonización Antioqueña*, Manizales, 1987, Universidad de Caldas, Manizales, in press.

Reviews

1947.   Review: *Les Nouvelles Hébrides*, by E. Aubert de la Rue, *Geographical Review*, Vol. 37, pp. 517-518.

1950.   Review: *Oil! Titan of the Southwest*, by Carl Coke Rister, *Geographical Review*, Vol. 40, pp. 157-158.

1950.   Review: *United States International Timber Trade in the Pacific Area*, by Ivan M. Elchibegoff, *Geographical Review*, Vol. 40, pp. 168-169.

1952.   Review: *The Aircraft Industry: A Study in Industrial Location*, by William Glenn Cunningham, *Geographical Review*, Vol. 42, pp. 675-676.

1953.   Review: *Colonial Placer Mining in Colombia*, by Robert C. West, *Pacific Historical Review*, Vol. 22, pp. 174-175.

1954.   Review: *Energy Sources: The Wealth of the World*, by Eugene Ayres and Charles A. Scarlott, *Geographical Review*, Vol. 44, pp. 320-322.

1954. Review: *Studien zur Klima und Vegetationskunde der Tropen*, by Wilhelm Lauer, Rolf-Diedrich Schmidt, Rudolf Schröder, and Carl Troll, *Geographical Review*, Vol. 44, pp. 468-469.

1954. Review: *Economics of Natural Gas in Texas*, by John R. Stockton, Richard C. Henshaw, Jr., and Richard Graves, *Economic Geography*, Vol. 30, p. 182.

1954. Review: *San Francisco-Oakland Metropolitan Area: Strukturwandlungen eines US-amerikanischen Grossstadtkomplexes*, by Fritz Bartz, *Erdkunde*, Vol. 8, pp. 340-341.

1955. Review: *Bosquejo Biográfico del señor Oidor Juan Antonio Mon y Velarde, Visitador de Antioquia 1785-1788*, by Emilio Robledo, *Hispanic American Historical Review*, Vol. 35, pp. 517-519.

1955. Review: *Industria y Protección en Colom-bia, 1810-1930*, by Luís Ospina Vásquez, *Hispanic American Historical Review*, Vol. 35, pp. 506-508.

1956. Review: *Disertaciones sobre la Papa*, by Mariano de Carcer y Disdier, *Hispanic American Historical Review*, Vol. 36, p. 416.

1956. Review: *Peasant Society in the Colombian Andes: A Sociological Study of Saucío*, by Orlando Fals-Borda, *Hispanic American Historical Review*, Vol. 36, pp. 388-389.

1958. Review: *Historia de la Gobernación de Popayán*, by Jaime Arroyo, *Hispanic American Historical Review*, Vol. 38, pp. 149-150.

1958. Review: *Shifting Cultivation in Africa: The Zande System of Agriculture*, by Pierre de Schlippe, *Geographical Review*, Vol. 48, pp. 137-138.

1958. Review: *La Obra de Alexander von Humboldt en México*, by Rayfred Lionel Stevens-Middleton, *Hispanic American Historical Review*, Vol. 38, pp. 130-131.

1958. Review: *The Pacific Lowlands of Colombia, A Negroid Area of the American Tropics*, by Robert C. West, *Economic Geography*, Vol. 34, pp. 373-374.

474

1959. Book Notice: *Una Excursión al Territorio de San Martín*, by Emiliano Restrepo E., *Hispanic American Historical Review*, Vol. 39, p. 346.

1959. Book Notice: *Jeografía Física i Política de las Provincias de la Nueva Granada* [1856], by Agustín Codazzi (director), *Hispanic American Historical Review*, Vol. 39, pp. 494.

1959. Review: *Conservation in the Production of Petroleum: A Study in Industrial Control*, by Erich W. Zimmermann, *Economic Geography*, Vol. 35, pp. 182-183.

1959. Review: *The Future Supply of Oil and Gas*, by Bruce C. Netschert, *Economic Geography*, Vol. 35, pp. 182-183.

1962. Review: *Industrial Activity and Economic Geography*, by R.C. Estall and R.O. Buchanan, *Economic Geography*, Vol. 38, pp. 181-182.

1962. Review: *Zonas de Vida Natural en el Perú*, by Joseph A. Tosi, Jr., *Economic Geography*, Vol. 38, pp. 278-280.

1963. Review: *Land and Water Use: A Symposium*, by Wynne Thorne (editor), *Science*, Vol. 141, p. 422.

1964. Book Notice: *Plantas Cultivadas y Animales Domésticas en América Equinoccial, Tomo I*, by Víctor Manual Patiño, *Hispanic American Historical Review*, Vol. 44, p. 447.

1964. Review: *Portugal's Other Kingdom: The Algarve*, by Dan Stanislawski, *Economic Geography*, Vol. 40, pp. 275-276.

1964. Review: *Los Quimbayas bajo la Dominación Española*, by Juan Friede, *Hispanic American Historical Review*, Vol. 44, pp. 414-415.

1965. Review: *Keith and Costa Rica*, by Watt Stewart, *Hispanic American Historical Review*, Vol. 45, pp. 313-316.

1965. Book Notice: *La Colonización Agrícola de Costa Rica*, by Gerhard Sandner, *Hispanic American Historical Review*, Vol. 45, p. 338.

1965. Review: *Flowers for the King: The Expedition of Ruiz and Pavón and the Flora of Perú*, by Arthur Robert Steele, *Hispanic American Historical Review*, Vol. 45, pp. 484-487.

1965. Book Notice: *Historia de Pereira*, by Luis Duque Gómez, Juan Friede, and Jaime Jaramillo Uribe, *Hispanic American Historical Review*, Vol. 45, p. 174.

1966. Review: *Struggle for Land*, by H.C. Brookfield and Paula Brown, *Landscape*, Vol. 16, No. 2, p. 37.

1966. Review: *Iberische Halbinsel*, by Hermann Lautensach, *Geographical Review*, Vol. 56, pp. 306-307.

1967. Review: *Middle America: Its Lands and Peoples*, by Robert C. West and John P. Augelli, *Geographical Review*, Vol. 57, pp. 585-587.

1968. Review: *Karl Theodor Sapper, 1866-1945: Leben und Wirken eines Deutschen Geographen und Geologen*, by Franz Termer, *Hispanic American Historical Review*, Vol. 48, pp. 462-463.

1969. Review: *Mexico's Natural Gas: The Beginning of an Industry*, by Freda Jean Bullard, *Economic Geography*, Vol. 45, pp. 374-375.

1970. Review: *La Familia y Cultura en Colombia*, Vol. 1, by Virginia Gutiérrez de Pineda, *Caribbean Studies*, Vol. 10, pp. 122-123.

1970. Review: *Die Westindischen Inseln*, by Helmut Blume, *Geographical Review*, Vol. 60, pp. 282-284.

1970. Review: *La Localización de la Actividad Manufactura en Chile*, by Graciela Uribe Ortega, *Economic Geography*, Vol. 46, pp. 107-108.

1972. Review: *Mexico: Eine Landeskunde*, by Hans G. Gierloff-Emden, *Professional Geographer*, Vol. 24, pp. 84-85.

476

1973. Review: *Atlantic Islands: Madeira, the Azores, and the Cape Verdes in Seventeenth-Century Commerce and Navigation*, by T. Bentley Duncan, *Journal of Interamerican Studies and World Affairs*, Vol. 15, pp. 383-385.

1974. Review: *A Guide to the Historial Geography of New Spain*, by Peter Gerhard, *American Historical Review*, Vol. 79, pp. 914-915.

1974. Review: *Between Land and Water: The Subsistence Ecology of the Miskito Indians, Eastern Nicaragua*, by Bernard Nietschmann, *Geographical Review*, Vol. 64, pp. 298-300.

1974. Review: *The Development of Tropical Lands: Policy Issues in Latin America*, by Michael Nelson, *Annals of the Association of American Geographers*, Vol. 64, pp. 453-454.

1976. Review: *Man and Earth's Ecosystems*, by Charles F. Bennett, Jr., *CoEvolution Quarterly*, No. 10, p. 53.

1977. Review: *Les Espaces Naturels Tropicaux: Essai de Géographie Physique*, by Jean Demangeot, *Geographical Review*, Vol. 67, pp. 245-246.

1977. Review: *El Café y el Desarrollo Histórico-Geográfico de Costa Rica*, by Carolyn Hall, *Hispanic American Historical Review*, Vol. 57, pp. 543-545.

1977. Review: *The Yanoama Indians: A Cultural Geography*, by William J. Smole, *Annals of the Association of American Geographers*, Vol. 67, pp. 280-282.

1978. Review: *Slavery on the Spanish Frontier: The Colombian Chocó, 1680-1810*, by William Frederick Sharp, *Hispanic American Historical Review*, Vol. 58, pp. 717-718.

1979. Review: *Spanish Red: An Ethnographical Study of Cochineal and the Opuntia Cactus*, by R.A. Donkin, *Journal of Historical Geography*, Vol. 5, pp. 361-362.

1980. Review: *Las Perlas del Caribe: Nueva Cádiz de Cubagua*, by Enrique Otte, *Journal of Historical Geography*, Vol. 6, pp. 103-105.

1980. Review: *The Spanish Lake*, by O.H.K. Spate, *Geographical Review*, Vol. 70, pp. 352-353.

1981. Review: *Carl Sauer's Field Work in Latin America*, by Robert C. West, *Hispanic American Historical Review*, Vol. 61, pp. 346-347.

1981. Review: *Agricultural Terracing in the Aboriginal New World*, by R.A. Donkin, *Agricultural History*, Vol. 55, pp. 416-417.

1981. Review: *Earlier Than You Think: A Personal View of Man in America*, by George F. Carter, *Economic Geography*, Vol. 57, pp. 182-183.

1982. Review: *Historia Doble de la Costa: I. Mompox y Loba*, by Orlando Fals Borda, and *Latifundio y Poder Político: La Hacienda Ganadera en Sucre*, by Alejandro Reyes Posada, *Hispanic American Historical Review*, Vol. 62, pp. 130-132.

1983. Review: *Man and the Mediterranean Forest: A History of Resource Depletion*, by J.V. Thirgood, *Geographical Review*, Vol. 73, pp. 356-357.

1983. Review: *Vanishing Landscapes: Land and Life in the Tulare Basin*, by William L. Preston, *Journal of Historical Geography*, Vol. 9, pp. 326-327.

1983. Review: *California Patterns: A Geographical and Historical Atlas*, by David Hornbeck, and *California: The Geography of Diversity*, by Crane S. Miller and Richard S. Hyslop, *California History*, Vol. 62, pp. 142-143.

1984. Review: *Cuando se Acaban los Montes*, by Stanley Heckadon Moreno, and *Panama Forest and Shore: Natural History and Amerindian Culture in Bocas del Toro*, by Burton L. Gordon, *Professional Geographer*, Vol. 36, pp. 509-510.

1985. Review Article: *The Canary Islands and the Americas: Studies in a Unique Relationship*, *Latin American Research Review*, Vol. 20, pp. 189-199.

1986. Review: *Zentralamerika und der Ferne Karibische Westen: Konjunkturen, Krisen und Konflikte, 1504-1984*, by Gerhard Sandner, *Geographical Review*, Vol. 76, pp. 334-336.

478

1987.   Review: *Frontier Expansion and Peasant Protest in Colombia, 1830-1936*, by Catherine Le Grande, *Journal of Historical Geography*, Vol. 13, pp. 223-224.

1987.   Review Article: *Cuba: Economía y Sociedad*, by Leví Marrero y Atiles, *Journal of Historical Geography*, Vol. 13, pp. 67-71.

1987.   Review: *An Atlas of Louisiana Surnames of French and Spanish Origin*, by Robert C. West, *Names*, Vol. 35, pp. 95-98.

1987.   Review: *Industrialization and Urbanization in Latin America*, by Robert Gwynne, *Annals of Regional Science*, Vol. 21, pp. 175-177.

1988.   Review: *La Arquitectura en dos Archipiélagos Caribeños*, and *Arquitectura de la Epoca del Canal, 1890-1914*, by Samuel A. Gutiérrez, *Hispanic American Historical Review*, Vol. 68, pp. 158-160.